STALIN'S SCRIBE

LITERATURE, AMBITION, AND SURVIVAL: THE LIFE OF MIKHAIL SHOLOKHOV

BRIAN J. BOECK

PEGASUS BOOKS

NEW YORK LONDON

STALIN'S SCRIBE

Pegasus Books Ltd.
148 W 37th Street, 13th Floor
New York, NY 10018

First Pegasus Books edition February 2019

Interior design by Maria Fernandez

Library of Congress Cataloging-in-Publication Data is available.

ISBN: 978-1-68177-874-7

10 9 8 7 6 5 4 3 2 1

Printed in the United States of America
Distributed by W. W. Norton & Company

*Dedicated to the past and present librarians
of Guadalupe County, Texas.*

A NOTE ON TRANSLATIONS, TERMINOLOGY, AND SOURCES

All translations presented here are my own. Where possible I have strived to distinguish between informal and official registers and to convey a sense of the tone and tenor of Soviet discourse. Since the translation process always involves a number of interpretive decisions and judgement calls I have erred on the side of making the text accessible to the widest possible audience. In a small number of cases I have deployed more easily understood or informal terms rather than the more formal official versions and their variations. The title of party 'secretary,' which conveyed a great deal of power and prestige in the USSR, presents a particular problem due to the connotations of the term in English. The fact that Stalin was a secretary too, should leave no doubts about its high status connotations. For continuity I have used a single recognizable political term, Politburo, rather than the other names for entities which served the same or similar functions at different times. Though

Sholokhov's epic novel is known in some English translations as *And Quiet Flows the Don*, I have opted for *Quiet Don* because it is closer to the original, which refers to both a quietly flowing body of water and the poetic personification of the river, Don Ivanovich, in Cossack folklore. Publishers in England added specificity to the title in order to avoid any suggestion that the book was about the life of a taciturn fellow at Oxford, a different kind of don altogether.

In a limited number of cases I have utilized oral or visual sources that do not easily lend themselves to citation. A number of aphorisms, turns of phrase, and anecdotes about Soviet history derive from my travels in Russia over the course of two decades. Visual descriptions of places rely partly on photographs and partly on my own experiences. For descriptions of people and historical interiors I have consulted photographic evidence that is close in time to either the person or event described. Illustrations 1–4 render historical photographs that were not available for publication. Only the first image would have been widely known to the Soviet public.

In order to reconstruct events as Sholokhov saw them, I have critically scrutinized the reminiscences of his friends, relatives, and assistants. Their accounts are often partial, protective, and chronologically imprecise. Nonetheless, they provide important insights into his mindset and key testimonies about how he narrated the story of his encounters with Stalin and other Soviet leaders. The dialogues presented here can be read both as vivid recollections of important meetings and as revealing reflections of Sholokhov's ongoing personal dialogue with the process of de-Stalinization. His strategic recall of aspects of his relationship with the dictator frequently responded to current Soviet controversies and political trends. A systematic reading of *Pravda*, *Izvestiia*, and *Literaturnaia Gazeta* for the period of Sholokhov's biography helped me to picture Sholokhov as a man of his time and avoid presentist biases of every imaginable variety.

PREFACE

This meeting was his only hope. A young man in a drab military tunic maneuvered his way through throngs of pedestrians. He was rushing to the most important encounter of his life. On that summer day in 1931 few could have guessed that this blond, baby-faced youth with a bashful, yet cunning, smile was Mikhail Sholokhov, the rising star of Russian literature. The twenty-six-year-old approached a mansion in the heart of Moscow with a mix of trepidation and forced bravado. His heart pounded as he reached the ornate gate.

This was the home of Russia's most famous living writer. By pleading with Maxim Gorky, Sholokhov hoped to save *Quiet Don*, the Soviet Union's epic equivalent of *Gone with the Wind*. The unfinished novel had already won him fame, controversy, acclaim, and envy. Bureaucrats had banned the latest installment as anti-Soviet. As he stepped inside the mansion, darkness confronted him. A rapid succession of footsteps brought him into a surreal space bathed in multicolored swatches of light emitted from stained-glass panels above. More darkness brought him to two tall, exceedingly imposing doors. As the doors opened, he could see a backlit silhouette at the end of a long, rectangular table. A lamp illuminated an astonishing profile and a bushy mustache. This was decidedly not the familiar silhouette of Gorky. The mustache belonged to a face made famous by newspaper engravings and grainy black-and-white photos of May Day parades.

That evening Joseph Stalin decided to discuss characters and scenes in *Quiet Don* rather than unravel conspiracies or analyze grain reports. Following introductions, Gorky receded into the background. Stalin beckoned Sholokhov to approach. In seconds it became clear that this was no social call. Stalin immediately accused Sholokhov of sympathizing with some of the revolution's most vicious adversaries. Resorting to one of his favorite tactics, he advanced a series of damning allegations. These were calculated to knock his adversary off balance and unmask his true character. Would his target retreat? Would he submit and become subservient? Or would he push back?

Sholokhov saw the dictator's eyes burning like those of a tiger ready to pounce. The snap decision he made in that instant had the potential to either influence his life for decades or to end it. He stood his ground. With his career on the line, he confidently argued with Stalin and vigorously defended his audacious decision to write sympathetically about the Cossacks, the former tsarist military caste that rose in rebellion against the Soviet government.

Stalin was impressed by Sholokhov's tenacity. Concluding his barrage of questions, he started to reminisce about his first, albeit temporary, taste of dictatorship in 1918. In Tsaritsyn—the industrial city on the Volga River that had recently been renamed Stalingrad in his honor—Stalin had encountered several Cossacks who now reminded him of characters in *Quiet Don*. The dictator and the writer bonded over conversations about battles that had faded from public memory but would soon become central to the emerging Stalin cult. Elated, Sholokhov departed from the mansion with the most coveted prize in the USSR—Stalin's personal telephone number. Though fate had smiled upon him that evening, he soon discovered that a dictator's favor comes with daily dangers and crushing burdens. As Stalin's prized protégé, he would have to become a new man.

That fateful meeting in a mansion forever changed the calculus of young Sholokhov's literary gambit. The instant Stalin revealed that he too was a fan of the novel, Sholokhov understood that he was in way too deep. The novel transformed him into a Soviet Scheherazade. His very fate now hinged on satisfying a dictator's literary cravings. He would have to become a great writer and a cunning courtier to stay alive during the Great Terror. An opportunistic, literary caper became a lifelong con . . . with no possibility of escape.

∞

In this, the first political biography of Mikhail Sholokhov, I tell the story of the brash young plagiarist[1] who fabricated Stalin's favorite novel and became one of the Soviet Union's most prominent political figures. While rivals for Stalin's attention resorted to flattery, Sholokhov chose candor and aloof availability. When I first encountered Sholokhov's letters to Stalin shortly after their first publication in the 1990s, I was stunned by their revelations. The dictator we like to think we know is a bloodthirsty monster with absolutely no redeeming qualities. Sholokhov's Stalin was a considerably more complex, though no less menacing, presence. How could anyone get away with speaking truth to a tyrant in such a manner? I puzzled. If the writer could pen such bold missives of protest and live to tell about it, then I didn't truly know either of them. I needed to understand how Sholokhov earned Stalin's respect and admiration. The combination of audacity and tenacity that Sholokhov brought to that unexpected meeting endeared him to a dictator who loved literature and craved the respect of writers. Sholokhov continued to mete out truths to Soviet leaders in deliberate, calibrated doses. An uncanny sixth sense always seemed to tell him which truths could be fatal.

I struggled to reconcile the bold, uncompromising, and sympathetic Sholokhov who emerged in the letters with the vindictive, mean-spirited man described in so many accounts of late Soviet history. He became so reviled in the West that Salman Rushdie could summarily dismiss him as a "patsy of the regime."[2] No patsy could have penned letters condemning party officials for setting villagers on fire, starving children, and force-feeding kerosene to recalcitrant farmers. No patsy would denounce the secret police at the height of the greatest wave of political terror of the 20th century. At the same time, there was indeed something deeply disturbing about the late Sholokhov and his vicious condemnation of political dissent. I craved to discover why an intellectual who was so deeply committed to speaking truth to power in the 1930s became a sterile mouthpiece of the regime in the Brezhnev era. As I delved into newly available archival documentation and the memoirs of Sholokhov's friends and assistants, I encountered a savvy survivor who drank his conscience into submission. He was saved by Stalin but crushed by the burden of the Kremlin's favor. It is my hopes that this book captures that story and gives us a better understanding and appreciation for this complicated man and his contradictory epoch.

Sholokhov's remarkable path both illuminates and clashes with our understanding of the Soviet system. His experiences provide a new and compelling perspective on the Great Terror. A single alleged utterance in a garage in the early 1930s was sufficient to set in motion a series of events that would endanger Sholokhov, derail writing of his epic novel, and ultimately change the course of Soviet history. The very notion that an individual could outwit the secret police and turn the tables on them seems impossible according to our understanding of the regime, but Sholokhov did just that. New evidence suggests that he intentionally delayed completion of the novel to save his own life and to help his friends who had been falsely condemned as enemies of the people during the purges of 1936–38. At the height of the terror, which claimed over a million lives, Sholokhov became a member of the most minuscule subset of the Soviet population, the handful of individuals whom Stalin personally intervened to save rather than mechanically dispatch towards death with the stroke of a pen. This fact alone makes him worthy of attention.

Though Sholokhov always remained committed to candor as he understood it, his life provides a stunning case study of the elusiveness of truth in the Soviet era. Even an individual who stood very close to the levers of power got lost in a labyrinth of untruths and half-truths. Privy to more of the regime's secrets than any average citizen, he still struggled to make sense of key events. Did Maxim Gorky die of natural causes as reported in 1936? Or was he poisoned by enemies, as new reports ominously revealed during the Great Terror? When the authors of those revised reports were subsequently unmasked as subversive agents of imperialism in 1953, did this invalidate their testimony? If so, did they kill Gorky? Sholokhov's persistent struggle to extract truth from the regime's official deceptions, aka fake news, forms an important aspect of my narrative.

In rankings of the most controversial recipients of the Nobel Prize in Literature, Sholokhov's name always appears at the top. The unsealing of the Swedish Academy's archive related to his nominations, which took place in 2015, makes it possible to tell the full story of this controversial Cold War event for the first time. An English knight, a French philosopher, and a Soviet hypnotist are among the odd cast of characters who contributed to his cause. Reflecting increasing Soviet openness to the Western world, in less than a decade the Nobel Prize went from being perceived as a "reactionary instrument of warmongering" to a coveted symbol of Soviet achievement. But Sholokhov's award was tainted by a dubious distinction. He became the only laureate to ever be accused of plagiarism by another recipient of the Nobel Prize in Literature. I reveal that there is a Cold War logic to this as well, by uncovering an alliance between two of Sholokhov's old foes: Aleksandr Solzhenitsyn and Harrison Salisbury of the *New York Times*.

Why tell this story now? The resurgence of Russia makes Sholokhov an important figure for our era. Under Gorbachev, alternative, unofficial aspects of Sholokhov's biography surfaced for the first time. After the USSR collapsed, Sholokhov's reputation took a precarious dive. It seemed as if the dissidents had triumphed and the Western, capitalist values he reviled would take hold in Russia. But in Putin's Russia, Sholokhov is a hero once again. The statist, illiberal ideology of Russian resilience that he advocated is more pervasive now than ever. The fact that he was one of the first major intellectuals to call for a Russian revival in the late Soviet era makes him a harbinger of today's Russian nationalism. In 2005 Vladimir Putin made a personal pilgrimage to the writer's home to mark the one hundredth anniversary of his birth.[3] In Russian official circles and academic institutions, Sholokhov the classic writer is continuously honored. The fears and flaws of the mortal man have been all but erased from official history. In order to better comprehend contemporary Russia's contradictory perceptions of a 20th century in which triumph and terror, disturbing fears, and improbable feats of achievement are inextricably interwoven, there is no better place to start than with the life of Sholokhov.

ONE

After forty-eight hours in a holding cell, the final hour arrived. A man with a rifle came to lead young Sholokhov away. Each step brought him closer to a hastily dug pit. The young communist had dreamed of acting, writing, and making his mark on the world. Now he would leave behind only a few handwritten plays.[1] His final testament, if it could be called that, was a bureaucratic report explaining why tax collection in his district was lagging. Only weeks earlier, in June 1922, he had written, "Every day dozens of people die. Even the roots of plants have all been eaten up and the only thing edible that remains is grass and tree bark."[2] One more death in a year in which hundreds of thousands of Soviet citizens had starved to death and in a decade in which war had consumed millions of Russians would certainly go unnoticed.

How did a teenager find himself awaiting execution? His father had suffered a sudden onset of mental illness and had had to give up his job in fall 1921. Young Sholokhov needed money to support his parents. This forced him into the most terrible teenage job imaginable—working as a tax collector during a famine. Several months later, in summer 1922, he was arrested for falsifying records.

He had tried to help the Cossacks of his district by being merciful. But those were unmerciful times. He had saved lives by falsifying tax lists and selectively lowering grain contributions. But he was caught and arrested. He was convicted of abusing his position of power.[3] Now a revolutionary tribunal could decree that he would lose his life.[4] Only a few formalities remained. An official began to read the judgement: "In the name of the People's Commissariat for Justice I hereby declare . . ." Sholokhov tried to protest that he admitted his mistakes and could still be useful to the Soviet government. Wincing in anticipation of the barrage of bullets that would tear into his flesh, he could picture himself falling backwards, downward, to his death.[5] Nothing happened. Suddenly, a voice started to speak again. Only the decisive word *probation* sunk in. He realized that at that moment his life began anew.

This was no revolutionary miracle. It was the result of a cunning deception.

His father had bribed a local priest to create a false baptismal record, which instantly transformed him into a minor under Soviet law.[6] This legal stratagem resulted in the lesser penalty of probation, but for the rest of his life this original sin against the Soviet regime would haunt him. He would dedicate his life to paying the Soviet government back for its mercy and making it proud of his achievements.

The arrest and conviction in 1922 became a decisive turning point in Sholokhov's biography. The blemish on his record meant that many communist careers would be closed to him. He would have to work considerably harder than others to fashion a loyal Soviet identity. There was no looking back. In fall 1922 he moved to Moscow, where he could become a new person.

The big metropolis would provide him with an opportunity for a fresh start.[7] In Moscow there would be no whispering about his mother's past indiscretions as a servant in a manor house. Local derision of him as a bastard boy born to a despised outsider and not a Cossack wouldn't matter to anyone in the capital. Nobody in Moscow knew that he began his life as Mikhail Kuznetsov, not Sholokhov, or could recall him as a small, sometimes sickly boy who was often teased. For all they knew he actually did run away to fight for the Bolsheviks during the civil war rather than just daydream about doing so.

He arrived in Moscow with little money and a few addresses of contacts who might provide him with a place to spend the night while he was getting on his feet.[8] Joining the thousands of out-of-work provincials and former Red Army soldiers who flooded into the capital in search of opportunity, he registered with the government labor bureau. This was supposed to be a first step towards getting a job. The offices, however, were crowded, understaffed, and ineffective. He discovered that his chances of joining a trade union and getting a steady job were minuscule. Skilled workers were in demand, but his range of skills was limited.

He spent months working odd jobs such as unloading train cars and laying bricks. Such menial tasks were both unsatisfying and uninspiring. He felt a compelling urge to exercise his intellect. Young men and women no better than himself were studying and starting professions. Sometimes a whole day of back-breaking labor earned him around a million rubles, but with that he could barely afford to buy more than a few potatoes. The Soviet Union was in the process of phasing out the hyper-inflated paper currency of the civil war era. One new paper ruble could be worth a million old ones.

In the evenings he started to hang around with young people from the provinces who were residing in dormitories in central Moscow.[9] Several of them were enrolled in special preparatory courses for workers and peasants who desired to obtain a higher education. Others were attending crash courses on journalism, literature, and history. Their conversations were of a different sort than those at labor sites. Was Lenin correct in arguing that hieroglyphs cannot reflect objective realities? Did Trotsky's neologism *Proletkul't*, an abbreviation for proletarian cultural strivings, suit the current cultural moment? Should the USSR seek loans and diplomatic recognition from hostile, capitalist countries? In the warm, welcoming company of these ambitious students he began to imagine a different life. Some of them were moonlighting as authors and writing articles for the burgeoning socialist publishing scene. Sometimes they earned more for publishing a short article than he made in a whole week of back-breaking labor. He had been considered something of a wit back home, and now he was holding his own in the company of these students. Why shouldn't he try his hand at writing? After all, one of his plays was so good that people in his hometown could hardly believe he wrote it. If only he could find the time, he resolved to give it a try.

His chances of success were slim. One contemporary observer estimated that there were around three thousand youngsters trying to make it as writers in Moscow.[10] They were staying with friends or sleeping in stairwells. Some even resorted to renting space in water closets. The "fortunate" ones ended up finding rooms in communal apartments, where they tried to write while surrounded by angry or amorous neighbors, hissing gas heaters, crying children, and cackling gramophones in adjacent rooms that seemed to play nonstop. To continue writing at night they pilfered lightbulbs from lamps in public stairwells.

After he spent almost a year stringing together temporary jobs and beds, his circumstances changed dramatically in summer 1923. His belief in better luck and brighter possibilities suddenly paid off. An acquaintance arranged for him to begin working as a clerk in a residential building that belonged to the Moscow housing administration. The job came with two enormous perks. On many days he finished work by the early afternoon. This provided him with precious time to write and to observe the moving panorama of Moscow life. It also came with a great rarity in those years—a room all his own.

Fortune also favored him with a mentor.[11] He got to know Vasilii Kudashev. Vas'ka, as Sholokhov called him, was only slightly older, but he was already slightly balding. In the ways of Moscow he was far wiser. He had arrived in the capital as a late teen from a peasant home during the civil war and had done his time as a day laborer as well. After a stint in the Communist Youth League he was admitted to a university preparatory program. Simultaneously he attended literary gatherings throughout the city. He honed his writing skills and was already a published author. He agreed to become Sholokhov's knowing guide to the Moscow literary scene. Vas'ka took him to lectures about literature and introduced him to editors. He provided advice and encouragement at a crucial crossroads in Sholokhov's life.

Only weeks after he left menial labor behind, Sholokhov's first story appeared in print under the name M. Sholokh. Entitled *A Test*, it was about a secret mission to test the loyalty and reliability of a rural Communist Youth League secretary.[12] A provocateur was assigned to share a carriage with the secretary and report back to his superiors. The provocateur dismissed a rural agricultural exhibition as idiocy, cursed young communists as hooligans and atheists, and condemned the financing of an air force. These declarations only provoked minor reactions. But when he began to assail Soviet leaders, the secretary could not contain his anger and pounced on the provocateur. The official passed the test. Sholokhov did as well. Other editors were now interested in commissioning stories from him. Sholokhov's sense that hidden provocations abounded and that certain red lines should never be crossed when talking about the Soviet government served him well on that occasion and would become deeply ingrained in his personal ideology.

Though things were going well in Moscow, a compelling force pulled Sholokhov back to the Don region. Her name was Maria Petrovna Gromoslavskaia.[13] She was no stunning beauty, but she had a pleasant, country appearance. She was full of tender, caring affection. He called her Marusia. She had worked with him when he was a local tax official. His arrest put an abrupt end to their courting. He corresponded with her from Moscow and promised to return. He came back for her in late 1923. Her father was a former Cossack leader who took one look at Sholokhov and dismissively declared, "*Golytba.*" This was an ancient Cossack word for a penniless, non-Cossack, migrant with no prospects. Marusia and her sisters pleaded with him for several evenings until he finally relented. There would be no financial support for the couple. They would have to make it on their own. Her family could only offer them a sack of grain and a few items to pawn in Moscow. With the occasional articles he published they could aspire to sometimes attend the theater in addition to paying for food and rent.

Only a few days after they arrived in the capital to start their new lives together the entire city was plunged into shock.[14] On the morning of January 22, 1924, hawkers and criers fanned out across the city. "Extra! Extra! Death of the Supreme Leader" and "Lenin passes away," they shouted in rhythmic repetition. A combined extra edition of the national papers reported that Lenin had lost consciousness and died from a brain hemorrhage. The most important piece of information was missing. Who would be in charge now? A day later Sholokhov began to suspect who had taken over the reins of power. The list of members of the honor guard for Lenin's coffin was announced. Curiously, it was not presented in alphabetical order. The first name on the list was Stalin, followed by Zinoviev, Kamenev, Kalinin, Bukharin, and others. Trotsky's name was nowhere to be found. This caused immediate speculations. Had he been killed? Was he imprisoned? Soon it became clear that he was in the Caucasus and would arrive later.

After the newspapers announced that the public would have the opportunity to say good-bye to Lenin, Sholokhov and Marusia headed to the House of Soviets.[15] The four classical columns of its façade were draped in black and red banners.[16] They saw a mass of people in dark overcoats, fur hats, and wool kerchiefs, who had braved extreme frosts. They joined a line that snaked for almost a mile across central Moscow. The conversations were subdued and somber. Red Army soldiers kept order and made sure the line continued moving. They entered a large hall and passed by hundreds of wreaths and banners from every corner of the USSR. An orchestra was playing funeral music, and they were surrounded by sounds of sobbing and occasional hysterics. Lenin's body rested in a raised coffin amid a sea of greenery. Members of the government and military officers stood at attention as an honor guard. It took them only about nine seconds to pass before the casket. They were not allowed to linger and were ushered forward. As they departed from a different door, the cavalry was there to make sure that the approaching masses remained separate from the departing masses.

A few months later Sholokhov would pay homage to Lenin in a short story about a little boy who heard about Lenin from his father and who repeatedly pours out his heart to a card with Lenin's picture on it.

In May 1924 they returned to the Don region and lived for several months with his parents. His abrupt decision to leave a steady job appears to have stemmed from a scheme to "improve" his biography.[17] Upon leaving Moscow, his finances were so precarious that he fretted he would not have the money to return to the capital if his latest short story was rejected. He had hatched a plan to join the Communist Youth League. This would open doors in the publishing world and enable him to pursue a higher education. After six months the plan spectacularly failed. The reasons remain murky. His Communist Youth League application was initially accepted at the local level and then subsequently voided at the district level. His father's merchant background, his wife's Cossack family, and his arrest were all strikes against him. This rejection meant that party membership would remain closed to him. He resolved to get by without it rather than to fight the decision.

He returned to Moscow. The assurance that at least he could stay with Vas'ka until he got on his feet again propelled him forward. Marusia remained behind with his parents. He brought with him several stories and a fresh backstory.[18] He took to wearing a Kuban' Cossack cap and a military tunic. This new form of self-fashioning became a key to marketing his latest stories.[19] The suggestion that he had a revolutionary past helped him stand out in the crowd. If editors jumped to the conclusion that his pro-Soviet tales of civil war scrapes and requisition detachments were autobiographical, he would not rush to disabuse them of such notions.

Though editors recognized his raw talent, they remarked that he was in too much of a hurry to publish.[20] His stories still needed work and careful reflection. One editor advised him, "Don't rush, it's worth taking the time to work on a story . . . Be more patient and deliberate." When he was introduced to the famous Cossack writer Alexander Serafimovich in spring 1925, he received similar advice. Serafimovich felt that the youngster needed to continue to learn, to polish each piece of writing and not be in a rush. Lamentably, Sholokhov didn't have time to follow such good advice. Without a steady stream of stories, he could not make ends meet. In summer 1925 he was forced to return to the Don region for several months to attend to his dying father. He soon learned that Marusia was expecting their first child.

By early 1926 he was enjoying moderate success as an author of short stories.[21] He traveled back and forth between Moscow and the Don region. Most of his new stories were finding their way into print. He was now able to send money home to both his wife and his mother. He was able to purchase a typewriter and could even contemplate moving Marusia back to Moscow. He was receiving various proposals to either submit new stories or to publish several stories together in a collection. By spring 1926 he was negotiating to publish reprints of his stories with two different publishers. Upon publication he could hope to net roughly two times the annual salary of a non-skilled worker, and he could expect to receive even more if subsequent editions materialized.

There were only two problems. He had promised the same stories to both publishers and didn't actually have in his possession typescripts of the stories he was expected to deliver. Fueled by his desire to succeed at any cost, he brashly and boldly plunged ahead with his plans for dual publication. He boasted to Marusia, "They might prosecute me for this sort of thing, but I'm not afraid."[22] In order to meet an impending deadline, he and Vas'ka showed up at the office of the publisher that issued the stories. He stood watch as Vas'ka tore pages out of bound back issues of journals. The tables were starting to turn in their relationship. Sholokhov was becoming more successful than his former mentor.

He realized that he was courting scandal, so he decided to come clean to one of the publishers. He showed up at the office and nonchalantly reported that three of his stories would also be published in another collection. The publisher got angry and categorically refused to permit this. But Sholokhov was ready for such a reaction. He confidently announced he would dissolve his publishing agreement and go to court if necessary. The stratagem worked. His only punishment was a nasty letter from one publisher.[23] Fortunately, he was still in demand at other publishing houses. Increasingly editors encouraged him to bring them something bigger. They said he needed a "larger canvas" to enhance his reputation. Without a novel to his name, he risked reaching a plateau in his career.

TWO

etween April of 1926 and September of 1927 Sholokhov performed a literary miracle.[1] Never before—and never again—would a similar feat be accomplished. During those incredible months he managed to generate hundreds of typed pages of some of the most engaging prose ever to appear in Russia, a country blessed with Tolstoy, Chekhov, Dostoevsky, and numerous other gifted writers. On an epic scale he narrated events that occurred in far-flung trenches of World War I, distant centers of power, and revolutionary meetings. He described multiple historical figures he had never met, and he painted vivid verbal pictures of battles that took place when he was still a boy. Brief periods of mad, feverish writing were sandwiched between moves, multiple trips to Moscow to meet with editors, and the birth of his first child.

His literary output during those months exponentially exceeded the accomplishments of his whole career up to that point and most decades of his career afterward.[2] The improvement in quality was incredible. None of his colleagues wept with rapture when they read his early, formulaic, communist short stories. Early editors sometimes had to apply a heavy, corrective hand just to get some of them into print. Suddenly seasoned editors were in awe of his prose. Even more mind-boggling is the fact that this rapid, unexpected literary metamorphosis occurred at the age of twenty-two.

How did he manage to pull off such an improbable literary feat? Some locals insisted that he acquired manuscripts that were left behind when the Cossack side was routed by the Red Army during the civil war.[3] At a minimum the archive he acquired appears to have included an unfinished novel that ended around 1919 and a trove of scrapbooks consisting of stories, sketches, newspaper clippings, and articles spanning over a decade of Cossack history.[4]

His first encounter with the materials he would weave into the fabric of his famous novel can only be imaginatively reconstructed. At first glance such a mélange of materials must have resembled a ragman's haul rather than a novel. Due to shortages during the civil war Russians resorted to repurposing every imaginable variety of paper. Stories were penned on pages ripped from old school notebooks or under imperial letterheads made obsolete by two revolutions. Memories were scribbled on the backs of long-forgotten proclamations. Missives in minuscule letters snaked across scraps of paper. A closer look at the materials betrayed the signs of a bygone era: the three letters of the Russian alphabet outlawed by Lenin in 1918.[5]

Sholokhov must have experienced both a rush of excitement and a sense of frustration in encountering this treasure trove for the first time.[6] He had to separate out and arrange pages into related groups by handwriting and content. He had to restore sequences and complete scenes which abruptly ended or trailed off without resolution. There were isolated fragments and reminiscences of varying length and quality. From a large pile an irritatingly beautiful story started to emerge. Like the young Michelangelo confronting the Apollo Belvedere, a Roman sculpture of impeccable quality that lost its head and limbs due to mutilation in late antiquity, he had to look past the defects and see the whole in his mind's eye. Applying imagination to restoration was just a first, tentative step towards intellectual appropriation.

For months he wavered about what to do.[7] Several of his own stories looked juvenile in comparison. Should he just draw inspiration from these materials? Should he mine them for facts? Or could he somehow give them new life? He had read enough philosophy to savor the existential irony of works of beauty lost to the world. At the same time he was pragmatic enough to realize that in its current form nothing from this trove could be publishable in the USSR. As he searched for an answer, the Soviet government offered him solutions. The realms of policy and law unexpectedly spoke to his literary dilemma.

In summer 1925 the government unveiled a dramatic policy shift.[8] The Cossacks would no longer be treated as a hostile, enemy population living under an occupation regime. The regional government determined that "indiscriminately negative" attitudes towards Cossack populations in southern Russia had impeded the growth of the Soviet economy. Many Cossacks believed that vengeance and spite were the driving forces behind Soviet policies. In order to boost the rural economy, local administrations were ordered to actively involve formerly hostile populations in local government. They were instructed to take into consideration Cossack "customs, habits, and traditions." After this directive Cossack traditions were talked about openly and positively in the Soviet press for the first time. The head of the regional administration even proclaimed that it was wrong to persecute the Cossacks after the civil war.

This was an important signal that it could be lucrative for Sholokhov to truly engage the "big thing" as he sometimes called it. Plans of cashing in on large honoraria and thoughts of hundreds of rubles accumulating page by page appear to have enticed him in the beginning.[9] After working with the "big thing" it became more than a book. It became a mission. From the moment he started to connect narrative threads and patch seams, he shifted from passive consumer to passionate cocreator. He moved, merged, and juxtaposed texts, combining them with new sections drawn from his own background.[10] He added communist threads and amplified communist characters. He wrote new scenes to connect together fragments and to create a grand tapestry. He feared that if something happened to him *Quiet Don* would "become orphaned."[11]

The result was a deeply tragic epic centered on two star-crossed lovers and a community in crisis. It offered much more than a romantic story beautifully told. The opening section provides a visceral, multi-sensory immersion into a small community where life is dominated by ancient traditions, agricultural rhythms, and old men who make the everyday decisions that govern the lives of all. Subsequent sections chronicle the twilight of a culture and a way of life swept up into a whirlwind of war and revolution. A society defined by honor, brutality, obedience, and hierarchy struggles to come to terms with individuals who go their own way. The Cossack military caste, which had served the tsars for centuries, fights to survive as its reason for existence vanishes and the revolution brings equality.

The narrative begins with the family history of the book's hero, Grigorii Melekhov. His grandmother was a Turkish captive brought from a military campaign by a Cossack. Her violent death sets the tone for the book. She was beaten to death by the residents of the settlement, who suspected her of being a witch responsible for the widespread death of cattle. Grigorii's father, who was born prematurely to the dying woman, rules the family with an iron fist. His explosive character, however, is starting to soften with age. A tall, swarthy teen with dark eyes and a nose reminiscent of a bird of prey, Grigorii begins to covet his neighbor's wife, Aksiniia Astakhova. She is a strong, beautiful, full-figured woman, with big dark eyes. Though she is a few years older than Grigorii, her "shamelessly-greedy, puffy lips" entice him. She had been raped by her father when she was sixteen and married off at seventeen to a man who viciously beat her on their first day of married life. Grigorii and Aksiniia's oft-thwarted desire to find happiness together drives the plot.

The novel follows the local Cossacks to the front lines of the First World War, where Grigorii witnesses the ugly sides of battle and others succumb to revolutionary agitation in the trenches. As a Cossack he is supposed to eagerly embrace the glory of combat, but he often he fails to see the sense of it. This sets the stage for a continuing series of vacillations about whom to serve and how to live. Taking a Tolstoyan turn, the novel depicts the coming of the revolution from different vantage points and introduces several real historical figures who fomented counterrevolution.

As Sholokhov contemplated publishing the novel, he likely discovered that a new Soviet law on intellectual property worked to his advantage.[12] The 1925 law on authorial rights made it nearly impossible for anyone to successfully lodge a claim against him and expect to receive financial compensation. The law explicitly stated, "It is not considered a violation of authorial rights . . . to use another person's work for the creation of a new work which is substantively different." The law did not explain either "new" or "substantively different." Since there was no case law to provide guidance, a very substantial gray area offered cover if anything went wrong. He could easily prove that the epic collage was substantially of his own making.

The vague provisions of the law created additional incentives for Sholokhov to claim sole authorship. The law provided no clear framework for recovering damages. It also established no criminal or civil penalties for infringement. By establishing a firm distinction between published and unpublished works, the law also created additional assurances that nobody could challenge him.

Assuming that the authors of texts used by Sholokhov died during the civil war on territory that was outside the control of Soviet authorities, the obstacles for anyone trying to assert intellectual property rights would be all but insurmountable. Soviet law ostensibly assigned heirs the rights to unpublished works for a period of fifteen years after the first day of January of the year after the author died. Any surviving relative would have to wade through a series of contradictory decrees on inheritance in order to assert rights. Just obtaining a death certificate could constitute a major ordeal, especially if none of the heirs had filed the proper paperwork to recognize the author as absent and presumed dead in accordance with the decree of June 17, 1918.[13] In a legal battle heirs would be required to prove that they included unpublished literary works in an inventory of property, which they were supposed to submit to Soviet authorities at the moment a death was recorded. If any of the heirs had ever concealed links to a relative who had served in a counterrevolutionary government or army—which, given the political sympathies of the materials, was highly likely—they would be even more reluctant to wage a fight they had little chance of winning.

If evidence ever came to light that he had used materials created by others, he could always claim to be experimenting with cutting-edge literary techniques.[14] He had attended lectures by the avant-garde literary theorist Osip Brik, who was advocating for a "literature of fact." In this new method, a literary work could consist of a creative montage of raw materials (documents, diaries, newspaper articles, or even overheard conversations). Many believed that revolutionary readers would in time grow to appreciate works in which real source material was creatively presented without significant alteration.

What did Sholokhov feel as he prepared to present the first volume of *Quiet Don* to fellow writers and editors? It seems probable that he was guided by thoughts of destiny rather than any nagging doubts or pangs of conscience. If such materials were being gathered by Don Cossacks for the benefit of a future Homer who would present their epic story to the world, then he was fulfilling their wishes.[15] He alone served as the arbiter between existence and oblivion: without his intellectual contributions the materials would in a best-case scenario end up under lock and key, gathering dust for decades in some museum. More likely they would perish. Stories intended for posterity would now be transmitted to posterity, regardless of who pocketed the honoraria. He must have also felt a sense of satisfaction. Deep inside him the boy who had been teased as a bastard and damned outsider, who was deprived of Cossack status from the moment his mother remarried, realized that he would no longer be an outsider looking in.[16] If his mission was successful, he would finally earn the respect of the Cossacks, and he would be the one shaping their narrative in the eyes of the world.

THREE

Nineteen twenty-seven was the perfect year to unveil the epic. As the tenth anniversary of the revolution approached, intellectuals were discussing whether its story could be told on a grand scale.[1] Debates raged in Moscow literary circles about whether Soviet writers should learn from the Russian classics or reject realistic, psychological portrayals altogether. One critic even spoke in early 1927 of a "fantastic belief in the coming of a 'Red Tolstoy,' who will unfurl the 'canvas' of a revolutionary epic." Sholokhov audaciously decided to step into that role.

He brought the manuscript of the first volume of *Quiet Don* to Moscow in summer 1927. Though Vasilii Kudashev and other young writers were enthralled with the novel, Sholokhov's submission was quickly rejected by a major state publishing house. The verdict was short and uncompromising: idealization of the Cossacks.[2] He took it home. He spent a few more weeks polishing it and producing a typed copy so that it could be under consideration at two presses. He returned to Moscow and submitted the manuscript to other presses in the fall.

The prestigious October publishing house agreed to consider the manuscript.[3] For several weeks it dragged its feet without announcing a decision. Behind the scenes a battle was raging. An aging Cossack writer, Alexander Serafimovich, was championing the book. He had joined the Communist Party before the revolution and had corresponded with Lenin, so his word carried weight. Having mentored Sholokhov on writing in 1925, he was surprised by the sudden transformation of an author who had previously written stories that in his opinion were small and "not bad."[4] Serafimovich nonetheless convinced a divided editorial board to publish the first volume of the novel in early 1928.[5]

The novel became an overnight success.[6] Sholokhov was immediately vaulted into the spotlight of Soviet celebrity. His public readings of the novel attracted crowds. Letters poured in from excited readers. Publishing houses started sending him lucrative offers of advances. Even the state publishing house, which was the first to reject *Quiet Don*, now offered to double what other houses were paying for rights to the next volume. From Moscow he wrote to Marusia, "My novel is resounding, this writer is rising to a zenith."

The reviews were overwhelmingly positive. Sholokhov was acclaimed as a rising star of Russian literature. The novel was hailed as a *War and Peace* of the revolutionary era. He was invited to the first Congress of "Proletarian" Writers. He was introduced to Maxim Gorky, the most famous Russian writer at the time. Serafimovich wrote a glowing endorsement in *Pravda*, the Soviet Union's most important daily newspaper. After that, print runs quickly ballooned into the hundreds of thousands. The days of Sholokhov's financial problems were over.

With fame came envy and suspicion. In Moscow, one of Sholokhov's first editors, Feoktist Berezovskii, became highly skeptical of his rapid metamorphosis. It just seemed too good to be true. He doubted that such prose could emanate from the pen of the same author whose promising, but problematic, short story he had laboriously edited just two years earlier. To fellow writers and editors he voiced his suspicions that something was fishy with Sholokhov's authorship claims. "How can anyone believe that a twenty-three-year-old without any education could write such a deep, psychologically true book?" he repeatedly asked.[7]

As the first volume reached ever larger Soviet audiences in book form in summer 1928, Sholokhov completed most of the second volume and searched for additional sources for the third volume. He planned to complete the trilogy by patterning Grigorii's experiences in the final book on the life of a Cossack named Harlampii Yermakov.[8] After leading a Cossack rebellion in 1919, Yermakov was captured by Soviet authorities in 1920.[9] Given an opportunity to redeem himself through service, he rapidly rose through the ranks of the Red Cavalry as it extinguished the last counterrevolutionary armies operating in Russia. He returned home in the mid-1920s but soon became embroiled in a series of local struggles to settle old scores. He was arrested in 1927.

Harlampii, the informant whom Sholokhov planned to rely on for the final volume of the novel, was shot as an enemy of the people before the writer could obtain a complete account of the uprising. Therefore he appealed to an organization that specialized in knowledge of all things anti-Soviet.[10] A secret police official agreed to help him obtain additional archival reports on the rebellion.[11]

By the time he secured those sources, he had already failed to submit the final installments of volume two to the publisher. Technically he was in violation of his contract. As he rushed to submit the final chapters of the second volume, he cut corners in sections devoted to Podtelkov and Krivoshlykov, two Cossack revolutionaries who were hanged in 1918 by a crowd of vigilantes. He borrowed heavily from a White Cossack journal published in 1918, a pamphlet published in the Soviet Union in 1920, and an unpublished memoir from the mid-1920s by a Cossack named Lagutin, which he discovered in a museum on a trip to the regional capital, Rostov.[12]

Oddly enough, this rash act would bring him to the attention of the most important man in the Soviet Union.[13] A prominent Moscow party official named Sergei Syrtsov had served in the Don region during the civil war and had closely interacted with both of the revolutionaries. In a conversation with Joseph Stalin about *Quiet Don*, the official complained about numerous inaccuracies in the recent installments.[14] The dictator, who was now starting to take an active interest in literary affairs and was beginning to imagine himself as a patron of the arts, resolved to keep his eye on the young author from the Don region.

Sholokhov soon came to the dictator's attention again, this time due to a plagiarism controversy.[15] In early 1929 rumors began to circulate in Moscow that an old woman had written to Soviet authorities claiming that her son, who disappeared during the civil war, had written a novel. She insisted that the recently published chapters of *Quiet Don* were identical to her son's book. As the story spread, it became more and more elaborate. In some versions the poor old woman was going from publisher to publisher hoping to arrange a tearful reunion with her missing son. In others, she was angrily demanding justice from the authorities. When the rumors reached Stalin and other members of the Central Committee of the Communist Party, out of curiosity they queried individual members of the Association of Proletarian Writers. The proletarian writers contacted state publishing houses. They could find no evidence to substantiate the fact that any publisher had actually been contacted by an old woman.

Nonetheless, the rumors persisted. Major publications continued to receive letters from readers inquiring about the controversy. Some of the rumors were so specific that they named actual prosecutors who were said to be investigating the case. Prosecutorial offices then started to receive queries. Phone calls flooded the switchboard of *Pravda* inquiring if the allegations were true. Censors at state telegraph offices started to notice. For the time being they deleted references to the controversy in telegrams being sent abroad.

In March 1929 the editorial board of *Pravda* (the Soviet Union's most important daily newspaper) convened an ad hoc tribunal to examine the allegations that Sholokhov had plagiarized *Quiet Don*. He was ordered to come to Moscow and bring manuscripts and any other evidence that could substantiate his authorship.[16] Upon hearing of the tribunal, he exploded in anger. "Despicable slander!" he exclaimed. As his anger subsided, he resolved to fight. He gathered up and packed several piles of manuscripts. Others would have to be retrieved from his editors in Moscow. He made plans to travel as soon as possible. Luckily the roads were still frozen and he would not encounter the mud, sludge, and flooded crossings that made them impassable with the spring thaw. The main thing was now to find out who the judges would be.

On his journey to Moscow he realized how far the rumors had spread and how dangerous they had become. During the long train ride he became so tightly wound that he could not relax. He worked himself into a state of nervous anxiety. This was a dangerous and dastardly attack on his reputation. Would he survive it? Would anyone ever publish him again?

Upon arrival his friends quickly supplied him with a list of names of fellow writers, or as he called them "bastard souls," who had expressed doubts. When he realized it was an organized campaign, he couldn't sleep. He completely lost his appetite after he found out that Stalin was inquiring about the plagiarism allegations. The words *extraordinary danger* kept coming to mind.

The tribunal that would examine his manuscripts included several writers. One of them was clearly his ally, Alexander Serafimovich. Several of the others had ties to the city of Rostov in the Don region (Fadeev, Stavskii, Kirshon).[17] One of the only published articles to insinuate doubts about his authorship of *Quiet Don* had emanated from there. On the one hand it seemed perfectly natural that writers familiar with his region would be asked to evaluate his manuscripts. On the other hand, Sholokhov could not completely rule out the possibility that someone there had discovered a secret about one of his sources. He had traveled to Rostov for a series of meetings and public readings in late 1928 and come away with the impression that he had conquered Rostov. Now he had to reassess that appraisal.

In Rostov he told his first public fib about the origins of *Quiet Don*.[18] When asked by a group of students about how he started working on the novel, he hastily improvised an answer. Obviously he could not say anything about a trove of texts and sources that fell into his lap. Instead he told the story backwards. He claimed to have started with a short story about the lynching of the two Cossack revolutionaries Podtelkov and Krivoshlykov in 1918. Upon reflection he decided that his readers would not realize how important this event was without an understanding of the deep divisions between the Cossacks who had returned from the trenches and the communities they had left behind when they went off to fight in the First World War. So he claimed to have widened the focus.

Then he went back further in time to start the novel on the eve of the war. In actuality, he had finished the section on the two revolutionaries only months earlier. It contained dialogues taken from a memoir that he had not yet seen at the time he claimed to have started working on the short story.[19] Did its author rat him out or lodge a complaint? Did that spawn new suspicions?

His meeting with the tribunal went well. He learned that there were no specific charges against him. No one had presented any tangible evidence that any part of the epic belonged to the pen of another writer. The members of the committee generally agreed that the persistent rumors needed to be quelled. They were not willing to put credence in vague suspicions about his age or lack of battle experience. They did, however, believe it was their responsibility to carefully examine his heap of manuscripts.

He presented the tribunal with several variant versions of early chapters with extensive evidence of editing and major stylistic revisions.[20] These demonstrated an evolution of both the characters and the plot. He also included a fragment of a story that appeared to predate *Quiet Don*, but which he later transformed for inclusion in the novel. Crucially he did not submit the chapters dealing with the two Cossack revolutionaries. Most importantly, there were hundreds of pages either written or corrected by his own hand. He also provided the names of witnesses who had seen him working on the manuscript of the novel in 1926–1927.

Several days later, *Pravda* published a lead article signed by five prominent writers.[21] It alluded to the rumors about plagiarism by Sholokhov and proclaimed them to be "malicious slander being spread by enemies of the proletarian dictatorship." Rumors were dismissed as an ancient and well-tested method of struggle deployed by class enemies. The writers expressed their full confidence in him: "The proletarian writers, who have worked with Sholokhov for years, know his entire creative career, his work during the course of several years on *Quiet Don*, the materials which he gathered and studied while working on the novel, as well as the rough drafts of his manuscripts." The article concluded that henceforth anyone in the USSR who perpetuated such slander could face criminal charges.

Sholokhov survived the plagiarism scandal, but he became convinced that envious writers were to blame for it. Henceforth, he resolved to avoid the viper's den of Moscow literary intrigues. He decided to put down roots in Vioshki, a market town of about three thousand residents in the northern Don region. It was more than a day's journey from the nearest railroad station, more if a change of horses was not readily available along the way. Letters from the capital arrived with a delay of a week or more. He was the only major Soviet writer who deliberately chose not to live in or near a large city.

FOUR

E ven after Sholokhov dodged the inquiry and the suspicion of his peers in the months after the initial publication of *Quiet Don*, a single article published in a regional newspaper in 1929 almost destroyed the reputation of the celebrated, if enigmatic, young author. The article, which accused him of aiding the enemies of communism in rural areas, precipitated two defining ideological moments of Sholokhov's career: his first brush with political denunciation and his transformation into a loyal Stalinist. He would have to negotiate for the first time the complex nexus of political controversies and draconian policies that were at the heart of Stalinization in the late 1920s. How did our author find himself walking the high-wire of Stalinist politics?

In 1929 the districts to the north of Sholokhov's home became one of the most important testing grounds for Stalin's rural revolution.[1] The last remnants of capitalism in agriculture were being decisively "smashed" in a vicious, experimental campaign unleashed by the Soviet government. Popular animosity and envy were deployed against an artificially created internal enemy—the *kulak*, literally meaning 'fist,' figuratively identifying hardworking and entrepreneurial peasants. A terrible tribute was extracted from the countryside. The poor were encouraged to pillage the more prosperous as a means of financing the first wave of industrialization and promoting the rapid collectivization of agriculture. In late spring 1929 the first victims of these new policies began to appear on Sholokhov's doorstep.

Why did victims clamor to share their plight with him? They had read *Quiet Don*. The novel's sympathetic portrayal of an agricultural community stirred up hopes that the author might become a voice for the dispossessed. Believing in the fairness of the Soviet system and thinking that he could rectify injustices, Sholokhov unwittingly stepped into the minefield of Stalinist politics.

Though the Communist Party succeeded in seizing control of the Russian countryside after the revolution, it failed to solve the problem of rural inequality. Lands belonging to the nobility, landlords, and tsarist officials were confiscated and redistributed to poorer peasants, but soil alone was no panacea for rural poverty. The balance of power remained in favor of households that owned draft animals. The poorest segments of the rural population—nearly one in three households in some areas—owned no horses, mules, or oxen. They remained dependent upon animals and equipment that they seasonally leased from their more prosperous neighbors (branded as *kulaks*). Though the old classes were gone, many rural residents resented the fact that exploitation still remained.

Unbeknown to Sholokhov, the new agricultural policies that destroyed so many households were part of a coordinated Stalinist effort to impose socialism on the peasantry. The countryside would be forced to serve Stalin's great vision of rapid industrialization, no matter the cost. When Soviet officials encountered resistance from people who did not want to sell their grain for paltry government prices, the Soviet machine unleashed a wave of terror from below that destroyed the most able, productive, and entrepreneurial members of the agricultural community. Stalin had declared war on the *kulaks*.

A Cossack with a solid Soviet biography who arrived on Sholokhov's doorstep embodied a typical victim of the senseless pillaging of this campaign.[2] In a matter of hours a man who had volunteered and served in the Red Army during the civil war and who had spent six years risking life and limb to defend the revolution had lost nearly everything. By every indication he was not a wealthy peasant. His land allotment was modest, and he neither owned machinery nor employed hired labor. When he was branded a *kulak* by his neighbors, everything that wasn't nailed down was confiscated from his home. Nearly all of his personal possessions were seized to pay a portion of his impossible tax burden. The socialist equalizers even ripped the blankets off the beds of his five children. His horse and team of two oxen were led to communal stock pens, where they perished from neglect and diseases due to overcrowding before they could be of profit to the "socialist sector."

In case after case, petitioners reported to Sholokhov that local communist officials did everything in their power to keep victims from exercising their rights as Soviet citizens. Throughout the campaign to smash the *kulaks*, party officials refused to issue travel documents. Postal and telegraph employees were prohibited from accepting any complaints or correspondence addressed to higher party officials outside the Volga region. By traveling to Vioshki, which was in a different administrative jurisdiction where such harsh policies had not yet been implemented, many Cossacks were able to send telegrams to Moscow detailing the injustices. Inevitably they received terse responses indicating that the matter had been forwarded back to local officials for investigation. Heartbroken by stories of such monumental injustices and deeply dismayed by these breaches of Soviet legality, Sholokhov helped a number of his visitors craft letters of protest to party officials in Moscow.[3]

Why was such horror visited upon the countryside in 1929? Since the rural economy was recovering to prerevolutionary grain production levels, Stalinist planners built increasing agricultural output and optimistic targets for export of grain into the calculations of their first five-year plan, which aimed to rapidly industrialize and modernize the Soviet economy and bolster the country's defense capacity. Finally, and most importantly, since the country had entered into a new stage of socialist construction, Stalin expected an intensification of the class struggle and more vigorous resistance from former capitalist elements.

This appeared to be confirmed when extraordinary measures to procure grain in several districts met with noncompliance. When peasants refused to part with their grain, their actions "confirmed" the official view that a *kulak* element was inciting resistance. The situation looked very different on the ground. In the face of dramatic shifts in Soviet agricultural policy, many farmers simply adopted a position of waiting. They kept their grain and refused to sell. This in turn caused a crisis for state procurement and foreign trade officials, who were locked into contracts to sell grain abroad to purchase industrial machinery. As it became clear that procurement targets would not be met, local officials resorted to improvisation. In some areas they promised credits or organized deliveries of manufactured goods such as tools and textiles to barter for grain. In other areas they resorted to "extraordinary measures" in order to fulfill their procurement quotas. "Extraordinary" in the Soviet context ordinarily meant extreme and violent. Technically pillaging was illegal under Soviet law, but soon violent expropriation became the defining feature of Stalinist revolution in the countryside.[4] Nondelivery now became an act of criminal conspiracy. Grain hiding or hoarding became markers of "*kulak* sabotage."

The dozens of Cossacks who journeyed to Vioshki in spring 1929 reported to Sholokhov that the campaign to smash the *kulak* had devolved into an all-out attack on the middle segments of rural society.[5] "Committees of the poor" were arbitrarily assigning households to the *kulak* category. This in turn triggered on-the-spot assignments of higher grain contributions. Those who were suddenly categorized as *kulaks* were ordered to surrender as much as 30 percent more grain than in previous years. When no hidden grain was surrendered, the poor then ransacked their homes and farms. In theory these confiscated items were to be publicly auctioned for payment of the extraordinary penalties. In practice many of them ended up in the hands of the poor activists.

Officially the Soviet government could maintain that it played no role in these outrages, which were ostensibly committed by the poor. But Sholokhov learned that Boris Sheboldaev and other party officials in the lower Volga region had colluded in these violations of Soviet law. In case after case, his visitors reported that party officials did everything in their power to keep victims from realizing their rights as Soviet citizens.

Deeply saddened and dismayed by these breaches of Soviet legality, Sholokhov helped a number of individuals craft letters of protest to Mikhail Kalinin, who was the Soviet Union's unofficial ombudsperson. Weeks passed without answer or acknowledgement. The silence from Kalinin hurt the writer particularly hard. His belief in the sincerity of Soviet legality was shaken. The press continuously promoted the myth that in Moscow a genteel, bearded, bespectacled man was constantly looking out for the little guy.[6] Articles insisted that Kalinin was working tirelessly to help individuals whose rights had been trampled on by callous local officials. Kalinin was depicted as a dynamo who resolved up to five hundred petitions a day and constantly chided careless and heartless local officials. According to press reports he acted quickly and decisively to correct wrongs. But Sholokhov began to realize that all of this was false. Numerous victims had sent urgent telegrams to Kalinin. Their compelling evidence of senseless pillaging and all-out lawlessness had been ignored. Not a single one of those cases resulted in restorative justice or "revolutionary legality."

Meanwhile the countryside was descending into lawlessness. In the middle of the night on June 17, 1929, Sholokhov heard an insistent pounding on the door of his house. Springing out of bed at two in the morning he opened the door and discovered that police had gathered outside. They were not there to arrest him. They only wanted to borrow a saddle. Reports indicated that a gang of armed bandits was approaching from an adjacent district. The police had been ordered to form mobile posses that would patrol the roads in case of an incursion. Sholokhov's thoughts continuously returned to the civil war era. Soviet newspapers were busy proclaiming that the spring grain procurement campaign had triumphed and that the pressure on *kulaks* had been accomplished. He was wary of such rhetoric because he had read similar proclamations from the White propagandists during the civil war. These often came on the eve of the total collapse of the White forces.

Under the impression of these traumatic events, Sholokhov wrote a letter to a friend in Moscow.[7] He detailed what his visitors had reported about the savage grain requisitions and their unsuccessful efforts to seek redress. He shared his fears that the region was full of "incendiary material" and that policies had led to the appearance of armed bandits for the first time since the civil war. He ironically spoke of the oblivious patter of the newspapers and openly labeled the party's position hypocritical. Incautiously, he shared his thoughts that those who had devised and implemented such policies "ought to end up behind thick bars, up to and including Kalinin himself." He even suggested that he was contemplating giving up—literally tossing aside—his literary work. As he penned the letter, he didn't know that in secret meetings of the Politburo Stalin had recently defended the very policies that he was criticizing.[8] Without knowing it, Sholokhov was now on record as opposing the wisdom of the highest leadership.

Soon thereafter Sholokhov saw his name vilified in the local press in an article accusing him of abetting the *kulak* camp.[9] Recognizing his status as an important writer, the article berated him for thinking that "politics is not his affair." He was depicted as an individual who closed himself off from Soviet society "behind the shutters of his house" while welcoming "whole delegations" of *kulaks*. He was abetting the enemy: when a former Cossack leader of a nearby settlement was proclaimed a *kulak* and threatened with the public auction of his property for nonpayment of the tax, Sholokhov stepped in to pay it for him. Furthermore, he intervened on behalf of his sister-in-law, who had been deprived of political rights due to her social origins as the daughter of a church psalm reader. Finally, the article accused him of not denouncing scandals in the local branch of the Communist Youth League.

When Sholokhov learned of these dangerous accusations, he initiated a vigorous defense of his reputation. At the time, anti-*kulak* rhetoric was reaching a feverish pitch and thousands of sympathizers were being arrested: the anti-Sholokhov exposé was now potentially a matter of life and death. A second wave of grain requisitions was due to culminate in October in honor of the anniversary of the revolution. As a result, rhetoric was becoming more martial and more violent. The newspapers were full of calls for the destruction of *kulak* resistance and the striking of death blows against the *kulak* enemy.[10] Anyone who expressed sympathy for the *kulaks* or even their innocent children risked being labeled a *kulak* abettor in fall 1929. Sholokhov penned a rebuttal to the article and submitted it to the editorial board of the newspaper that in his opinion had defamed him. For over two weeks he waited in vain for a reply. His only recourse was to travel to the regional capital and lobby on his own behalf to party officials.

Upon his arrival in Rostov he discovered that the mood in the regional capital was even more militant than he'd anticipated. Important national and regional leaders had converged there for a conference on agricultural affairs.[11] In unison they proclaimed that a new front needed to be opened in the struggle against the *kulak*. All of the problems with the fall grain procurement campaign were now blamed on "*kulak* sabotage" and "*kulak* slander." In pursuit of justice Sholokhov visited party officials to proclaim his innocence. They could only be of limited help, since he was not a member of the Communist Party.

He petitioned the North Caucasus Association of Proletarian Writers to investigate the allegations against him. He also penned a new rebuttal of all the allegations and demanded that it be published prior to the completion of the investigation. He declared, "I consider it my duty to declare that I am in full and complete agreement with party policy and the Soviet government in the peasant question. I am firmly convinced that in the period of reconstruction of agriculture, pressuring the *kulak*, who has withheld surplus grain, is the only correct line. For that very reason alone I cannot be a defender of *kulak* interests." The declaration appeared in print on October 6, 1929.[12]

Though Sholokhov was permitted this brief, public proclamation of loyalty, he was not allowed to openly refute any of the specific charges. Within days of his public embrace of the party line, the North Caucasus Association of Proletarian Writers took up his request for an investigation. Journalist and literary critic Ivan Makar'ev was sent on a fact-finding visit to Vioshki.[13] Having authored a brochure entitled "Why the *Kulak* Is Our Enemy" in 1928, well before the escalation of the current campaign, Makar'ev was the logical choice for the mission. If anyone could sniff out a *kulak* sympathizer, it was him.

Makar'ev interviewed Sholokhov and judged him to be politically illiterate. He concluded that the writer was without a doubt a sincere supporter of the Soviet cause, but one who was remarkably naïve about current party policies.[14] Makar'ev also came to believe that Sholokhov was only partially to blame for his political mistakes because the writer had been left to his own devices in a large Cossack settlement where no constructive ideological influences were present. In his opinion the best hope for saving Sholokhov's writing career was to convince him to become more involved with the Communist Party.

Sholokhov returned home to await the results of the investigation. If Makar'ev decided to cast a wide net, he would surely uncover the fact that Sholokhov had provided consultations to multiple individuals who had been branded as *kulaks* by "committees of the poor." If the letter to Moscow had been opened and perused by the local postmaster or the secret police, Makar'ev might even discover that the writer had disseminated "*kulak* slander" and had vigorously criticized the Stalinist position. The anti-*kulak* investigator could easily turn against the writer and destroy his career.

Luckily for Sholokhov, Makar'ev began his investigation by interviewing the journalist who wrote the exposé. He discovered that the story was based entirely upon rumors. Makar'ev was able to clear Sholokhov's name by dismissing the charges to be the "most vile slander." The final report proclaimed that since Sholokhov had given the country one of the best works of literature in recent years, there could be no basis to any charge that he was disconnected from society.[15] Due to his fame, Sholokhov often received uninvited visitors, but the overwhelming majority of them were from the poor and middle segments of the rural population. Even if there were a few cases of *kulaks* bringing complaints among those visitors, the important thing was how he reacted to them. He had never interceded for *kulaks*.

Within weeks Sholokhov returned to working on the remaining installments of *Quiet Don*. He also made plans to submit an application for candidacy to the Communist Party. Though he emerged unscathed from the campaign to smash the *kulak*, the novel was not so fortunate. In order to assert his loyalty, he incorporated an anti-*kulak* rant into one of the new chapters of *Quiet Don*.[16] This was a sad, but seminal, choice for the writer and for the novel, especially given his genuine attempts to help those who were being persecuted. By initially sympathizing with the victims of Soviet oppression, Sholokhov had unwittingly risked ruining his writing career. By changing his tune, he took a decisive step towards becoming a Stalinist writer.

FIVE

O nly weeks after the *kulak* controversy died down, critics attacked Sholokhov again. This time he was the recipient of blows intended for Maxim Gorky. Before Sholokhov could even obtain a copy of the offensive article that labeled him a counterrevolutionary, a decree from the Central Committee appeared in the press. It rebuked the journal for "hooliganism" and fired its editor. What caused the Kremlin to intervene decisively and heavy-handedly against a small clique of provincial literary critics? How did invisible bonds come to connect Sholokhov, Gorky, and Stalin?

Maxim Gorky was the most prominent Russian writer to embrace the revolution. Rising to prominence in the 1890s, he was arrested in 1905 and after release went into exile abroad for eight years.[1] Though he sympathized with the Bolshevik cause in 1917, he nevertheless criticized Lenin's commissars for dispersing peaceful demonstrations and unleashing violence against their rivals. His influence helped gain support for the revolution among intellectuals in Russia and abroad. In return, the Bolsheviks permitted him to protect cultural monuments and intercede for various intellectuals who had fallen afoul of the new regime. As he increasingly expressed pessimism about Lenin's despotism, he faced humiliating rebuffs from state publishing bureaucrats. A mutual parting of ways took place in 1921, when Gorky was permitted to leave the USSR. Officially he was leaving to restore his health and strengthen ties between Soviet and foreign intellectuals. In actuality, he had become a thorn in the side of the regime and was pushed into exile.

Upon Lenin's death in 1924 Gorky wrote a conciliatory obituary. This was a tentative first step towards his rapprochement with the Soviet government. Generally shunned by Russian émigrés, he feared irrelevance. He yearned to mentor young writers and to reach a Russian audience larger than a few hundred like-minded exiles. He watched with great interest the rise of a new Soviet literature that thrived in hellish and hungry conditions.

Before Stalin took control of cultural affairs in the late '20s there was considerable criticism of Gorky in the Soviet Union. For many avant-garde figures Gorky was old, stale, and out of touch with present realities. While they were radically changing the world, he remained on the sidelines. In 1926 the famous poet Vladimir Maiakovskii mocked Gorky for trying to provide advice to people in the Soviet Union:

> I feel great pity, for you comrade G
> Thinking that from Capri you can see
> More clearly and in ever more comprehensive ways,
> While absent from the construction sites of our days?[2]

Capri was a conscious reference to his tsarist exile between 1906 and 1913. It pegged him as an eternal émigré.

As Stalin consolidated his power, he increasingly clamped down on intellectual experimentation and promoted conservative cultural trends. After expelling Trotsky from the party in 1927, he sent signals that he was now in charge of Soviet literature. He began courting Gorky to play a crucial role in his transformation of Soviet culture. He permitted Gorky's works to be republished, thus ensuring that Soviet royalties would became the major source of revenue for the exiled writer. In turn Gorky was expected to celebrate Stalin's policies. As a living link to the great prose of the 19th century and a bridge to "progressive" public opinion in the West, Gorky would also be expected to lend legitimacy to Stalin's dictatorship.

Just weeks before Gorky embarked on his first visit to the Soviet Union since his exile, in 1928 one of his correspondents informed him about the remarkable transformation of the budding young writer named Mikhail Sholokhov.[3] Gorky was intrigued that in only a year this youngster had transformed himself from a novice in need of constant editorial guidance into an accomplished writer. Upon his return to Italy he resolved to read *Quiet Don*. In December 1928 he wrote to a friend, "Judging by the first volume Sholokhov is talented. . . ." He made arrangements to meet Sholokhov on his next visit to Moscow. In 1929 he praised Sholokhov in public on multiple occasions.

One of those statements of praise contributed to the scandal that brought Gorky, Sholokhov, and Stalin together. The meticulously staged pageant of Gorky's triumphant return trip to Russia in 1928 was correctly interpreted in literary circles as the harbinger of a new era in Soviet literature. Gorky, who was now portrayed as Stalin's friend, would set the tone, his every word would be trumpeted in *Pravda* as marching orders for other writers. Though there was widespread disaffection, there were few outlets for expressing it. A defiant minor literary journal in Siberia rallied those who identified Gorky with "reactionary forces." A war of words ensued and Gorky brought out the big guns.[4] He labeled one editor of the journal an anarchist and dismissed another as a wrecker in the field of culture. In the same article he praised Sholokhov's talent and lauded him as an example of how traditional approaches rather than experimental writing had earned the appreciation of the working class.

With a few words of praise in a national newspaper Gorky undermined several months of carefully orchestrated criticism of Sholokhov by a faction of proletarian writers. They claimed that he idealized and romanticized Cossacks. They complained that his sympathies were not unequivocally on the side of the proletariat. They accused him of humanism, pacifism, and, worst of all, objectivism. By portraying class enemies without expressing over-the-top hatred for them, he risked having his readers sympathize with those enemies.

In late 1929 the Siberian literary journal *Nastoiashchee* published a series of articles attacking Gorky. It also devoted one to his perceived protégé—Sholokhov. An inflammatory article entitled "Why Sholokhov Is Pleasing to White Guardists" compared his novel to books that had been condemned by the party. More dangerously, it revived the charge that Sholokhov was a *kulak* abettor. "Even having the very best subjective intentions, Sholokhov objectively carried out the mission of the *kulak . . .*" it proclaimed.[5] Sholokhov found out about the article only after the Central Committee upbraided the journal in a resolution. Though he was not mentioned in the resolution, a prominent article in the *Literary Gazette* condemned the article about him in passing.[6]

The resolution signaled that henceforth attacks on Gorky would be "impermissible." Soon after the resolution was published, Gorky wrote to Stalin to intercede for his former enemies: "Joseph Vissarionovich, I truly beg of you don't punish those cursers."[7] The authors of the Siberian articles avoided arrest . . . for the time being.

In January 1930 Sholokhov completed new installments of *Quiet Don*. He delivered them to Alexander Fadeev, the new editor of *October*.[8] Fadeev gained fame for writing a partly autobiographical story called "The Rout," which focused on a small partisan detachment fighting in the Soviet Far East during the civil war. It provided a compelling psychological portrait of a small group of fighters who were constantly surrounded by danger and hardships. Under the command of a resolute, iron-willed leader, the partisans developed a quiet confidence in their revolutionary cause. They sacrificed and fought on in spite of incredible odds against them.

Fadeev believed that a writer needed to be intimately acquainted with the subject he was writing about. Sholokhov more than met this requirement. Fadeev's own books were based on personal experiences and displayed detailed knowledge of regional settings. There was no question that Sholokhov knew his region. Fadeev was open to the blending of fact and imagination, and he greatly valued the realism and psychological depth of Leo Tolstoy's stories. Such tastes should have united the two writers. But Fadeev preferred a narrative arc in which revolutionary leadership turned the weak-willed and the wavering into stronger, more dedicated, and more committed supporters of the communist cause. The chapters Sholokhov handed over to him were highly deficient in this regard. Grigorii Melekhov was drifting further and further away from communism.

Acting on his revolutionary intuition and understanding of the "laws" of creative fiction, Fadeev demanded major changes to the novel.[9] To the wider Soviet public it appeared as if *Quiet Don* suddenly fell out of favor overnight. The novel had been serialized each month in *October* until it abruptly disappeared. A month went by and publication did not resume. Half a year came and went, but there was still no word on the continuation of the novel. Publication had ceased without any explanation whatsoever.

Soviet readers wondered why the book was banned at the very moment when the main protagonists were in motion. Aksiniia returned to her husband, who came back from captivity. Grigorii abandoned the Bolshevik detachment he'd briefly joined and fought for a local Cossack unit defending the district from incursions by Red forces. After becoming pessimistic and indifferent to the larger struggle, he decided to go home to his neglected wife, who had tried to commit suicide. Literary bureaucrats had accidently created a dramatic cliff-hanger by ceasing publication. Would the ill-fated pair rekindle their affair? Would Grigorii return to the side of the revolution?

Those in the literary world knew that Sholokhov was arguing with Fadeev. Sholokhov took offense at Fadeev's categorical tone. Fadeev was not so much offering collegial guidance as dictating major changes. Sholokhov refused to bow to such pressure and would not contemplate any changes to his vision of how the novel should continue. He complained to a friend, "I cannot turn Grigorii into a committed Bolshevik in the end . . . I would prefer not to publish at all, rather than publish in a way that goes against my wishes, to the detriment of the novel and myself."[10]

Sholokhov decided to forge ahead. "To hell with them!" he exclaimed. His attempt to circumvent Fadeev's mentoring by publishing chapters in Rostov only resulted in more criticism. Even Makar'ev became less vigorous in his support.[11] He still defended Sholokhov against charges that his prose was counterrevolutionary, but he believed that the third volume's point of view was all wrong. It portrayed the Whites and their struggle against the Red Army rather than adopt the politically appropriate Red perspective. His appraisal of the third volume was blunt: the plot appeared to be falling apart, and certain sections were written in a "nervous" manner.

The stalemate between Fadeev and Sholokhov lasted for almost a year. At that point an elder statesman decided to intervene. Gorky wrote to Stalin in early November 1930. He asked the dictator to grant Sholokhov permission to visit him in Italy.[12] Among other things Gorky wanted to involve Sholokhov in his project to produce a popular history of the civil war. Given his interest in *Quiet Don*, he must have also planned to find out why the novel was still in limbo.

Sholokhov was delighted to receive Gorky's invitation. He was summoned to Moscow to discuss his travel arrangements. At a meeting in the Kremlin he requested permission to take his friend Vasilii Kudashev along. His request was granted. They were instructed to immediately travel by train to Berlin.[13] There they would apply for Italian visas. Since the first two volumes of *Quiet Don* had just been published in Germany, interviews with the socialist press were being arranged for Sholokhov. On the eve of their departure, they learned that a third writer, Artem Veselyi, would be joining them. Sholokhov had savored his short stories, especially one about civil war veterans facing bureaucratic indifference in the early 1920s. As representatives of Soviet culture, they were issued new overcoats and hats for their journey to the capitalist world. After nearly two days in transit they arrived in Berlin.

A few days in Germany unexpectedly turned into a prolonged stay. Their visas were delayed by the Italian embassy. After several days it was unwilling to provide them a clear sense of when, or even if, their visa applications would be approved. They spent the first days walking, visiting museums, and attending meetings with left-leaning German intellectuals. As days dragged on they looked for new ways to pass the time and traveled to other parts of Germany. At the Hamburg port Sholokhov tasted a banana and observed exotic sailors from distant locales.

In Berlin he also came face-to-face with militant fascism. All of Berlin was talking about the premiere of the film adaptation of Erich Maria Remarque's novel *All Quiet on the Western Front*. In spite of the book's pacifist message, the film was being acclaimed as the best war movie ever made. The war scenes involved hundreds of extras, and many of them were veterans of the First World War. This ensured that the battle scenes were highly realistic.

On the day that Sholokhov went to see the film, National Socialist zealots shouted slogans, set off stink bombs, and released mice in the theater that was showing it.[14] Outside they staged massive street marches and demonstrations against the film, believing it to be part of a radical, Jewish-sponsored plot to diminish the honor, masculinity, and fighting spirit of the German nation. The police were overwhelmed and struggled to contain the disorder in central Berlin. Tens of thousands of angry demonstrators took to the streets on subsequent evenings. The German government quickly capitulated and banned the film. Sholokhov had witnessed one of the ugliest incidents in the early rise of fascist power.

Witnessing how the authority of the state could suddenly weaken and become helpless in face of vicious, persistent provocations made a profound impression on the young writer. It reinforced his adolescent anxieties forged during the civil war. For a second time he observed the fragility of civil order. The gossamer-thin thread upon which peace persistently hangs could sever at any point, letting bloodshed and brutality loose. Like many conservatives, his deep aversion to disorder would lead him to value stability higher than either prosperity or liberty.

As the money allocated for their trip began to run out and news of total collectivization of agriculture reached Berlin, Sholokhov and Kudashev began wondering whether they should still travel to see Gorky. Ultimately, they decided to return to Moscow. Sholokhov sent a telegram to Gorky expressing his regrets.

Upon returning to the Don region, Sholokhov threw himself into the thick of collectivization.[15] He toured dozens of collective farms, which had been rapidly created in the preceding months through rousing exhortations, intimidation, and class warfare in the countryside. As he traveled through the region he encountered the same disturbing pattern in almost all of the collective farms. The horses and draft animals, which had been appropriated from their former owners to provide labor power for the collective farms, had been grossly neglected. They were dying from exhaustion and malnutrition. The fulfillment of the grain requisition plan assumed that very little grain needed to be put aside for winter animal fodder, since a normal hay harvest was expected. When bad weather limited hay production and diminished the nutritional value of the hay that could be harvested, a crisis resulted.

Sensing that a "catastrophic" situation was developing, Sholokhov embarked on a bold step. He decided to write a letter to Stalin to inform him.[16] He reported that the problem was widespread in both ordinary and exemplary collectives. He expressed his view that it was damaging to collective agriculture and risked demoralizing collective farmers. By starving animals and working them to exhaustion, farm directors contributed to a crisis that could have been avoided: "With such 'management' one can't demonstrate to individualists [private farmers who did not join collectives] the advantages of collectives over individual farming." In order to save ten rubles' worth of grain, farm leaders were destroying horses worth ten times that amount. He asked Stalin to form a commission to examine the issue.

He returned to working on *Quiet Don* in late spring 1931 and signaled to Fadeev that he would be willing to compromise. Fadeev was delighted with his change in attitude. Their communications became more cordial and collegial. By then, however, Fadeev had received additional appraisals of the third volume from other writers.[17] He returned the manuscript to Sholokhov full of markings and marginal notations. Now the writer faced a new problem. Ten different readers were demanding ten different kinds of changes. The majority of the third volume would have to be substantially reworked.

In an ironic twist of fate, this obstacle turned into a remarkable opportunity. Fadeev insisted that he needed blessing from "above" to publish anything related to the civil war. Sholokhov decided to go all in: he wrote a letter to Gorky seeking support for publication. Stalin had recently enticed Gorky to return to the USSR for good and had awarded him a home in Moscow in a prestigious area not far from the Kremlin.

Sholokhov's long letter begged for a meeting and countered the various objections to the new volume. His critics were accusing him of being derogatory towards the Red Army. They were claiming that he overstated the scope and significance of the Cossack rebellion in 1919. They alleged that he exaggerated abuses committed by Soviet officials against Cossack communities on the eve of rebellion. He vigorously defended his audacious decision to write sympathetically about the Cossacks and the extensive, dangerous, anti-Soviet rebellion they mobilized.

The letter worked. Gorky invited him to a meeting to discuss the novel. His house was well known in Moscow.[18] It was the former mansion of a tsarist merchant. When Sholokhov arrived, Gorky was not alone. An astonishingly familiar mustachioed face filled the large room with its presence.

SIX

After the men exchanged greetings and pleasantries, Stalin beckoned Sholokhov to sit down next to him. Well-informed about Sholokhov's problems with literary bureaucrats who wanted to ban the novel, he was there to decide whether to solve them or compound them.[1]

"Why did you represent General Kornilov in such a soft way?" Stalin demanded.

Sholokhov felt a tongue-numbing rush of trepidation. As he searched for words, Stalin continued the barrage: "How is it that someone who was prepared to spill the blood of the people is not depicted more harshly?"

Taken aback by the dictator's aggressive interrogative style, Sholokhov realized in an instant that he could not tell the truth. Stalin had immediately honed in on a significant ideological weakness of volume two. An honest answer could imperil his literary career.

The truth was simple. In a rush to weave together incidents and narratives into a publishable volume, he had relied too heavily upon anti-Soviet sources. In hindsight he should have been more cautious. He'd borrowed from the memoir of a tsarist general named Lukomskii.[2] The general was not merely an eyewitness to Kornilov's march on St. Petersburg in July 1917 but also a passionate devotee of his cause. By appropriating speeches and dialogues verbatim, Sholokhov had introduced unfiltered counterrevolutionary voices into several passages of the novel. In addition, he'd taken an entire scene devoted to Kornilov's arrival in Moscow and his enthusiastic reception there from a tendentious 1917 newspaper article that lauded his popularity with various segments of the Russian population.[3] Though Sholokhov had injected irony and absurdity into the scene, his lapse in judgement had apparently crossed a line.

He decided not to contradict Stalin outright. He had to find an alternative way to exonerate himself.

"Objectively speaking, of course Kornilov was an enemy who was prepared to spill the blood of the people,"[4] Sholokhov replied. "But from a subjective perspective, he was a brave man who was true to the principles of his caste."

Stalin, who by then was unaccustomed to hearing contrary opinions voiced in his presence with confidence, cast a feline gaze upon the writer and demanded, "But why did you give such humane traits to an enemy such as Kornilov?"

Why was Stalin insistently zooming in on Kornilov? Deep down Stalin knew that if Kornilov had more capably organized a coup in July 1917, the entire history of the Russian revolution could have been very different. An alternative history would have spawned a different dictator. This possibility both fascinated and repulsed him.

Stalin had obviously taken the time to acquaint himself with recent criticisms of *Quiet Don*. One critic in particular argued that Sholokhov's heroes were indistinguishable from those of a recent novel that had been publicly condemned as anti-Soviet.[5] Moreover, class consciousness was completely absent from chapters devoted to Kornilov's "black conspiracy." To make matters worse, no Red commander rose to the stature of Kornilov in the published installments of *Quiet Don*.

Sholokhov was compelled to immediately find a way to justify his non-negative portrayal. "Kornilov distinguished himself on the Austrian front with acts of bravery, he was captured by the enemy and managed to escape from captivity and return to Russia. He could even be described in some sense as honorable."

"Honorable?" Stalin smiled. "A man who went against the people? Such a man could never be considered honorable."

"Subjectively speaking he was honorable. From the point of view of his class he behaved honorably. He was motivated by a strong sense of duty. He possessed an officer's sense of honor. He risked his life to return to Russia. He loved his motherland."

These pronouncements must have intrigued Stalin. He was pondering whether ideology alone could bring cohesion to the Soviet Union.[6] He was starting to have doubts about the mobilizational potential of proletarian internationalism for inspiring the masses to defend the country. The emotionally resonant concept of "motherland," which had gone out of fashion with the October revolution, now intrigued him.

Sholokhov continued, "I also portrayed how Kornilov gave orders to lynch the entire Petrograd council of workers' and soldiers' deputies. I demonstrated that in the end the people, even the Cossacks, were against him."

Sholokhov had comported himself well under Stalin's first barrage of questions. He had passed a literary litmus test that the dictator developed during an earlier foray into the field of literary censorship.[7] A year earlier Stalin was asked to decide whether or not to ban a play by Mikhail Bulgakov. Censors complained that it heroicized White generals who had been vanquished by the Soviet side. Although Gorky did not find it objectionable and interpreted it through a satirical lens, several major Soviet theater figures were appalled by its contents. They appealed to Stalin to suppress it. By this action they invited him to assume the role of censor of last resort. He took on the role with relish and would never relinquish it.

In the Bulgakov affair Stalin reasoned that the Whites were portrayed as "honest in their own way," but the playwright did not depict their rejection by the people.[8] The playwright failed to create any scenes, even minor ones, that acknowledged the exploitation of the people. Stalin ultimately decided to ban the play because it evoked empathy for individuals who supported a counterrevolutionary cause. Sholokhov, on the other hand, had passed the first test, but there were several more to come.

Stalin then inquired how an "objective" book about the Cossacks could serve the Soviet cause. A question of this sort seemed deceptively simple. Nonetheless several writers and literary critics had recently come under fire for taking wrong positions on the issue of Stalinist objectivity.[9] Literary authorities pilloried one group of writers for their excessive "objectivism." The writers had supposedly provided an artistic platform for disseminating the views of enemies of the Soviet state and ideology. Another group had been castigated for excessive "subjectivism." They had allegedly doubted the party's ability to actively reshape reality. The first group suffered from too little Marxism, the second one from too much of the wrong kind. The Stalinist position demanded a dialectical synthesis of reality and ideology, ideas and experiences, class struggle and history. The "subjective" and "objective" had to be perfectly aligned, but only a privileged few ideologues around Stalin knew what the current recommended doses were.

Familiar with such dangerous undercurrents, Sholokhov searched for an appropriate answer. He declared, "By portraying the White Generals objectively I demonstrated the achievement of our Red Commanders. I showed readers how hard it was to defeat such committed, well-trained, and militarily capable enemies."[10]

This clever answer appeared to please the censor-in-chief. The tenacity of the interrogation started to soften. Stalin declared something to the effect of "I knew one White officer who became a distinguished Red Commander. He came over to us in Tsaritsyn."[11] Sholokhov was one of the few Soviet intellectuals whom Stalin could expect to immediately appreciate the strategic importance of Tsaritsyn during the civil war.

Sholokhov undoubtedly understood far more than he let on that evening. While working on the second volume of *Quiet Don* he had thoroughly combed through back issues of a White Cossack literary journal published during the civil war. One of those issues featured the report of a secret agent who had infiltrated the Soviet side. This exposé of Stalin's first taste of dictatorship labeled him the "evil genius of Tsaritsyn." It characterized him as cunning, smart, and capable of maneuvering his way out of any situation. It credited Stalin with bringing order to a chaotic region. He immediately became a force to be reckoned with, and he energetically took control of grain requisitioning, railroad administration, water transport, propaganda, and military affairs. When others panicked, believing that Tsaritsyn would fall to the Cossacks in August 1918, Stalin stood firm and refused to leave the city. He consolidated his power by unleashing a reign of terror against both real and imagined enemies. Uncovering conspiracy after conspiracy, he took hostages, ordered shootings, and requisitioned the labor of class enemies to dig trenches for the defense of the city. The threat of constant conspiracies in turn helped him rally the workers to vigorously defend the city.

Stalin's devotees were just starting to mythologize those days as the turning point of the civil war.[12] In time a new, revised official history would insist that in 1918 Soviet Russia was facing a catastrophe from counterrevolutionaries in the south who were depriving Petrograd workers of grain. The struggle for bread became a struggle to save the revolution, so Lenin sent Stalin to Tsaritsyn in mid-June with unlimited powers. A nest of saboteurs had infiltrated the rail hubs there, and all the trains had ground to a standstill. They made such a mess of things that it took Stalin days to untangle it and avoid the collapse of the front.

Sholokhov's interest in Tsaritsyn spurred Stalin to share a highly revealing reminiscence.[13] It was a tale of life, death, and discernment. He told of how he intervened to save a captured White officer from death during the civil war. After considerable back and forth about whether the officer had actually been serving the fatherland, he decided to let the man live. "I took a risk and he turned out to be a brave Red Commander. He occupies a high office in our military even today," Stalin declared.[14]

Stalin revealed his belief in his own powers of discernment. He had staged such interrogations before when much more was at stake. He was convinced in his ability to read a man's character from the way he answered questions. He took risks that others did not dare to take.

Having had enough discussion of a key historical event, Stalin turned to the Cossack rebellion. He now demanded to know where Sholokhov got his information about deviations against Cossack middle peasants leading to the outbreak of a wide-scale rebellion. Sholokhov realized where the interrogation was going. Several literary figures accused him of exaggerating the scale of the Cossack rebellion in 1919 after reading drafts of volume three of *Quiet Don*.[15] Some had even alleged that he made up events that had never happened. Furthermore he was accused of causing his readers to sympathize with the rebels rather than with the Red Army men whom they killed.

"Comrade Stalin, everything I wrote about the rebellion is historically accurate. Histories of the civil war acknowledge its significance but say little about its causes."

Stalin at this point must have cunningly queried, "So how can you prove to your critics that the Cossacks were persecuted by our side?"

Sholokhov played his trump card—Soviet archives: "Our archives are full of materials about those events, but historians have avoided those documents in their accounts of the civil war. Even today there is almost nothing in print about the causes of the rebellion. I represented the brutal realities when I told of how arbitrary violence and senseless excesses inflamed hostility not only towards those errant extremists in our ranks but towards the whole idea of Soviet power."

Gorky quietly followed the exchange. Lighting matches in silence, he watched them burn in the ashtray.

Stalin continued, "But won't your readers sympathize with the rebels?"

"No. They will comprehend how the rebellion came about and why so many Cossacks were initially willing to support it. Excesses and errors made folks believe that our side was not out to destroy classes but to destroy the entire Cossack way of life. I didn't exaggerate in depicting extremists such as Commissar Malkin. But he is counterbalanced by multiple representatives of Soviet power who did not distort our ideals."

Stalin appeared to be satisfied with these answers. He was no longer concerned about millions of impressionable readers. Instead his thoughts turned to thousands of tenacious enemies in foreign lands. "Speaking of our ideals, won't the third volume of *Quiet Don* give our enemies, the White Guard émigrés, a great deal of pleasure?"

Here Stalin repeated one of the charges advanced by the disgraced Siberians in December 1929. He was practically citing the title of their article. Realizing this, Gorky perked up and interjected. "That's true, but no matter what you write they'll find a way to get their pleasure. They are already capable of distorting and contorting the most positive things against Soviet government."

"They won't find much to enjoy," Sholokhov insisted. "After all, I depict how they were utterly and completely routed in both the Don and Kuban' regions."

For Stalin this was a commendable answer. It conformed to his view that a Soviet literary work needed to leave a lasting impression. Stalin had decided that borderline works needed to demonstrate the "crushing force" of the Soviet side.[16] Enemies should either be vanquished or forced to surrender their arms and submit to the will of the people, accepting that theirs had been a lost cause. Sholokhov had passed the final test.

Satisfied, Stalin turned to Gorky: "Aleksei Maksimovich, what do you think about volume three of *Quiet Don*?"

"In political terms the novel is sufficiently objective. Overall, it advances our cause."

"I agree," Stalin declared. His agreement, however, was conditional.

As the discussion of *Quiet Don* wound down, Stalin proposed a deal that Sholokhov would be wise not to refuse.[17] If Sholokhov would agree to write about collectivization, the dictator would have a talk with the obstinate editors who were obstructing publication of *Quiet Don*. Though unexpected, the offer was flattering. Stalin chose him, a twenty-six-year-old, to write about the most important political issue of the era.

Sholokhov had already pondered writing about collectivization for over a year. He had even mentioned this to some friends in Moscow and had discussed collectivization with a high-ranking ideological official. Confident he could meet the challenge, Sholokhov accepted the deal.

He left the meeting with a new understanding of the dictator and an assurance that the third volume of the novel would be published. He was also granted a talisman that would eventually save his life. Stalin handed him a piece of paper with the contact information of his personal secretary, Aleksandr Poskrebyshev, and the number of his direct phone line.[18]

SEVEN

When Sholokhov actually sat down to write the collectivization novel, he faced a quandary. The problem was neither inspiration nor plot lines. It was politics. How could he present his own views of forced collectivization as a risky policy with uncertain consequences while adhering to the party line? Would he be willing to conform to new restrictions on literary representation? He planned the new novel as a carefully constructed dialogue with the dictator. Crossing the boundary between literature and policy, the novel warned Stalin of the serious challenges that he ignored when he embarked on the rapid and complete collectivization of agriculture.

Though he had missed crucial weeks of collectivization while in Berlin and Moscow, Sholokhov was confident that he could depict the complicated policy in a novel.[1] He could also rely on the compelling testimonies of a trio of local officials who helped to implement the policy in 1930. Their experiences would provide textured authenticity to his account.

The first of this trio was Petr Lugovoi.[2] He was sent from an adjacent district to lead the local Communist Party committee in summer 1930. He was a short man with a slightly elfish appearance. He had a pointy, upturned nose, ears that were slightly too large, and deep-set eyes that lit up in a good-natured, penetrating way. He proved to be a tireless, energetic, and hands-on boss.[3] He immediately set about learning the names of local leaders and ordinary farmers. He quickly mastered the intricacies of agriculture. He excelled in making sure that others understood precisely what was expected of them. Soon after arriving he helped revive the local newspaper and worked to bring telephone service to Vioshki. He also brought in credible specialists from outside to help develop the district's economy.

Sholokhov was intrigued with the new arrival and invited Lugovoi over to his house for dinner. After several subsequent visits they quickly developed a friendship.[4] They traveled together to collective farms, hunted, played cards, and sang folk songs on various occasions. For a brief time, they even shared an automobile. More importantly they shared a belief in the power of technology and party leadership to transform a backward rural economy into a profitable bastion of socialism. Lugovoi encouraged Sholokhov to apply to join the Communist Party and served as one of the sponsors of his candidacy.

The second was Petr Krasiukov, a party activist who arrived on the recommendation of Lugovoi after 1930.[5] For Sholokhov, Krasiukov became both a party associate and a friend. They shared countless yarns and downed numerous bottles. He stood nearly seven feet tall, and his hefty frame awkwardly lumbered from side to side as he walked. His prominent, but not quite Neanderthal, brow line betrayed his peasant origins. Despite having enormous hands, he became an expert in penmanship. This practical skill favorably distinguished him from the ranks of semiliterate party activists. His ability to operate a tractor was a skill that was in high demand in the early 1930s. He quickly rose through the ranks of collective agriculture and was eventually made responsible for grain procurements. He played a prominent role in forced collectivization and could recount many harrowing episodes of both local resistance and communist mobilization.

The final member of the collectivization trio was Andrei Plotkin, a short, stocky former sailor and factory worker.[6] He was sent to the region by the party on a temporary assignment to force recalcitrant farmers into collectives. He became so successful at his job that he stayed on to lead a collective farm. He was a colorful character who gained the trust of locals by both learning from them and leading them with a peculiar mix of charisma, memorized party directives, and quotes from books about economic innovation. Having arrived in the area with no knowledge of either agriculture or Cossack culture, his perspective was particularly illuminating for Sholokhov. It provided a starting point for representing the experiences of the thousands of urban party activists who were suddenly thrust into impossible situations in the countryside. The novel's main communist hero would be based on him.[7]

The implementation of complete collectivization had followed a general pattern throughout the region.[8] Between November of 1929 and January of 1930 each settlement hosted a series of agitation meetings. Orators gave thunderous speeches about the happy, prosperous life that complete collectivization would bring, and orchestras played militant marches as locals listened in stunned silence. If locals refused to voluntarily surrender their land and livestock, methods of coercion were used. Grain requisitions and tax contributions were sharply increased. Agricultural loans made in previous years were suddenly recalled. In February the *kulaks* were liquidated. Hundreds of families were deported from each district. Remaining residents were summoned to the local party headquarters for recruiting and cajoling. If that didn't work, threats and shaming were deployed. Then mass meetings were held. They commenced with fanfare, proceeded to haranguing, and usually culminated in an exclamation of the sort, "Whoever is against complete collectivization raise your hand!" In settlement after settlement few risked raising public hands of defiance. As a result, motions to embrace collective farming carried the day. Soon thereafter party activists came to each household to seize horses, cows, tools, and implements as locals wept and confronted them with sullen stares. Sham acts were signed to legalize these transfers. Lands were reapportioned, households were assigned to brigades, and new names such as Lenin's Path, Banner of Communism, or Gift of the Red Partisans dotted the landscape.

In March, Stalin's article "Dizzy with Success" was published. Scrutinized intensely by all, it seemed to suggest that zealous local party officials had mistakenly rushed to collectivize all farms and that the central government would relent in the drive to collectivize. Days later in many settlements women staged upheavals. They gathered together in large organized groups to take back horses and cattle. They staged meetings to demand the return of their land. In places they encircled local government buildings and refused to leave until they were threatened with retribution. Cossack men met in secret to lament their lost world and to hide weapons that might come in handy at some point. In spring of 1930 sometimes as many as a quarter of the Cossacks who had joined the collective farms abruptly withdrew from them. In order to save the system, taxes were seriously reduced for those who remained, and individual garden plots and barnyard animals were legitimated.

The first planting season was extremely difficult. In places where party leadership was lacking or local resentments were acute, collective farmers worked with no alacrity, habitually arrived late, took long breaks, and sat down whenever brigadiers moved on to supervise other fields. In order to save the harvest that year, large numbers of students and city party activists had to be sent to assist in planting. This "assistance" also included house-to-house searches for grain that could be contributed to the collective farm's "seed fund." Collective farming survived through a combination of coercion, concessions, and charisma of local leaders.

For Sholokhov, the psychological turmoil caused by the sudden break with private property in the countryside was one of the major unintended consequences of rapid collectivization.[9] The long-established bonds between rural people and animals were more complicated than ideology would ever admit. Based on the testimonies of locals, he wrote two powerful scenes devoted to a farmer's sleepless nights. The first scene presents a farmer's last night as a private property owner before joining the collective farm, and the second narrates a night in which he fights with his own regrets and longing for the animals he gave up. His internal monologues reveal both his resolute commitment to a new way of life and his inability to fully overcome his concern for his own farm animals and his fears that in collective hands they'll suffer. He even goes to say good-bye to his plow ox and talks to it: "For four years we worked together, the ox for the Cossack and the Cossack for the ox, and nothing productive came out of it for us . . . Because of that I'm trading you in for a collective life." His regrets and doubts, which were artfully expressed as a series of questions in the first scene, return in the second scene. He cannot stop himself from going to look after his former horse and tries to give it a better handful of hay to make its life a little sweeter. He continues to question whether it was necessary to collectivize all the chickens. When his former ox tries to return to its former home after a long day of work, he has to block its path and herd it back toward the common pen. Even animals could not escape old mentalities and behaviors.

Sholokhov also wanted to write about gut-wrenching incidents that caused even dedicated communists to doubt how collectivization was implemented. As appropriations accelerated and whole households were evicted, even supporters were wavering. The anguish over imposing notions of collective guilt on families became palpable. Even a committed party activist declares, "I'm not trained! I . . . I . . . I'm not trained to wage war on little children! . . ." Davydov, the novel's communist hero, has to rally doubters with memories of past exploitation and the myth that *kulak* children will be reeducated in distant places of exile.

From witnesses Sholokhov had accumulated materials for several powerful scenes, but he had to find a way to fit them into a larger structure that still validated collectivization. This would not be an easy task. By late 1931 anyone who expressed doubts about collectivization risked being accused of slandering the Soviet government. The well-publicized example of the writer Andrei Platonov made this painfully apparent.[10] In summer 1931 Platonov published a sarcastic short story about a fictional journey to several collective farms in south central Russia. It depicted a strange province where ordinary people aped Soviet slogans without understanding them and local officials eccentrically subverted party polices while claiming to adhere to them. It depicted a series of collective farm leaders who were occupied with absurd plans such as the creation of an electric sun or promoting radios to replace religion. Platonov did not even spare the heroes of the civil war—they had become odious hypocrites. The only character who was truly committed to world revolution was the village idiot who was "dumber than dirt."

Literary circles were buzzing about how such a cynical story could have slipped by the censors. Though it was hilarious in places, its tone was all wrong for 1931, and Platonov would pay for it. The big question was, What was Platonov thinking? Perhaps he was too confident in his ability to discern Stalin's intentions.[11] After all, many had noticed that Stalin occasionally quoted from prerevolutionary satirists such as Saltykov-Schedrin, who ridiculed provincial officials and social conventions. Others observed that Stalin had recently included two prominent literary references in his widely circulated answer to letters he had received from collective farmers. He invoked Don Quixote's attack on windmills, errantly imagined as enemies; he also mentioned Gogol's "dead souls" in reference to collective farms that existed only on paper. These literary signals seemed to suggest that at least some aspects of collectivization lended themselves to satire.

The Moscow literary rumor mill insisted that Stalin sent the editorial board a note about Platonov that simply read, "Fool, idiot, and vile creature."[12] Fadeev, who had a hand in the publication, immediately shifted to damage control.[13] In a nationally circulated article he ferociously denounced the story as counterrevolutionary and called Platonov a "*kulak* agent" who hid behind the mask of a harmless, well-intentioned simpleton. The old hand at denouncing *kulaks*, Ivan Makar'ev, also joined the fray. He called the story a shameless outburst of the class enemy and labeled Platonov a *kulak* writer who had slandered Soviet society.

The scandal was so explosive that it generated a new litmus test for writing about Soviet society.[14] A long review of the story in a journal dedicated to communist enlightenment proposed a new Soviet definition of truthful representation. A true story had to depict a "great movement towards a new life" and steer clear of "distortions, stupidities, humiliations, and mistakes." Henceforth every author would be wise to subject his or her work to an adversarial eye examination. How would a narrative, play, or novel appear to enemy eyes?

The Platonov scandal had long-lasting repercussions. It led to a hardening of the rules governing all literature in the Soviet Union. The new framework was emphasized to satirists by a high-ranking official: "The enemy benefits when the maximum possible number of elements of Soviet life are mocked and we benefit when that number is kept to a bare minimum . . . never put forward a satire without contrasting that which is being made fun of to the glorious and healthy aspects [of our society]."[15] Avoidance of slander became a major preoccupation of both writers and censors.

Writing soon after the Platonov affair, Sholokhov comprehended that he had to be attentive to both objective and subjective realities: a realistic portrayal of events witnessed by knowledgeable, local informants would not be sufficient for a Stalinist novel about collectivization. He would need to study party directives and read Stalin's speeches from 1929 and 1930. He would have to perform a balancing act by constructing a plot that both derived from Stalinist ideology and reflected the harsh realities of collectivization in the Don region. He would have to find a way to balance triumph, tragedy, and treachery.

He made the specter of rebellion important to the plot in order to make the novel thoroughly Stalinist. In 1929 Stalin advanced the idea that as socialism became stronger, the class struggle would further intensify rather than diminish, as some of his rivals expected. Sholokhov needed a rebellious conspiracy to conform to this postulate. For a second time in his brief career, the secret police came to his assistance. It furnished him with a worthy villain. In 1930 it had foiled a counterrevolutionary network headed by a Cossack named Senin, whose goal was to stage a rebellion during collectivization. Sholokhov acquired direct testimonies from Senin, who curiously had been mentioned by name in a minor scene of *Quiet Don*, shortly before his execution.[16]

Having carefully calibrated his hero, his villain, and his Stalinist plot, Sholokhov furiously began writing. To a friend he half ironically wrote, "I'm working like someone engulfed in and enflamed by socialist competition."[17] He was indeed engaging in a competition, one to create the novel about collectivization that would be most valued by Stalin. Others were much faster out of the starting gate, but catching up and surpassing rivals was a Stalinist virtue as well. Sholokhov finished the book in only a few weeks. He was confident that it would silence fellow writers who had snickered that he was merely a plagiarist from old diaries and memoirs who could never measure up to the task of dealing with contemporary issues.

Sholokhov began the book by introducing one of the oldest and most compelling plots in all of literature: the arrival of a stranger. A Cossack named Polovtsev arrives in an area of the Don region undergoing collectivization in 1930. Almost simultaneously, another stranger, a communist factory worker and former sailor from Leningrad named Davydov, arrives in the same area to bring party leadership. While one plots at night and plans a rebellion, the other tirelessly works by day to lead the reluctant and the recalcitrant to a new socialist life.

The publication of Stalin's 1930 speech "Dizzy with Success" is the decisive moment in the narrative. Sholokhov first introduces the dictator's article as a matter of concern for the Cossacks intent on organizing a rebellion. Upon reading it, a group of Polovtsev's former supporters announce to him, "Because of that article in the newspaper *Pravda*, we have decided not to rebel. Our paths and roads have diverged from yours." He flees, presumably to his allies abroad. For Davydov, the arrival of the article at the Stalin Collective Farm brings about a new struggle to consolidate the committed farmers and recover from mistakes caused by zealous regional officials. Just as he starts to succeed, Polovtsev returns. The book ends ominously: "The old started again anew."

Several scenes in the book were inspired by party directives. These included depictions of mistakes by local officials who forced collectivization and demanded the expropriation of cows, chickens, and tools. The suffering middle peasants and "left" deviationists of party pronouncements became living, breathing characters. Stalin's proclamations about locals who feared admitting mistakes and avoided self-criticism became interesting scenes. Even words that the dictator uttered in passing about the struggle for seed planting shaped a whole chapter. Satire was consigned to its newly proper place. A coarse, foolish, old character named Shukar' provided both comic relief and fleeting, insightfully biting appraisals of Soviet policies.

The novel, which he titled *With Sweat and Blood*, fully embraced Stalin's suspicions that enemies of collectivization would continue their efforts to subvert the farms from within and wage a clandestine, counterrevolutionary struggle against the Soviet regime. At the same time, it cautioned the dictator that even the most loyal supporters of collective agriculture could succumb to old mentalities. Local party officials were simultaneously a source of strength and a weak link that could cause the Soviet chain of command in the countryside to weaken. The book demonstrated that forcing peasants into collective farms could not turn them into socialist farmers overnight.

In late fall 1931 Sholokhov delivered his manuscript to the journal *Novyi Mir.* The editor evaluated the work as a talented and powerful treatment of collectivization but was afraid to publish it.[18] The editorial board was extremely skittish after coming under fire from Stalin for allegedly not defending Bolshevik policies in publishing. The journal had been criticized for several articles displaying "rotten liberalism." Under such circumstances no editor wanted to be seen as anything other than zealous. The editor demanded that the scenes depicting the destruction of the *kulaks* be removed in order for the novel to be published. In those scenes Sholokhov gave voice to both "*kulaks*" and the communities that expelled them. More than one point of view emerges in a series of tragic episodes in which *kulaks* are kicked out of their homes and all of their possessions are socialized and confiscated by others. Their futile protests—one mentions that he fought for the Soviet side in the civil war, another presents his receipt for a full grain contribution, yet another claims to have labored honestly—are met with hostility from within the community.

Sholokhov protested that the novel's depiction of class conflict would be diminished without those scenes. When his protests were ignored, he decided to appeal to Stalin. For the first time he turned to his talisman. Nervously, he dialed that precious phone number. He explained the situation to Aleksandr Poskrebyshev, Stalin's secretary. Since Sholokhov was in Moscow, the secretary asked him to bring over the manuscript.

Stalin read the manuscript over the course of three nights. Then he summoned Sholokhov to a meeting in the Kremlin.[19] Arriving at the corner office building, which housed the Central Committee, he was taken upstairs. After a few questions and a brief inspection by a guard, he was led to a waiting room adjacent to Stalin's office. At 8:30 P.M. he went in. Stalin was there with three associates: Lev Mekhlis, the editor of *Pravda*, Sergo Ordzhonikidze, who was in charge of economic development, and Kliment Voroshilov, the People's Commisar for Military and Naval Affairs. The Politburo members were there to witness Stalin's verdict. The dictator showed both superiority and magnanimity. He assured Sholokhov that the novel would be published, and he fumed to the Politburo members about bunglers sitting on editorial boards: "We weren't afraid to de-*kulak*ize the *kulaks*, so why should we now be afraid to write about how we did it."[20] Stalin continued to believe that depriving *kulaks* of productive resources was an essential element of breaking down resistance in the countryside.[21] Only the liquidation of the last bastion of rural capitalism could clear the way for a true socialist economy. The brief, informal meeting was over in minutes.

Sholokhov was confident that he had cleared the last hurdle before publication, but he was wrong. The editorial board asked him to provide a more fitting title than *With Sweat and Blood*. He reluctantly agreed to give the novel a Stalinist name: *Virgin Soil Upturned*.[22] Though "virgin soil" was only mentioned in passing in a few minor passages of the book, those particular passages were a major concession to Stalin's view of agriculture.[23] The dictator believed that collective farms would open up new "virgin" lands, which could never be productively exploited under individual, capitalist farming. This myth only died under Khrushchev in the 1960s.

EIGHT

n 1932 a curious invitation landed on Sholokhov's doorstep. No Soviet citizen could contemplate rejecting such an unusual request. Genrikh Yagoda, the head of the Joint State Political Directorate, invited him over for the evening. What could the man in charge of the secret police, prisons, and labor camps want from Sholokhov? Was this a matter of literature or politics?

When Sholokhov arrived in Moscow he found out that Fadeev had also been invited to Yagoda's residence.[1] His curiosity deepened. Would Yagoda try to recruit them for some kind of secret operation? That didn't seem likely. Many writers had visited Yagoda's home. Would he be interested in the new installments of *Quiet Don*, which were scheduled to be published in the coming months? Due to Stalin's great interest in literature, Yagoda felt obliged to keep abreast of literary affairs. The commissar was known for throwing lavish soirees, so this would probably be a simple social occasion. On the other hand, when dealing with the secret police nothing was ever simple.

In person Yagoda could have been mistaken for an inconsequential local functionary. He had a small frame, a corpuscular nose, and a hairline that had started to retreat from his forehead long ago. He wore a toothbrush mustache like the ones made famous by Charlie Chaplin and Adolf Hitler. His residence was filled to the brim with all sorts of luxuries that were unimaginable for ordinary Soviet citizens.[2] He could offer his guests an assortment of imported cigarettes and an unparalleled selection of fine, foreign wines. He could entertain them with an impressive collection of the latest records and risqué photos from abroad. Looking around, Sholokhov couldn't help but notice that Yagoda had surrounded himself with countless trappings of prosperity: curtains, clocks, carpets, coins, and antiques. Among the items of greatest interest to Sholokhov were a collection of hunting rifles and foreign fishing lures.

Yagoda put his guests at ease and plied them with alcohol. He was such an obliging host that Sholokhov started to let his guard down. Fadeev followed suit. Soon they were calling their host by name rather than Comrade Yagoda. Relieved by the absence of explicit recruiting overtures or sensitive political inquiries, they both got drunk and went wild. What happened next is impossible to reconstruct from available sources. They did something that was so outrageous or so irresponsible that Yagoda cursed them out. At the time they both laughed it off. Days later, Fadeev, however, started to experience bouts of regret, and he wrote to Sholokhov to say that his recollections of the evening were starting to become "burdensome."

Sholokhov's letter to Fadeev only provides opaque hints of what happened. Weeks later he still continued to find their behavior more humorous than offensive. His literary reference to "the style of the sub-urbs across the river [from the Kremlin] in Moscow" suggests an early 19th-century short story about a bureaucrat who became a perpetual alcoholic.[3] His phrase "broad natures" echoes a late-19th-century story featuring characters who became wild and shameless, who sang loud drunken songs, who broke dishes and mirrors, and then got down on their knees in front of Gypsy women in taverns.[4] Sholokhov urged Fadeev to reassure Yagoda that they were just having a good time in the Russian folk manner. He also insisted that his hands had not touched a shot glass since his return to Vioshki.

The encounter in Moscow helped Sholokhov to see Fadeev in a new light and to empathize with his plight as an editor. It was becoming increasingly difficult for Fadeev to publish anything of quality, due to a series of pronouncements from Stalin and party ideologues.[5] Fadeev was expected to be ever vigilant against idealistic rubbish, anti-party slander, reactionary outbursts, slobbering humanism towards class enemies, petty bourgeois individualism, contraband Trotskyite sorties, and masked Menshevik pronouncements. He could not publish works that either presented a deformed view of present-day realities or distorted the past as it was presently understood by the party. Stories should neither be too dark nor so excessively optimistic that they underestimated the challenges of building socialism. Too much irony was harmful, dispirited works threatened popular morale, and the prevalence of the old over the new was a sure sign of an ideological lapse. As an editor he was expected to get into the minds of Soviet enemies and constantly ask himself whether anything in a work could serve their goals or heighten their spirits.

Fadeev was also deeply involved in literary factional struggles in the capital.[6] A few months earlier the Association of Proletarian Writers (henceforth RAPP) had gotten into feuds with both the editorial board of *Pravda* and a competing literary faction. The Central Committee intervened and warned RAPP that its purpose was merely to lead and educate, not to command or act as an administrative wing of the party. It ordered the organization to create a "comradely atmosphere" for all groups that supported the party line. Fadeev had cautioned other leaders against mandating that stories feature heroic efforts to fulfill the five-year plan. He turned out to be right. Only days before he met Sholokhov, the Central Committee secretly criticized the association for going overboard. Everyone was expecting some kind of drastic action.

On April 24, 1932, news began to spread in literary circles that Stalin had decided to liquidate RAPP. What exactly did liquidate mean? No one knew. The RAPP leaders were smarting from both anxiety and insult. In the wake of the liquidation of their organization, Stalin delegated a Politburo member, Lazar Kaganovich, to implement the decision. For writers who had visited with Stalin on several occasions, this seeming demotion of their stature smacked of disfavor rather than mere reorganization.

In early May 1932, against his better judgement, Sholokhov involved himself in this Moscow literary intrigue.[7] Fadeev, Makar'ev, and other leaders of RAPP sought his assistance. Their apprehensions about Stalin's disfavor seemed to be confirmed when a literary bureaucrat approached them with the prepared text of an open letter and demanded that they sign it.[8] It contained a humiliating confession that for several years they had dedicated themselves to factionalism. In doing so the RAPP leaders had lost sight of the struggle for socialism. The letter also contained dangerous insinuations that their mistakes had harmed the party. Putting a signature on such a letter would always hang over the RAPP leaders like a sword of Damocles.

Sholokhov knew enough from recent press articles to realize that these were serious charges. Harm to the party, whether intentional or not, could also mean wrecking. The country had just gone through a series of widely publicized show trials in which wreckers admitted to participating in counterrevolutionary, conspiratorial efforts to harm and sabotage Soviet industry. In a recent trial, former Mensheviks admitted to both economic wrecking and attempting to discredit the government by sowing doubt about Soviet achievements.[9] After the trial Gorky labeled such behavior "moral wrecking."

Sholokhov penned a note in defense of the party loyalty of Fadeev, Makar'ev, and the other RAPP leaders and sent it to the Central Committee.[10] Within hours a response arrived. A highly placed official advised him to withdraw his letter. There was no point in compounding one political error with another political error. Would he really want to go on record as the only writer, a non-party one at that, to support the RAPP leaders? The business of the open letter was being carefully considered "up there" in the Kremlin and would be resolved soon. Sholokhov did as he was told. He immediately retracted his note of support. A few days later, the *Literary Gazette* published the open letter.[11] All of the former RAPP leaders had caved in and signed it. Sholokhov could take solace in the fact that the final version seemed more moderate.

While literary factions jockeyed for power and influence in a new Writers' Union being organized in Moscow, Sholokhov fully shifted his attention to local affairs in summer 1932.[12] His friend Lugovoi had suffered a major misfortune. When his car stalled during a flash flood, he ended up stranded in a car filling up with water. Realizing he had to get out before it was too late, Lugovoi waded through water up to his chest to reach higher ground. To get back to Vioshki, he had to ride a horse in soaking wet clothes. He came down with malaria and was transferred to a job near a city where he could be closer to medical attention. The regional government dragged its feet in naming a replacement.

This deficit of leadership could not have come at a worse time. In early July 1932 a government car arrived in Vioshki. A man of taller than average height, with a robust head of dark hair, emerged from the car. He wore a thick mustache. As he approached closer, Sholokhov could see the mustache presiding over lips that were pursed in either annoyance or dissatisfaction. The face seemed very familiar. This imperious official introduced himself as Boris Sheboldaev, the head of the regional government.

The party boss was conducting an inspection tour of grain-growing districts.[13] He demanded to see forecasts for the grain harvest in Vioshki, and he intensely scrutinized the local government's plans for allocating the grain. Based on what he saw from his car window during his journey and the calculations completed in the regional capital, he predicted an optimal grain harvest. To his chagrin local leaders estimated that in a best-case scenario only two thirds of his grain target might actually be harvested. He voiced suspicions of sabotage, dismissing the local plan for using grain for seeds, feeding cattle, and compensating collective farmers as a *kulak* concoction. There was no reasoning with him. He wouldn't hear of differential yields in different areas of the district. He couldn't countenance the notion that sown seeds could subsequently perish due to frost, birds, or rot. He was dismissive of Sholokhov, who was not even a full member of the party.

Convinced that the locals were deceiving him, he announced that he would be sending a fact-finding commission.[14] Shortly thereafter several urban party officials arrived in Vioshki. They lacked even rudimentary knowledge of agriculture. They continuously quarelled with local leaders. They completely ignored the grain needs of children and the elderly. After considerable discussion, they finally relented and agreed to revise the grain requisition plan downward. This new plan would still leave virtually nothing for locals to consume in the winter or put aside for seed stocks.

This suspicious second visit of regional officials set off a wave of panic in the district.[15] Rumors spread that the regional government planned to seize the entire grain harvest. Stalin's public boasting about grain exports the previous year only exacerbated the situation. Locals assumed that foreigners would be eating their grain while they and their children would go hungry. So they started making plans to hoard grain. Grain that was too ripe or had been damaged by moisture could not be sold or transported over large distances. They delayed harvesting in hopes that grain which did not meet government quality standards would be left behind.

Uncertainties in both literature and regional affairs weighed heavily upon Sholokhov during those months.[16] He even revealed his deep anxieties in a comment to a friend about "deviation." Stalin had vanquished Trotsky by accusing his rival of left-wing deviation from the party line. He had triumphed over Bukharin by exposing right-wing deviation from the party line. Recently, a "left-right bloc" had been uncovered and routed. The abrupt zigzagging of party policies even spawned a popular anecdote about Stalin ordering his soldiers to vigorously march in place out of fear that if they paraded they might start to veer either to the right or to the left. Sholokhov joked that he too was in danger of being "stitched up" on charges of deviation, in his case "Cossack deviation."

His comments about his work on *Quiet Don* during that period also revealed a number of anxieties. On one occasion he stated, "In the first volume I ambitiously took on far too much, introduced way too many characters, and initiated such a giant literary enterprise that now I am facing the difficult challenge of how to most easily be done with all of it."[17] Then he declared, "In *Quiet Don* I got myself involved with such a big thing, that I am getting tired to death of it. It can be expanded for a couple of five-year plans, but I'm running out of steam."[18] During the same meeting with fellow writers he hinted of his intention to "crush and do away with all the [novel's] heroes in such a manner that the reader will be horrified." He often delivered such provocative declarations in comical form to study the reactions of his audience. Such comments were a prelude to his biggest announcement thus far. *Quiet Don* would not end with the third volume, which was about to be published, but with a fourth volume, which was yet to be written. He decided it would be wise to buy himself more time.

In October 1932 he received another invitation to come to Moscow. A very important meeting would be held at Gorky's house.[19] It was no secret in Moscow that Gorky was now very close to Yagoda. Anyone who scrutinized Gorky's recent publications could detect a secret police agenda emerging. Gorky warned that the Soviet Union was facing a constant counterrevolutionary threat: "Within [our] country most cunning enemies are organizing a famine against us, the *kulaks* are terrorizing the peasants who support the collective farms with murders, acts of arson, and various kinds of underhanded acts. Everything which has outlived the lifespan allotted to it by history is against us and that gives us the right to consider ourselves still in a state of civil war. One natural conclusion follows from this: if the enemy does not give up, he is annihilated."[20] Gorky also affirmed that anyone inside the Soviet Union who dared to question or diminish the country's positive achievements was aiding the enemy. To deal with this, the USSR was already in the process of purifying its shortcomings. "However little by little we are purifying and when we purify, we do so mercilessly."[21] Would the meeting announce a wave of literary purges?

Upon arrival at Gorky's mansion Sholokhov discovered that around forty writers were expected. As the evening progressed, Gorky came out occasionally from his office to greet writers who just arrived. He appeared to be preoccupied, anticipating the arrival of an important guest. After a while Stalin showed up, wearing a military overcoat. He was accompanied by several high-ranking officials. He was immediately shuttled into Gorky's office, and the doors quickly closed behind them.

Then Gorky's assistant ushered the writers into a dining room. They filed in and took seats in front of a large art nouveau window, which was elaborately carved with floral and geometric decorations. The room buzzed with excitement and nervous energy. Soon the doors opened again. Stalin, Gorky, and others entered. As Stalin looked around the room, he inquired, "Where is Platonov?" Though Platonov had not been invited, this casual statement helped to rehabilitate him. If Stalin publicly inquired about a writer, editors could no longer treat him as if he did not exist.

Gorky began the discussion with some general talking points about literature. These were a prelude to a plea for leniency for the former leaders of RAPP. He emphasized that they had admitted their mistakes and were ready to productively contribute again. He stressed that everyone needed to cooperate: "Now we need to talk about out how together we can create a Soviet literature which is worthy of the great fifteenth anniversary [of the Revolution]." He then opened the floor to discussion.

Some of the speakers were tentative and nervous. After Stalin intervened to correct an error by one of the first speakers, the atmosphere became even more tense. The boldest was Lidiia Seifullina. She objected to including the former RAPP leaders in the organizing committee for a new, official writers' organization. She reminded every one not to forget the "RAPP cudgel" that had been wielded against writers of all stripes in recent years. As she began to list names of writers who had been berated or persecuted, a commotion broke out. "False!" the RAPP supporters began to shout. Others defended Seifullina. "Let her speak," Stalin insisted. This renewed rancor made Gorky uncomfortable. His smooth rehabilitation campaign had gone off the rails. As the discussion dragged on, several individuals went out to the corridor for smoke breaks and returned. When Makar'ev's turn to speak came, he began to argue that RAPP's minor deviations would never be repeated. At this point Stalin got up with his pipe in hand and headed for the door. Gorky, sensing Makar'ev's discomfort, immediately halted the proceedings and announced a break.

The writers were encouraged to relax outside while the room was prepared for a banquet. During the break writers crowded around the members of the Politburo. Stalin appeared ill at ease with people pushing into his personal space. At every turn some writer eagerly accosted him. Sholokhov realized that this was the least productive way to earn the dictator's favorable attention. Aloof proximity appeared to be a far better strategy. When the doors of the dining room opened again, the tables had been set for a banquet. Stalin took a seat next to Gorky and across from Fadeev, who had arrived late. Apparently he had a good excuse, since the conversation continued on convivial terms.

After a feast and considerable drinking, several writers read poems or recited short excerpts from their work. Fadeev stood up to propose a toast for "the great man" Lenin. The writers delightedly clinked their glasses in unison with members of the Politburo. Another stood up and loudly declared, "Let us drink for the health of Comrade Stalin." A writer named Georgii Nikiforov exclaimed, "I'm fed up with this. A million times we have drunk to the health of Comrade Stalin. He himself must already be fed up with hearing this." Stalin extended his hand to Nikiforov. "Thank you, Nikiforov, that's right. I'm fed up with it already."

Fadeev then tried to get Sholokhov to sing a Russian folk song with him. Sholokhov declined and merely smiled awkwardly. Fadeev sang alone. Then Stalin stood up. Turning to Gorky, he asked, "Must I speak?" "You must! You must!" the writers shouted. For twenty minutes Stalin delivered an oration. His words were slow, measured, and confident. He criticized RAPP and praised Seifullina for speaking truths others did not dare to voice. His most intriguing comments were devoted to the themes of partnership and purges. He proclaimed that non-party members were of great value in purging the Bolshevik party, and the party provided guidance to non-party members. "Thus we purge one another." He articulated his view of partnership. "Let each defend his own [opinion], but as soon as a directive has been issued [by the party], then [let everyone] defend the party's opinion." To be strong the party always had to be willing to purge "vile individuals" and chameleons hiding their true intentions.

After Stalin sat down, the room returned to drunken revelry. Another round of toasts ensued. At one point an inebriated Fadeev stood up, glass in hand. "Let us drink to the most modest of all writers, for Misha Sholokhov." Stalin raised his glass. Commanding the room, he started to pontificate again. "There's one more thing I wanted to say. There are many kinds of production: artillery, automobiles, machinery. But you are also producers. You produce an essential product . . . human souls. The production of the entire country depends on your production." The room was once again buzzing.

The dictator continued: "Your production is very important. You are the engineers of human souls." This was a highly intriguing statement. Stalin had only recently rehabilitated engineers as a valuable segment of society. After a series of high-profile arrests and trials in which engineers were charged with wrecking the Soviet economy and undermining central planning, he announced a new policy of caring for engineers, even those trained under the old regime. First engineers were purged, then they were lauded. In this case literary engineers were being lauded immediately after a declaration about purges. Could that be a coincidence? If not, literature and terror were on a collision course.

The proceedings that evening cemented Sholokhov's reputation as a favorite of Stalin. Others had not been personally honored by a toast. Stalin had raised his glass for Sholokhov, saying, "Let us drink for writers and to the most modest of them all, for Comrade Sholokhov!" At one point Stalin even initiated a discussion of *Quiet Don*, telling a group of writers that Grigorii Melekhov could never be considered a typical representative of the peasantry. While other writers vied for the dictator's attention, at times Stalin appeared to be seeking out Sholokhov.

The plans lurking behind Stalin's brief words about purges became manifest in a few weeks.[22] The government announced that "alien elements" and "double dealers" had infiltrated the party during its massive growth. In order to reinforce iron discipline, the party would now systematically purge itself of enemy elements, deceivers, careerists, and morally suspect individuals. The purges would start in Moscow, Leningrad, and key border regions, and other areas would soon be "purified" as well.

NINE

When the fall harvest of 1932 turned out to be in line with dire local predictions, a severe crisis resulted. Rather than admit that the party's regional grain harvest estimates were bogus and based on false assumptions, Sheboldaev decided to terrorize the population. Savage efforts to seize every ounce of grain deeply appalled Sholokhov. The writer watched in horror as hundreds of families were kicked out of their homes and deprived of all sustenance as winter approached. A wave of terror pushed the region's population to the brink of starvation but yielded only a fraction of the "missing" grain. Sholokhov decided to throw caution to the wind. He would denounce the regional government and the illegal wave of terror it unleashed. He would risk everything in a plea for Stalin's help. He insisted to friends that he could not remain silent. He would either prevail or perish in defending the local government against charges that it had criminally mismanaged the planting and harvesting of precious grain.

When Sholokhov returned from Moscow in late fall 1932 he witnessed firsthand the crisis that he knew was coming after the fall harvest.[1] The regional government insisted that the revised grain requisition plan be fulfilled regardless of the actual amount of grain production in the district. In November a factory manager and party leader named Grigorii Ovchinnikov arrived from Rostov with a mandate from the regional government to accelerate grain requisitions. He berated local officials for not believing in the reality of the plan. He warned that they were presently on target to deliver less than half the grain that the party demanded. In late December 1932 Ovchinnikov returned.[2] He brought credentials from the regional government granting him "extraordinary powers." Even though the district had met three quarters of its grain obligations, nothing less than full compliance would suit the regional boss. Ovchinnikov waved a revolver and screamed at local officials. "Grain must be seized by any means!" He expelled twenty local officials from the party for failing to dramatically increase grain collection and threatened all the rest with a similar or worse fate if they did not comply. When Sholokhov tried to intervene, Ovchinnikov labeled him a "little lord" and kicked him out of a meeting of the local party committee.[3]

Sholokhov watched in horror as nearly half the households of his district were harmed in some way by Ovchinnikov's henchmen. Operating with the regional government's estimate of "missing" grain, Ovchinnikov divided up the remaining amount between all households in the district. Any household that could not deliver its quota would be targeted for immediate repression. He ordered party officials to unleash a wave of torture, psychological intimidation, and terror against the entire population.

Nearly one in ten families in the district was rendered homeless as a result of failure to pay the new grain contribution. Often all grain, including grain that loyal collective farmers had legitimately earned as compensation for their diligent labors, was confiscated.[4] Those who were suspected of hiding grain were ruined. Their homes were ransacked and torn apart under the assumption that grain might be buried under the floors or immured behind walls. Everything edible was confiscated under the premise that only starvation would force suspected grain hoarders to reveal their secret caches.

Surrounded by suffering, in early 1933 Sholokhov quit working on the novel. The population of the districts around Vioshki continued to be terrorized by regional officials even though residents displayed bloated stomachs, gaunt faces, and other signs of severe starvation. They resorted to fishing, hunting varmints, and gathering edible herbs to survive the winter. The families who were tossed out of their homes could find no succor. Ovchinnikov and his henchmen forbade their neighbors from providing them any assistance. The cities were off limits for them as well, since a new passport law prohibited all travel out of rural areas. Many simply perished out in the open. Sholokhov wrote to Lugovoi, "Events in Vioshenskaia have taken on a monstrous character."[5]

Because he had provided advice to local officials and attended party meetings about grain forecasts, Sholokhov found himself in potential danger as well. Ovchinnikov insisted that a criminal conspiracy was to blame for the poor harvest in the district. Local party officials would become the fall guys for the regional government's faulty estimates. Sholokhov's friend Krasiukov was arrested. This meant that his family would be deprived of rations as winter approached. To Lugovoi Sholokhov wrote, "We're all going to be framed as counterrevolutionaries." He resolved to fiercely contest this. "I'm going tell about all this in Moscow, to you know who," Sholokhov declared.[6]

In early April 1933 Sholokhov wrote a long letter to Stalin describing in graphic detail the astonishing savagery of Soviet officials who had evicted families from their homes and forced them to wander in the bitter frosts of January and February because they could not pay arbitrary grain contributions. He was appalled by the case of a mother with a newborn infant who froze to death just steps away from the heated homes of her neighbors because communist officials had prohibited anyone from providing assistance of any kind to families punished for not handing over enough grain. He chronicled how thousands of loyal collective farmers were starving because of policies that seized the very grain they had earned from the Soviet state for their labors. He proclaimed that productive workers were getting weaker and weaker by the day because they were forced to share their bread rations with children and the elderly, who did not receive any rations because officially they did not work. He raised the specter of whole villages of half-dead laborers collapsing in the fields during spring planting.

He condemned the "extraordinary measures" that Ovchinnikov deployed in his furious search for hidden grain. He exposed a series of grotesque manifestations of "medieval torture."[7] Party officials set villagers on fire, made them stand outside naked in the cold, forced them to drink kerosene, and staged mock executions. This arbitrary and illegal wave of terror punished everyone indiscriminately. By equating loyal citizens who had worked hard and supported the government with loafers and true enemies, such policies threatened to alienate broad segments of the population. Since nearly everyone in the district was starving, spring planting was lagging and future production was sure to decline even further.

His letter was both a multifaceted analysis of the situation and a personal appeal to a higher power. From it one could get a clear sense of the motivations of both local farmers and regional officials. It demonstrated that faulty estimates and indifference to local expertise had caused an unnecessary crisis. It mobilized government statistics and data from the secret police. Nonetheless throughout the letter Sholokhov repeatedly communicated a belief that "dear Comrade Stalin" would share his view that the situation was unacceptable. "You are our only hope" he pleaded. Sholokhov concluded with a request for an investigation and insisted that he could not remain silent. He placed his hopes in the dictator: "I decided that it is better to write to You, rather than use this material to create the second book of *Virgin Soil*."

Shortly after receiving the letter, Stalin sent an urgent telegram to Sholokhov: "Your letter received fifteenth. Thanks for message. Doing all that is required. Inform about amount of necessary assistance. Name a number. Stalin."[8] The dictator also began consulting with the Politburo. His initial reaction was that they needed to "make Ovchinnikov and all the others who caused these deformities to answer for their actions."

Stalin's telegram exhilarated Sholokhov. The news that aid would be sent reinforced his conviction that Stalin trusted and respected him. Now he needed to provide a number.[9] How much grain was sufficient, and how much would be seen as too much? He did not want to look greedy. At the same time his decision would have dire implications for people in need. He decided to consult with Andrei Plotkin and other local officials. They argued about how different numbers would look to Moscow. They considered everything they knew about grain stockpiles and infrastructures. They discussed how many people they might be able to save. There were fifty thousand individuals in the district, who would each need around thirty-six pounds of grain per month for several months. Such an amount was simply not available and could not be transported in time. They eventually settled on a number that would be realistic, given transport conditions and grain on hand in government silos. They decided to ask for enough grain to fully feed around twenty thousand people for four months. If officials distributed assistance wisely, based on local conditions such as the availability of non-grain foodstuffs, then many more would be helped.

When Sholokhov telegraphed his number, Stalin immediately contacted members of the Politburo to secure their approval for providing aid to Sholokhov's district.[10] He wrote to Molotov, "I think we should satisfy Sholokhov's request in full . . . it is decisive right now for the population of these two districts." He pushed for an immediate vote. In the following weeks aid was distributed to thousands of families in Vioshki and adjacent areas.

Stalin also decided to send a fact-finding commission to investigate the allegations in Sholokhov's letter.[11] Matvei Shkiriatov, a high-ranking specialist in party purges and procedures, arrived in Vioshki on May 10, 1933, and spent ten days interviewing local witnesses. He asked Sholokhov to accompany him during the investigation and also invited a regional official to participate. He visited six areas mentioned in Sholokhov's letter and interviewed dozens of locals. After gathering testimonies from individuals who had suffered from illegal repressions, he then interviewed the party officials who had persecuted them. His inquiries "completely confirmed the accuracy of Comrade Sholokhov's letter." He reported to the Politburo that there had indeed been widespread cases of mass evictions and confiscations of property and that loyal, active collective farmers had suffered. Sholokhov was impressed by Shkiriatov's commitment to finding out what had happened and his

willingness to provide redress to those who had suffered. Shkiriatov recommended that Ovchinnikov be held responsible, but the final decision
would be made by the Politburo.

Sholokhov's delight with the results of his petition was short-lived.

In May 1933 Stalin also sent him a stern follow-up letter.[12] It was his
only attempt to explain his view of the grain requisitions crisis to anyone
outside the Central Committee.

Stalin wrote:

May 6, 1933

Dear Comrade Sholokhov.

Both of your letters were received, as you are aware. The help,
which was requested, has already been sent.

To get to the bottom of this affair Comrade Shkiriatov will
be sent to Vioshenskii district. I very much request that you
provide assistance to him.

But that is not all Comrade Sholokhov. The fact of the
matter is that your letters create a one-sided impression.
Regarding that I would like to write you a few words.

I have thanked you for your letters because they expose one
of the defects of our party-soviet work, exposing how sometimes our agents in desiring to keep in check [literally bridle]
the enemy accidently beat friends and can even descend into
sadism. But that does not mean that I agree with you *in all
matters*. You see one side of the affair. In order not to make
a mistake in politics (your letters are not *belle lettres* but are
infused with politics) one has to be able to observe, one has to
know how to see the *other* side. The other side consists of the
fact that the respected grain-growers of your district (and not
only your district) carried out an Italian [strike][13] (sabotage)
and would have no qualms about leaving the workers, the
Red Army without bread. The fact that sabotage was quiet
and in external appearances harmless (without blood)—does

not change the fact that the respectable grain growers in effect carried out a "quiet" war against Soviet power. This, dear Comrade Sholokhov, was a war of extermination by starvation.

Of course this circumstance cannot to any degree vindicate those disgraceful practices [literally deformities] which were allowed to happen, as you insist, by our agents. Those who are guilty of those disgraceful practices should receive their due punishment. But it remains as clear as day that the respectable grain growers are not such harmless individuals as it might seem from a distance.

Well, best wishes. I shake your hand.

Yours,

J. Stalin

Though the tone was friendly, the message was blunt. Sholokhov had unwisely strayed into politics. Stalin cleverly chided the writer in a series of parenthetical statements for committing a very serious political error. Sholokhov had dispassionately described popular resistance without explicitly outlining the potential political consequences of such actions. He failed to look at the situation from a larger, macro-political point of view. The writer had failed to call sabotage by its name. Stalin believed that he was so focused on local affairs that he did not consider the countrywide implications of the struggle he was witnessing.

Why did Stalin admonish Sholokhov for perceiving local grain growers "from a distance"? Sholokhov was arguably closer to the events than any central official. Here the dictator hinted that Sholokhov had distanced himself from the party's view of the crisis by privileging the local over the global. The party had already decreed that resistance to grain requisitions was sabotage. Sabotage was a *kulak* action caused by class enemies or individuals who had fallen under their pernicious influence. Sholokhov's letter provided no indication that he believed *kulaks* were real. He provided no acknowledgement that destroying the population's will to resist was a central feature of breaking sabotage. Sholokhov talked about the crisis in his district as if it existed in a vacuum. He displayed no awareness of the political significance of the fact that hoarding, hiding, and deceiving had been decisively vanquished, never to return. He dared to provide a different view of events than party ideologues.

Sholokhov realized that Stalin was attempting to strike a balance in his own peculiar way. Though the dictator was clearly dissatisfied with how his letter framed popular resistance, at the same time he communicated an appreciation of the writer's candor. Yet Sholokhov could not ignore the fact that Stalin was clearly sending him serious warnings. Did such a letter require a response? Should he admit any mistakes? Such a move did not seem warranted. The dictator's letter began and ended on a positive note, and Joseph Vissarionovich was restrained in his criticism. The writer decided to wait for a while.

In June he was summoned to Moscow for a meeting. He was invited to take part in the Politburo's discussion of the Shkiriatov report and its recommendations. One of the items on the agenda was a discussion of whether his friend Andrei Plotkin should be expelled from the party for vicious actions and mock executions during the grain requisition campaign. Ovchinnikov's fate would also be considered. Sholokhov decided to attend.

At 2:50 P.M. on July 2, 1933, he was called into Stalin's office, along with Ovchinnikov, Plotkin, Sheboldaev's second deputy, and another local official accused of excesses.[14] Sholokhov watched as Stalin dominated the proceedings. The Politburo faulted the regional leadership for failed oversight of the grain requisition campaign. Sheboldaev had cunningly never issued any written orders that could link his name to the campaign of terror, so the regional government shifted accountability for illegal actions to its representative, Ovchinnikov, who would now be blamed for initiating the deviations.

Ovchinnikov was summoned to Moscow because multiple local witnesses confirmed Sholokhov's allegations that his arrival coincided with outbreaks of terror. One of Ovchinnikov's deputies had even questioned in writing why he always avoided issuing official, written directives approving the harsh methods he demanded.[15] He operated in a gray area outside the law.

Ovchinnikov's optimal defense strategy was to emphasize success and confirm the official narrative of the regional crisis. He had participated in an important meeting with Politburo member Lazar Kaganovich in Rostov in November 1932.[16] This gave him an intimate understanding of how the crisis looked to the Kremlin. When he and his deputies arrived in the region, grain deliveries were completely lagging. Secret police reports confirmed that the collective farms were riddled with "anti-Soviet elements." Roughly one in ten residents of the district was engaging in some kind of rural, counterrevolutionary activity. There was no denying that tons of grain had been hidden from the party.

He must have sensed that he could neither refute nor deny the various testimonies that Shkiriatov accumulated against him. Therefore, he had to provide a convincing context for his actions. Operating with instructions to deliver the grain in the shortest possible time frame, he simply could not investigate in depth each and every household and identify the precise origins of all grain that was on hand. In an ideal world it would have been possible to verify which households had legitimately earned specific amounts of grain by working in the collective farms, but this would have taken too long. There was simply no effective way to quickly determine whether or not locals were eating hidden, contraband grain in order to hoard legitimate grain for later sale or exchange. If he permitted any category of the population to be exempted from searches and seizures, then he would have been handing the cunning *kulak* element a dangerous weapon to use against the state. They could coerce others into hiding grain for them. Even in Sholokhov's novel there were examples of such tactics.

He must have admitted to committing a series of mistakes in a sincere and zealous drive to bust coordinated sabotage. His pleas for leniency needed to be political, not personal. Without extraordinary measures, collection of grain in the district would not have doubled in just a few weeks.[17]

Since Sholokhov was there as a witness, there was little need for him to introduce any new information. Shkiriatov's report vindicated his letter. Stalin's response had closed off several talking points and prompted him to exercise a degree of caution. His main goal going into the meeting was to help Plotkin, whom he introduced as the real-life inspiration behind Davydov. If Stalin proved to be in a good mood and the proceedings went well, he would also request that Lugovoi be reinstated as local party leader and that items illegally confiscated from local farmers be returned.

For Plotkin everything was at stake that day.[18] There was no way to know whether or not he would leave the room a free man. Sholokhov pledged to help him but was not quite sure what he could expect. If Stalin liked Plotkin and found no reason to doubt his motives, that would help his case. His best bet was to emphasize that he was following orders and heroically confronting real enemies. Regional officials had helped to prepare the way for such a defense. There was no point in denying that on several occasions he resorted to extreme intimidation. The initiative was not his however.

Plotkin was prepared to portray the enemy as both cunning and ruthless. A story from the grain requisition campaign would suffice for this purpose.[19] There was one outlying cluster of farmsteads, where one of the family members of a local Cossack died. They insisted on a closed casket funeral. And so it was. But one of the relatives, who was carried away by grief, couldn't resist saying good-bye and taking one last look at the dearly departed. When he lifted the lid of the coffin, it was filled to the brim with grain! Such a narrative strategy was advantageous, since several members of Politburo already believed that nothing was sacred for *kulaks*, who plotted day and night to deceive the government.

Clearly referring to the Shkiriatov report, Stalin asked Plotkin to tell about the incident with the revolver. Plotkin began to tell about a late-night confrontation. The element of surprise was always crucial when confronting *kulaks* suspected of hiding grain, so night was the best time to strike. When a door opened there was little time to determine the best course of action. Sometimes, standing there in the dark, you just went with your instincts. You might claim that neighbors had written a denunciation about hidden grain and that the only way to avoid arrest was to reveal it immediately. Other times, it was best to just skip the formalities and come in brandishing a weapon to show who was in charge. This was one of those times. Goriunov was a stubborn individualist, the kind who repeatedly resisted joining the collective farm. With those kinds you couldn't appeal to any sense of social duty.

Plotkin narrated the crucial moment:[20]

"So I pointed my revolver at him [and started demanding the grain. He kept playing dumb], so I screamed: 'Either you are gonna take this revolver and shoot yourself or I'm going to shoot you [right now].' So he takes the revolver, puts the barrel right up to his neck and pulls the trigger."

Stalin interrupted: "And he fell to the ground?"

"No, he didn't fall."

"How is that? Did the trigger get jammed?" Stalin impatiently inquired.

"Not quite. When the barrel just clicked, he fainted."

Plotkin explained that the gun was not loaded.

"What if a bullet for some reason remained in one of the chambers?" Stalin asked.

"I excluded the possibility that could happen. I took out and counted the bullets before I went in."

Stalin appeared to be savoring the story of how a vigilant party member had deceived a deceiver. He started recalling incidents from *Virgin Soil Upturned* and quoting passages from memory. He delightedly asked both Sholokhov and Plotkin to confirm whether they were based on true events. From behind the dictatorial façade a fan emerged. Did Plotkin have tattoos on his breast like Davydov? Did he really confront a mob of angry women? It was a good sign that they were soon regaling him with stories.

"Aren't you afraid that if you return to that area they'll, excuse me for saying it, rip your balls off?" Stalin asked.[21]

Before Plotkin could answer, Sholokhov intervened. "I'll vouch for their safety, Comrade Stalin."

"In such a serious matter . . . we trust Sholokhov," Stalin joked.

Minutes later Stalin adjourned the meeting and announced that the Politburo would deliver its decision in the coming days.

Two days later they were summoned to the Kremlin again. The second meeting was purely a formality. The decision of the Politburo was read to Sholokhov and the others.[22] It pronounced that the second secretary of the regional party committee did not exercise adequate control and did nothing to restrain Ovchinnikov. At the same time it affirmed that the policy of putting pressure on those who were sabotaging the grain requisitions was "absolutely necessary" even if in Vioshki it was implemented in a distorted manner.

Plotkin's performance in front of Stalin and the Politburo was a great success. Shkiriatov's report had recommended that Plotkin be expelled from the Communist Party. Instead the Politburo decided to reinstate him and issue him a stern reprimand, while forbidding him from working in Vioshki district. Though this news was encouraging, Ovchinnikov also succeeded. He managed to remain a party member in good standing. He was removed from his leadership post in Rostov and was forbidden from working in rural areas for a year. So the contest ended in a tie.

For Sholokhov the best news was that his friend Lugovoi, who had now recovered from his illness, would be reinstated as local party leader.[23] Upon his return he would spend many months attempting to find and return property that was illegally confiscated from loyal collective farmers during the savage grain requisitions. While Lugovoi made attempts at restitution, Sholokhov gave himself over to grim reflections.[24] To Plotkin he wrote, "It's as if a wheel is turning and on one half there is an inscription that says 'good,' while on the other it says 'bad.' It is uncertain when the wheel will stop and which word will end up on top." In classical mythology, fortune's hand turned the wheel of fate. Sholokhov wisely refrained from speculating in writing about who made it spin in Soviet Russia.

TEN

In late 1933, *Kino*, a Soviet cinema magazine, published a scoop. It announced that Sholokhov was working on a screenplay. A Georgian director had convinced him to collaborate on a film version of *Virgin Soil*.[1] They were in the advanced stages of preparing for production. The movie would be finished in 1934. The news was greeted with great interest in the Soviet Union. However, soon all talk of the film abruptly ceased. The studio stopped production. This minor mystery would in time be eclipsed by the greatest unsolved mystery in the history of the USSR.

Sholokhov was looking forward to mastering the art of cinematography. He and the director Nikolai Shengelaia scouted locations in the Don region for film shoots. They studied Cossack songs for the sound track. They debated camera angles for key scenes. After laboring for several months on the screenplay, Sholokhov even agreed to give the film a different ending than the novel. It would conclude with a scene of the heroes plowing the virgin soil.

Sholokhov never found out for sure why the film was suddenly cancelled. There were good reasons for suspecting that a journalist was to blame. While working on the screenplay, Sholokhov and the film director had taken a photo together to commemorate their work. It showed Sholokhov holding a quill and Shengelaia brandishing a pistol. A representative of the *Literary Gazette* acquired the photo—exactly how became a subject of controversy—and published it on February 6, 1934, with the caption "N. Shengelaia 'convinces' M. Sholokhov to hurry up and finish the screenplay of *Virgin Soil*."

A copy of the newspaper would only reach Sholokhov a few days later, but a friend in Moscow must have immediately phoned to warn him. He telegraphed a letter of protest to the editor within hours of the paper's hitting the newsstands in the capital. Sholokhov insisted that he did not give the picture to anyone from the newspaper and did not provide permission to publish it. He wrote, "In my view no Soviet writer needs such low quality popularization of his work, much less myself."[2] Though the newspaper printed his letter and an apology in the next issue, the damage had been done.

How were Soviet readers to interpret a photo of two major cultural figures horsing around with weapons that were illegal for the vast majority of the population? Since 1918 all guns were under strict control of the police and could not be kept by private individuals without special permission. Only party officials were exempt. Since no announcement had ever ceremoniously proclaimed that Sholokhov had become an official of the party, this raised even more questions. Finally, there was the threat that foreign propaganda might exploit an image of a major Soviet writer being forced to write by an armed Georgian.

This lapse in image control coincided with Sholokhov's preparation for his appearance before the party purge commission.[3] It was scheduled for a date in July 1934. He was expected to spend months studying the party's bylaws, reviewing important ideological statements, and memorizing phrases from key policy documents. It would also be wise to ingratiate himself to the regional party leadership. A commission consisting of two members, a chair, and a secretary would be approved by the regional government. In theory the commission could ask about anything relevant to policy or ideology. Questions might include "Define democratic centralism"; "Name all of the forms of party discipline that can be imposed on a member"; "Explain the major achievements of the Communist International in the routing of Trotskyism and right opportunism"; "Outline how the party fulfilled its goals for the development of blast furnaces in the first five-year plan"; "According to Comrade Stalin, which four lines of attack shape the struggle against bureaucratism?"

During those months the regional party leader Sheboldaev repeatedly sought to mentor Sholokhov.[4] He advised him to devote more attention to the urban working class. He lamented that the writer was spending too much time getting involved in local agricultural affairs. He feigned concern for Sholokhov's literary career and offered to facilitate his move to a larger, industrial city. He insinuated that the writer risked becoming an ideologue of counterrevolutionary Cossacks and candidly advised him to switch to a safer topic.

Sholokhov responded to Sheboldaev's persistent prodding with defiance. He used interviews with the national and regional press to push back.[5] Rather than leave Vioshki, he decided to acquire a larger house there. Instead of retreating from agricultural affairs, he intervened more frequently. He doubled down on the very topics that Sheboldaev found objectionable by announcing new projects: a play devoted to collective agriculture and an operatic version of *Quiet Don*. He urged young writers to "bind" themselves to a particular place and to tell the story of socialist construction there over time. He insisted that writers needed to be immersed in the real world rather than ensconced in writers' clubs in big cities.

Sholokhov's direct access to Moscow officials threatened Sheboldaev's total control over the region.[6] So he resorted to various strategies to reign in the writer. These strategies only made the writer more determined to fight back. When Sheboldaev lashed out at local leaders, Sholokhov insisted in the press that he owed various debts to district leaders because they helped him make *Virgin Soil* more realistic. When Sheboldaev issued a regional decree to oust Lugovoi from local party leadership, Sholokhov put in a call to Moscow to have it annulled. When allies of Sheboldaev used district party meetings to obstruct initiatives, Sholokhov alerted the Central Committee that officials in several districts had ignored the 1933 directive to provide restitution to collective farmers.

As the date of his appearance before the party purge commission approached, he learned more about how the process worked. The first wave of public purge sessions in Moscow and Leningrad provided a preview of what he could expect.[7] The commissions were digging deep into the biographies of everyone who had recently joined the party. They were eager to uncover any evidence that a communist had concealed information or deceived the party in some way. They combed through every single item in a member's personnel file and reviewed every public statement on record. Their goal was to uncover inconsistencies. At the session they would hone in on discrepancies and seek to catch you off guard. As you struggled to recall what you said in a meeting or wrote on some form several years ago, they were laying a trap. If your memory was faulty, they would confront you with contradictory evidence. If you ever changed your story, they would accuse you of cunningly concealing information from the party. The opportunity to recite an autobiography at the beginning of the session was both an opportunity to shape the proceedings and a potential pitfall. You had to recall everything you had ever said about your biography and your background. You needed to anticipate any potential dirt they could dig up on either you or your relatives. You had to remain calm and collected rather than tense and apprehensive.

At times during those months Sholokhov got the distinct impression that he was being followed. Odd sounds and background noises hinted that his telephone conversations were being listened to. He began to suspect that Sheboldaev was monitoring him. Though he could not be certain, he had to take precautions. He had to be careful not to reveal anything that could be deployed against him at the purge session.

For Sholokhov his arrest in 1922 presented a thorny problem. Should he reveal it to the purge commission, or should he avoid any mention of it? There was only a handful of people who knew all the details, and he was still on friendly terms with most of them. As soon as the purge was announced, Sholokhov decided not to leave matters to chance. He renewed his acquaintance with the most significant witness and codefendant in his case.[8] It was vital to secure his goodwill . . . just in case. There was no way to know whether or not the purge commission would go back that far.

The meeting of the purge commission was held at the local May Day movie theater in late July.[9] Hundreds of people crowded in to get a glance at Sholokhov. When the chair of the commission announced, "The next to be examined is Mikhail Aleksandrovich Sholokhov," the crowd burst out in vigorous applause. He stepped up to the front of the room and stood next to a modest table draped with a red banner. He handed his party candidacy card over to the chair of the commission. He would only get it back if the purge commission passed him. As he looked out into the audience, he noticed that Sheboldaev had unexpectedly shown up.[10] The potential for an ambush amplified his anxieties about the proceedings.

The ritual demanded that first he recite his autobiography. He began:

> I was born in 1905 in Kruzhilin hamlet. My father was at first employed as a clerk in a trading firm, then he later worked as the administrator of a mill. I studied in the parish school in Karginskaia, then I went on to study in the men's advanced secondary school of the town Boguchar. I was not able to finish and only completed the fourth level.

Here the only significant bone of contention was his father's social status. The term *clerk* or *white-collar worker* seemed more palatable than *merchant*. He continued:

> In 1920 I worked as a filing specialist in the Karginskaia executive committee. From there I was sent to a course for grain requisitioning workers and after that I worked in Bukanovskaia as a *prodinspektor* [assessor of taxes which were paid in kind with food]. In 1923 I left for Moscow.

Here he failed to mention that in 1922 he had been relieved of his duties, held in custody for several weeks, released on surety to his father to await trial, then convicted and sentenced to probation.

At this crucial point in his personal narrative, he deployed humor to deflect attention from his failure to explain the circumstances under which he left local administration. He associated himself with the thousands who suddenly found themselves with obsolete skills when the civil war and the policy of war communism ended:

> In Moscow I ended up in the situation of one of the heroes of [the writer] Artem Veselyi. This man came after the civil war was over to register at the government labor bureau. 'What is your profession?' They asked him. 'Machine-gunner,' he answered. But no one needed machine-gunners anymore. I registered as a *prodinspektor*, but that profession wasn't needed any more either. After two to three months of unemployment, I worked as a day laborer doing manual labor, a bricklayer, a porter and as a book-keeper in the administration of a residential building.

This tactic made tax collecting one of several occupations, all of which served as a prelude to a life in literature. He continued:

> Starting in 1923 I began to devote myself to learning how to write. I wrote articles and feuilletons for the newspaper *Youth Pravda*. After the publication of a book called *Don Stories*, I became a professional author. I am still one today. I became a candidate for party membership in 1930 and was enrolled as a member from 1932. That's my whole biography.

The chair of the commission then opened the floor for questions. Immediately dozens of hands were raised. The chairman decided to call on a young man. Sholokhov was ready to start answering questions about party policy and recent events. Instead literature instantly became the focus.

The young man began, "Tell us, how did you gather your materials . . ." Before he could finish, someone in the hall shouted, "With a basket." The hall erupted in laughter.

The chair of the committee intervened:

"You don't have to answer that question. It would be better if you tell about the social and party work that you are doing."

A relieved Sholokhov started to list examples.

"Do you maintain contacts with collective farmers?"

"I frequently visit collective farms. Without such contacts I would not have been able to write *Virgin Soil*. The novel itself is the [best] answer to that question."

"You, it would seem, are listed as a member of the editorial board of the team which is writing the history of the Lenin [locomotive] factory in Rostov. What have you done up to this point as part of that work?"

This seemed like the kind of question that Sheboldaev would plant in the audience. It homed in on an obligation that he had neglected in recent months. It was an urban, working-class obligation. Should he say that he had not really done much? That would mean publicly admitting that he had ignored one of the country's most important constituencies.

Sholokhov pondered the matter for a moment, then declared:

"Being connected to the editorial board of the committee which is responsible for composing the history of [all] factories and manufactures [throughout] the Soviet Union, I have not received any directives from that [national] editorial board about [how and when] to begin work."

His answer adroitly deflected the question. If the question came back, he could mention that he would meet with Gorky during the upcoming Writers' Congress and that if they had any doubts they could contact the classic.

The next questions returned to *Quiet Don* and his early stories. Then the vexing challenge came back again in a different guise from a different questioner.

"Are you thinking of writing something about factory workers?"

Sholokhov responded, "It is difficult to answer that question" while fumbling for a better answer. Then he declared:

"I am not thinking of limiting myself to peasant topics. But since I am tied up with two books and a play, I simply can't give an answer about when I will switch over to a topic related to factory workers."

Sheboldaev had urged him to switch topics and move to the city in order to bolster his credibility as a proletarian writer. Would the party boss now stand up and insist that the writer had ignored clear guidance from his party superiors? If so, how should Sholokhov respond? Remarkably, Sheboldaev sat still. Why was he waiting to intervene?

The next round of questions was concerned with how Sholokhov benefited from criticism of his novel *Virgin Soil*. He tried his best to appear self-critical. The ritual required that he recognize some kind of flaw that had been uncovered through criticism. He conceded that he could have provided a stronger portrayal of female collective farm workers.

"Are you aware that when *Virgin Soil* was published abroad they cut out five chapters?" someone demanded.

This was a deceptively simple question with dangerous subtexts and political permutations. It had to be handled with care.

"Yes, I am aware of that," Sholokhov replied.

He needed to prove that he was in far better command of the facts than the questioner:

"In France the publishing house Gallimar tossed out seven chapters. Because there is no diplomatic literary convention between the USSR and several western European states, they are able to publish our works in any form that is convenient for them. I energetically protested at the time. In particular André Gide [the French writer and socialist fellow traveler] supported me."

"How are you guided by Stalin's letter 'Some Questions Concerning the History of Bolshevism'?"[11]

Sholokhov trolled through his memory for appropriate responses. Should he talk about all the egregious ideological errors that German Social Democrats had committed since 1903? Would it be better to address Lenin's pamphlet from 1916, or Stalin's reinterpretation of it in 1931? The letter had also launched a search for disguised Trotskyite rubbish in literature. Maybe that was the right answer. If he took that tack, however, a follow-up question could demand to know what he had personally done to combat "rotten liberalism." He decided to stick with a safer answer:

"Being guided by Stalin's letter is important not only for me but for all writers. I continue to learn, to the extent that my energies and capabilities permit, from the works of Marx, Lenin, and Stalin."

He waited for Sheboldaev to stand up and demand a citation or clarification. But the party boss didn't budge.

After a few additional questions, including a query about whether Grigorii Melekhov had survived the civil war and succeeded as a collective farmer, the question session was over. Not a single probing question about his biography or party policy had been asked. He was not out of the woods yet. The time had come for the commission members to confront him with evidence of deficiencies in his party work. As they started, the audience drowned them out. Sholokhov's supporters had packed the hall.

"We know Sholokhov!" "He grew up before our very eyes." "He's from around here." They shouted.[12]

The chair of the commission was forced to conclude the proceedings. The standard notation "passed the examination" was added to his file. After the session, Sholokhov and Sheboldaev held a long and tense private meeting. Neither the writer nor the regional boss was willing to admit any mistakes.[13] Nor could they come to an agreement about Sholokhov's role in local political and agricultural affairs.

Relieved that the purge was behind him, he could turn his attention to preparing for the long-awaited Congress of Soviet Writers. It was held in Moscow in August 1934, and it turned out to be more burdensome than stimulating.[14] There were too many empty ceremonial speeches. Pompous declarations were all too plentiful and often started with the predictable phrase "We need to . . ." Writers eagerly compared themselves to workers, soldiers, and engineers. Every imaginable form of special pleading was employed to advocate for the extraordinary value of children's books, literature of the formerly backward peoples, and inspiring stories about aviation and arctic exploration. Many speeches offered little more than long lists of names. In the presentations devoted to literature, Stalin was mentioned more times than Leo Tolstoy. Several different definitions of "socialist realism" were offered. In most of them, realism was subordinate to socialism. When reality and socialism clashed, the noble ideal was always preferable to inconvenient truths.

Considerable time was devoted to welcoming delegations. Among them there were highly efficient milkmaids, young pioneers, and herders from the far north who for some reason brought their reindeer along.

Representatives of Soviet society were also allotted speaking time to discuss literature from the perspective of ordinary people. Sholokhov was forced to endure an appraisal of *Virgin Soil* delivered by two women who had become highly successful collective farmers. The first urged Sholokhov to turn Lukeria, who is portrayed in the novel as a frisky, libidinous woman, into an exemplary shock worker for collective agriculture. The second noted that she had become an award-winning farm director while her husband remained an ordinary worker. She attributed this to his fondness for cigarettes and alcohol. "Though men might be honest people, they tend to get a little drunk at times and every sort of thing can result from that," she declared to the delight of the audience.[15] Sholokhov couldn't quite tell if the last comment had been planted as a message to him to tone down his own drinking.

Gorky's idiosyncratic performances at the congress raised concerns about his commitment to conformity. He said relatively little about recent works in a speech devoted to Soviet literature.[16] His opening remarks were full of tangential comments ranging from primitive culture to folklore to why detective novels retarded the growth of class consciousness in western Europe. He quoted obscure pamphlets from the 18th century and made strange references to *vozhdizm*, the striving for supreme leadership, labeling it a "disease of this epoch." He lashed out at the editors of the *History of Factories and Manufacturing Plants* for not finding the time to do their job. He insisted that out of the fifteen hundred individuals who had joined the new Soviet Writers' Union, only about forty-five could truly be classified as talented. The fact that he praised "the genius" of Lenin and the "iron will" of Stalin did not go unnoticed by the delegates. At the close of the conference he stood below a two-story-tall banner featuring his own portrait and insisted that his name had been mentioned far too often in combination with lofty epithets.

The problem of *Quiet Don* also unexpectedly resurfaced around the time of the literary congress. A man named Ivan Elankin had started to claim that Sholokhov had appropriated texts from him.[17] Elankin was a native of the Vioshki area who was about a decade older than Sholokhov. He had spent much of his adult life drifting from place to place. His background in poverty, service in the civil war, and education in a series of communist crash courses was sufficient to get him hired as inspector of this or instructor of that, but after a few months his paranoid schizophrenia would always flare up. He was habitually transferred to another job somewhere at the margins of his previous boss's network. He bounced around between various towns in southern Russia and even managed to spend two brief periods in places not far from Moscow. He changed jobs over a dozen times in two decades. The total would no doubt have been higher if not for his two confinements in mental hospitals. He returned to the area in 1934 after being ousted from a teaching job.

Only a few months after his return, Elankin's paranoiac fixations shifted. He had been prone to suspecting that a hidden, worldwide center had taken control of Stalin and was using him to undermine the revolution and deprive the workers of power. In the summer of 1934, he started to suspect that Sholokhov was the cause of all his personal misfortunes. He took to carrying around an iron rod to defend himself in the event that Sholokhov mounted a physical attack against him. To anyone who would listen, he would express his antagonism and share his suspicions that Sholokhov had appropriated his texts.

If persistent plagiarism rumors had not already circulated about volume one of *Quiet Don*, Sholokhov could have easily dismissed Elankin's allegations as the ravings of a local lunatic. The problem was that in moments of clarity, Elankin talked about the theft of a suitcase and a basket filled with all kinds of manuscripts devoted to the Cossacks between 1912 and the end of the civil war. The materials had been deposited for safekeeping with one Sholokhov's distant relatives, named Georgii Borisov, who lived for a time in the town of Maikop in the North Caucasus. Upon investigation, certain aspects of Elankin's story would check out.[18] The fact that in 1930 Elankin was expelled from the party for openly espousing "opposition rhetoric" severely diminished the danger that anyone would take him seriously. Nonetheless, some residents of the area clearly believed him, something that would continue to fuel Sholokhov's own anxiety.

In spite of the fact that on several occasions Elankin made threatening statements about Sholokhov, the local NKVD failed to arrest Elankin.[19] For Sholokhov and his friends, this uncharacteristic leniency raised suspicions that someone powerful was protecting Elankin for some kind of nefarious purpose.[20] They wondered whether Sheboldaev could be manuevering him against the writer as an act of vengeance for the complaints to Moscow.

This uncertainty did not deter Sholokhov from embarking on his second trip abroad. He had been granted permission to go on a long business trip to negotiate with publishers and establish international contacts.[21] He visited Sweden, Denmark, England, and France. He met writers, took part in official receptions, and signed hundreds of copies of translations of his books. In England and Denmark he gave brief lectures on the state of Soviet literature. In Scandinavia he arranged visits to local farms to learn about cutting-edge agricultural practices.

He was in Sweden on the evening the embassy received an urgent cable.[22] It read:

> On December 1 at 4:30 in the afternoon in Leningrad in the building of the Leningrad Council Comrade Sergei Mironovich Kirov . . . [lofty epithets] . . . was killed by the hand of a murderer who was sent by the enemies of the working class. The person who fired the shot has been detained. His identity is being investigated.

In the days that followed it became apparent that the murderer had used a revolver and had fired directly into the back of Kirov's head. One of the highest-ranking members of the Soviet government, the head of the Leningrad party organization, had been gunned down by a terrorist. How could such a horrible crime have happened?

By the time Sholokhov arrived in England, embassy officials were discussing a secret letter from the Central Committee which alleged that a counterrevolutionary Leningrad center affiliated with Zinoviev was connected to the assassination. Grigorii Zinoviev? He was a prominent member of the Soviet government until 1927, when he was expelled from the party, then later readmitted after confessing mistakes. The foreign press was full of wild speculations about arrests and rebellions. There was much discussion of whether Kirov's murder was a political assassination or a crime of passion resulting from an adulterous affair between Kirov and his suspected assassin's wife.

Between spending his royalties and filling eight suitcases full of things he had purchased in London, Sholokhov met on various occasions with the Soviet ambassador, Ivan Maiskii.[23] Maiskii was particularly upset that British Labour Party activists doubted that the Soviet Union was actually confronting a widespread terrorist conspiracy. They had even protested the application of the death penalty to individuals caught infiltrating the Soviet border. Maiskii was convinced that many terrorists had been sent with bombs, grenades, revolvers, and other weapons to carry out attacks on Stalin and other leaders. The Kirov murder was just the beginning. He even feared that a return of Red Terror might be necessary to confront the mounting threat.

ELEVEN

Sholokhov was in Moscow on the day that a horrific, fiery blaze engulfed Maxim Gorky. Small children screamed in panic and seasoned officers ran for cover. Dozens of dismembered bodies were strewn amid smoking shards of molten metal. Immediately there were suspicions of terrorism. Witnesses insisted with certainty that *Pravda* was to blame. As the authorities prepared for a massive mourning march through the heart of Moscow in May 1935, everyone wondered whether Stalin would show up for the funeral.

Sholokhov arrived in Moscow only days before the tragedy. He was hoping to outfox Sheboldaev, whom Sholokhov believed was having him followed. Sheboldaev was accusing Lugovoi of obstructing regional policies and pursuing his own agenda. "Sooner or later you're going to have to leave Vioshenskaia," he ominously warned. Though directed toward Lugovoi, the statement reminded the writer of earlier suggestions that he relocate. Sholokhov decided that complaining to Stalin about Sheboldaev would only weaken their hand in the event of future problems.[1] It was better to save that trump card for a situation that was truly desperate. They didn't want to look like small children running to complain against a bully to an adult.

Sholokhov was scheduled to meet with Stalin for other reasons, and he resolved to use the meeting to their advantage.[2] After his return from Scandinavia he trumpeted a series of ideas for agricultural innovation that he brought back from abroad. At the meeting he could make a case for agricultural innovation and Lugovoi's role in promoting it.[3]

When Sholokhov arrived in the capital, everyone was preparing for a huge celebration in honor of the grand opening of the Moscow metro system.[4] For months Soviet propaganda celebrated the heroism of the workers building the first lines of an extensive underground system. An official slogan proclaimed: "Victory in building the metro is a victory for Socialism!" There were constant reports about engineering challenges and upbeat stories about how brigades competed with each to advance the tunnels a few extra inches. Even children could recite statistics about dirt removal, tunnel reinforcement, and square meters of marble and granite paneling. There was a palpable pride in the fact that palaces for the people were being created underground. The first test trains started to run in February 1935, and in April workers who had received commendations were permitted to ride. Later that month Stalin took an unplanned ride, to the delight of ordinary Russians. The Moscow papers featured interviews with giddy ordinary folks who proclaimed that seeing Stalin waving at them from afar in the metro was the best day of their lives.[5]

Walking around the capital, Sholokhov noticed that images of Stalin were everywhere. The dictator simultaneously appeared on the covers of magazines, on posters, on banners, and on the front pages of newspapers. The new metro stations were draped with gigantic banners of Stalin and his words. Even the station named in honor of Kirov, one of the first to receive a name, was adorned with huge portraits of both Stalin and Kirov. These were several stories tall and towered over the pedestrians below.

There was also something disquieting about the coverage of Stalin's speech at the official opening of the metro system.[6] It was as if propaganda officials were providing stage directions for the proper public reaction to his future appearances. These were highlighted in bold and represented as spontaneous, collective responses to each of his actions. When he came up to the podium, the audience "exploded into frenzied ovation." In unison everyone suddenly poured out cries of greeting. They screamed phrases such as "Long live the Supreme Leader of the World Proletariat!" and "Hurrah for dear Stalin!" At various pauses during the supreme leader's speech—it was now becoming proper protocol to employ this term—everyone rose to their feet and engaged in stormy applause. When Stalin left the podium, the applause did not subside for a long, long time. An "indescribable enthusiasm" seized the entire audience. With "happy faces," everyone continued applauding. After such stage directions, just imagine being the person in the crowd who missed his cue.

To his great surprise, Sholokhov was called in for a brief meeting with Stalin soon after his arrival. He interpreted this as a sign of great favor, since all the papers were reporting that Stalin was busy conducting crucial talks with French foreign minister Pierre Lavalle. They were negotiating an important mutual aid and assistance treaty, which was obviously intended as a bulwark against Nazi German aggression.

The ostensible purpose of the meeting was a discussion of an anti-fascist writer's conference that would take place in Paris in a few weeks.[7] Sholokhov had been selected along with Gorky and others to represent the Soviet Union. But he was there to petition Stalin for permission not to attend. His excuse was highly personal, not political. His wife was expecting their third child and would give birth in a matter of days. He wanted to be with his family. Moreover he had just recently returned from abroad. Stalin granted his request and ordered the head of the delegation to find a substitute. Sholokhov then discussed several ideas for innovation in agriculture. He spoke highly of Lugovoi, who was helping him to implement them. Without mentioning or criticizing Sheboldaev, Sholokhov asked the Central Committee to give them some additional time to test new methods. Stalin agreed. This would cushion them from any regional interference for several months.

At that meeting Stalin appears to have shared with Sholokhov some thoughts about a new constitution for the Soviet Union.[8] He likely consulted the writer about whether former White Guard supporters should still be deprived of the right to either vote or be elected to office. Stalin was reviewing Lenin's writings from 1919 to the effect that upon the strengthening of socialism it would be possible to introduce universal suffrage without any restrictions whatsoever.

The talk about lifting of restrictions spurred Sholokhov to remind Stalin that fifteen years after the end of the civil war the government still placed severe restrictions on Cossack service in the Red Army.[9] Large numbers of them were still not permitted by the government to volunteer for military service because their relatives had served in counterrevolutionary armies. Those with "clean" backgrounds still faced exclusion from sensitive military specializations. Sholokhov alluded to the fact that Trotsky and his followers had provoked a Cossack rebellion back in 1919 by banning Cossack traditional clothing and threatening to shoot people who still called themselves Cossacks.[10] This appeal to a historical injustice caused by a hated rival provoked Stalin to pick up the phone and call Voroshilov. He ordered him to look into the issue and report back.

After the official business had been transacted, Sholokhov built up the courage to ask Stalin a question that had been bothering him for days.[11]

"Joseph Vissarionovich, why is it that you permit all this praising of you beyond measure? I mean all of the portraits which are cropping up at every turn." He also said something about subservient lackeys glorifying Stalin in countless ways. This was a literary reference to the Russian fabulist Krylov, who opined that subservient lackeys can sometimes be more harmful than enemies.

Stalin looked at him intently and without malice. A cunning smile came across his face. "What can one do about such matters? . . . The people need a *bashka*." He watched intently for Sholokhov's reaction.

Sholokhov didn't quite know what to make of this comment. He pretended to comprehend but avoided Stalin's gaze. A *bashka* is a head. Several Russian proverbs use the term, but often in a derogatory sense. No definition quite seemed to fit this context. Not sure about what to say, he felt uneasy. He was relieved that the conversation concluded after a few minutes. Only later did he realize that he had not heard Stalin correctly because of the leader's Georgian accent. Upon further reflection he determined that Stalin had actually said something to the effect of: "The people need to believe in a *bozhka* [a godkin or little idol like the ones pagans in Siberia worship]." This put the dictator's declaration in an entirely different light. He was suggesting that he permitted worship not because he enjoyed it but because it was in the nature of the people to yearn for idols.

Although Sholokhov did not realize it at the time, Stalin was also alluding to a bitter ideological and philosophical dispute between Gorky and Lenin that took place several years before the revolution.[12] Gorky believed that some elements of religion could be useful in the process of creating a socialist society because they were so deeply ingrained in the population, particularly in Russia. Lenin sharply disagreed and labeled the idea "dangerous vileness." He called the construction of any kind of "little gods" to be an act of "necrophilia alien to Marxist ideology" and wrote two acrimonious letters about the subject to Gorky.

Forty-eight hours after their meeting concluded, all of Moscow was speculating about the fate of Gorky. At 12:45 on the afternoon of May 18 the pride of the Soviet Union perished in a blaze of fire in front of hundreds of stunned residents of the capital.[13] The giant Maxim Gorky airplane was hailed as a triumph of technology and mobilization. It was built in less than two years and paid for with contributions sent by thousands of ordinary citizens. A country enthralled with giant factories, giant farms, and giant hydroelectric dams needed to have a giant airplane as well. It had the longest wingspan of any plane ever built up to that point, and its eight powerful engines had already set a world record for payload lifting capacity. The underside was emblazoned with MAXIM on one wing and GORKY on the other. As the world's first propaganda plane, it possessed a loudspeaker that could be heard from half a mile away while it was in the air. It boasted a printing press that could churn out thousands of leaflets and even print newspapers while flying. To the awe and delight of Soviet citizens, it flew low over the Kremlin for the May Day parade only weeks earlier. Its shadow appeared to envelop the huge space of Red Square.

On the day of the tragedy the authorities waited for nearly nine hours before releasing an official statement.[14] This left ample time for rumors to spread. Some claimed to have seen explosions in the air. Others disputed this. There was general agreement that billows of black smoke appeared and bodies suddenly started to fall from the sky in a suburb north of Moscow. A giant wing crashed into a house. an enormous engine crushed a man riding a bicycle. Some insisted that many of the heroic builders of the Moscow metro and their families were on board. Others speculated that high-ranking members of the government were supposed to be testing the plane. Those near the scene swore that Gorky collided in the air with a small airplane, which looked like a gnat in comparison with a soaring eagle. This small airplane was apparently being filmed from a third plane, the *Pravda*, for a newsreel.

For hours a palpable tension gripped a population primed for fear. The Kirov assassination had unleashed anxieties about a vast terrorist conspiracy against the USSR. Was this the beginning of a relentless wave of attacks? Ambassador Maiskii in London had warned of infiltration of the country by enemies intent on assassinating the country's leaders. Was Stalin on the plane? Is that why the radio said nothing about the tragedy even though all of Moscow was talking about it? Sholokhov tried to remain calm while awaiting the official announcement.

The first statement late that evening acknowledged that the *Maxim Gorky* had crashed.[15] In addition to twelve crew members, there were thirty-six passengers on board. They were mainly engineers and technicians who had worked on the plane and a few members of their families. The next day, May 19, *Pravda* proclaimed that an investigation had already conclusively determined that the pilot of the small plane was solely to blame for the accident. Against orders the undisciplined pilot performed a looping stunt manuever and lost control of his plane and collided with the giant plane. A day later the papers noted that Stalin had reviewed the findings. Sholokhov was left wondering what kind of investigation could have been initiated and concluded in less than twenty-four hours.

An elaborate public funeral march through the center of Moscow was organized for the victims of the crash. Thousands lined the streets to honor the crew. The two most prominent mourners who were expected to attend failed to appear at the burial.[16] Stalin delegated an upstart official to take his place at the head of the funeral procession. This official was Nikita Khrushchev, whom the dictator had brought from Ukraine to

Moscow to help oversee the completion of the metro and the expansion of the capital. The other egregious absentee was Maxim Gorky.[17] In Moscow literary circles there were soon whispers that Gorky was severely distraught by the mere thought of the catastrophe. His name was now associated with the worst disaster in aviation history up to that point.

When Sholokhov returned to Vioshki, the struggle with Sheboldaev continued. The regional boss had sent three new officials to the district.[18] One was named second party secretary, another was appointed editor of the district newspaper, and the third was appointed to head the local NKVD office. The first could manipulate party procedures, the second could influence public opinion, and the third could unleash fear. It was no secret that they sometimes received visitors from the regional government who never even bothered to stop at the district party headquarters. They held secretive meetings and acted as a clique.

As Sholokhov plotted his next move, he found ammunition among the large stack of letters that had accumulated during his absences. One particularly intrigued him. It was from a group of Red Partisans in the Kuban' region.[19] The Red Partisans were a category of citizens who were entitled to special privileges as a result of their service during the civil war in local partisan armies that fought for the Soviet side. In the 1920s local commissions were established to review applications and certify revolutionary service. These commissions issued identity cards entitling Red Partisans and their children to preferential access to loans, land, improved housing, health resorts, education, and employment. Partisans were also given pride of place in local parades and public meetings as exemplary citizens who were among the first to embrace the Soviet government in places where it was very dangerous to do so.

The partisans urged Sholokhov to expand *Quiet Don* southward to their territory. They sent him some stories they had written about their own experiences during the civil war. They resolved to fight for the Soviet side even though they were surrounded by counterrevolutionaries. Against all odds they managed to take control of an armored train and evacuate to the central Caucasus. There they were forced to blow up the train and retreat even further. Only a few dozen of them survived and eventually returned home. Sholokhov immediately realized the dramatic potential of the subject matter. It would simultaneously kill two birds with one stone. It would answer Gorky's call for collective forms of authorship incorporating the voices of common people, and it would send a signal to Sheboldaev that the writer was expanding his interest to encompass all Cossack territories during the civil war.

He visited the partisans to find out more about their experiences and their novice literary efforts. The visit was a success. He decided to continue working with them. Though they were likely subtle enough not to overemphasize it during his visit, the partisans were seeking to involve Sholokhov in a bureaucratic struggle that was unfolding during those months. The Soviet government had instituted a second wave of purges of Red Partisans.[20] The first wave in 1932 investigated whether all card holders had actually fought for the Soviet cause and whether they had ever subsequently deserted it. Now the government assumed that various pretenders had falsely acquired Red Partisan identity cards. The new procedure would involve investigations similar to the party purges.

After a two-day visit to the partisans, with great fanfare Sholokhov announced to journalists in Rostov that he would either write or edit a book devoted to the heroic struggle of the Kuban' partisans. By putting their suffering and heroism in the public eye again at a time when partisan identities were being questioned, Sholokhov would be taking on the role of their patron and protector. He was clearly aware that literature could help advance their social claims. He particularly emphasized that "the majority of the partisans are invalids now."[21]

Only weeks later, however, he quietly abandoned the partisan project. He never said anything about it again in print or provided any explanation for his abrupt decision. In August 1935 a party directive ordered regional governments to close down commissions for the affairs of Red Partisans.[22] A subsequent directive annulled registration files and deprived the partisans of all of their special privileges. Signed by a Politburo member, the directive was considered at the highest levels. Sholokhov had narrowly avoided a political error.

What happened after that was uncanny. A Kremlin official asked Sholokhov to organize a Cossack choir for a series of high-profile performances in Moscow.[23] They were to prepare songs with rousing martial melodies. They were to wear Cossack uniforms, which had been banned since the revolution. There could be no coincidence that so soon after he had spoken to Stalin about Cossack clothing he was suddenly assigned such a task. Even Sheboldaev was given a supporting role. He would greet them in Rostov and help organize their trip to Moscow. Something important and unusual was afoot.

By the time Sholokhov brought the choir to Moscow a few months later it was clear that the concerts were just one of a series of test runs designed to feel the pulse of the Soviet public for a return of the Cossacks to a role in the military.[24] The secret police were carefully recording public reactions and reporting back to the Kremlin. In order to confront the looming threat from Nazi Germany, Stalin was implementing a revival of military traditions from the tsarist era. From exile, Trotsky proclaimed that the restoration of the Cossacks was the surest sign that a Stalinist Thermidor was consuming the revolution.

Though Sholokhov could claim some credit for this reversal of Soviet policy towards the Cossacks, it was highly ironic that Sheboldaev and his deputies were responsible for the actual revival of Cossack traditions.[25] The same officials who for years had terrorized and disparaged the Cossacks suddenly started to effusively praise them. Individuals who only weeks earlier had insisted that the Cossacks no longer existed now penned long articles emphasizing their distinctive traditions and culture. Absurdities abounded. The imprisoned leader of the Communist Party in Germany, Ernst Thalmann, was named an honorary Cossack. Stalin was now lauded as "the supreme leader of peoples and friend of Cossackdom."

An elaborate ceremony was staged in Rostov in March 1936 and was dedicated to Cossack folk songs and cavalry traditions. The proceedings were chaired by Ovchinnikov.[26] Nothing more cynical could be imagined. The man who was directly responsible for starving thousands of Cossacks to death stood on stage and pretended to be a connoisseur of Cossack culture.

Later that summer the literary world became preoccupied with an odd and unsettling coincidence. Starting on June 7, 1936, the Soviet media began publishing daily reports on the condition of Maxim Gorky's health.[27] The first report noted that a week earlier the classic had contracted a serious case of the flu and that his lungs and heart were compromised. From his meetings with Gorky, Sholokhov recalled that the classic's breathing was always a concern, due to an old case of tuberculosis and a pernicious habit of chain smoking. After a week of mixed reports, which provided daily measurements of Gorky's pulse and body temperature, on the morning of June 18 the medical bulletins took a dramatic turn for the worse. The previous day Gorky had lost consciousness. His pulse was fading. On June 19, the Soviet government announced that Gorky had died.[28] The papers published a surprisingly detailed and technical medical assessment of the causes of his death, in addition to a summary of the autopsy conducted in the presence of seven distinguished doctors. It was as if they were trying exceptionally hard to emphasize that his death was natural.

By an extremely strange coincidence the same day a darkness descended upon the land. The Soviet Union experienced a total solar eclipse, and its full phase was centered over Siberia. Some insisted this was no coincidence. Not everyone in Moscow literary circles believed that Gorky and Stalin were still on amicable terms in 1936.[29] Some claimed that Gorky became a captive and that his mansion served as a gilded cage. It was disturbing to think that the correlation between Gorky's death and a very rare astronomic event might have been more than accidental.

Sholokhov was forced to put aside such questions for the sake of political expediency. On June 20, 1936, he sent a short and highly cautious telegram to *Pravda*. It read, "I mourn the enormous loss which is being endured by the country and Soviet literature."[30] That was it. The communication was strangely distant and impersonal.

In comparison with the over-the-top outpourings of grief sent by others, Sholokhov's telegram was odd. He avoided any characterization of Gorky's contribution to the cause of communism. He said nothing about Gorky as a mentor or genius writer, beloved by all. He omitted the standard tropes: friend of Lenin and Stalin, revolutionary fighter of worldwide stature, creator of an immortal body of work. He soon realized that his caution was misplaced. *Pravda* published a large photo of Stalin serving as the lead pallbearer for the urn with Gorky's ashes.

TWELVE

n the mid-1930s, a minor character vanished from all new copies of *Quiet Don* printed in the Soviet Union.[1] Under normal circumstances the presence of a marginal protagonist in a novel would not imperil an acclaimed author or endanger the lives of those associated with him. When that character is Leon Trotsky, the reviled, exiled leader of opposition to Stalin and enemy number one of all the world's toiling masses, and when the year is 1937, the height of the paranoid hunt for hidden Trotskyists across the Soviet Union, all assumptions about literary normalcy evaporate. The purging of Trotsky from the novel's fabric foreshadowed the disappearance from Vioshki of hundreds of innocent individuals dramatically "unmasked" as Trotskyists. As the purges approached nearer and nearer to Sholokhov, and arrests first engulfed acquaintances, then consumed close associates, then seized his best friends, Sholokhov became dangerously despondent. He abandoned his work on the novel and awaited his own doom.

Until late 1936 Sholokhov was on track to finish his Cossack epic.[2] He would bring about a final resolution to the dramatic cliff-hanger—the ultimate fate of Grigorii Melekhov and his family at the end of the civil war—that Soviet readers had been anticipating for several years. In an article published in *Izvestiia* in May of 1935, Sholokhov insisted that he was "laboring day and night" to finish *Quiet Don*. He confidently proclaimed, "By next spring I will hand it over [to the publishers]. There is just one more tale to be told and that's it." In a letter written in October 1936 to a fellow writer he declared, "This month I'll have to work myself into a bitter sweat. If I don't finish *Quiet Don*, I'll gain the glory of being the world's biggest rogue teller of tall-tales."

While millions could be expected to wait, there was one reader to whom false promises could not be made. Stalin too was eagerly anticipating the climax of the novel. Despite his best efforts to coax Sholokhov into revealing the ending, and in spite of inquiries about whether reconciliation with communism could be expected from its Cossack protagonists, Sholokhov remained evasive. During a visit to Stalin's cottage in late May 1936, Sholokhov gave Stalin his assurances that the book would soon be finished.[3] Delighted with the news, the dictator presented him with a precious bottle of cognac from his personal collection.

Around the time that Sholokhov was visiting Stalin, a carnivorous craze seized the NKVD. In summer 1936 it declared open season on anyone who was even remotely connected to Trotsky. The hunt for hidden Trotskyists would define the first stage of the Great Terror.[4] Any utterance favorable to Trotsky, whether printed or spoken, could instantly transform a loyal party activist into a target. Even casual, factual remarks reviving memories of Trotsky's former role in the revolution or the Soviet government marked a person as anti-party prey. Thousands of people ensnared that summer became the human bait that would lure others out of their conspiratorial lairs and into the open.

Sholokhov was initially skeptical of the hunt for hidden Trotskyists and did not hesitate to share his views with others. Many of those arrested that summer were ordinary party activists ensnared by a changing definition of Trotskyism. On a hunting trip with the local newspaper editor in early August 1936, Sholokhov strongly objected when his companion started to name numerous locals as Trotskyists and began to urge that they be excluded from the local branch of the party.[5] Not only was it odious to mix politics and pleasure on a hunting trip, but most of the individuals on the list were practical people who rarely uttered political statements of any sort. The editor was likely taking his cue from the secret letter of July 29, 1936, to first secretaries of city and district committees. It instructed local officials "to evaluate from top to bottom . . . and purge the apparatus of persons of questionable or wavering [loyalty] and in any way connected, in the present or past, with Trotskyism or Zinovievism."[6]

Sholokhov was still operating within the parameters of the old definition of a Trotskyist as someone who had actively and openly supported the opposition in party meetings or publications. He tried to warn the editor to be more cautious and not to make such sharp accusations. Regarding one individual he insisted, "You defame him for no good reason. He's no Trotskyist."

Arrests in the literary world also gave him great cause for concern. Ivan Makar'ev had recently been exposed as an agent of Trotsky.[7] For some unexplained reason, Sholokhov's portrait was published right next to an article condemning former RAPP leaders who had also been arrested. For years Sholokhov had known Makar'ev and never detected any signs that he could be an enemy of the party. Did he miss some kinds of subtle clues of deception or double-dealing? Could he have let his guard down out of gratitude for Makar'ev's help in 1929? Such a lapse of vigilance on his part was disconcerting. Perhaps the NKVD had made a mistake? In 1934 Makar'ev had written a thoroughly Stalinist appraisal of *Virgin Soil*. He appeared to always be in synch with the party line. Could it all have been a cunning disguise? It just didn't seem to make sense. None of it did.

The first wave of local arrests that summer passed over Sholokhov's inner circle, but early victims would soon point fingers at others in an attempt to somehow mitigate their punishment. A Communist Youth League activist named Bondarenko, who was "unmasked" as a Trotskyist and arrested in the local library that summer, publicly accused one of Sholokhov's friends of disloyalty. As he was being apprehended by agents in their telltale leather jackets he exclaimed, "Why are you singling me out when Krasiukov himself said that Trotsky was a good man?"[8] Never forgotten by the NKVD, this exclamation would bring the Great Terror into Sholokhov's inner circle.

This explains why Sholokhov took that first arrest so close to heart. As a twenty-two-year-old budding author, he had stood by, powerless and dejected, as Harlampii Yermakov, his main informant for volume three of *Quiet Don*, was arrested, summarily convicted, and shot. Now a famous author who had traveled abroad and even visited Stalin, he might hope to intervene on behalf of an individual who had served both Soviet agriculture and literature.

The allegations against Krasiukov were unveiled at a party meeting in August by the head of the local NKVD, a man who in available sources is ominously known by a single name—Timchenko. Allegedly in summer 1930 the Communist Youth League activist Bondarenko had overheard Petr Krasiukov talking to others in the garage of the local branch of the party saying, "Trotsky was truly a hero. He knew how to speak well. I saw him and heard him, and after his words Red Army soldiers confidently marched into battle, because they knew what they were fighting for."[9] Whether actually uttered as quoted, this casual comment in a garage—the kind of statement that had been trumpeted in the Soviet press on thousands of occasions before Trotsky's disgrace—now became a dangerous political declaration.

Sholokhov dismissed the allegations as slander. Lugovoi, in his role as head of the local branch of the party, promised a full investigation. In closed meetings of the local party leadership, Lugovoi insisted that for years he had known Krasiukov and that his friend had never deviated from the party line. Confidently he declared that the allegations were false. On September 12, the leadership of the local branch of the party vindicated Krasiukov. It concluded: "Bondarenko's statement could not be confirmed. Krasiukov was not yet in Vioshki during summer 1930 and the supposed location of the meeting contradicted the actual location of garages at that time."[10] Sholokhov and his allies were playing by the old rules of party discipline, which still demanded actual evidence to convict a fellow party official of disloyalty. Nonetheless two factions were forming. Timchenko was joined by the local newspaper editor and a few others in pressing for the dismissal of Krasiukov from the party. It didn't help that Timchenko and Krasiukov engaged in a drunken public argument and fistfight during festivities devoted to the anniversary of the October revolution.

The town was clearly not big enough for both of them. What ensued was not only a battle of personalities but also a battle of biographies. Timchenko and his secret police allies portrayed Krasiukov as the son of a major *kulak* who, prior to the revolution, owned and rented large amounts of land, invested in a windmill and steam-operated machinery, and who always used hired laborers—read exploited workers—in his operations. They emphasized that under the New Economic Policy Krasiukov owned a tractor and that he profited from an industrial food oil press. Both facts testified to means far beyond those of a normal peasant and implied odious connections to capital. In contrast Sholokhov portrayed Krasiukov as an exemplary individual raised up from rural obscurity by the party.[11] He emphasized his voluntary enlistment in the Red Army as a late teen during the civil war and his more recent service to collective agriculture. Dedicated heart and soul to the party, he never wavered and was among the first to embrace collective farming. The truth was no doubt somewhere in between.

Krasiukov was arrested in mid-November. This event coincided with a trip by Sholokhov to Moscow on party business and opera affairs. The Bolshoi Theater was staging an operatic version of his unfinished epic and needed consultations. He viewed the arrest of Krasiukov as the first step in a campaign to take over control of the local branch of the party and to potentially destroy him.

Lugovoi avoided discussion of the arrest in local party meetings in December 1936. He refused to dismiss Krasiukov from the party. In party meetings he thundered against generic Trotskyite-Zinoviev gang members and urged vigilance against counterrevolutionary Trotskyist bastards in the district, but no names were mentioned. He managed to convince most of the local party elite to suspend judgement until all the facts were known.

Sholokhov in turn spent much of December 1936 trying to assess the gravity of the situation. He traveled to Rostov to find out from higher officials what was going on. There he learned that Krasiukov's case had been linked to multiple cases of "counterrevolutionaries" operating in the Don region.[12] His fate was now intertwined with dozens of others, and his guilt no longer hinged on any alleged utterance in a garage.

In early January 1937 news from Moscow dramatically changed the dynamic in Vioshki. The Politburo suddenly removed Boris Sheboldaev from his post as regional boss.[13] It announced that a Trotskyist center had operated with impunity under his nose and carried out espionage, sabotage, and terrorism. In an attempt to save himself, Sheboldaev shifted into full confession mode, admitting the charges and proclaiming that he was blind to the fact that he was surrounded by "the vilest of enemies." Sheboldaev was assigned to a district closer to Moscow.

When several of Sheboldaev's other deputies were condemned as Trotskyists, anyone who owed their appointment to him now had good reason to worry. The party secretaries of almost all major cities in the region were arrested. Communist Youth League branches, trade organizations, and major factories were also "liberated" from the hands of Trotskyists. There were rumors that Ovchinnikov shot himself when they came to arrest him.[14]

The dismissal of Sheboldaev emboldened Sholokhov to move against the Timchenko faction.[15] In meetings held in January 1937, Sholokhov presented a speech blaming Sheboldaev and his clique for all the region's problems. Lugovoi accused Second Secretary Chekalin, newspaper editor Videlin, and Timchenko of being Sheboldaev stooges. In turn the other faction responded by demanding that Krasiukov be expelled from the party and criticized Sholokhov for lack of dedication to party affairs and acting "like the lord of a manor house." Lugovoi sprang to Sholokhov's defense and reminded everyone that the NKVD had failed to notice the first Trotskyist who was unmasked in Vioshki—Yelankin. On January 17 Lugovoi confronted Timchenko and once again accused him and other "Sheboldaev appointees" of conspiring against Sholokhov. This confrontation set off a cascading series of Soviet self-defense maneuvers. The "Sheboldaev appointees" began sending denunciations to higher-level party authorities and regional secret police branches. These denunciations implicated Sholokhov and Lugovoi in the protection of Trotskyists.

In fact, at the very time that they were confronting Timchenko, the NKVD agent already knew that his interlocutors were the focus of an ongoing investigation into collusion with Trotskyists. Lugovoi's own act of individual mercy towards an alleged Trotskyist several years earlier would strengthen the allegations against him during the Great Terror. In 1931, when one of Lugovoi's subordinates, Ivan Slabchenko, was accused of not authoring but receiving a six-page letter criticizing collectivization of farms, Lugovoi declined to have him arrested, believing him to be a rude, semiliterate hothead who lacked Bolshevik restraint but was not a Left oppositionist.[16] The investigation he led at the time only determined that the letter could not be found and its anti-party content could never actually be confirmed. Slabchenko was allowed to resign without prejudice and leave the district.

In 1937 this cluster of facts provided ample evidence of an ongoing Trotskyist conspiracy. According to testimonies procured by the secret police under duress at the height of the Great Terror, Lugovoi and Sholokhov had both collaborated to steal the Trotskyist's letter in 1931 in order to destroy evidence of conspiracy. Further revelations suggested that Slabchenko was also present in the garage on the very day that Krasiukov was overheard praising Trotsky.[17] Thus in the eyes of the local NKVD, for half a decade Sholokhov had helped foster a vile nest of dangerous Trotskyists.

The NKVD bided its time. Although Lugovoi's name was already included on a list of suspected Trotskyists compiled in summer 1936, nearly a year would pass before his arrest. Slowly and methodically it built a case against him. It also solicited compromising testimonies that could be used against Sholokhov if he tried to protest. In February 1937 it attempted to turn one of Lugovoi's former associates against him. After a grueling fourteen-hour interrogation, the associate was ordered to gather compromising material on Slabchenko, Lugovoi, and Sholokhov. "Visit Slabchenko and get him good and drunk on vodka," the inspector ordered, "then, when he lets his guard down, bait him into confirming his Trotskyist leanings."[18] Threatened with torture for noncompliance and a swift demise if he revealed secrets about the investigation to anyone, upon release the associate immediately warned Sholokhov. Within weeks, both that associate and Slabchenko would disappear.

In March 1937 a dejected Sholokhov ceased all work on *Quiet Don*. Convinced that his enemies were "weaving a black web around him," he put down his pen. Stalin's Scheherazade refused to spin another tale while his enemies were spinning webs of intrigue. Since the fate of his friends occupied his imagination, he could not ponder the lives of his literary creations.

By May 1937 the Timchenko faction gained the upper hand. The intervention of the territorial NKVD proved decisive. In a closed meeting of the local party elite, Genrikh Liushkov, one of the highest-ranking security officials in the region, revealed that both investigative materials and Krasiukov's own confession proved that he was a major counterrevolutionary. He was the crucial, criminal link between Socialist Revolutionaries, Trotskyists, and Don counterrevolutionaries. This was too much for Evdokimov, the new head of Territorial Committee of the Communist Party. "Look whom you've been defending!" he screamed at Sholokhov.[19]

Following that meeting Krasiukov was expelled from the party. Even Sholokhov had to relent in the face of such pressure. For his role in abetting and protecting such a dangerous enemy, Lugovoi was removed from his leadership position. District officials promised that he soon would be "enlightened," a euphemism for seeing the error of his ways and any punishment that those errors might merit.

On June 6, 1937, a telegram arrived in Vioshki. It ordered Lugovoi to come to Rostov.[20] When he arrived, his party superiors ordered him to submit by the end of the day a comprehensive written record of his connections with Krasiukov and several other recently unmasked enemies of the people. The next morning, he was arrested.

The news that his best friend had been arrested alarmed Sholokhov and spurred him to travel to the territorial capital too. An audience with the regional party leaders brought disturbing news. Intercession was out of the question. One party leader ominously declared, "Your friends are in jail. Testimonies are pouring in from all directions. The Vioshki case is just the start of a larger affair that will thunderously resound throughout the whole country!"[21]

After hearing these statements, Sholokhov was in motion again, this time towards Moscow. During the journey to the capital, which lasted as long as twenty hours, he must have repeatedly mulled over those cryptic comments. What did they mean? Was this a sign that he would share the fate of his friends? Did it mean that he would become the object of a show trial? What kind of "larger affair" was being fabricated?

Upon arriving in Moscow, he checked into his hotel and immediately began beseeching Stalin for a personal audience.[22] On June 19, 1937, he sent a note that read:

> Dear Comrade Stalin!
> I have come to Moscow for 3–4 days. I would very much like to see You, even for just 5 minutes. If it is possible, please receive me. [your secretary] Poskrebyshev knows my telephone [number].
> M. Sholokhov.

Hour after hour passed, but the phone did not ring. No unmarked black car appeared in order to whisk Sholokhov into the Kremlin or away from Moscow to one of the leader's retreats. No bellhops bearing messages knocked on the door of his hotel room. Stalin declined to meet with him.

Sholokhov was left alone to contemplate why Stalin failed him. Much had happened since their last meeting.[23] André Gide had published a slanderous book about the USSR, Genrikh Yagoda had been relieved of his duties as head of the NKVD, and the whole country had commemorated the first anniversary of Gorky's death. None of these events had anything directly to do with Sholokhov, but any of them could be distorted to incriminate him. From the limited information available in the Soviet attacks on Gide, Sholokhov could glean that he had become a servant of fascism and had somehow insulted Stalin. The same publishing house in France that published *Virgin Soil* had published Gide's screed. Unwisely Sholokhov had defended himself at the party purge in 1934 by invoking the support of Gide. Did Stalin find out about this? In theory Genrikh Yagoda's arrest should not have distressed Sholokhov. They were never very close. Nevertheless there was a tangible paper trail linking the two. Had Stalin discovered that Sholokhov had met with and accepted gifts from the disgraced leader of the secret police? The first anniversary of Gorky's death directly coincided with Sholokhov's request for a meeting with the dictator. Did the anniversary cause Stalin to recall Sholokhov's cautious and lukewarm words? He could not stop second-guessing his actions of the previous years. His trip to the capital of fascism, Berlin, in hindsight now looked like a bad decision.

Although Stalin might have simply been too busy with the purge of the country's top military brass to grant anyone a private audience, for Sholokhov this first failure was crushing. Instead of traveling as scheduled to the International Writers' Congress in Spain, he headed home in despair. If the end was coming, then at least he would savor a few final days with family and familiarity. But before leaving Moscow he signed a letter by the Soviet Union's leading writers demanding death by firing squad for eight military leaders who had just been unmasked as spies and vile creatures. [24]

His mind could imagine countless rational reasons why Stalin rejected a meeting, but in fleeting moments of fear his thoughts must have returned to the Vanished Commissar. Why did one of his Cossack characters have to elevate Trotsky to second in rank behind Lenin? Had the damned accursed phrase, "Lenin, Trotsky, and tsarist tools, they all trampled on us fools" doomed him? [25]

The very fabric of the novel could be made to testify against him. He'd included a document issued by Trotsky in the text. Why worry, though? He had portrayed Trotsky as a coward in one passage and had excised him from all recent reprints. But then again, thousands of copies of the un-purged text were in circulation. They portrayed Trotsky as an orator who inspired Red Army soldiers. Such comments were dangerously close to the utterance that had resulted in Krasiukov's arrest. Moreover, he had sent other documents authored by Trotsky to Gorky in 1931 in order to convince him of the scale of the Cossack rebellion in 1919. Almost certainly the secret police had rifled through Gorky's papers.

Bad news also awaited Sholokhov on his return to Vioshki. Timchenko revealed that his relative would soon be arrested. This was a calculated attempt to put psychological pressure on the writer and bully him into submission. Timchenko insisted that the relative, who was the principal of a local school, had engaged in both sabotage and ideological diversion. [26] He had propagated Trotskyism, fascism, and Christianity—truly an unholy trinity if there ever was one—in one of the best schools in the region. Sholokhov would later characterize the allegations as "monstrous make-believe and wild nonsense," but at the time he could not prevent the local branch of the party from relieving his relative of his duties and passing a resolution urging the NKVD to pursue the case.

In late July 1937, a note surreptitiously delivered to Sholokhov's house begged for a secret meeting. It was from an acquaintance whose son, Andrei Tiut'kin, worked for the secret police. At the meeting Sholokhov received even more disturbing news: "My son expects to be arrested at any moment," his acquaintance related, "and he insists that you are in danger too."[27]

The son was now caught up in the web of purges. Hoping that Sholokhov might intervene, he disclosed to his father that he overheard Timchenko extracting a confession from an arrested Cossack. The prisoner was forced to testify that Sholokhov had tried to recruit him to take part in the assassination of prominent members of the government when the local Cossack choir gave a performance in Moscow. Multiple other individuals had been coached to claim that Sholokhov was planning to assassinate Stalin and even made arrangements for one of the members of the Cossack musical ensemble to hide a pistol inside his accordion.

Could Stalin have refused to meet Sholokhov because he believed such preposterous allegations? Did one of the NKVD's many thick files land on Stalin's desk? Then why didn't they arrest him in Moscow? Perhaps there was some hidden logic to the "larger affair that will thunderously resound throughout the whole country." Cursed was the day he'd left a photographic proof of his ownership of a revolver lying around for a journalist to find and publish back in 1934.

There was no way for Sholokhov to know whether testimonies against him were extracted "just in case," to be hidden away in a file somewhere, or if they were part of an active, ongoing investigative dragnet that could close in on him at any moment. While such accusations strike us as absurd today, they were part and parcel of the NKVD's machine of terror.

With little time and quotas to meet, generic plots with preconceived criminal contours helped investigators dramatically increase the number of cases they processed. Such fill-in-the-blanks prosecutions proliferated the vast array of plots foiled by vigilance. Two dozen or so agents working in Vioshki and adjacent districts would process hundreds of cases in 1937.

Although he might not have known it at the time, only weeks after Sholokhov was informed of the danger to him, the elderly conductor of the Kuban' Cossack choir was arrested for essentially the same cookie-cutter plot.[28] He was accused of attempting to organize the assassination of Stalin and prominent members of the government during a gala concert of his choir in Moscow. The decrepit seventy-year-old musicologist likely went to his execution protesting that he was the victim of some kind of horrible misunderstanding.

Sholokhov viewed the multiple cases as an interconnected web of conspiracies against him. If the Krasiukov and Lugovoi cases fell apart, the terror plot against Stalin might stick. If that case disintegrated, the secret police could still try to coerce his threatened relatives into betraying him. If that strategy didn't work, his literary contacts and past statements provided abundant opportunity for fabricating charges. Any one of the cases could finish him. He would be labeled an enemy and disappear into jail. If all were woven together into the larger affair that had been promised, he might even disappear forever from the history books. He would be stripped of authorship of *Quiet Don* in favor of either a local lunatic or some mystery man who left behind a suitcase of papers in Maikop.

During the last days of July 1937 Sholokhov nervously awaited a summons from the secret police. Every knock at the door seemed sinister. Every phone call portended doom. He could not write. He could not sleep. Deprived of rest, he became edgy to an extreme. His despondency began to trouble his wife and disturb his remaining friends. At times he appeared on the verge of despair. His muse failed him. His days were wasted and faded away unproductively. Dark thoughts pervaded his restless nights. Hour after excruciating hour, he waited.

Finally in early August 1937, Sholokhov received a message. It originated in an NKVD dungeon, but it wasn't an order for his arrest. It was a letter from his friend Krasiukov. Against insurmountable odds, a faint message scribbled in coal dust or pencil fragments on cigarette paper traveled over a hundred miles from the regional prison to Sholokhov's doorstep.

The letter's author was crammed with sixty other unfortunate souls into a cell designed for eight individuals.[29] The heat was reported to be more intense than in the engine room of a steamship. The prisoners slept on their sides and were packed so tightly next to one another that in order for any one of them to change position they all had to turn over in coordinated waves. The deficit of oxygen was so acute that only the door sill provided any relief. Prisoners took turns every few hours spending a few minutes there breathing air from the corridor.

The letter must have navigated its way through the prison's informal postal service. Inmates would exchange messages from cell to cell by means of a matchbox loaded with a few pebbles for weight and attached to a long string.[30] On the outside of the box they might indicate a name, floor, and cell number. In succession other inmates would repeatedly toss and re-toss the matchbox until it reached the designated addressee. If it wasn't confiscated by guards, a message might be expected to reach one of the few prisoners who were given the privilege of daily walks in a court-yard adjacent to the prison's tall outer walls. Krasiukov's "letter" must have worked its way successfully from stage to stage within the prison until it was surreptitiously cast over the wall. There it was snatched up by one of the wives, mothers, or friends who kept a constant vigil near the prison lest one of their loved ones appear near a window or shout to them from an exercise yard. One of them must have delivered the letter to Sholokhov.

After overcoming his initial surprise, with hands trembling and heart racing he began to read the "letter." For months there had been no certain news. In an instant all the reports that Krasiukov had broken down and that his confession had destroyed himself and countless other were proven false. Here in his own hand Krasiukov declared, "I am not guilty!"[31] Through the smudges Sholokhov could make out a few additional phrases. "Investigation improper . . . interrogators are criminals . . ." Krasiukov was not only alive but defiant. If he could remain defiant in such circumstances, so could Sholokhov.

THIRTEEN

The grimy sides of the bug box were spattered with burgundy blotches, the cumulative chronicle of the nightly battles between the one and the thousands. The thousands shunned the light of day, disappearing to bide their time and plot their return. Their impenetrable citadel was impervious to all assaults by the one. There they safely awaited the retreat of the sunlight, which pierced the darkness through a single opening and bathed the asphalt in a flood of light. As that lone light diminished, the box began to teem with life. Under the cover of darkness, the thousands would stream out from the cracks and crevices of their stronghold. Attacking simultaneously from all directions, they aroused the one from stillness. With arms flailing vigorously in all directions, a hopeless defense was mounted. As soon as their first casualties were crushed into a bloody pulp, they were already pouring into his boots. By the time boots were flung away, a frenzy of backbiting commenced. If the one retreated towards a corner, they were waiting there too, amassed as legions. The thousands always prevailed. Retreating satiated and bloated, the army of bedbugs abandoned the one to contemplate the crimson canvas of his skin and clothing.

For seven nights in September 1937, Petr Lugovoi confronted the thousands.[1] Sholokhov's best friend was just one individual out of more than a million swept up by the Stalinist machine of terror. The bug box was just one horror in the horrific chain of dungeons operated by the NKVD. The thousands deprived countless men and women of their dignity and their sanity. The box was often the final obstacle on a path from condemnation to confession and damnation.

Few individuals could endure the gauntlet of torment without breaking down. Barrages of questions were punctuated by physical stress, psychological distress, midnight awakenings, bright lights, tempting offers, and torture. Around the clock a different cast of investigators would grind down an individual with the same questions and varying tactics. The official transcripts of Lugovoi's case file contain polite phrases along the lines of, "The investigator urged the accused to cease his stonewalling and give truthful testimony."[2] In actuality, investigators thundered phrases such as, "We'll break your arms and when they heal we'll break your legs. After that we'll crush your ribs. You'll be so mangled that you are going to be pissing and shitting blood. When I'm finished with you, you'll be crawling around in a pool of your own blood, groveling at my feet, begging for a quick death."[3] Despite several rounds of increasingly hostile interrogations, Lugovoi never confessed to any of the absurd charges of his involvement in Trotskyist conspiracies.

Sholokhov had passed the months since Lugovoi's arrest in agitation. In the weeks after his friend was taken into custody, he realized that the terror was gaining momentum. Both the local and the national newspapers simply stopped mentioning scores of names. Celebrated one day, a prominent individual became an un-person the next. More often than not there was complete silence about his or her subsequent fate. Occasionally a major arrest would be heralded in the press, but thousands were disappearing without notice. The locals even joked about which "round of the draft" certain individuals had been taken in.

He all but ceased attending local party meetings and rarely visited collective farms. He occasionally went hunting, but all too often he identified with his prey and returned home empty-handed.[4] Only a visit by Vas'ka Kudashev temporarily lifted his spirits. Mostly he sat at home. He engaged in heavy drinking and occasionally spent nights away from home. This happened whenever he panicked or suspected that this was the night they would come for him. Every time he picked up his pen, he put it down again in frustration. To make matters worse, an article in the *Literary Gazette* drew particular attention to the fact that he had not handed over the fourth book.[5]

Krasiukov's letter had temporarily emboldened him, but then he realized that there was no one to whom he could turn for help. Local and regional party officials were openly hostile towards him. There was no way to know whether Stalin actually believed the absurd allegations against him. Hadn't Stalin said in one of his speeches that silence is also a form of criticism? For a while Sholokhov befriended a new high-ranking official of the territorial government. They drank vodka and caroused amiably for several days. Then suddenly this new official disappeared. Yet another enemy of the people had been unmasked. Sholokhov withdrew from the world and interacted only with a small group of trusted individuals, mainly relatives.

Then in early September 1937 a visitor arrived in Vioshki. He was Vladimir Stavskii, the general secretary of the Writers' Union. Stavskii was a journalist and writer who had been active in the Don region after the civil war and who made a name for himself by penning a series of politicized, literary sketches about the first wave of collectivization of agriculture in the Kuban' region. A portly man with a round, bejowled face, he resembled a provincial baker or butcher more than a man of letters. He was a writer in favor with Stalin. His literary skills were average, but his unwavering loyalty to the party line had earned him authority as a party mouthpiece in literary matters.

Stavskii spent several days with Sholokhov. Since the two writers had last met, Stavskii had eagerly and militantly embraced the Great Terror. He claimed to have narrowly avoided death on a recent trip when a train that was traveling along the same route as his suddenly derailed, no doubt due to the actions of Trotsky's terrorist saboteurs.[6] After Kirov's death there was no such thing as an accident. Indeed, every unfortunate event had to be linked to the name and surname of a specific enemy of the people. He was utterly convinced that only the vigilance of the NKVD had prevented hundreds of thousands of deaths that would have inevitably resulted throughout the Soviet Union if spies, secret agents, and terrorists had been permitted to carry out their dastardly designs.

He brought news from Madrid as well as Moscow. The International Writer's Conference in Spain had provided him with an opportunity to gain a more expansive view of the Soviet Union's struggle against its vast array of enemies.[7] He had visited the front lines of the Spanish civil war, toured the ruins of devastated factories, and praised the Spanish workers for their valiant contribution to the international struggle against fascism. He had witnessed German airplanes raining down death upon ordinary people, initiating a new, evil era in the history of warfare. The more he talked about such matters, the more Sholokhov was reminded of his own inaction.

By the tenor of his questions, it was clear that this was not simply a collegial visit or courtesy call. Stavskii was on a mission of some sort.[8] His friendly disposition and sympathetic demeanor poorly cloaked the true purpose of his visit. Stalin had evidently sent him to find out what was going on with Sholokhov. Conversations constantly turned to political matters, and Stavskii seemed to be sounding out Sholokhov's loyalty to the party line. "Didn't you think about the fact that it is in the interest of your enemies that you aren't writing anything? Since you are not writing now, that means that the enemy has achieved his objective."[9] Stavskii's repeated insistence that his colleague relocate to an industrial town seemed highly suspicious and reminded Sholokhov of Sheboldaev's urgings.

During the days of Stavskii's visit, Sholokhov was on his best behavior. He remained vigilant and sober, lest lips loosened by alcohol provide any pretext to condemn him. He couldn't tell whether his colleague's benevolence masked malignant designs. In recent months, as Sholokhov knew from various sources, Stavskii had participated in a series of ugly incidents exposing fellow writers as enemies of the people.[10] He had embraced the view that they were Trotskyist agents who had infiltrated the literary establishment in order to commit sabotage among Stalin's "engineers of human souls."

Stavskii repeatedly inquired about the manuscript of the final part of *Quiet Don*. Why hadn't it been handed over to the publishers? Didn't the writer realize that he had already been publicly chided in a leading literary publication for missing his deadline? How would it end? Did Grigorii finally become a Bolshevik? Evidently Stalin had tasked him with this second mission too. Sholokhov finally relented and permitted his visitor to peruse the manuscript. But before handing it over he reminded Stavskii that foreign publishers were also inquiring about it and that some were even expressing concerns that something might have happened to him. "The general tone," Stavskii recorded, "is destruction and a certain sort of hopelessness on all three hundred pages." All of his attempts to stage a literary intervention were thwarted by Sholokhov, who stubbornly insisted, "I cannot turn Grigorii into a Bolshevik."

Days after leaving, Stavskii penned a secret report and sent it directly to Stalin. It portrayed Sholokhov as a man on the brink. Not satisfied with his two-story house, his car, his two "household laborers" (officially there were no servants in the USSR), his assortment of horses, cattle, and hunting dogs, the writer occupied his days by sitting idly at home and bemoaning his fate. Sholokhov was alternately despondent, then seething with anger. Sometimes he appeared to be writhing with some kind of hidden guilt. To Stavskii the writer at times appeared to be almost paranoid, convinced that a wide-ranging conspiracy pitted local and regional party officials and the NKVD against him. He was blind to the fact that wreckers and enemies were using him as a shield to defend themselves. Stavskii ominously concluded that Sholokhov "is engaging in [literary] sabotage."

After Stavskii's departure, Sholokhov pondered whether redemption or damnation awaited him. He had tried to convince his visitor that his friends Lugovoi and Krasiukov had been unjustly arrested and illegitimately framed in violation of Soviet law and party procedures. Neither had uttered an anti-party word in all the years of their acquaintance. But each day that passed without news heightened his anxiety.

Meanwhile, Lugovoi had endured yet another interrogation in which he was accused of being a Trotskyist conspirator. Within days of being transferred to a new cell, he was threatened with a second blood-sucking bout in the bug box.[11] Not long after that he suddenly found himself being escorted to a waiting car and deposited on a train. Upon arrival in Moscow he was whisked away in a waiting vehicle and transported directly to the NKVD's central prison. He lost count of how many days had passed in interrogations. Each day his new cellmates became increasingly more prominent individuals in their former, irretrievably lost, lives. In the faces of these haggard and half-crazed men he even identified a few whose portraits had featured prominently in *Pravda* in previous months. Each night brought encounters with increasingly more vicious and prominent NKVD officials.

Languishing in jail in Moscow, Lugovoi discerned a regular rhythm of physical distress alternating with psychological pressure. Deprivation of sleep was usually followed by some new charge or revelation.[12] He was shown a pile of dossiers. "They all contain testimonies against you!" an inspector thundered. More physical distress followed. "Your wife and seven-year-old son have testified against you!" a tormentor proclaimed. Eventually a high-ranking investigator revealed to him late one night that Sholokhov had betrayed him: "He's in Moscow at this very moment to sign statements." This would amount to his death warrant. In a moment the rumors reported by other prisoners of Sholokhov's arrest were substantiated.

After a marathon interrogation lasting nearly forty-eight hours, Lugovoi was relocated to a different cell.[13] There he was fed breakfast for the first time in weeks. Suspiciously, they started to provide palatable portions of meat for lunch. Soon he was taken for walks in an enclosed rooftop terrace, where he renewed his acquaintance with the sun and the sky. He was also given books to read. What kind of signs were these? The collective wisdom of the jail decoded these portents as positive signs that fortune had turned in his favor, but one could never discount the possibility that he was being returned to a more or less human appearance in advance of a public show trial. Everyone knew that show trials had a tendency to culminate in shootings. Would he be forced to testify against Sholokhov? Or had Sholokhov become the keystone in the NKVD's case against him and countless others?

Then one day they came for him. He was led through a series of passageways and corridors. The piercing screams, gutteral groans, and frantic murmurings of the condemned faded away as a series of secure metal doors clanged shut behind him. He was taken up in an elevator. They walked him down a long, almost endless corridor. Slowly it dawned on him that he had walked this path before. It ended at the offices of the NKVD's highest officials. He was led to an imposing office door. As he stood in the reception area waiting to be admitted, it was impossible to fathom the fate that awaited him on the other side of the door. Minutes seemed like hours.

As the door opened he could see two figures sitting at a table.[14] On the left he could clearly identify the diminutive, impish silhouette of Commissar Yezhov, the head of the NKVD. On the table in the center there was a teapot, some fruits, and a bust of Stalin. To the right sat Mikhail Sholokhov. Without even scanning the expression on the writer's face, he instinctively reverted to the hardened habits of prison self-preservation. His eyes intensely scrutinized Sholokhov's midriff. Was it there or not? Without it they were both doomed. If only he could discern it, there was hope. In a millisecond the simple army belt that Sholokhov ordinarily wore in public became the arbiter between life and death. The moment Lugovoi spotted it, he knew that Sholokhov was a free man. The meeting in Yezhov's office was neither an interrogation nor a judicial confrontation between arrestees. No prisoner was ever permitted to retain his belt, lest he wind it around his own neck to strangle the life out of his body before interrogators had the opportunity to wring from his mouth testimonies that would destroy the bodies of countless others. Before he knew it, Sholokhov was embracing him. Then he noticed tears flowing from the writer's eyes.

Shedding tears of joy mixed with horror, Sholokhov studied his friend attentively. Since they'd last seen each other a few months earlier, the energetic, thirty-four-year-old Lugovoi had been transformed. Now he resembled a gaunt, sallow, bearded ancient who had emerged from some primordial cave. Even Yezhov appeared to be moved by the pathos of their reunion. He ordered Lugovoi to be immediately taken for a shave and a haircut. Mere days before this encounter Lugovoi stood powerless before his tormentors, trembling and nearly delirious from lack of sleep.

How did one from the bug box manage to escape the precinct of terror? What had happened to retrieve him from the dark abyss? Stavskii's report had landed on Stalin's desk. And there was something in the report that deeply disturbed the dictator. Sholokhov admitted to having thoughts so terrifying that "it anguished him to merely contemplate them."[15] Stavskii decoded these cryptic statements as hints about suicide. Learning that Sholokhov was on the verge of despair, Stalin displayed a rare act of empathy.

Stalin's attitude towards suicide was complex. When his political adversaries or perceived enemies committed suicide, Stalin became enraged. Not only did they deprive him of his power over life and death but they also appropriated from the party the means and time of their demise. At one party meeting in December 1936 Stalin called suicide one of the "most cunning and easiest means by which one can spit at and deceive the party one last time before dying, before leaving the world."[16] But he had also endured the suicide of his wife. He took it hard and at times blamed himself, reasoning that if only he'd behaved differently on that fateful evening, she would still have been by his side.

His hand, which up to that point had mechanically signed over a hundred lists containing the names of thousands of individuals who would be shot, moved with a sense of urgency. It scribbled on the report: "Comrade Stavskii! Try and summon Comrade Sholokhov to Moscow for a day or two. You can refer to me. I would not be adverse to speaking to him."[17] Confident in his ability to pull the writer back from the brink, he ordered his secretary Poskrebyshev to ensure that a slot in his schedule would be kept open for the writer.

The dictator's message was communicated to Sholokhov, who immediately started making plans to visit Moscow. Would he face the stern face of a dictator or the warm embrace of a friend? How would he behave? What would he say? Where would he start? Upon arrival in Moscow he learned from Stalin's secretary that he had been granted an audience of thirty minutes with the Boss.

On September 25, 1937, they met.[18] No transcript of that meeting exists. But its subject matter can be reconstructed from subsequent references in their correspondence. Two pertinent facts testify that this was more than a social call. The visitor's log indicates that Viacheslav Molotov, commissar of foreign affairs, and Commissar Yezhov were both present in the room.

Stalin must have reassured Sholokhov of his friendship and favor. Thereafter the writer behaved as if his own life was no longer in danger. He hastily shifted the focus to saving his friends. "I don't believe in Lugovoi's guilt, and if he is found guilty, that means I am guilty too," Sholokhov declared on more than one occasion. "After all, we worked jointly in everything that was done in the region." He probably mentioned the letter from Krasiukov, since he considered it an important piece of evidence in favor of the innocence of his friends. His emotional state was hurried and nervous. He would later apologize to Stalin that during that meeting he could "neither coherently nor systematically tell about everything that took place earlier in our territory and what is taking place at the moment."[19] We know the topics he couldn't bring himself to talk about because he later wrote a long epistle to the dictator devoted to what he didn't say on that day.

As a result of that meeting Sholokhov was introduced to Nikolai Yezhov, the architect of the Great Terror. Yezhov had become the public face of the Soviet Union's struggle against internal and external enemies.[20] His rapid rise from a minor party leadership position was due to his uncanny ability to anticipate the direction in which Stalinist winds were blowing. At the time Stalin was declaring that cadres solve everything, Yezhov had distinguished himself as an expert in selection of personnel. When Stalin was looking for scapegoats in the wake of the Kirov murder, Yezhov made himself indispensable in purging both the party and the police and in issuing new regulations for the NKVD. When Stalin became preoccupied with Zinoviev and Kamenev's nefarious intentions, Yezhov was already at work on a book about their conspiratorial activities and plans to assassinate Stalin. When Stalin began to doubt Yagoda, Yezhov was ready to amplify those doubts with dubious revelations.

Standing only 151 centimeters (less than five feet) tall—slightly taller when he brushed his hair upward—in person he was the opposite of the strong, powerful individual portrayed in propaganda posters, the most famous of which depicted him in iron gloves choking a multiheaded hydra of Soviet enemies. He spoke with a soft, pleasing, high-timbred voice and agreed to look into the cases of Sholokhov's friends.

In the hours after Sholokhov's departure from Stalin's office, multiple telegrams and telephone calls were exchanged between central NKVD headquarters and agencies in the Don region. Moscow urgently inquired whether the writer's closest associates had confessed or been convicted. Agents frantically rifled through card files to determine whether Lugovoi, Krasiukov, and Logachev could still be counted among the living. By the time forty-eight hours passed, special car number 942 had been added to the daily Rostov-Moscow train. The car was guarded by an NKVD security detail. Its cargo officially consisted of "particularly important state criminals." Among them were Sholokhov's friends.

Almost simultaneously with his meeting with Stalin, Sholokhov made his next move in the high-stakes chess game to save his friends. Any miscalculation or weak move could potentially jeopardize their survival. He handed over an excerpt of *Quiet Don* to *Pravda* for publication.[21] But this was not just an ordinary excerpt, it was his protagonist's most precarious moment since WWI. *Pravda* published the excerpt without any accompanying material about the writer. It simply noted that this excerpt was from the fourth volume of the novel "which is being prepared for publication."

The excerpt is pervaded by a heightened sense of anxiety. It takes place on an autumn day tinged with signs of decay and transition, such as the smell of rotting oak bark. As leaves fell to the ground and geese flew south, a church bell ominously tolled for hour after hour, honoring the village's dead from a recent civil war battle. Grigorii's sister watched from the window as the dead were brought back to their homes: "Here's another dead man they're bring back from the front," she would report. In an instant the family's curiosity turned to horror as she exclaimed, "They're bringing Grigorii! It's his horse." Sholokhov the master storyteller then gave the tale yet another twist. Grigorii's family suddenly learned from a neighbor: "He's alive, alive! He's got typhus." Millions of Soviet citizens were again left to contemplate a cliff-hanger, wondering whether their hero would make it out of this latest scrape alive.

Sholokhov's stratagem worked. Stalin ordered Yezhov to review the case files of the writer's friends. He also mandated that the head of the NKVD schedule a second meeting with the writer in person in October and arrange for him to see his friends. This was the meeting where Sholokhov saw Lugovoi for the first time in months. Yezhov clearly prepared for the meeting by assiduously combing through their case files in addition to questioning Sholokhov's associates.

The long conversation between Sholokhov and the head of the NKVD likely occurred according to a preplanned scenario.[22] Yezhov probably sat behind an imposing desk arrayed in his costume of power—a powder blue dress uniform with prominent, gleaming gold stars emblazoned with the hammer and sickle on both its sleeves and collars. He likely welcomed Sholokhov into his office and turned to some of his routine talking points about the sharp crisis facing the USSR.[23] These usually unfolded as terrifying troikas: spies/saboteurs/subversives; assassins/terrorists/coup-plotters; fascists/capitalists/remnants of the old regime in Russia; Germany/Japan/Poland; or Trotskyists/Zinovievites/Bukharinites.

Sholokhov described the events that had taken place in Vioshki over the past two years. Yezhov brought in Sholokhov's friends one by one for brief reunions. Each was given a few minutes to state his case or proclaim his innocence. Yezhov assured each that he would personally conduct a thorough reinvestigation of the facts of the case. After they departed, Yezhov confidentially shared with Sholokhov a few details from their case files demonstrating that the sloppy work of local branches would be corrected by the vigilance of central investigators. For example, he revealed to Sholokhov that among the twenty-seven individuals who had testified against Lugovoi there were individuals who had never met him before and had never been to Vioshki.

Impressed by Yezhov's feigned concern and rehearsed diligence, Sholokhov pressed the commissar to look into the fate of those who had been arrested solely due to their connections to his three friends. At the end of the meeting Yezhov indicated that the writer's friends would be liberated as soon as all procedural matters concerning their cases were concluded—the USSR was, after all, a society of laws and procedures. We know that Sholokhov came away from that meeting confident in the commissar's competence and concern. For months he continued to believe that Yezhov was responsible for the first "disentangling of the Vioshki knot."[24]

He was wrong. Yezhov was too busy ramping up the Great Terror to genuinely look into the circumstances of their arrests.[25] During those weeks he was involved in implementing the so-called national operations in the east and in the west. Anyone connected with Poland in the past or present was subject to arbitrary arrest and deportation from western border areas. In the Far East Koreans were being rounded up and "relocated" deep into central Asia. The disposition of several hundred thousand lives was at the forefront of his agenda. Any further investigation of Sholokhov's claims would also have compromised his close subordinate Genrikh Liushkov, who was involved in the prosecution of Krasiukov. But in order to placate Stalin, he nonetheless had to find some solution.

Emboldened by the success of his meeting, Sholokhov wrote to Stalin. "The things that I have endured these ten months give me the right to request of You, that you permit me to see You for a few minutes after Comrade Yezhov reports to you about the Vioshki case, or at any other time which You consider to be convenient."[26] After twenty-four excruciating hours without a response, Sholokhov realized that no one had the right to demand anything of Stalin. He made a second, more modest "request" to schedule a meeting when he returned to Moscow in a few weeks.

Sholokhov departed for Vioshki confident that his friends would soon return home too. He could now shift his focus to the novel and start to prepare the final chapters for publication. To his great delight he soon learned that his friends had been released from jail and were staying at government expense in hotels in Moscow. His initial euphoria gradually gave way to apprehension. In the weeks that followed, the long-awaited telegram announcing their imminent return to the Don region never arrived. Had Stalin changed his mind? Was he displeased with the new excerpts from *Quiet Don*?

Within days a favorable sign appeared. After months of silence, the country's leading literary publication, the *Literary Gazette*, published an extensive article devoted to Sholokhov in mid-October 1937.[27] The article provided an enthusiastic review of his entire career and positioned him as an exemplary citizen who was uniquely in touch with the Soviet people. It began by reminding the world that Sholokhov was indeed finishing the novel and that thousands of impatient readers had written to the publication inquiring about the fate of Grigorii Melekhov.

Oddly the article defended Sholokhov against a series of charges that no one had publicly advanced since 1929. It reminded readers that an unspecified group of "enemies" had repeatedly tried to cast aspersions upon Sholokhov. They had insisted that *Quiet Don* was not a true example of Soviet literature and even claimed that it was not written by him. In response the Communist Party had "smashed those rotten Trotskyist attempts to discredit the most significant Soviet writer." Although these unnamed enemies admitted that he was a talented writer, they proclaimed that he was "no Kirshon or Chumandrin." These two recently discredited names were retrieved from the dustbin of history in order to provide the greatest possible distance between Sholokhov and the literary dead—the group of writers whom Stavskii had denounced and doomed a few months earlier. The article also drew sharp distinctions between Sholokhov and his living comrades of the pen. Unlike other writers, who had to undertake "business trips to study everyday reality," Sholokhov was deeply involved in party affairs and collective agriculture.

The only recent events addressed in the article were his two trips abroad. Under different circumstances these could have been twisted into suspicious confirmation of either his capitalist contamination or his imagined subversive connections. But this article provided him with ideological inoculation. It reassured readers that these trips were dedicated to exploring cutting-edge agricultural practices and finding better ways to "equip farms, construct animal pens, and put dung to better use."

Was Stalin reminding Sholokhov of the razor-thin line between favor and infamy? Or was Sholokhov working behind the scenes to return to favor? Or was this a tango in which both made moves in tandem? There were much easier ways for Stalin to remind Sholokhov of the bonds that tied them together since 1931. Moreover Sholokhov had already returned to favor by publishing new chapters from *Quiet Don*. Most likely the article was intended to deflect criticism in literary circles about his recent aloofness and rash rejection of the invitation to travel to Spain.

After well over a month of waiting passed, there was still no sign of his friends. Yezhov had outmaneuvered Sholokhov. He'd decided to find prestigious jobs for them in Moscow.[28] This made it easier for the NKVD to suppress any hint of error. Keeping them in Moscow meant that they remained securely in his power. If they returned home, mistakes would have to be publicly admitted to both local and regional officials. But as everyone knew from the press, under Yezhov's watchful eye the NKVD didn't make mistakes.

While the writer anxiously awaited news of their return, his friends had entered a surreal netherworld. Their former tormentors were now buying them new suits, paying their restaurant bills, and taking them on tours of resort villages in the vicinity of Moscow. The terror had emptied thousands of summer cottages by sending their occupants to labor camps or the bottoms of hastily dug pits. Now, in one of the most perverted and peculiar reversals of fortune in Soviet history, three victims of the terror were being coaxed into joining the side of those who had systematically humiliated and dehumanized them.

In early November 1937 Sholokhov finally received word that Stalin would be able to meet with him. He traveled to Moscow determined to find out why his friends had not returned home. On the eve of his meeting with the dictator, he reunited with his friends for the first time since those brief and awkward reunions in Yezhov's office. Although they sat in the same hotel room, the writer and his friends exchanged messages from mutually exclusive worlds.[29] Sholokhov told them about his previous meeting with Stalin and described his efforts to secure their release. He told of how he had provided material help to their wives and families, who had been driven from their homes and fired from their jobs. In response Sholokhov got his first stark glimpses of the dark doings of the Soviet security apparatus.

Krasiukov told of how he had endured ninety-six hours of interrogation without respite or sleep.[30] As a result of his constant refusals to provide a confession, the interrogators worked in tandem to prolong his agony to beyond the limits of ordinary endurance. Exhausted, delirious, and drenched in his own urine, he stood until his legs finally collapsed underneath him. He also related how his nearly seven-foot-tall frame was crammed into a damp, stone cell so narrow that he could never stretch out his legs. There he persisted through twenty-two solitary days of cramps and utter darkness. Occasionally he had a visitor. A sweet seductress sang the siren song of an easy and quick death, but she was only an illusion. In vivid details he described his bouts with bloody diarrheas that brought him to the verge of death. Only the summons to Moscow saved him.

Logachev narrated how he succumbed to the conveyor belt of terror. Eight straight days of interrogation were followed by a week in solitary. Only in his case, solitary was full of rats. After multiple bitings, beatings, and nights without sleep, he confessed. "In the state I was in at that moment, if they would have told me to sign a document saying that I am the pope I would have signed it," he declared.[31] He shamefully recalled how he was forced to provide testimony against Sholokhov as well.

Lugovoi related the story of his nightly battles in the bug box.[32] Sholokhov listened in disbelief as Lugovoi told of a special isolation cell teeming with "millions" of bedbugs. Their nightly attacks left his clothing a crimson canvas and his mind an even bigger mess. The biting was bad, but the waiting was worse. The mere anticipation of the nightly onslaughts drove most men mad. As Sholokhov shook his head in disbelief, Lugovoi advanced his theories that somehow jailers brought the bedbugs in each day, scooping them portion by portion into the wooden box. Where could they get all those bedbugs from? How had they mastered them or bent them to their will? All of this simply defied rational explanation. Although the bug box was a very real place, in his mind it also became a metaphor for how each night a few thousand NKVD agents terrorized and convulsed the whole Soviet body politic.

Sholokhov left the hotel room that night utterly shocked and fully convinced that he had to press for the full rehabilitation of his friends. On November 4, 1937, he met with Stalin. The occasion dictated that they briefly discuss the operatic version of *Virgin Soil* that had just been staged. For Sholokhov this required some diplomacy, since he found it ridiculous that choreography could be devoted to *kulak* resistance or that arias could address the exclusion of enemies from the party.[33]

His main goal was to plead with Stalin for full rehabilitation of the trio. The entire populace of his hometown had witnessed their humiliation and public disgrace. Unless a public rehabilitation was staged, doubts would persist about their innocence. People needed to know that they had been cleared of all charges. A real rehabilitation would mean that all three would be returned to their previous positions of leadership. Any other solution would cast a shadow over their careers and social lives. Remarkably, Stalin agreed.

During that meeting Sholokhov also named two officials who, in his opinion, had obstructed the investigation of his friends' cases.[34] On multiple occasions he had beseeched Yevdokimov, the head of territorial government, to check into their cases. But instead he had delegated that task to Genrikh Liushkov, the very NKVD official who had helped to condemn them in the first place. As a result nothing had changed in their cases until Stalin himself intervened. Stalin listened attentively but made no assurances. Toward the end of this meeting Yezhov joined the two and confirmed the decision to rehabilitate the writer's friends upon filing all the necessary paperwork and getting the necessary signatures from regional party officials.

Before leaving Moscow, Sholokhov sent a telegram to his wife to start elaborate preparations for a celebration to welcome his friends home.[35] She quickly spread the news from house to house. Cellars were scoured for aged bottles of wine from the sandy banks of the northern Don. The right people were recruited to secure the right bottles from local distilleries. Chickens were chased around courtyards with axes. The last fruits of the fall harvest were gathered and distributed across several kitchens for preparations. The population was preparing for a celebration. Sholokhov soon returned home to coordinate the travel arrangements and public reception of his friends. He arranged to personally pick them up from the nearest railroad station in his car. Hundreds turned out to meet the writer and the three men who had defied all odds. They were greeted with gusto by the assembled crowd. For some reason the district party leadership and the new head of local NKVD were conveniently out of town on business that very day.

A few weeks later, Sholokhov made a momentous announcement. He proclaimed to the world that after twelve years of creative struggle, he had finally finished *Quiet Don*. He insisted to a journalist from *Izvestiia* that his work on the novel had been delayed by his party work, his participation in public affairs, and "life itself."[36]

FOURTEEN

With his friends no longer incarcerated, Sholokhov could embrace his predetermined place in what Soviet propagandists were calling "the most democratic electoral system that exists or has ever existed in the history of the world." The 1936 Stalin constitution mandated that Soviet citizens select a parliament called the Supreme Soviet in a nationwide election. For the first time in history neither gender, nor race, nor nationality, nor educational attainment, nor health status, nor property ownership nor lack thereof would prohibit a single citizen from voting. All adults, except those individually deprived of voting rights by courts or psychiatric commissions, would be expected to participate. The Soviet Union would now hold the first of many ritual parliamentary elections in which nearly 99 percent of the electorate voted and in which all nominated candidates won. As a member of the election commission, Sholokhov would join a small army of officials charged with overseeing both the uncontested elections and the concomitant universal, public performance of civic duty.

In November 1937 he also learned that he would be standing for election to become a deputy to the Supreme Soviet. In Stalin's elections you did not nominate yourself to stand for office. Instead nomination was by a process jokingly referred to as "volunteering against your will." Representatives of the workers and peasants could nominate candidates. When the revolutionary populace asked, candidates complied. In many cases candidates were not directly selected by the local branch of the Communist Party. No, things were not always so crude. Instead, open public meetings were held in farms, factories, and schools. Propaganda had already preselected an acceptable pool of candidates. The newspapers and radio programs continuously trumpeted clusters of names. The constant, compelling repetition of these names replaced the need for crude administrative directive. By these means the party could ensure that local electorates would select a Supreme Soviet which reflected a proper balance between political figures and cultural figures and also embraced heroic tractor drivers and lathe operators, liquidators of illiteracy in Uzbekistan, pilots who had soared to unprecedented heights, polar explorers, and women who harvested record yields of red beets in Ukraine.

On November 13 a telegram arrived in Vioshki informing Sholokhov that the electorate of Novocherkassk, the former Cossack capital, had nominated him to "defend the interests of the laborers and the interests of the home country of socialism." Nine hundred individuals had voted unanimously to propose his candidacy. Keeping with the spirit of the times, they also proclaimed that his candidacy would bolster the Great Terror. "Your books," they insisted to the writer, "help to unmask and utterly uproot low-down enemies of the people, the tail end dregs of Trotskyist-Bukharinite bandits."[1]

Only a day later, the NKVD issued the official document that rehabilitated his three friends. It read: "Investigative agencies have established the complete non-involvement of comrades Lugovoi, Logachev, and Krasiukov in counterrevolutionary activities involving enemies of the people."[2] Because they had been "maliciously defamed by participants of the counterrevolutionary and right-Trotskyist and Socialist Revolutionary-White Guard organizations" they would be restored to previous jobs and their replacements would be reassigned to other duties. For Sholokhov this official victory was sweet, but the blatantly deceptive formula left a lingering bitter taste. Why did the document emphasize their "non-involvement" rather than outright innocence? Even if his friends were the victims of malicious enemy types, he knew for certain that party officials and NKVD officers had also colluded in discrediting and almost destroying them.

An article published in December 1937 gave him a degree of hope that the guilty might eventually be punished. Among a list of fascist interventionists and Trotskyite-Bukharinist conspirators there was a familiar name: Boris Sheboldaev. The former regional boss had been convicted of planning terrorist attacks and spying for a foreign government.[3] The article noted that Sheboldaev had recently been shot. Unfortunately, there was no indication that agricultural affairs even featured in the verdict.

Instead of editing the typescript of the final chapters of *Quiet Don* as planned, Sholokhov dedicated the next few months to participating in an election whose results were a foregone conclusion. Nevertheless, he was obliged to give speeches, meet with voters, and study the issues that concerned his constituents. Every signal indicated that these elections would be taken very seriously. Initially, there had been some fears among the Soviet political elite that enemies of the people would take advantage of open public meetings and election rallies to agitate against the party. There were suspicions that foes of the regime might collude to obstruct or, even worse, rig the elections. But the Great Terror had liquidated those concerns.[4] The electorate had been thoroughly purged of unreliable elements. One of the little-known facts about the purges is that the largest arrest "operations" were scheduled to end just before election season was set to begin. By depriving thousands of life, the dictator could maintain that technically almost no one was deprived of a vote.

Predictably Sholokhov decided to campaign for Stalin on a platform of patriotism and party loyalty. His young age enabled him to proclaim, "Both as a person and as a writer I have been instructed and reared by our great Communist Party." In a speech to voters in early December he declared, "Being a patriot of our great, mighty motherland, I can proudly declare that I am also a patriot of my native Don region." He emphasized the preparedness of Soviet Cossacks to confront fascism on the field of battle, and he lauded the region's Stalinist prosperity, but he also donned the mantle that his electors had prepared for him. He became a mouthpiece for the Great Terror. Standing before two thousand citizens from his electoral district, he declared,

"The 170 million strong laboring population [of the USSR] loves our motherland. And if out of those 170 million there happen to be a few thousand vile individuals, people who have prostituted themselves politically—all of that Trotskyite-Zinovievite-Bukharinite scum, who put up for sale not only themselves, but also their motherland—then those people do not evoke surprise in us, but revulsion which can have no equal."[5]

He was consciously speaking the Stalinist lingo of purification. "Vile individual" was one of Stalin's favorite words for those who antagonized him. Sholokhov employed the language of revulsion, filth, and contagion that predominated public pronouncements of the era. He embraced the epoch's expression of political outrage in terms of physical and moral impurity. He even deployed one of Yezhov's terrible troikas. No longer a passive recipient of formulas created by the terror machine, he now became a producer of them. Under these conditions it was only logical that he concluded his speech with the exclamation: "Long live the great Stalin!"

In early 1938 he traveled to Moscow to take part in the opening of the Supreme Soviet. As he suspected, it was largely an occasion of boring, long-winded speeches and endless bureaucratic reports. When Stalin's name was mentioned, deputies would spring to their feet and erupt in thunderous applause. When speakers returned to droning statistic after statistic about barley forecasts or blast furnaces, eyes would glaze over. Since deputies were expected to merely rubber-stamp proposals that were prepared in advance by the Central Committee, almost all of the business was transacted in the corridors. A veritable who's who of Soviet life engaged in celebratory handshaking by day and carousing by night. During one of those sessions Sholokhov bumped into a nemesis.

A stocky, well-dressed man with a cleft chin approached him and slapped him on the back. "Misha! Why did you have to over-paint me to excess in that novel of yours?" the man inquired. "If I had written about everything that happened and all that you did back then, you wouldn't be standing here right now." Sholokhov retorted and walked away. He had just intersected with one of the villains of volume three of *Quiet Don*.[6] This was Commissar Malkin, the communist whose beastly reprisals had provoked the Cossack uprising narrated in the epic. After the suppression of the rebellion, Malkin had left the Don region but continued his work in the secret police. He had helped implement the new security procedures at Stalin's vacation home in Sochi after the Kirov assassination. In a strange twist of fate, he was elected to represent the Kuban' region, the other major Cossack territory of the USSR. A man who had nearly brought the Cossacks to the brink of extinction stood face-to-face with the man whose literary acclaim had restored their humanity and dignity.

For Sholokhov the Malkin incident provoked disgust. Liars like Liushkov and bloodthirsty fanatics like Malkin were now occupying some of the most honored places in the Soviet hierarchy. Men like these had destroyed countless good people. The very thought that such swaggering, boastful executioners in their fine suits had also infiltrated the people's parliament ate away at him. "The innocent are incarcerated, while the guilty live well," he kept thinking.[7] None of the officers who persecuted his friends were even punished. They simply continued their careers in other districts. NKVD careerists had been able to sweep under the rug how they had mangled multitudes of innocent lives. Now they were even rewriting history to cover up their own mistakes.

Sholokhov decided that when he returned home, he had to inform Stalin of the actual state of affairs. He would expose the regional NKVD. On February 16, 1938, he completed a letter to Stalin.[8] At over six thousand words, it was one of the longest texts he had written in nearly two years. The first few pages chronicled the situation in Vioshki since 1933. It described how the previous regional leadership had slandered him and his associates because they had opposed efforts to sabotage agriculture. Then he narrated the events that led to the arrests of Krasiukov and Lugovoi and chronicled the various attempts to discredit and persecute him. In graphic detail he decried the horrific conditions prevailing in the region's jails and denounced the ways in which investigators fabricated cases and forced individuals to confess. Uncovering revelation after revelation about the dungeons operated by the NKVD in the Don region, he urged, "It's time to put a stop to the shameful system of tortures being used against arrestees."[9] The investigators had little interest in the truth. They just methodically and mechanically moved cases to a deadly conclusion. Such "inquisitorial methods" were in his view "shaming the glorious name of the NKVD."

The letter contained multiple direct addresses to Stalin. These reminded him of facts that they had discussed previously or that were expected to solicit his sympathy or his censure. "Our hopes were placed on You, Comrade Stalin, and on the Central Committee." "Dear Comrade Stalin, I am personally beseeching You—You have always been attentive to us." It also portrayed the suffering prisoners as loyal Stalinists. In solitary confinement they cried out, "Long live Comrade Stalin!" In interrogations they confidently confronted their tormentors: "When Stalin finds out about this I'll be set free."

Sholokhov saved his most personal revelation for the last section of the letter. The Great Terror had derailed *Quiet Don* and had deprived him of his creative powers. "In five years I have with great difficulty written half a [section of the final] volume. Under the circumstances as they were in Vioshki, it was not only impossible to work productively, but it was also exceedingly difficult to live at all."[10]

He concluded by making two specific requests: that Stalin send M. F. Shkiriatov, the specialist in party procedure, to investigate the arrests of communists, and that an investigation closely look into the conduct of Yevdokimov, the head of the territorial administration. "He's crafty, that old lame fox," Sholokhov declared and enumerated the names of eight individuals linked to this official who had already been unmasked as enemies of the people. "Can such a leader really be a good fit for a territory in which the political situation is extremely complicated and in which enemies have excelled in messing things up?" he inquired.[11]

Since the Soviet postal system was a crucial node of NKVD surveillance, Sholokhov probably avoided it and hand-delivered the letter to Stalin's secretary, Poskrebyshev. We know that the letter reached Stalin. He wrote on the last page a brief note: "1) the persecution of

Sholokhov." To save time, he must have communicated further instructions to Poskrebyshev. Either he or Yezhov made a number of markings in the margins identifying passages to be investigated. As a result of this preliminary evaluation, over two thirds of Sholokhov's letter was excluded from further investigation. None of the horrific descriptions of torture or medieval conditions prevailing inside jails were marked for scrutiny. Not even Sholokhov's mention of a special isolation cell teeming with bedbugs elicited curiosity. Stalin knew about much of this. Many of the passages highlighted for investigation pertained to the efforts to frame Sholokhov. Others delineated specific factual claims that could be cross-verified. For some reason, the case of Sholokhov's relative, the school headmaster who was accused of propagating fascism and destroying seedlings of fruit trees, provoked interest. Stalin knew something about horticulture, having planted fruit trees at his summer home near Sochi. Perhaps he was intrigued by the absurdity of the charge that someone could both plant ten thousand seedlings on half a hectare of land and subsequently destroy them in a wanton act of sabotage.

A few weeks after sending the letter, Sholokhov learned that Shkiriatov was on his way to Vioshki with a fact-finding commission. He was accompanied by a high-ranking NKVD official appointed by Commissar Yezhov. Upon arrival they informed Sholokhov that they were there to investigate some of the claims in his letter. They would neither reopen nor reconsider the cases of Lugovoi, Krasiukov, and Logachev. Instead their mandate authorized an investigation of other cases arising in Vioshki that were mentioned in the letter to Stalin. They would conduct their investigation in Sholokhov's district and the Rostov jail, but they would not be able to summon large numbers of individuals from other jails.

Sholokhov correctly deciphered the subtext of this Aesopian introduction to the investigation.[12] He had to prioritize. They were urging him to make up his mind then and there. This was the time to name individuals who were worthy of salvation. When they asked him something along the lines of, "Do you still insist that we investigate *all* of the case files of individuals arrested during the *kulak*–White Guard operations carried out in 1937–38?" he replied, "No. I no longer have doubts about whether or not all the arrests carried out in Vioskhi were justified." He limited his list to eleven individuals and requested that Lugovoi be given an opportunity to name others. Those additions brought the total to eighteen.

Then the investigators turned to the question of the alleged persecution of the writer. "Who specifically is presently engaging in such persecution of you?" they asked.[13] Again Sholokhov must have sensed that the investigators were hinting that they had already determined that this line of investigation would not be productive. Following their lead, Sholokhov declared that he no longer considered the matter worthy of a detailed investigation. Having complied, however, he requested that they evaluate the circumstances of arrest of Andrei Tiut'kin, the young NKVD employee who before disappearing had revealed to his father the plot to implicate Sholokhov in a conspiracy to assassinate Stalin. He also implored them to look into the inappropriate activities of Timchenko when he was head of the local NKVD.

The final matter was an investigation of the letter of a certain collective farmer named Blagorodov to the Vioshki party committee in December 1937, which Sholokhov had handed over with his letter to Stalin.[14] Sholokhov must have included this document because it identified a man named Sidorov as the source for the false allegation that Sholokhov was plotting to kill Stalin. Otherwise the epistle represented a jumbled litany of accusations running the gamut from drunken hell-raising to neglect of communal cabbages, which were left to rot in a field. It provides a mildly interesting mini-portrait of a low-level tyrant who threatened to arrest anyone who crossed him and who delighted in debauching local women.

Because both of the principal figures in this additional letter still resided in the vicinity, Sholokhov could keep abreast of this part of the investigation and was even permitted to take part in interviews with some of the witnesses. Within days it became clear, however, that he had made a huge mistake in tying his reputation to the author of the letter. Neither the author of the letter nor the accused turned out to be exemplary citizens.[15] The two had put aside old scores and were now drinking buddies. None of the witnesses could confirm any of the letter's allegations. To make matters even worse, the letter's author turned out to be a *kulak* who had escaped from arrest. His name was not even Blagorodov. He had clandestinely hidden out for a time near the Persian border. There he'd obtained false documents, which enabled him to return to the Don region with a new identity. During a second interrogation, in the presence of Sholokhov, the author of the letter even admitted that he made up the whole story about the efforts to implicate the writer in a plot to assassinate Stalin. Confronted with this new information, Sholokhov declared that he had been deceived by a swindler and requested that the case on persecution be closed. Before the investigators departed for Rostov, Sholokhov also asked them to look into the recent arrest of one of his wife's brothers. They agreed to look into the case in spite of the fact that it had not been mentioned in his missive to the dictator.

It did not take long for Sholokhov to find out that the commission was starting to deliver real results. In May 1938 Andrei Tiut'kin suddenly came home after spending months in jail. From his reports, Sholokhov learned that the investigators were meeting with and interviewing the people on his list. The investigators had requested that Tiut'kin be transferred to the jail in Rostov. There they interrogated him about the reasons for his arrest. When he didn't name the alleged plot against Sholokhov as the reason, they asked, "What did you tell your father about materials being gathered against Sholokhov?" "I told him that there were in fact materials against Sholokhov in the local NKVD."[16] When pressed to explain, he indicated that there was no connection between the charges that were presented against him during his detention and the writer. By the time the commission interviewed him, his file had been purged of all materials relating to the writer.

In fact he had been prosecuted for giving a lecture in which he declared that Hitler was the worldwide leader of the fascists who was engaged in a struggle against Stalin, the genius leader of the Soviet Union and world revolution. He had mistakenly equated a cosmic force for evil with a communist force for good.

Although there is no evidence that Sholokhov received a copy of the commission's report to Stalin, his subsequent actions suggest that he was aware of the general outlines of its contents. It seems likely that either Shkiriatov or Poskrebyshev briefed him about the results.[17] The prosecutions of five individuals on his list were upheld as justified on the basis of either their own admissions of guilt to the commission or the existence of numerous witness statements that were deemed credible. Three arrests were declared unjustified, but pronounced unrelated to any alleged persecution of Sholokhov. Among these were Tiut'kin and two others who were liberated and returned home. Ten individuals could not be interviewed because they had either been shot or sent to distant labor camps. Their files were nonetheless extensively reviewed. Of the ten, only two cases were deemed worthy of further inquiry. No evidence was uncovered that the writer had been persecuted. The investigators did find that local NKVD officials had on several occasions discussed the writer's close relationship with various arrestees. The former local NKVD man Timchenko, who now worked in another district, categorically denied the charges that he ever persecuted Sholokhov. He even produced witnesses who could testify to their friendly relations. Finally, not a single one of the individuals who were still in custody confirmed that any "physical methods of influence" (i.e., torture) were being practiced within the jails in the region.

For Sholokhov the results must have been hugely disappointing. Although the NKVD had clearly engaged in a cover-up, it was equally clear that from the outset the commission had committed itself to hearing and seeing no evil. How could they expect any individual still in the clutches of the NKVD to admit that he or she had been subjected to torture? A year of suffering and weeks of agonizing over how to report to Stalin had culminated in these modest, but nonetheless tangible, results.

He soon learned, however, that another injustice addressed in his letter had suddenly received a positive resolution. His relative the school headmaster and several teachers were reinstated to their jobs. It turned out that Stalin's interest in their case was more than horticultural.

Then even bigger news broke. Through party channels Sholokhov found out that the "old lame fox" had been deprived of his role as a shepherd. Yevdokimov had suddenly been relieved of his duties as regional party boss. He was officially reassigned to serve as Yezhov's assistant in the Ministry of Water Transport.[18] Stalin had obviously considered and granted Sholokhov's second request.

This "promotion" put Yezhov in a very precarious position. He had managed to steer the Shkiriatov commission away from uncovering any systematic flaws in the work of the NKVD. The commission concluded that "only isolated mistakes took place and we have corrected these." None of the NKVD officers involved in the arrest and prosecution of Sholokhov's associates faced criminal charges, and only a few individuals were transferred to other assignments. But by the time the report reached Stalin's desk, the decision had been made to recall Yevdokimov. This means that there must have been a parallel inquiry. In deciding which of his protégés to support, Stalin had sided with Sholokhov rather than Yezhov.

Yezhov came to power by investigating and exposing the mistakes and missteps of his predecessor, Yagoda. Now he had been dealt a major blow. One of his most trusted lieutenants had been compromised by Sholokhov. For several days after he received the news of the transfer, he came to work in a foul and anxious mood. His attitude towards Yevdokimov was extremely cautious. After nothing dramatic transpired for several days, Yezhov ensured that Yevdokimov was closely watched and given few responsibilities. Then he learned that the Central Committee had decided to also recall Genrikh Liushkov to Moscow. Yezhov had protected Liushkov when he purged the NKVD of individuals loyal to his predecessor.[19] More recently he had transferred him from southern Russia to oversee purges in strategically important areas of the Far East, where the threat of war with Japan was looming.

Could it be a coincidence that the only two individuals who were directly identified in Sholokhov's letter to Stalin as linked to enemies of the people were now being summoned to Moscow? No. This was no coincidence.[20] There were also rumors that investigations were being conducted in areas where the two had previously worked.

Acting on a prior agreement with his lieutenant, Yezhov sent Liushkov a message. It must have included a code word signifying that suicide was his sole option. This was the most convenient solution to the problem that both were facing. Liushkov's quick and painless death would ensure that his secrets went to the grave with him and Yezhov would be rid of a subordinate who had fallen afoul of the Boss. But Liushkov, who had followed orders to a T in extinguishing the lives of countless others, decided to save his own life.

For several days Liushkov worked on an escape plan.[21] He sent his family to Moscow, from where they unsuccessfully attempted to flee to Poland. He acquired two pistols and 4,153 Japanese yen. He made official arrangements to conduct an inspection of a troublesome border sector between the Soviet Union and the Japanese puppet state of Manchuko. On June 12, 1938, he took a detachment of border guards into the forbidden zone adjacent to the Soviet border. He disguised his uniform by putting on an overcoat and hunting cap, claiming that these were necessary for individual reconnaissance. Fog provided cover. By the time the border guards became suspicious that he had not returned, he had already slipped across the border. After wandering as far as he could into Japanese territory, he found a hiding place and spent the night. The next morning he was apprehended by Manchurian police officers. He became one of the highest-ranking defectors to ever escape from the Soviet Union.

Yezhov greeted the news of Liushkov's defection with despair.[22] He confided to a close associate, "I'm doomed." He wavered about whether or not he should report to Stalin. He knew that this defection would signal to the Boss that the NKVD was still infiltrated by dangerous and unpredictable enemies. Several of his subordinates began making plans for their own suicides. When he finally reported to Stalin that Liushkov had gone over to the Japanese, business carried on as usual for some unfathomable reason. Just in case the affair would somehow blow over, Yezhov ordered the immediate executions of numerous prisoners who might be able to compromise him and his close associates. He also began making plans to neutralize his new enemy, Sholokhov.[23]

But Sholokhov himself knew nothing of Liushkov's defection and his new enemy, Yezhov, which was kept top secret. He too was preoccupied that summer with matters of life and death—in this case, those of one of his main protagonists. He had returned to working on the novel and completed a draft of the section on the death of Aksiniia. Before he could complete the section to his satisfaction, agricultural matters impeded upon his work. Lugovoi and the restored district leadership were attempting to prove to regional bureaucrats that earlier planting dates would lead to greater harvests.[24] To do this they needed to secure fuel, seeds, and bureaucratic buy-in from central authorities. Sholokhov traveled to Moscow to meet with ministers and to secure permission for a local initiative that might enhance future harvests.

While he was away, his enemies laid the groundwork for his fall. In autumn of 1938 Sholokhov received an anonymous letter from a Cossack who lived in the vicinity of Vioshki.[25] The letter proclaimed that once again NKVD officials were gathering false testimonies against him. This time they were coercing arrestees into declaring that he was the mastermind behind a planned uprising and was actively organizing guerilla groups throughout the region. Lugovoi soon reported that he had received a similar letter from a different Cossack, who had been threatened with a pistol to provide similar testimony.

In view of the damage to his credibility that had resulted from his trust in unverifiable allegations by a former *kulak*, Sholokhov decided to bide his time. There was nothing to be gained from panicking or relying for a second time on a source that could not be trusted. Perhaps these anonymous letters were just a ruse designed to push him into some kind of rash action that would further discredit him. For weeks he agonized about what to do.

In early October during a visit to Rostov, Sholokhov's fears were confirmed. Lugovoi was driving him back from a meeting when he suddenly stopped the car to pick up an individual on the side of the road. This man had worked in Vioshki for part of the year on the installation of the new electric station. His name was Ivan Pogorelov.[26] Lugovoi knew him well and insisted that they should give him a ride to a factory district on the outskirts of town. There Lugovoi stopped the car and told Sholokhov that the passenger had something very important to tell him. Pogorelov explained that months earlier he had been fired from his job and excluded from the party for failing to condemn dozens of individuals during the first wave of terror. Now NKVD officials had approached him with promises of rehabilitation. He could regain his job and reclaim his place in the party if he succeeded in a special operation to ensnare Sholokhov. These NKVD officers were convinced that the writer was collaborating with foreign intelligence officers, no doubt individuals who had recruited him on his trips abroad, to coordinate an uprising of Cossacks throughout the North Caucasus region. Pogorelov had been assigned to entrap him and collect evidence that would lead to his arrest, as well as the arrests of his three friends released in fall 1938 and several of his family members.

Sholokhov's first reaction was disbelief. "Their goal is to kill you," Pogorelov insisted. Sholokhov was still incredulous. Standing by the side of the road, he simply didn't want to believe that his ordeal had resumed. Seeing this, Pogorelov became more animated and more insistent: "Don't tell anyone. Especially not any regional officials. If anyone finds out about this, both of our lives will be in danger." To save his life, Sholokhov would have to leave Vioshki and go to the Central Committee. Pogorelov explained that because he was often followed by NKVD tails, it would take him several days to plan his escape. He too would go to the Central Committee.

Sholokhov and Lugovoi resumed their car journey. Lugovoi insisted that Pogorelov was an honest and reliable individual. His sudden appearance in Vioshki and the manner in which he had easily gained the confidence of several locals seemed to reinforce his story. Sholokhov and Lugovoi would be risking everything by ignoring his warning. The possibility remained, however, that this was an elaborate provocation and that Pogorelov was also trying to discredit Sholokhov.

They returned to Vioshki and said very little to their families. They quickly packed their bags and announced that they would be away on business for as long as necessary. Rather than drive to the nearest railroad station, they headed to a different station that was significantly farther. This station had considerably less passenger traffic and was consequently of less interest to the NKVD. Flagging down a passing train and claiming urgent business as a Supreme Soviet deputy, they were able to travel onward and then make a connection to Moscow. The whole trip Sholokhov sat in silence, interrupting his nervous chain-smoking only to repeatedly mutter, "Those lowlifes!"[27]

Upon arriving in Moscow, he contacted Poskrebyshev. Reporting that his life was in danger, he urgently requested to see Stalin. Poskrebyshev insisted that an immediate meeting was out of the question, but he inquired about the details. He advised the writer to take a room at the Hotel National and await further instructions. Day after day the writer's mornings began with a call to Poskrebyshev and a phrase such as "Is today the day?" The invariable answer was "No, not today."[28]

There are few worse places for waiting than central Moscow, where the chimes of the Kremlin painfully mark the passage of each hour. A whole week passed with no word about either Stalin's schedule or Pogorelov's fate.[29] Had he been apprehended by the NKVD handlers who, he insisted, were constantly following him? Had he met with the unfortunate "accident" he predicted? Even Poskrebyshev couldn't locate him. Without his testimony, the writer appeared to be sounding false alarms. But after two weeks, Pogorelov finally showed up at Sholokhov's hotel room. He had hidden for over nine days in a reed-swamp not far from Rostov, subsisting on Riesling and candies. He had hitchhiked to Ukraine claiming to be on the way to his mother's funeral. From there he had traveled by train to Moscow. But he couldn't get his petition to the Central Committee past the gatekeepers and goons who guarded the doors at various party institutions. He had no choice but to place his petition in a drop box for appeals to the Central Committee. Then he departed Moscow and returned to one of his civil war–era hideouts, but soon had to move on. Poskrebyshev finally located him, but when he was called to the telephone he didn't believe that he was actually speaking to Stalin's secretary and showered his interlocutor with a series of expletives. Only a trusted party comrade convinced him to travel to Moscow. Now he was a nervous wreck, and Sholokhov tried to calm him.

Even though Pogorelov had been found, the summons to the Kremlin still did not arrive. Poskrebyshev ordered them not to leave the hotel for any reason. Days of waiting took a toll on Sholokhov. Finally he decided to get drunk out of his mind. Fate decreed that on that very day the phone rang.[30] Poskrebyshev was on the other end of the line. "The car is waiting for you downstairs." "But we didn't know . . ." Sholokhov protested with slurred words, "We're in no . . . condition." "The car is waiting downstairs, come down!"

They were driven across Red Square past Lenin's somber, modernist mausoleum and St. Basil's Cathedral with its whimsical onion domes and their carefully concocted swirls of confectionary color. Passing through the heavily guarded Savior gates with their famous clock tower, they entered the Kremlin. The car stopped in front of the former Senate office building, which now housed the offices of Stalin and his most important subordinates. They were taken upstairs and guided to a waiting area. A few minutes later several officers from the local and regional NKVD entered the room. Sholokhov protested that he did not even want to be in same room as "those bastards," but Poskrebyshev insisted that the wait would only be a few minutes.

At precisely 4:15 P.M. Poskrebyshev entered the waiting area and told Sholokhov and the others to follow him. Two tall, large, wooden doors were opened into an expansive room.[31] Stalin met his friend at the door. Seeing his condition, he admonished him, "Comrade Sholokhov, I've received reports that you've been drinking too much."

"From such a life, Comrade Stalin, anyone would turn to drink," Sholokhov replied.

"Your life isn't so bitter as to turn to drinking. You have not yet finished your epic." Stalin's words contained a double entendre. In Russian the word for *bitter* sounds the same as the last name Gorky. In fact a famous newspaper cartoon entitled "Bitter life/Gorky's life" played on this double entendre and depicted the writer Maxim Gorky constantly being hounded by an adoring Soviet public. Stalin's simple statement both chided the writer and reminded him that he had not yet reached the pinnacle of Soviet success.

In the center of the room a long wooden table abutted a big wooden desk. At the other end of the room a wooden mantel was decorated with a few vases. If not for a few crucial elements of decor, this meeting room might have been mistaken for a late-19th-century provincial English gentleman's club. On the left side above the mantel there was a painting of Lenin at his desk poring over a newspaper. The table in the center was stacked with papers, inkwells, files, a fruit bowl, and a few bottles. There was also a large, prominent rubber stamp of the kind that speeded the drying of ink and affixed permanence to important signatures. Seated at the table were several members of the Politburo of the Central Committee. Among these was a man whom Sholokhov didn't quite recognize. This was Georgii Malenkov, who was just starting his meteoric rise from junior secretary to party hierarch.

A regional official named Grechukhin was given the first opportunity to address the Politburo. He opened with a wide-ranging report about agricultural affairs and party discipline in Vioshenskii district. He laboriously painted a portrait of a dysfunctional district administration headed by Lugovoi. Comrade Molotov, the second most important man in the Soviet hierarchy, attempted to remind him that the matter at hand was not the state of agriculture but allegations about the practices of the regional NKVD. Grechukhin nonetheless continued in the same vein.

Lugovoi contested the negative assessment of affairs in his district. He insisted that the local NKVD must have applied its hand to falsifying reports of planting and harvesting too. Since the first speaker relied so heavily on such reports, he had just demonstrated that he knew even less about agriculture than his NKVD colleagues. Intrigued by the allusion to discipline, Stalin inquired, "Comrade Lugovoi! Why didn't you inform the territorial party secretary that you were going to Moscow to the Central Committee? You departed without even informing anyone, without requesting permission from your superiors. As you know, this is very bad. Indeed it is a most egregious violation of party discipline."[32]

Lugovoi responded, "I could not have acted any differently. Not with the life of a very dear friend, our Sholokhov, hanging in the balance. If I told anyone about the trip to Moscow, our enemies would have been forewarned and could have tried to interfere."

"You should have known better than to think that we would believe slanderers," Stalin retorted. "More than once Yevdokimov came to me asking for sanction to arrest Sholokhov because he engages in conversations with former White Guardists. But I told him he doesn't understand anything in politics or in life. How can a writer write about White Guardists and not know what makes them tick [literally: what air they breathe]?"

Sholokhov was stunned to learn that when he thought Stalin was indifferent, the dictator was actually supporting him.

Sholokhov was invited to speak next. This new information astounded him. Only the personal intervention of Stalin had averted his arrest. Trying to calm his nerves and desperately searching for the right words through the daze of his inebriation, he averred that NKVD officers were once again soliciting false testimonies against him in order to frame him as an enemy of the people. Pogorelov had been engaged to entrap him and others had been threatened to concoct charges against him. "They are slandering/discrediting honest people who are dedicated to the party. I beseech you to put an end to this. I request that the Central Committee shield me from such arbitrariness."[33]

Stalin then asked Pogorelov to speak. He related how regional NKVD officials had recruited him and ordered him to frame Sholokhov. He had been forced to sign a statement that he would never divulge to anyone the details of this secret operation. His handlers insisted that their orders came directly from the very top—Comrades Stalin and Yezhov.

Upon hearing this Stalin started to interrogate the regional NKVD officers.[34] Approaching one named Kogan, he inquired, "Did you receive orders to frame Sholokhov? Did you assign Pogorelov to perform a secret mission?"

"This is a provocation. I've never even seen him before. Nor did I give him any orders," Kogan declared.

Desperately trying to get Stalin's attention, Pogorelov waved his arms like a pupil in school. "Comrade Stalin, I have proof they're not telling you the truth." Pointing to a page in his notebook he said, "This is where he recorded the address of the conspiratorial apartment where our meeting took place."

Stalin looked attentively at the notebook.

Stalin thundered at Kogan, "Is this your handwriting? Does this apartment exist? You know . . . it would be very easy to find out."

Kogan remained silent. At this point Stalin decided to turn up the pressure on Kogan. "Who is telling the truth here?" he repeatedly inquired.

Finally Kogan relented. "Yes, it's mine."

"So you and the others have given false testimony?"

"Yes."

"I'm asking, now answer truthfully, who gave you orders to frame Sholokhov?"[35]

Silence ensued. Stalin gazed intently into his face. "By whose orders did you concoct this plot against Sholokhov?" he asked.

Kogan attempted to name a regional NKVD official who had been recently arrested. Under the withering intensity of Stalin's gaze, however, he broke down. "It was all coordinated with People's Commissar Yezhov."

At that moment Yezhov sprang to his feet and screamed, "Slander! This is slander! I've never given such orders to anyone, and I didn't know about any of this."[36]

Stalin directed his gaze to Yezhov. "So how is it then that such things are being kept secret and hidden from you, from the Politburo, from everyone?"

Stalin returned to the table and started to thumb through a file. "Let me read this aloud. 'I, I. S. Pogorelov, do hereby declare to the Regional NKVD that the operation entrusted to me will be guarded in the strictest secrecy and will not be revealed to anyone. If I so much as reveal any detail of the special operation entrusted to me, I will be immediately shot on the spot without trial or investigation.'[37] Why does your NKVD go about soliciting such frightening affidavits?"

Yezhov started to address the legality of the document and began to enumerate the various kinds of signed documentation that could be solicited by the NKVD officers in the normal course of investigative work.

Stalin interrupted him. "Haven't I warned you? Why aren't you doing anything to put an end to this disgraceful disorder?"[38]

Molotov broke the silence by redirecting the focus to Pogorelov.[39] "One thing that's not clear to me, Comrade Pogorelov, is why you didn't report this whole affair directly to Comrade Yezhov. I just can't understand your behavior."

Pogorelov began to explain his distrust of Yezhov, but Stalin motioned him to halt. "What's not to understand?" Stalin interjected.

Pointing at Kogan and the others, who must have sensed that their luck had completely run out, he exclaimed, "They scared him with this affidavit. If not for Pogorelov, they would have put away our writer Sholokhov." Approaching Pogorelov, he exclaimed, "I see in his eyes that this man is honest, I can tell from perusing his file that he is a loyal communist. I think that everything is clear."

Sholokhov, who was still tipsy, sensed the shift in Stalin's mood. "That reminds me of the rabbit who was running around like a lunatic."[40] When all eyes turned to him, he continued:

"Bear approaches and asks, 'Rabbit, why are you running around like crazy?' 'I'm running because they're going to catch me and castrate me,'

Rabbit replied. 'But haven't you heard?' said Bear. 'They aren't capturing and castrating rabbits. It's camels that they're after.' 'True, but once they get hold of you and start cutting your nuts off, try and convince them then and there that you're not a camel.'"

Many of the Politburo members erupted in laughter. Sholokhov had just had the last laugh by casting the secret police officials in the role of the blundering castrators.

"Whom are we to believe in this matter?" Stalin asked the Politburo members.[41]

Turning to Yezhov, he declared, "I trust them [Sholokhov's side of the room], I don't trust your careerists and concocters anymore."

"The discussion of this matter has exhausted itself, let us conclude. Comrade Sholokhov, return to Vioshki, and continue to work on your novels as passionately and with as much inspiration as in previous years. No one will ever trouble you or impede your creative work."

With those words, the session adjourned. The proceedings had vindicated Sholokhov, but he was in no condition to discern the weight of what had just transpired. He was even mildly irritated at Pogorelov for publicly impugning the reputation of Yezhov. Upon returning to the hotel he even declared it an "unforgivable act of stupidity."[42]

Sholokhov did not realize it, but on that fateful day one of the most important scenes in the last act of the Great Terror had taken place. Stalin had stage-managed the session to finalize doubts about Yezhov's competence in the minds of the Politburo. Stalin didn't need such a spectacle to save Sholokhov. He used the meeting to decisively dispense with Yezhov. The encounter was a trap to ensnare the head of the NKVD, and it worked perfectly. The moment Yezhov declared, "I've never given such orders to anyone and I didn't know about any of this," the commissar demonstrated that he was either incompetent in keeping his house in order or he was lying to the Politburo. In either case he was finished.

The Politburo meeting with Sholokhov represented the tipping point in the downfall of Yezhov. A few weeks before the meeting the Politburo had decided to appoint a secret commission to study arrests and investigations. Malenkov, the rising star who observed the Sholokhov session, was one of its leaders. Within a week after the meeting, the Politburo issued a top-secret decree criticizing a series of major deficiencies in the work of the NKVD. It railed against simplified investigative procedures and declared an end to mass arrests. Two weeks after the meeting, a regional NKVD head turned against Yezhov and provided testimony that he had ignored various warnings from other NKVD officials about the suspicious behavior of several individuals. Three weeks after the meeting, Yezhov resigned from his post as head of the NKVD, and Lavrentii Beria was appointed as his successor.

Purges would now be redirected against those who were formerly doing the purging. Yezhov would soon become a denizen of one of his own dungeons. Many NKVD officers was either arrested or fired in the months after the meeting. During the course of 1939 thousands of individuals were released from jails and regained their freedom as a result of reviews of their cases. The experience of Sholokhov's friends now played out on a national scale. Issued with documents that didn't quite proclaim their innocence, they attempted to reclaim their jobs and restore their severed family ties. Often they were forced to work side by side with those whose slanderous accusations had nearly destroyed them.

FIFTEEN

I n the days after the Politburo session, Sholokhov struggled to decode Stalin's hints. Would he have to pay a price for his salvation? How in good conscience could he reconcile himself to the thought that innocent people were still suffering and that he could do nothing for them? Why did Stalin insinuate that he was not yet Gorky's equal? The two Sholokhovs, the one who seethed inside about the injustices committed by the NKVD and the one who was expected to publicly embrace the terror, engaged in a daily clash. All too often only the bottle kept them in their respective corners.

It was highly puzzling that Stalin would allude to Gorky. One of the most explosive revelations of the Great Terror involved the Soviet classic.[1] In 1938 a new and sinister explanation of Gorky's death alarmed and outraged Soviet citizens. Members of the "Right-Trotskyist bloc" confessed to killing Gorky in a conspiracy to overthrow Stalin, undermine the revolution, and terrorize Soviet citizens. At the trial several defendants insisted that the plot was coordinated by Yagoda, the former head of the NKVD.[2] Yagoda had established a special chemical laboratory in order to continuously enhance his arsenal of death. A Kremlin doctor and a professor of medicine were recruited to join the plot. They used their intimate knowledge of biochemistry and Gorky's medical history to ensure that no poisons could be detected. The death appeared to be completely natural to observers in 1936, even to expert pathologists.

Sholokhov found out about these shocking confessions along with the rest of the Soviet population from riveting court testimony presented in the Soviet press. Did he believe these revised claims? To believe anything else was both dangerous and unconscionable. It was easy enough to become convinced that the two versions of Gorky's death were somehow compatible. The prism of terror had merely brought new clarity to bear upon the same series of facts. It had unveiled a true, more vile cause.

Stalin's ambiguity was disconcerting. Sholokhov continued thinking about Gorky for days. Before leaving Moscow he attempted to discern the dictator's latest disposition towards the Soviet literary legend by touring the new museum dedicated to Gorky.[3] It was full of artifacts—yellowing old school certificates, leaves ripped from clandestine revolutionary notebooks, lithographed leaflets, pages from tsarist police files, watercolors of jail cells and places of exile, and books in all major languages of the USSR—but devoid of insights.[4] None of the objects provided any hints about whether Gorky fell from Stalin's favor, and thus causing suspicions over his "natural death."

The cantankerous man seemed to be missing from his sterile shrine. Even the centerpiece of the exhibition, the bronze rendition of Gorky's death mask, failed to capture his essence. Crafted by the Kremlin's court sculptor and elaborately framed by a whole room dedicated to a calculated display of mourning, the result was instead a disconcerting simulacrum. Gorky's visage had been assiduously retouched by the sculptor to conceal signs of age, distress, or blemish. Even his devil-may-care mustache had been neatly trimmed and obediently coiffed to convey a diminished sense of ego and attitude. A younger, more content Gorky rested on a pillow as if sleeping. One of the exhibition narratives even implied that this peace derived from satisfaction that his life's work had culminated in the Stalin constitution. The main message thus far was that the party controlled your image even after death.

Stalin's friendship with Gorky was omnipresent in the later rooms. A bust of Stalin even presided over the last stage of the classic's life. A large marble plaque was inscribed in gold with the dictator's words to Gorky in 1932: "Dear Aleksei Maksimovich, from the bottom of my heart I greet you and firmly shake your hand. I wish you many long years of life and work for the joy of all laborers and instilling fear in the enemies of the working class." Sadly, enemies had prevailed and those many long years never materialized. Why? If Stalin's friendship provided the key to both longevity and productivity, how did enemies manage to outwit him?

As Sholokhov walked through the exhibition, he couldn't help but notice that Gorky's last major literary effort was conspicuously absent. Heralded as a remarkable literary experiment only a few years earlier, now it was completely taboo.[5] A series of writers had collaborated with Gorky and the NKVD to produce a literary celebration of the construction of the White Sea canal. Lauding the heroic, transformative power of correctional labor, while overlooking the slavelike conditions and deadly excesses that surrounded the project, it heralded the canal as a great Stalinist achievement. In a curiously postmodern method of working, each writer's prose was circulated to several others and in the process acquired additional layers of artistic accretions. Acclaimed as the first truly collectively authored work in the history of world literature, it was handed out by the thousands at the 1934 Writers' Congress and subsequent party gatherings. It was a sensation . . . until it became odious. Its coeditor was condemned as an enemy of the people in 1937, and the book disappeared from public memory after Yagoda confessed to his role in the murder of Gorky.

Upon exiting the museum, Sholokhov did what duty demanded of him. He left an inscription in the guest book.[6] It read: "One departs from this museum with a feeling of profound gratitude to those who gathered everything relating to the life and activities of Aleksei Maksimovich. The millions of people who love Gorky will say thank you." It was a typical example of the white lies and half-truths that all public figures were forced to pronounce. Rumors circulating in the literary world suggested that Gorky's archive had been confiscated by the secret police and might never again see the light of day. Any perceptive person would surely interpret the word *everything* as "everything fit for display under given circumstances."

Perhaps Stalin's allusion to a "bitter life" was not even about Gorky. As Sholokhov learned during his stay in Moscow, life could become savagely bitter for any writer who disappointed Stalin. Could the dictator have been alluding to his colleague Andrei Platonov? Platonov's experiences provided ample proof that there was indeed a fate worse than death—literary oblivion coupled with bitter agony over a vanished loved one. Though the two writers were never close friends, the terror briefly brought them together in 1938–39.

Platonov had spent much of the past decade out of literary favor. At times shunned by the entire Soviet literary establishment, he continued to write, knowing that he could not publish. Then one day in late April 1938 his fifteen-year-old son disappeared. Platonov spent days searching for him. Neither the hospitals nor the morgues had a record of any individual fitting his son's description. A more sinister Soviet institution had claimed him. His early efforts to seek the assistance of the Writers' Union in finding out what happened to the boy had proven to be futile. Learning of this, Sholokhov offered to make some inquiries.[7] The results were devastating. The boy had been sentenced to ten years. Only his young age saved him from being immediately shot as an enemy of the people.

As Sholokhov told Platonov everything he had learned about fabricated testimonies and indiscriminate use of torture in the cases of his friends, he could see his colleague struggling to accept the existence of the NKVD's dark, terrible parallel world. "What kind of game is this?" Platonov kept muttering.[8] From doubt and disbelief he descended into severe agitation. While he struggled to accept that a teenage boy could be condemned for so long, Sholokhov knew that belief in the dictator was his only hope.

In late 1938 Sholokhov coached Platonov on how to write a letter to Stalin. His colleague was accustomed to penning sophisticated, even philosophical, prose. The letters he drafted had proven to be excessively complicated. Sholokhov's advice was to be simple and direct. Platonov had to boldly request that the boy be freed.[9] This was not the occasion for elaborate arguments or effusive emotions, promises, or justifications. Above all his colleague needed to communicate a belief in Stalin's benevolence.

On a subsequent visit to Moscow in early 1939 Sholokhov learned that Platonov's letter to Stalin produced results.[10] The boy's case was being reexamined, but he had severely compromised his chances of release by affixing his signature to charges that he was involved in a plot to pass on state secrets to a German newspaper correspondent. Platonov's son and his playmates had been convicted of involvement in a fascist youth organization that plotted to overthrow the Soviet government and had allegedly discussed contaminating a major Moscow water reservoir with cholera bacteria.

Sholokhov continued to make inquiries with the NKVD and the prosecutor's office.

It did not take long for Stalin to clarify his plans for Sholokhov. Multiple signs indicated that the dictator was grooming him to become Gorky's successor. His membership in the Soviet Academy of Sciences was formally proposed in late November 1938. It was hastily ratified in January 1939. Days later he received the Order of Lenin, one of the Soviet Union's highest honors, for his achievements in advancing Soviet literature. Then he received an even higher honor. He was commissioned to give a keynote speech at the upcoming eighteenth Congress of the Communist Party. Sholokhov had never delivered such a high-profile national speech. The whole country would be listening.

He faced a choice between two alternative paths. Choosing the path of Maxim Gorky meant relinquishing his conscience and candor in order to retain fame and fortune. If he took the hard, candid road of Andrei Platonov, he would retain his good name but would languish in isolation and penury. Even though he had enjoyed a life of plenty, he pondered the path of suffering. It would not be an easy choice.

As he prepared for the speech he received letters from all parts of the Soviet Union. A deluge of testimonies suggested that the terror had not just cut a swath through his district. It was eviscerating every district. In late 1938 the writer confided to a friend that he was buckling under the burden of "human misfortune which has been heaped upon me in such abundance."[11] Although the archive of Sholokhov's correspondence from this period was destroyed during the Second World War, the kinds of letters he must have received can be deduced from those received by another major writer who had become a deputy and public figure, Aleksei Tolstoi.[12] During the terror he received over six hundred letters. Four hundred of them complained of injustices, begged for intercession, or excoriated him for supporting the regime. Ordinary Soviet citizens shamed their deputy for "shouting hurrah for Stalin and applauding Yezhov." Brave individuals whose commitment to the truth was stronger than their fear of repression denounced torture and dehumanization. "Throughout our much-suffering Russia the screams and moans of victims of sadists continue to resound," one letter proclaimed ". . . knowing this . . . you remain silent." Even in the depths of their despair people doggedly pursued the lost causes of their disappeared loved ones. Letters recounted how ordinary people became detectives. They located former cellmates or camp comrades who provided snippets of information about the fates of the lost and the damned. They implored him to find out the truth. Some begged him to hand their petitions to Stalin, while others ridiculed the dictator who had destroyed the revolution. Some lamented the senseless deaths of thousands, while others hoped to save a single individual who was dear to their heart. There were also those who proclaimed that Russia had lost its conscience now that its writers routinely resorted to bootlicking. As a recipient of similar letters, it is no wonder that Sholokhov complained that it was too much for one person to cope with.

At the Party Congress Sholokhov was expected to pay the price of his deliverance. His keynote speech was supposed to emphasize that the Great Terror, which was now winding down, had strengthened the safety and security of the Soviet populace by vanquishing vile, dangerous, and persistent enemies. He would have to embrace a series of odious talking points about literature. He would have to endorse the official rhetoric of societal purification. But could he bring himself to publicly utter such words?

Somewhere deep inside him there was a defiant desire to speak out. Should he denounce the institutions that unleashed the terror? Should he expose the absurd allegations that destroyed the lives of innocent people? Could he find the right words to expose the tragedies occurring throughout the country? If the "competent organs" were so competent, why did it take them months to determine that an underground, teenage cholera conspiracy could hardly have functioned in the heart of Moscow? Why was a boy who was convicted of bizarre charges in a secret trial still languishing in a labor camp in one of the most remote regions of Siberia? Such thoughts were quickly cancelled out by equally compelling thoughts. Wouldn't enemies rejoice if he spoke out against the NKVD? They would twist his words. They would allege that everyone was innocent and everything was in vain. What good would it do to alienate Stalin? A few minutes of compromise could help a lot of people. If he didn't deliver the correct remarks, he would never be able to help anyone else. He also had to think about his family.

He convinced himself that the enemies were real. The conspiracies were real. Traitors had indeed infiltrated the highest levels of the government and the NKVD before being exposed and eliminated. To justify his acquiescence, he summoned to mind various peculiar incidents from recent years. One of them continued to trouble him. As he mulled over it, he began to count himself among those who had been targeted for liquidation by the vanquished Trotskyist opposition. After all, in those years you were only someone important if THEY were after you.

He recalled an incident that occurred in Moscow.[13] One time Yagoda invited him over. Enticed with the promise of a hunting dog, he agreed. After drinking and dining with the head of the NKVD, he returned with the puppy to the hotel. That night he became extremely ill and was seized by unbearable abdominal pain. His friend Vas'ka Kudashev rushed him to the hospital, where the doctor on duty diagnosed him with an acute appendicitis requiring an emergency operation. At the operating table, he noticed that a nurse was intently gazing at him. Something in her eyes kept telling him not to go through with it. He got up from the table and left the hospital. He soon recovered.

Now he saw clearly that he was supposed to die there that day. It would all be made to appear normal. Hadn't one of Yagoda's assistants testified about a whole cabinet full of ampules and vials of poison? Didn't the Kremlin doctors collude in the death of Gorky? His reconstructed memory was compelling.[14] It was a curious amalgam of revelations from the great show trial of 1938 and rumors about the death of the defense minister Mikhail Frunze in 1925, who was said to have suspiciously died as a result of an operation in the Kremlin hospital.[15]

Whether or not one of Yagoda's deadly vials was surreptitiously emptied into his shot glass or infused into the fish he ate on a frightful evening in the mid-1930s, it is undeniable that Sholokhov was poisoned. The toxins of the terror years took root in his mind. He would no longer confront and expose systemic evil. Instead he would extol the regime while striving to save individuals as best he could without subjecting himself, his career, or his family to too much risk. Whenever the occasion demanded, he would don a new mask if he could continue to help his district. When the narrative changed, he would be among the first to change with it. Yet deep inside he still seethed that the NKVD had destroyed so many innocent people. To mitigate this poison he increasingly turned to another—alcohol. He decided to march in step with the regime and drink his conscience into submission.

In March 1939 he stood up in front of two thousand delegates and the entire Soviet populace and proclaimed that the Great Terror was a worthy triumph.[16] Although he delivered his speech at the Party Congress with aplomb and was met with generous applause, he gave away more than he might have wished. While introducing himself, he made light of one of his greatest anxieties. He embraced his identity as the author of two unfinished, multivolume novels. "When you heard my name you probably said to yourselves, 'Ha, that's the very same Sholokhov who takes a long time to write and doesn't ever get to the end.'" After laughter died down, he reassured his audience that he would actually finish this speech and that he wouldn't have to be interrupted or reminded of his allotted time by the chair.

He returned to an issue that had been a major concern since Gorky's time: how the scarcity of paper imposed severe limitations upon literature. He also poked fun at the state publishing monopoly, which used the awkward acronym State-lit-print. He jocularly remarked that it should be renamed State-lit-reprint or State-lit-no-print, judging by its recent output. The joking was just a prelude to the major theme of his speech: the terror's beneficial influence on Soviet society.

He delivered the proscribed talking points, which reinforced the refrain of the congress:

> As in all precincts of our life, Soviet literature, having gotten rid of enemies, has become healthier and stronger. . . . We got rid of spies, fascist intelligence officers along with all of that scum, all of which were in essence neither human beings nor writers in the true sense of those words, they were to put it simply, parasites, which were sucking the life blood of the living organism of Soviet literature. It is clear, that having purged itself, our literary environment has only benefited.

He lamented that nonetheless unnamed enemies had "managed to deliver a very weighty blow to us: with their involvement the great writer of our present era, Gorky, was killed." At the very moment he delivered the speech he appears to have fervently believed this. Subsequently he vacillated.

The fascist threat to the Soviet Union constituted the other major theme of the speech. He echoed Comrade Voroshilov's earlier remarks about the Soviet Union's defense capacity. In a rousing military pronouncement, probably uttered off the cuff, Sholokhov made one of the most peculiar declarations he ever made in public: "We are going to beat the enemy in such a manner as no one has ever beaten him. I can assert to you comrade delegates of the congress, we will not leave behind his field bags—no for us that Japanese custom is not appropriate. We will gather up those alien bags, because in our literary enterprise the contents of those bags will in time be put to good use. Having utterly liquidated the enemy, we will then write books about how we beat those enemies . . ."

In an act of verbal juggling, the Stalinist acrobat extraordinaire appears to have accidentally revealed his most guarded professional secret. Were there any examples in Soviet literary history of works that claimed to be based in part on a written legacy left behind by vanquished enemies? No works had ever been publicly acknowledged to consist of reworked raw materials left behind on the field of battle. In fact Sholokhov's statement closely mirrors the allegations that some were making about his own "literary enterprise" in 1929.

After his speech, the flow of critical, scathing letters must have increased. Hundreds of writers are presumed to have perished in the purges. It seems inconceivable that none of their close friends, surviving spouses, or children took objection to their being labeled as pernicious "parasites" by the country's most famous writer.

He turned to the bottle once more to help him cope. He justified his actions by imagining the future good that could result from his performance at the congress. He consoled himself by admitting that the higher goal of building socialism outweighed individual suffering. One of the first letters he penned after the congress emphasized his newfound submission to the will of a higher power. Invoking the traditional Russian proverb that states, "We are all under God's jurisdiction and his ways are inscrutable," he updated it, writing, "We are all under the jurisdiction of the Central Committee, and its ways are inscrutable."[17] The Central Committee was often a euphemism for Stalin.

After months of bending, the breaking moment for Sholokhov came.[18]

In early June 1939 he sought consolation in solitary engagement with nature. During those years the Don River provided his only secure refuge and place of respite. One morning he headed for the banks of the river and rowed his boat into the current. Maneuvering it into the middle of the river's course, he drifted. Eventually he dropped anchor to savor the solitude. As the fish started to bite, the sun became hotter and hotter. Soon he noticed that his bowl of bait, probably a mixture of grains and secret scent ingredients, started to dry out. Without thinking, he took off his hat and covered the mixture. As he started to fish he didn't notice that the sun had become scorching. Although he didn't admit it in retellings of the incident, his extreme sun exposure seems to have been precipitated by excessive consumption of alcohol. By the time he started towards home several hours later there was ringing in his ears. Then he was seized by a throbbing headache. As he staggered to the house, his family recoiled in horror from the sight of him. His eyes were bloodshot red. His recently shaved head was breaking out in blisters. His speech was becoming incoherent . . . These were signs of acute sunstroke.

He collapsed into bed and did not rise. In Vioshki the news spread like wildfire. The locals whispered in hushed tones about the direness of his condition. Dozens came to his house daily to inquire whether he would recover. His family managed to keep the story out of the press by telling visiting journalists that he had succumbed to a recurring bout of malaria.[19] As he laid inert and immobile, unable to even raise his head without experiencing severe vertigo, Sholokhov was tortured by the thought that he would die without finishing *Quiet Don*.

SIXTEEN

For weeks Sholokhov languished in a mental fog. Slowly, all too slowly, the fog lifted. Each time he attempted to sit up, he collapsed back into bed. His incoherence and immobility caused severe consternation in his household. Marusia openly voiced her fears and frustrations. She chided him for imperiling his literary career. She couldn't contain her dissatisfaction that he severely threatened his family's livelihood. In one pointed conversation she even declared, "Now you'll never write anything again. As you well know those who have been touched (i.e., damaged in the head) don't write, and if they attempt to do so, the results are always bad."[1] At first this ominous declaration disturbed him. Then it angered and motivated him.

As his head recovered, literary choices that had previously caused him agony now appeared to be crystal clear. He understood for the first time in years that he would finally finish the novel. It had been almost twelve years since the first installment was published. The elixir of favor made him feel invincible.[2] He was not "touched," as Marusia had insisted, but untouchable for as long as he fervently believed in Stalin's benevolence. Sholokhov realized that the normal rules no longer applied to him. He had been saved during the Great Terror for a higher purpose, and completion of *Quiet Don* was just one facet of his salvation. To Stalin he was a symbol of the dictator's own self-perceived magnanimity. His continued existence reinforced the dictator's confidence in his own benevolence and powers of discernment. The writer resolved to take advantage of this. As one of the few who had peered behind the curtains in the palace of the Kremlin's Oz, he understood Stalin's self-perception and decided to capitalize on it. He timed the conclusion of *Quiet Don* to coincide with Stalin's sixtieth birthday celebration.

On December 11, 1939, he sent Stalin a letter and a birthday contribution to *Pravda*.[3] It read:

Dear Comrade Stalin!

On May 24, 1936, I visited you at your cottage. If you remember, on that occasion you gave me a bottle of cognac. My wife took it away from me and firmly declared, "We can't drink this, this is a memento." I spent an enormous amount of time and deployed every rhetorical flare I could think of to convince her otherwise. I said that the bottle might accidentally get broken, that in time its contents would become sour, and tried every conceivable stratagem. With annoying stubbornness, which probably all women have, she declared, "No. No and no." In the end, however, I finally wore her down. We agreed to drink the bottle when I finish *Quiet Don*.

Over the course of these last three years, in difficult moments of life (and like for every person there were more than a few of these) more than once I plotted to violate the intact contents of Your gift. All of my attempts were methodically and furiously beaten back by my wife. In the last few days, after thirteen years of work, I am finishing *Quiet Don*. Since that big event will coincide with Your birthday, I will wait until the 21st, and before taking a sip, I will wish you the very same [thoughts as] the old man in the article that I have enclosed wishes you.

I'm sending it to You, because I don't know if *Pravda* will publish it.

Yours,

M. Sholokhov

As he wrote the letter, he must have been aware that Stalin was preoccupied with far more grave matters than the ending of his novel. On November 29, 1939, Viacheslav Molotov, the People's Commissar for Foreign Affairs, delivered a speech via radio to the entire populace.[4] He emphasized that the Soviet Union's repeated diplomatic efforts to ensure the security of Leningrad had failed due to Finnish animosity and imperialist intrigue. In the past few days Finnish military hawks had carried out a series of provocations along the Soviet border and had even killed Red Army soldiers with artillery fire. From that very moment the Soviet Union was freed from its obligations under the non-aggression pact signed between the two countries. Though Molotov avoided the word *war*, preferring instead to speak of "measures for ensuring security," Sholokhov understood that this speech was a declaration of war.

The next day the newspapers announced the formation of a Finnish People's Government. It immediately signed a treaty with the USSR and invited the Red Army to assist in the "liberation" of the Finnish people. Over the next few days the media was filled with reports that the anti-Soviet Finnish regime was on the run and that soon even Helsinki might be liberated. Then the reports began to get considerably smaller and less specific. The early reports mentioned major towns, the later ones could only be deciphered with the help of meticulously precise topographical maps. Initially bad weather was blamed. Then it became clear that the Soviet advance had completely stalled. The later reports tersely stressed that "nothing notable" took place at the front. Sholokhov correctly surmised that the Mannerheim defense line had presented a major obstacle. The war in his view would turn out to be "no cheerful walk in the park."

During those blistering winter weeks of December 1939, Anatolii Kalinin, a correspondent from the national Communist Youth League newspaper, suddenly appeared in Vioshki.[5] From his military overcoat Sholokhov immediately deduced that his guest had flown in from the front. The transfer of a war correspondent in the midst of a campaign suggested that the war was not going well and the editors were hoping for a scoop that could temporarily divert readers' attention. Sholokhov responded to each of the correspondent's questions about the final volume of the novel with questions of his own about conditions at the front. This was a cat-and-mouse game. The war correspondent was bound by the rules of military censorship not to reveal the true situation at the front. The writer talked about the novel but revealed "nothing notable" about its ending. The desired preview of the ending of *Quiet Don* was not to be.

Though Stalin was too busy to discuss the end of the novel with the writer, he must have enjoyed Sholokhov's letter. He wrote on it: "[For] My archive. J. Stalin." The article was forwarded to *Pravda* with instructions to publish it.[6]

Out of over thirty articles in honor of Stalin's birthday that were published by leading political figures, shapers of Stalinism, and foreign fellow communists, Sholokhov's was the most discordant.[7] Although he was part of the orchestra of praise, his tune was composed in an altogether different key. Most of the others contained profuse praise of Stalin's role as a shaper of history and theorist of communism. They eagerly quoted Stalin's own words about cadres, industrialization, collectivization, and a happy prosperous life for ordinary folks. Most frequently he was called the supreme leader, teacher, or genius. His roles as Lenin's friend, partner, and political equal were paired with his function as "today's Lenin." Flatterers proclaimed him to be the "great machinist of the locomotive of history," "father and friend of the people," "brain and heart of the party," and "[Caucasian] mountain eagle of our party."

Sholokhov's article was purposefully devoid of fanfare. It consciously rejected hyperbole and avoided the profuse, but empty, phrases of the state propaganda machine. He defied every convention by declaring, "Speaking of Stalin, it is possible to express thanks without resorting to an overabundance of words, to express love without resorting to frequent references to it, and to evaluate the achievements of this great man without abusing epithets." He continued, "It just so happens that one word straight from the heart pronounced meekly can substitute for all other words, especially when there are so many of them."

While the other articles celebrated Stalinist triumphs, Sholokhov broke every rule in the book by invoking tragedy. He wrote, "In 1933 enemies in the territorial leadership of the former Azov-Black Sea region under the guise of battling with sabotage in the collective farms, deprived the collective farmers of grain. All of the grain, including stocks which had been distributed as an advance towards labor-day payments, was confiscated. Many communists, who pointed out to the leadership of the region the incorrectness of the policies that they were implementing, were expelled from the party and arrested." Next he dared to use a word that was generally taboo until the fall of the USSR—*famine*. When Stalin was informed that people were starving, he sent a telegram inquiring how much grain was needed. The grain was sent. Thousands were saved. Afterwards the guilty parties were shot. The next December the chairman of a collective farm wanted to write a long-winded resolution about Stalin's gift of grain. A 58-year-old blacksmith stood up and declared, "None of that is necessary. We need to write just one word to Stalin. Write 'thank you' and he will understand everything." His proposal carried the day, and for the first time since collectivization the chairman's proposal did not prevail. The resolution simply read: "Thanks Comrade Stalin."

Sholokhov claimed that the act he depicted became an annual ritual occasion. Each year on Stalin's birthday the blacksmith continues to put on a new shirt, gathers everyone at the table, pours a shot of vodka, and says a toast to Stalin. "He's a good man," he proclaims, "God grant him a bit more health and to live as many years in this world as he has already lived." Then those in the room silently reflect on how hard it must be for Stalin to live with the great weight of caring for the people on his shoulders.

Sholokhov celebrated his Stalin, or rather the Stalin he chose to believe in—the responding dictator. The incident was fictional but loosely based on the writer's request for grain for his home district in

1933. Sholokhov structured the anecdote to play upon the dictator's self-image as a leader who was elevated to guide and guard his people in a world filled with cunning enemies and incompetent local bunglers. The emphasis on simplicity, patriarchal solemnity, and ritual toasts was calculated to speak to the values that Stalin still cherished from his upbringing in the Caucasus. The most remarkable feature of Sholokhov's article was the notion that Stalin too was worthy of empathy. He was more than a magnet for epithets and metaphors, he too was a man who carried burdens.

Along with numerous birthday panegyrics, a short, intriguing article appeared in *Pravda*. It announced the creation of a new award called the Stalin Prize.[8] The prize would be awarded for outstanding achievements in science, literature, and culture. Since Sholokhov had just completed *Quiet Don*, he would be eligible for the inaugural round of prize awards. The winners in each field would receive 100,000 rubles, which was roughly thirty times the annual salary of an ordinary Soviet worker.

While in Moscow a few months later, Sholokhov decided to inquire about his chances of receiving the inaugural Stalin Prize for literature. Rumors in the literary world proclaimed him to be the odds-on favorite to win the award.[9] After the Gorky Institute of World Literature endorsed his nomination, it seemed like a foregone conclusion that the inaugural prize was his. He nonetheless arranged a meeting with Aleksei Tolstoi, the head of the selection committee for literature. The two had never been close friends, but they had encountered one another at various events.

Tolstoi agreed to meet him at the restaurant of the Hotel National.[10] Arriving together with his wife, Tolstoi hoped that her presence would ensure a pleasant evening. But as the discussion became more serious and contentious, he sent her home. Returning hours later, he was blind drunk, disgusted, and in a foul mood. He proclaimed to her that if he had a gun at that very moment he would first kill her, then turn the gun on himself. Fortunately, gun control in the Soviet Union was very strict.

Evidently Tolstoi revealed to Sholokhov that the literary selection committee would likely not endorse *Quiet Don* for the Stalin Prize. Fadeev was conspiring to sway the committee against the novel and had introduced other works into consideration that could lead to a split vote. He was even pressuring Tolstoi to write a negative evaluation of the novel. Tolstoi shared this information in confidence with Sholokhov so that the writer would not be shocked when the decision was announced. He evidently tried to reassure Sholokhov that in time he would become a laureate. Sholokhov reacted badly to the news. He became rude and angry. The meeting concluded with him yelling at Tolstoi, "You're a person who is finished," which had ominous implications of "You're a dead man." The two writers would not speak to each other again for nearly two years.

The preliminary deliberations of the prize committee had not only questioned whether the novel was worthy of the prize, they had challenged the finality of the book's ending and impugned Sholokhov's judgement.[11] Tolstoi complained that Sholokhov had committed a serious mistake by having his protagonist, Grigorii, join up with a group of anti-Soviet bandits in the final volume. The literary hero of millions of Soviet citizens should not be permitted to exit from the literary stage in the guise of an outlaw. But this is "only a mistake if *Quiet Don* ends with the fourth volume." A fifth volume could be written "by the will of the masses of readers who are demanding from the author a continuation of the life of Grigorii Melekhov."[12] In effect he turned a finished novel back into an unfinished one. This made it ineligible by the terms of Stalin Prize criteria.

Sholokhov left no written traces of his reaction to the news. It seems likely that he wasted no time in following through with his threat to Tolstoi. Before leaving Moscow he must have complained to someone in the Kremlin that his candidacy was being sabotaged by Fadeev and Tolstoi.

The next round of prize deliberations took place on November 18, 1940, and involved the wider committee for the arts. Opinions about Sholokhov were polarized. While some debated whether Sholokhov's body of writing was sufficiently Stalinist, others criticized the ending of the book while endorsing its artistic merits.

The strongest arguments against Sholokhov were voiced by the Ukrainian film director Aleksandr Dovzhenko, who was close to Stalin and had worked with Fadeev on a film adaptation of one of his novels.[13] Dovzhenko believed that such an honor would be premature for Sholokhov. The novel's fourth volume left lingering dissatisfaction. The revolution brought fratricide, syphilis, dirt, and enmity, it turned the strongest people into bandits, and that was it. The ending lacked a positive or constructive message. Depriving Sholokhov of the first award would serve as a stimulus for raising his creative activity. He would still be eligible to receive a future prize for the unwritten, but politically palatable, fifth installment of *Quiet Don*.

The Ukrainian playwright Aleksandr Korneichuk spoke forcefully in favor of the novel, arguing that some of Sholokhov's passages even rivaled Leo Tolstoy's ability to create literary images that were so lifelike that the reader imagined he could touch them. He contended that awarding Sholokhov the prize could actually spur him to do even greater things and widen his horizons. He was one of the few to openly declare that he would be voting for Sholokhov.[14]

One of the most penetrating assessments was provided by the poet Nikolai Aseev. He spoke to the essential dilemma of the committee: a remarkable work of art could be deemed ideologically harmful.[15] Was the committee created to assess artistic merit or ideological worth? As a young writer and "provincial lad" Sholokhov was still honing his craft at the very moment when he was unexpectedly thrust into the limelight. Fame and scrutiny from all directions might have negatively impacted his work. A novel centered on a specific region should not be expected to reflect all of the greater truths of the revolution. Grigorii could not be faulted for the fact that he did not become a flesh-and-blood embodiment of communist ideals, because there were too few leaders and revolutionaries in the Cossack lands.

Sholokhov's allies must have learned of the substance of the deliberations. They tried to tilt the scales back in his favor. An article in *Izvestiia* countered several points that were made in the confidential discussions.[16] It affirmed the world historical importance of the novel. It claimed the regional focus was an advantage because it helped to show how the history of humanity is contradictory. It asserted that for the first time people of the land were represented in a deeply insightful way by a truly Bolshevik writer.

In early January 1941 the Stalin Prize committee took a vote. On January 14 it sent its ranked list of finalists to the Kremlin.[17] Stalin carefully reviewed the committee results. He struck four names from the committee's list and introduced three new names, leaving only one of the committee's original rankings intact. His final ranking shifted all of the others names downward. Intriguingly the work that emerged in first place in the dictator's ranking had actually been withdrawn from consideration by its author due to its unfinished status. It did not feature in the committee's initial discussions or ballot. Stalin decided to send everyone a message. He would remind the committee and Sholokhov that this was *his* prize.

On March 15, 1941, *Pravda* published a list of winners of Stalin Prizes.[18] Among the awards for prose literature there were three names: "1 [A. N.] Tolstoi, 2 Sergeev-Tsenskii, 3 Sholokhov." Of the three winners, only Sholokhov was depicted on the front page. His portrait appeared with winners in fields other than literature. This was a compromise of sorts, but Sholokhov could take little delight in the fact that his name was listed under number three. He did not agree to give any national press interviews about the award.[19]

Soon a letter arrived in the mail. The envelope was from the "Committee for Stalin Prizes in the area of literature and arts." Inside there was a letter on tan, bureaucratic stationery dated April 11, 1941.[20] It read:

> Most respected Mikhail Aleksandrovich! The Stalin Prize which has been awarded to you will be transferred to your current account. For the processing of the transfer it is necessary to receive from you a [filled out] copy of the attached declaration with your bank account information. Secretary of the committee O. S. Bokshanskaia.

It was insulting that the first official communication was from some low-ranking bureaucrat. He ignored the request. Additional efforts to contact him failed. Eventually he was summoned to speak with Molotov, who was puzzled that the writer had refused to provide the required information.[21] "Why won't you accept the prize money?" he asked. Sholokhov replied, "I don't need money." Molotov countered, "But you could build yourself a new house." "I already have a home," Sholokhov retorted. After such back and forth Molotov finally proclaimed, "It's your business what you do with money, but you are required to officially accept the prize that has been awarded to you. The Central Committee has already decided to set up a special account for you in Moscow." Sholokhov neither agreed nor disagreed with this decision. The next time he heard Molotov's voice, it was delivering a gut-wrenching radio announcement.

SEVENTEEN

On June 22, 1941, Molotov announced that at four o'clock that morning Hitler's forces invaded the Soviet Union. Sholokhov was shocked to hear that Nazi soldiers launched surprise attacks against Soviet borders and *Luftwaffe* bombers raided Soviet territory. A great patriotic war had commenced. Molotov went on the radio to urge Soviet citizens to defend the motherland and to close ranks around Stalin. Claiming that only two hundred Soviet citizens had been killed or wounded that morning, he proclaimed, "Our cause is just. The enemy will be defeated. Victory will be ours."[1]

After the shock wore off, Sholokhov immediately started working to support the war effort.[2] He wrote to a top military official, volunteering to serve in the army. He donated his entire Stalin Prize to the Soviet war effort. Then he gave a rousing speech to Don Cossacks mobilizing for the war. In an article reminding his readers of the first "German" war, he emphasized that the hatred of the enemy remained fresh in the minds of many gray-haired old men who were now sending their sons and grandsons off to fight. A mysterious delay in the processing of his officer's commission kept him away from the front during the early, most savage months of the war.

Before he experienced the war firsthand as a war correspondent, he struggled to comprehend the war from a distance.[3] He strived to discover the truths buried in the daily briefings from the military command. From the very beginning Soviet censors included so few facts in the official bulletins that reading between the lines became a daily national obsession. Sholokhov had read too many memoirs and studies of the First World War while working on *Quiet Don* to fully trust the military scenarios offered by Soviet propaganda during the early months of combat. They were too implausible.

The early reports exuded confidence. They stressed that enemy planes were being destroyed in large numbers and that German ground forces were sustaining huge casualties due to the valiant resistance of the Red Army. Regarding Soviet casualties there was complete silence, except for those two hundred mentioned by Molotov and isolated others who always died heroically and in small batches. The tone of subsequent reports became more formulaic and less specific. Shorthand phrases such as "savage battles" masked combat realities. Only hours into the war even the official reports had to concede that fighting now stretched from the Baltic Sea in the north to the Black Sea in the south. The oddest early event of the war was Stalin's silence. He didn't address the populace or publish any rousing statements.

Patterns of absence and presence revealed uncomfortable truths. Censors were too preoccupied with the present moment to pay close attention to what they had tried to conceal in previous days. Occasional slips revealed a more brutal and less successful war. By carefully reading stories from the front, Sholokhov could piece together a hazy picture of an enormous catastrophe that unfolded in late June 1941.[4] No maps of the German advance were printed. The capture of Soviet cities was usually not announced. They simply stopped being mentioned in reports. When new cities suddenly began to be trumpeted as heroic centers of resistance or linked to "area commands" or "previously prepared defensive positions," the geographic contours of the German advance and the Soviet retreat started to become discernible. It appeared as if the Germans had invaded the Baltic republics and were advancing to the east. They were also attacking from Finland in the north in the direction of Leningrad and from Romania in the south in the direction of Kiev.

Subtle shifts in the war coverage usually portended disaster.[5] Articles heralding Soviet air raids on German factories and Romanian oil fields gradually became fewer in number. Then it became clear that Stalin's falcons of the air were no longer capable of preventing air raids first on Kiev, then on Moscow. Did this mean that the entire Soviet air force was devastated? For no apparent reason the navy receded into the background of war coverage. Did that mean that the Baltic fleet was finished? Occasionally small stories about heroic Soviet doctors tending to wounded appeared. If at one station there were hundreds of wounded, that meant that similar dramas were unfolding all along the western frontiers of the country. One only needed a school geography textbook to project that there were hundreds of such stations near the shifting front lines. In the absence of hard facts wild rumors ruled the day.

On July 3, 1941, Stalin ended his silence with a speech that was widely transmitted over loudspeakers in public spaces.[6] Sholokhov learned that a grave danger threatened his country. The dictator began the speech in a highly unusual way, addressing the Soviet people for the first time as "brothers and sisters" and "my friends." Stalin spoke in a calm and deliberate voice. He read his speech in staccato, pausing after a few words, then uttering a few more. He spoke of the life-and-death struggle in a casual, confident manner, like a father at a dinner table explaining some pressing matter of family business. He repeatedly used the words "we" and "our" and almost never alluded to himself or spoke in the first person. He admitted that the Germans had occupied Lithuania, most of Latvia, western Belorussia, and western Ukraine.

The main points of the speech were calculated for comprehension by even the most simple folk. Our motherland is in danger. The German attack was perfidious. History shows that there is no such thing as an invincible army. The fascists want to seize our grain and oil, restore landowners, and enslave the Soviet population to German barons. There will be no mercy for deserters, sowers of panic, and rumor mongers. Only our united energies will rout the enemy and bring about victory.

The speech provided Sholokhov with a measure of reassurance. It stressed that mobilization was on the upswing and that the Red Army's best days were still ahead. It admitted that further evacuations of territory could be necessary but provided a framework for action. The goal was to leave behind nothing of use to the enemy. A widespread partisan war would be waged anywhere and everywhere that the German fascists set foot. Most importantly the speech communicated a confidence that the country would prevail as it did in 1812 when Napoleon invaded.

For Sholokhov, a more dramatic personal event overshadowed Stalin's reappearance. He found out that right after Stalin's speech Vas'ka Kudashev enthusiastically entered the regular army.[7] Impatient to contribute to the epic struggle, he marched to an enlistment office to volunteer. A more shrewd operator would have waited for an appointment as a war correspondent. This could have entitled his family to an officer's rations. Assigned to a fighting unit at the front, he started to regret his decision almost immediately. His nearsightedness, which could have qualified him for a deferment, hampered his ability to fight and put his life in danger.

While Sholokhov chafed on the sidelines, other writers were filing frequent stories from the front lines. He noticed in August 1941 that the propaganda war was entering a vicious new phase. On a daily basis the Soviet media churned out new stories about atrocities committed by inhuman German cannibals, barbarians, and depraved sexual deviants.[8] Sholokhov's old rival Aleksei Tolstoi penned a lead article for *Red Star*, the major military newspaper, claiming that German sadists ripped babies from the arms of their mothers and brutally cast them to the ground, raped women and cut off their breasts, and buried alive both Soviet prisoners and wounded Nazi soldiers. Lesser authors followed his example and reported various, vicious atrocities. Joseph Goebbels was so outraged that he went on German radio, which could now be heard deep within Soviet territory by those who did not comply with the Soviet government order to hand over their radio receivers to Communist Party functionaries. In an attempt to refute the story, he denied the atrocities and accused Tolstoi of having a dark imagination worthy of the devil himself. Tolstoi in turn responded by publishing a series of testimonies naming specific witnesses and locations and calling for an international investigation.

Simultaneously, Soviet newspapers started to publish highly curious articles about Nazi policies to increase the German birth rate.[9] They portrayed Hitler's leadership as so concerned about German casualties and so single-mindedly focused on maintaining racial purity that they were turning to desperate measures to replenish the population. Women of childbearing age, whether married or not, were to be registered and assigned to government-run local "breeding centers." Soviet publicists had a field day railing against the fascist destruction of the family. Indignant Soviet women condemned policies that allegedly turned German women into machines for the production of soldiers and lamented that their German sisters were being subjected to involuntary insemination by full-blooded Aryan storm troopers from the S.S.

Two months into the war, Soviet propaganda officials produced a detailed assessment of casualties for dissemination to the population.[10] It continued Stalin's strategy of both acknowledging a few setbacks and trumpeting several successes. The Red Army had successfully thwarted Hitler's plan to destroy it within the first six weeks of combat. Admitting that German bombers were now reaching Moscow, it assured citizens that the city's defenses were nonetheless becoming stronger every day. The territories that had been lost were not of decisive significance, and important reserves were just starting to enter the struggle. Most importantly the Red Army's forces were constantly increasing, while Hitler's forces were rapidly diminishing. To illustrate this, statistics of Soviet and German losses were announced for the first time. Soviet officials claimed that two million Germans had been killed, wounded, or taken prisoner. The invaders had lost 8,000 tanks, 10,000 artillery pieces, and 7,000 planes. The Red Army lost 150,000 men to death, 440,000 had been wounded, and 110,000 had gone missing. Soviet forces had lost 5,500 tanks, 7,500 artillery pieces, and 4,500 planes.

From his extensive reading about the First World War Sholokhov could sense that something was seriously wrong with these numbers. They were too good to be true. The number of missing Soviet soldiers was many times fewer than one could have predicted based on the kinds of retreats and large-scale infantry, tank, and artillery battles that were being mentioned in the press. The total number of Red Army deaths was utterly unbelievable. There was no conceivable way that multiple German soldiers were consistently being killed for every single Soviet soldier who died in battle. Very few campaigns during the first German war resulted in remotely similar ratios. The battles with such skewed numbers reflected a completely different reality. If these numbers were true, then Soviet soldiers should be advancing deep into German territory rather than retreating towards their own capital.

After two months of waiting, Sholokhov's summons to the front finally arrived in August 1941. It came at a moment when it appeared as if the Red Army might stop the German advance and launch a significant counteroffensive to the west of Moscow. He received an assignment to travel as a war correspondent to territories that had recently been liberated from German occupation. This would provide an opportunity to see the war up close.

In preparation for his first assignment as a war correspondent, Sholokhov came face-to-face with elaborate military censorship rules.[11] Geographic locations where fighting was taking place could never be mentioned. Neither numbers of units nor names of regiments could be revealed. Instructions mandated that all battles took place at N location and involved N military subdivision, which was commanded by an officer invariably named N. Even stories not directly related to battle had to be censored so that no valuable information about transportation, infrastructure, supply, substitute materials used in production, morale, or shortages could be revealed to the enemy. The rules were so draconian that war journalists joked that even the author of Russia's medieval epic "The Song of Igor's Host" could be arrested for revealing to the enemy both the name of a commander and the fact that he led an army rather than a corps or a division.

He met his old rival Fadeev in Moscow, and they journeyed together to the front. Fadeev was responsible for helping writers who had fled from the western areas of the Soviet Union.[12] Many had ended up in provincial Russian towns, where they had to sleep on floors or share single rooms with their whole families. Local officials had done very little to welcome them or put their intellectual talents to use for the war effort. From such accounts, Sholokhov understood how important it was always to be prepared for the possibility of sudden evacuation.

Traveling by train and jeep to battle lines only 150 miles west of Moscow, Sholokhov realized that the Germans had advanced much farther than he had ever imagined. He entered a world profoundly structured by war. The train lines were operating around the clock to move important productive resources—jokingly referred to as the "Great Migration of Factories"—away from the front and to deliver reserves and military supplies to the front. Each railroad station was the site of daily logistical miracles. A complex ballet of prioritization determined whether a train moved or sat on a side spur for days, depending upon the perceived urgency of its cargo. On the roads military police with colored flags regulated the flow of traffic, forcing thousands of refugees with carts, cattle, and children to wait by the side of the road while military vehicles passed. Every few miles, a checkpoint ensured that only those with special credentials inched onward.

As Sholokhov got closer to the front he saw devastated villages, unharvested crops, and fields littered with corpses.[13] In places dust kicked up by tanks covered nearly everything in sight. Mangled machinery dotted the landscape for as far as the eye could see. He was taken to meet with commanders in that area. They impressed him with their ability to put a brave face on a very difficult situation, and he penned an article about General Konev, who led the offensive.

In candid conversations with drivers and ordinary soldiers he was able to learn new details of both the military collapse in the early weeks of the war and the recent offensive.[14] Members of the Nineteenth Army had started the war in central Ukraine but were quickly withdrawn to near Kiev. From there they were hastily transported by rail to western Belarus', which became an unexpected defense line when the Soviet frontier forces were overwhelmed by the German blitzkrieg. They faced continuous air assaults from German planes, which dominated the skies after the Soviet air force was quickly decimated. During the early hours of the war, Nazi air raids destroyed large numbers of Soviet planes before they could even get off the ground. By early July the Nineteenth Army arrived at its destination, the city of Vitebsk. Parts of the city were in flames and fiercely defended by citizen volunteers and remnants of units that had chaotically retreated from border areas. Uncoordinated actions by the Soviet command enabled the Germans to pick off the Soviet regiments one by one and take the town. In helping to stabilize the situation at the front, roughly one in five of the Nineteenth Army's men died. Twice as many were believed to have been either captured or wounded. The survivors were augmented by additions from other decimated divisions. It was widely rumored that 100,000 Red Army soldiers were killed in that general area and that hundreds of thousands had been taken prisoner. They told of the brutal recent offensive that had pushed the Germans back as far as twelve kilometers in a heavily defended sector and had enabled the city of El'na to be liberated. Concentrated howitzer and artillery fire, combined with coordinated Soviet air strikes on German positions and the dumping of white phosphorous and self-igniting bombs on motorized columns, had helped clear the way. Fighting was so fierce that on some days thousands of men died in order to advance only five hundred meters. Some believed that the purpose of the offensive was to improve morale in the rear and to create the appearance of a turning tide. Others mustered arguments about controlling strategic points and transport junctions, probing enemy defenses, and testing tactics for future offensives.

Sholokhov's visit to the front provided revelations of a different sort. He toured the recently liberated city of El'na, which had been under occupation for over a month. He interviewed dozens of residents, but no article about atrocities would result from his fact-finding visit.[15] He could not find anyone who could confirm the kinds of sadistic atrocities that Tolstoi had decried only weeks earlier. Local women had not been forced en masse into brothels. No tanks were used to grind up vulnerable victims. He could not securely document a single act of wanton, vicious torture and barbarous dismemberment of noncombatants. If systematic atrocities were not taking place, the Soviet Union's international credibility was being needlessly being put at risk by Tolstoi and his ilk.

At the front he asked a commander for authorization to talk to a group of German POWs. They too would not confirm the reports. He continued asking them questions in order to discern their fighting spirit and level of dedication to the fascist cause. Since he had an interpreter, he also decided to take a different tack and find out what they thought about their wives at home being subjected to SS studs. His inquiries about the Soviet press accounts were met with grins and laughter rather than outrage or indignation. This intrigued him. Most of the prisoners guarded their silence. One, a former Social Democrat, was willing to talk.[16] He explained that a Soviet journalist must have gotten hold of a comical prank letter that was circulating among German soldiers at the front. It had many of the same elements as the Soviet stories, such as district "breeding points" and housewives whose husbands were at the front. The Soviet press had taken the Nazi equivalent of an April fools' hoax at face value. Using it in propaganda could only discredit the Soviet war effort.

When he filed his first story from the front, which was about German captives, he omitted any mention of sexual politics. Instead, he emphasized that German soldiers were starting to understand that it was futile to wage war with the USSR.[17] This reinforced the official view that the Red Army's fierce resistance would bring about the inevitable collapse of the German army.

Bad news awaited him when he returned to headquarters. His story about Konev was in limbo. An editor revealed that Stalin had personally called him and barked, "Enough publishing about Konev already!"[18] The problem was not so much Sholokhov's text as its subject matter. A series of publications about the general had exaggerated the scale of the counteroffensive and given him too much credit. The risk to Moscow was still too great to give the impression of a turning tide.

While returning to Moscow, Sholokhov spent some time chatting with a group of writers from Rostov who were heading to the front. He had known some of them since the 1920s. A few days later they all went missing and were never heard from again.[19] This helped Sholokhov understand his special status. An invisible hand kept him a step away from the most savage fighting on the front lines, but he still beheld devastation up close.

When he returned to Moscow, he visited Matilda Kudasheva to find out if there was any news from Vas'ka. By October 1941 Vas'ka had sent several letters with increasingly urgent appeals. He pleaded for Sholokhov to have him summoned from the front to Moscow for a few days. Sholokhov wrote back to him, expressing his confidence that "fate will bring us together again" and sharing his hopes for "a meeting in the near future."[20] Since much of Moscow was contemplating evacuation and rumors insisted that Kiev had fallen, this was merely a wish under existing circumstances.

Sholokhov also dropped by the Central Committee in hopes of arranging a meeting with Stalin. The note he wrote to request a meeting was unspecific.[21] Stalin was too preoccupied with the impending defense of Moscow to entertain visitors. There could be no meeting. Sholokhov was forced to address his concerns about the dubious atrocity stories to a high-ranking official in the Soviet information service.[22] His other concerns—problems with the quantity and quality of hand-held mortars and other weapons issued to Soviet front-line infantry and Vasilii Kudashev's temporary leave pass—would have to wait for another occasion.

On the long train ride from Moscow, he mulled over how to present the shocking situation at the front to the people back home. Could he actually reveal that Soviet troops were being sent into battle with very little training and poorly functioning weapons? Could he talk publicly about strategic mistakes? He decided to emphasize that in the first months of the war the Red Army had learned lessons from the enemy that would be of value in future battles but that many more lessons still needed to be learned.[23] After his arrival, a public gathering was organized at the local theater. Two kerosene lamps illuminated a small part of the stage as Sholokhov provided a candid appraisal of the strategic situation to a packed audience partially shrouded in darkness. The long, somber faces of those in the front rows indicated they were hoping for a very different message.

When an audience member urgently inquired about whether Leningrad would be surrendered, Sholokhov was gripped by a moral conflict. The appropriate answer had already been repeated countless times in Soviet propaganda: "The Fascists will never, ever set foot in Leningrad." The second-best option was to declare, as so many others before him had, that the cradle of the revolution was being turned into an impregnable fortress by masses of citizen volunteers and that yesterday's hairdressers and bookkeepers were fighting as today's patriotic snipers and antiaircraft gun operators. He could neither state his true opinion of how dire the situation was, nor provide false reassurances. Evasion offered the only way out. "I have not been authorized to provide answers to such questions," he declared. Realizing that this answer smacked of defeatism, which was increasingly becoming a focus of secret police investigations, he quickly added, "I can only state that everything possible will be done to make a decisive stand and prevail in the defense of Leningrad."

For days, he fretted about his remarks. He second-guessed much of what he said during the meeting. Who knew how the audience might have misunderstood him? Had the secret police informers in the room already reported to their superiors? His acquaintances tried to reassure him. Days of uncertainty were dispelled in an instant by a phone call from Moscow. The front in eastern Ukraine was collapsing. It was no longer safe to remain in the Don region. It was time for him to evacuate his family.

EIGHTEEN

Sholokhov had planned ahead. His two private cars were already fueled and ready to go in the event of evacuation.[1] He managed to secure a truck and the necessary papers for crossing military checkpoints. He would guide his wife, children, and a number of female relatives to a safe location, while his male relatives would stay behind to guard their houses and wage partisan warfare if necessary. A small caravan of vehicles took off in the direction of the Volga River. Their destination was Nikolaevsk, a provincial town two hundred miles east of Vioshki and one hundred miles north of Stalingrad on the other side of the Volga. It would be vulnerable only in the event of the absolutely unthinkable—the fall of Stalin's city. The only amenity it offered was safety. It was a small town with little industry, and it was far enough from railroad lines to be of little interest to German bombers.

In Nikolaevsk Sholokhov and his entourage were accommodated for a few days in temporary quarters while local officials scrambled to find him a house.[2] They allocated a four-room apartment to him and his extended family of around twenty people. It was located on the second floor of a government building, with a shared toilet in the courtyard. The children were enrolled in school. A telephone line was soon installed. He made arrangements to set up an office in a different building around the corner from where his family was housed.

Something resembling normalcy set in. It was a highly apprehensive kind of normalcy. Moscow was in grave danger. The reports indicated that the entire city was preparing for a decisive stand. At first it seemed as if the Germans might encircle the city, but gradually the defenses stabilized. New and better tanks helped stall the German advance around eighteen miles from the Kremlin. Cold weather neutralized Hitler's advantages in the air, and fresh Red Army reserves helped turn the tide. Counteroffensives began to push them back in early 1942.

After the situation in the capital stabilized, Sholokhov's contacts started to reach out to him. They shared devastating news.[3] Vas'ka Kudashev's unit was among several that had been encircled by the Germans in fall 1941. Even highly informed officers could report very little about the fate of the unit, other than the ominous term *reconstituted*. This meant that it was so depleted that it continued to exist only on paper.

For months this news pained him. The more he found out, the more he was haunted by thoughts of his own inaction. It turned out that Vas'ka's unit was trapped very near El'na, the liberated trophy city Sholokhov had visited. The thought that his friend was stationed only a few miles away when he toured the front weighed on him. Doubts about the military value of the fall offensive lingered. What if it was all a deadly publicity stunt which he had willingly participated in? Sometimes when he closed his eyes, he could picture Vas'ka with his poor vision, blindly wandering straight into captivity, or far worse. This trauma made it very hard for him to embrace the heroic vision of the war. He didn't write anything substantial for months. In spite of calls from editors, he missed important deadlines.[4]

Nonetheless, he continued making brief trips to the front and renewed his visits to Moscow. On one of those trips he procured the transcript of an interrogation conducted by Soviet military intelligence. A Soviet officer named Iakov Zinovievich Ferdman had been captured by the Germans and managed to escape from captivity. He told in stunning detail of his experiences as a prisoner of war and the appalling conditions of Soviet prisoners.[5] Such information was of great interest to Sholokhov after he learned that Vas'ka Kudashev was now officially listed as missing in action. Often this designation signified capture by the enemy. He desired to draw attention to the plight of captive soldiers.

Though dozens of brief personal accounts of captivity had been published by journalists in previous months, Sholokhov crafted a story that would add new dimensions. He would allude to the Holocaust by describing how Germans singled out and shot anyone they considered to be Jewish. He would highlight how Soviet populations living under German occupation displayed solidarity with Red Army captives. He would turn trauma into a powerful impetus for vengeance.

A speech by Stalin gave him political cover to turn a rehabilitated prisoner into a literary hero.[6] On May 1, 1942, Stalin published an article to mark two years since the start of fighting in Europe. He claimed that Hitler's army had been significantly weakened and that the Red Army had achieved a substantial breakthrough. The liberation of Soviet lands had commenced. In Stalin's view, one of the major factors that accounted for recent successes was a breakthrough in the mind-set of ordinary Soviet soldiers. He wrote:

> Feelings of benign disposition and nonchalance towards the enemy, which were not uncommon among the fighting men during the first months of the Patriotic war, have disappeared. The atrocities, plundering, and violence committed by the German-fascist occupiers against civilian populations and Soviet POWs have healed our fighting men of this infirmity. The fighting men have become angrier and more merciless. They learned for real how to hate the German-fascist occupiers. They have understood that it is not possible to defeat the enemy without having learned how to hate him with all the forces of the soul.[7]

This statement provided a template for Sholokhov. Virtually every sentiment emphasized by Stalin made its way into his story. Sholokhov's hero even echoed Stalin's words by proclaiming, "We have learned for real how to fight, how to hate, and how to love . . . we always carry hate on the tip of our bayonets."

In order to write the story, Sholokhov had to acknowledge German atrocities. Through the eyes of his hero he would portray the war as a war of extermination from the very beginning. Germans would be seen as sadists and merciless tormentors. His early sense that the Soviets needed to learn from the Germans came full circle. They had learned how to hate.[8]

The story begins with a landscape ravaged by war, pervaded by the smell of pine trees and decomposing corpses. The narrator introduces a mysterious Russian lieutenant Gerasimov, who is a master killer with the bayonet and the butt of a rifle. Over the course of two encounters Gerasimov tells his life story. A man who once admired German technology, read books by German authors, and could even imagine ordinary Germans as comrades could no longer stand the sight of living Germans. He came to hate them with every fiber of his being. Arriving at the front in Ukraine from Siberia, he was transformed by the sight of mutilated bodies and ravaged communities. The image that stood out the most in his mind was the corpse of an eleven-year-old girl who was raped by Nazi soldiers and killed on her way to school. She was still clutching her school bag. Gerasimov's unit fought to defend the local population. Nonetheless it had to retreat and was encircled. He was wounded and lost consciousness. Though he was subjected to horrors, degradation, and dehumanization in captivity, his spirit could not be broken. Soviet civilians behind enemy lines helped keep him and others alive by leaving bread and boiled potatoes by the side of the roads on which prisoners were marched into captivity. He killed a guard with a shovel and escaped while on a work detail and returned to the Red Army. He transformed his trauma into a single-minded dedication to exterminating Germans. By 1942 he had by his own count killed nearly a hundred. Like the cracked trunk of an oak tree hit by a shell earlier in the story, this half-dead hulk of a man showed signs of new life. When his narrative of Russian resilience was published to great acclaim, Sholokhov's career revived as well.

In late June 1942 Sholokhov was invited to a dinner at Stalin's apartment in the Kremlin.[9] Several high-ranking officials were gathered there. After a wide-ranging discussion of the war and some particularly critical remarks about Russian generals, the conversation turned to literature. On that evening Stalin was especially disparaging about Fadeev, whom he called a "nonentity as a writer and debauched person." After their joint visit to the front the previous summer, Fadeev had disappeared from view for several days, and reports had reached the Kremlin that he had descended into a state of drunkenness. The Boss didn't miss the opportunity to use this example to chide Sholokhov about his own weakness.

"By the way, I've received reports that you've started to drink more," Stalin said to Sholokhov.

"More than whom?" Sholokhov jokingly inquired.

In response Stalin diverted the conversation. "You know it's the responsibility of the party to look out for good writers like yourself. Our Kremlin doctors insist that you would benefit from some time off to restore your health. Why don't you visit a sanatorium. I can recommend an excellent one in Georgia."

"That's out of the question," Sholokhov declared. "What would I do? You know how many good wines they have there, but my doctors refuse to let me drink. A person would hardly be able to withstand such an ordeal," he joked.

"Nonetheless, we'll arrange for you to have some time off from your duties as a correspondent."

The conversation then turned to other matters. Towards the end of the evening, as the guests began to disperse, Stalin motioned for Sholokhov to remain.

Stalin praised Sholokhov's latest story.

"Literature needs dedicated laborers. It is essential to our war effort. I hope you will take full advantage of your time off and think about that."

As Sholokhov was voicing his general agreement, Stalin inquired, "How many years after the conclusion of the first war was Remarque's novel *All Quiet on the Western Front* published?"

"I believe it appeared in Russian translation in 1929, so he must have finished it a little before that," Sholokhov replied.

"That's too long," Stalin pronounced. He started to fidget with his pipe. After a pause, he continued. "Ten years is much too late. This war needs to be written about now, don't you agree?"

Sholokhov was starting to understand the purpose of his invitation that evening. Stalin's remark about Remarque's book was not accidental. The book had appeared around the same time as *Quiet Don*. Sholokhov realized that Stalin was cunningly directing the conversation.

He did his best to avoid being backed into a corner. Neither agreeing nor disagreeing, he declared, "Tolstoy only started working on *War and Peace* decades after Napoleon was routed . . ."

"Remarque is no Tolstoy. He was clearly not as talented, but he responded to the events much quicker," Stalin declared and began to pound the tobacco that he had placed into his pipe. "*War and Peace* appeared far too long after the events. You should really give some thought to writing a novel about this war. You should consider the events of this war, which is a sacred war for the fatherland for our times as well. I'm sure you will be able to do it."

Once again Sholokhov tried to lower Stalin's expectations. "Under conditions as they are at the moment, it would be extremely difficult."

"Just give it a try."

Before he even realized it, Sholokhov replied, "I will."

Hearing those words, Stalin commanded Malenkov to facilitate Sholokhov's time off and then signaled that it was time to adjourn.[10] Malenkov inquired about Sholokhov's plans for the coming months. The writer indicated his desire to return home to Vioshki. Malenkov promised that his assistants would be in touch and would help to arrange whatever the writer needed.

Based on his conversations in Moscow, Sholokhov believed that the front had stabilized and that the German advance had been stopped. He returned to Nikolaevsk to prepare his family for the long-awaited return home. The seriousness of what had transpired in Moscow was soon confirmed when an official stepped out of a sleek sedan.[11] As he approached closer, Sholokhov identified him as a major from the NKVD insignia on his uniform. A few steps behind him, a subordinate was carrying a very large package. "Comrade Sholokhov! This is for you," the major said.

The writer puzzled over this special delivery. What was so important that it needed to be personally placed in his hands during wartime? As Sholokhov opened it, he found a note inside.[12] It was in Poskrebyshev's hand. It read: "Comrade Stalin asked me to ensure that your family receives this package." It contained canned goods, a bottle of wine, and two items which were in very short supply: cheeses and sausages. The writer's family enjoyed some of these delicacies and stored the rest of the treats for a future occasion.

Returning to Vioshki, Sholokhov and his family were relieved to be reunited with friends, classmates, and comrades. Their joy was short-lived, however. Military vehicles started appearing in increasing numbers.[13] A steady stream of traffic crossed the pontoon bridge near the settlement. The radio continued to insist that the situation at the front was stable, but the appearance of more and more military vehicles, including tanks, became worrisome. There could be no other explanation than retreat.

This time Sholokhov decided not to take any chances. He decided to pack up his archive. He consulted with Lugovoi, and they agreed that it would be best to hand it over for safekeeping to the local NKVD.[14] Other household goods would be buried in the vicinity of the family home.

An officer approached and urged Sholokhov to leave. The Soviet defense lines were faltering, and the Germans would soon be advancing towards Vioshki on their way to Stalingrad. As Sholokhov was packing his literary archive, he heard a faint hum. As it become louder, he recognized a terrifyingly familiar sound from the front. The rounded hum was made by German plane engines grouped in an attack formation.[15] There were only seconds to spare before those planes would dive low to either drop bombs or strafe the ground with powerful guns. He screamed to his wife and children to run to the root cellar. Since he was too far from the house, he and Lugovoi ducked down in the yard. The humming came closer and closer. Four planes were approaching, and the humming was reaching a siren-like crescendo. They dipped down to a height of only two hundred yards above his home. Loud screeching sounds preceded a series of explosions about fifty yards away. As the hum receded, he jumped up and started to check on the household. The bombers had not taken out the bridge to deny Soviet forces their only exit route. They would no doubt be back again.

He gathered his wife and children in the car and looked around to find his mother.[16] She was in the barnyard. She stubbornly refused to get in the car, claiming she would stay to look after the cow. Since there was no time to lose, he didn't argue. He drove the car into the steppe as far away from the bridge and other critical infrastructure as possible. After a short time a messenger arrived. By his looks he came bearing bad news. The writer's mother was dead. She was torn apart by shrapnel during a second bombing raid. Sholokhov returned to oversee the burial of her remains in the family garden. To his horror, he learned a few days later that the grave was soon disturbed by marauders searching for valuables.

On July 15, 1942, he wrote from Nikolaevsk to Malenkov to complain that his "time off turned out poorly."[17] He described how the Germans conducted two days of bombing and strafing raids of Vioshki without meeting resistance. The raid had directly targeted his house. "I had a very heavy heart as I was laying there in the damned grass, weaponless, and powerless to wage any sort of defense against such impudent enemies, who were able to do whatever they pleased." For unknown reasons the division stationed near Vioshki didn't do anything during the attack. "Dear Comrade Malenkov I have just one request. I don't need provisions, I'll manage as things are, so please send an automatic machine gun. This thing is more necessary at the moment than all the vitamins which I brought back from Moscow."

Reporting the death of his mother, he could not conceal his grief. At the same time, he communicated how happy she had been to hear about his last meeting with Stalin. She insisted that he write to Stalin and Malenkov to thank them on her behalf for the time off. He now claimed to be fulfilling her wishes posthumously. This was a calculated effort to play upon Stalin's belief in the esteem in which simple people such as his barely literate mother held him.

After sending the letter he learned of subsequent air raids.[18] Bombs had destroyed parts of the upper floors of his house. Shelling had pierced the walls and windows. His library had not been immediately evacuated as promised, and only after the fact were the books gathered and shipped to somewhere near Stalingrad. In subsequent raids much of the settlement was destroyed. The pontoon bridge across the Don was taken out, dooming hundreds of Red Army vehicles waiting to cross the river. A bomb dropped on a gasoline tanker truck ignited an inferno that caused ammunition stores to explode. Hundreds were burned beyond recognition. The remaining civilians were evacuated from the town. The Germans occupied the right bank of the Don River. Vioshki was now on the front line. Petr Lugovoi was now the commander of a group of partisans.

Sholokhov once again took to the road and headed off with his family into the unknown. In Nikolaevsk he found out that his former apartment had already been reassigned. The collapsing front created great uncertainty about areas near Stalingrad, so he consulted with regional officials about a more distant destination. He decided to travel on to an area beyond the point where gravel roads ended. He would drive across the open steppe into western Kazakhstan.

NINETEEN

I t seemed as if Sholokhov mysteriously vanished after publishing *Science of Hatred*. He rarely appeared at the front. He filed no stories as a war correspondent. Though Stalin proclaimed a great victory at Stalingrad in early 1943, there was no celebratory article by Sholokhov. His name was one of the few missing from the honor roll of writers who lauded the epic battle. Only a handful of high-ranking officials knew that Sholokhov had been granted a creative leave to produce a war novel. While other war correspondents struggled to obtain permission to take only a few weeks off, in effect he was granted unrestricted creative leave. This came, however, with smothering restrictions.

Eager to write about the crucial battles that were unfolding at Stalingrad, Sholokhov arrived in the area in early October 1942.[1] For over a month the Germans had been trying to take the city. While important tank battles were raging on the outskirts and in pockets throughout the city, in the center there were savage fights to control key streets and buildings. Soviet propaganda was already creating a heroic narrative.[2]

The defenders of Stalingrad comprehended that there could be no more retreats. They swore to never take even a single step backwards. They resolved to fight to the last man, to the last drop of blood. Every building would become a fortress that would have to be stormed by the Nazis at an exceptionally high price. Every day amid bombed-out buildings and smoldering ruins new Soviet heroes were emerging to take the place of those who had fallen the previous day.

The situation in the center of the city was so dire and so dangerous that military officials could not risk permitting Sholokhov to travel there. His blood was too precious for the cause. He chafed at the official obligations that kept him far from the fighting. He was stuck handing out medals while others were right there in the middle of the war, witnessing it and writing it. While a decisive and "titanic" battle was raging all around him, he had to be content with watching distant actions through the lenses of binoculars. This sense of detachment frustrated him.

It did not help that he arrived in Stalingrad at the worst possible time.[3] During his visit the situation was extremely dire. Soviet reserves had not arrived yet, and the Germans were widely believed to have every advantage in machinery and manpower. There were fears that traffic across the Volga might soon cease due to constant attacks from German planes and artillery. Ammunition needed to be ferried across the river on small boats, which were constantly bombed from the air. The lucky units had only lost half their men. From across the river, Stalingrad looked like a bleak wasteland. It was shrouded in a heavy layer of gray and brown ash, which blanketed the city after oil cisterns were set ablaze. Dozens of fires smoldered in residential areas. In the foreground he could see dozens of forlorn chimneys of flattened houses and lone smokestacks of factories that no longer existed. In the distance, showplaces of Stalinist architecture had been reduced to crumbling ruins.

The crews of the river flotilla, which were responsible for ferrying supplies to the defenders of the city, told of tragedies unfolding on the other side of the Volga.[4] In mid-September 1942 a battalion of almost eight hundred battle-tested men was ferried across at night with orders to take and hold the building of the Stalingrad central railroad station. They successfully made it into the heart of the city and after several hours reported back that they had taken the station. Then they were given orders to advance from the station towards adjacent buildings. Moving out into the open several times, they were mowed down by machine gun fire from their flanks. Only a few made it back alive to the other side.[5] As Sholokhov parsed these events in his mind, he couldn't stop thinking about the fate of those men who were slaughtered for the symbolism of saying that Stalingrad had not actually fallen. He left in a pensive mood a few days later.

He appears to have returned to his usual behavior in times of crisis—heavy drinking.[6] The situation with his health became so worrisome that the Central Committee ordered him to come to Moscow for hospitalization. He spent over a month in the Kremlin hospital in late 1942. He revealed to no one why he was there or how he was treated. He jokingly called it "a mid-level overhaul."

By late January 1943 he was fit enough to start writing again. His mood was greatly lifted by the daily war briefings.[7] Names of settlements all around Vioshki started to appear among lists of places liberated by Soviet forces as they advanced westward from Stalingrad. By late January Millerovo and its important railroad junction was firmly in Soviet hands. Though there were still pockets of German resistance in the area, all the reports suggested they were weakening by the day. Long lists of trophies enumerated the number of tanks, planes, guns, cars, motorcycles, and even horses that Soviet forces captured each day.

After the liberation of the Don region, Sholokhov longed to hear news of his literary archive.[8] The fate of the priceless manuscripts of his literary works was not his biggest concern, however. If his other papers got dispersed, he could even be in danger. He had retained copies of his letters to Stalin about the famine and the terror, along with Stalin's responses. If those fell into enemy hands, they would prove to be an enormous bonanza for anti-Soviet propaganda. Though there was no specific intelligence that the Germans had obtained the archives before their retreat, the fact that the papers had gone missing was highly alarming. Upon contacting the second-highest-ranking officer in the Soviet secret police, he received a response that was not consoling. Six months after the disappearance of his archive, no traces of it had yet been located.

As the first anniversary of his rash promise to Stalin approached, he came under intense pressure to provide some kind of proof that he had commenced working on a new novel. In May 1943 he handed over several middle chapters of a novel entitled *They Fought for their Motherland*. They were quickly slated for publication.[9] The censors deleted only a few phrases in which Soviet soldiers teased one another as "allies."

The new chapters were ostensibly set somewhere near the Don region during the retreat towards Stalingrad in 1942. Amusing banter between soldiers and comical hijinks substituted for action and suspense. The biographies and backstories of these soldiers who were brought together by war were not entirely clear. There was a surprising lack of specificity to the military context. Tobacco was talked about more often than either tanks or trenches. Ideology lingered somewhere in the background. Death somehow seemed distant as well. Stalin was not mentioned.

The reaction from fellow writers was lukewarm at best. They could discern that Sholokhov had avoided painting himself into any corners. He had signaled that his characters were heading for Stalingrad, but he left himself considerable room for developing the otherwise absent plot. The response from ordinary soldiers was enthusiastic.[10] They were constantly surrounded by casualties, explosions, and political exhortations. They craved diversion and light entertainment. The lack of specificity helped them recognize kindred souls in Sholokhov's characters.

Sholokhov's move was a calculated effort to stall for time. He knew that several other writers had a far better command of the military situation at the front. In particular, Vasilii Grossman had excelled in writing vivid, sometimes lyrical descriptions of the Soviet front lines. After reading one of Grossman's articles, Sholokhov half-jokingly proclaimed to an acquaintance, "Very well written. I would get great satisfaction from signing my name [to that article]."[11] His joke concealed a deep-seated fear. The war was slipping away from him. Others were living it and capturing it while he was rarely more than a celebrity visitor to the front. He consoled himself with thoughts that returning home would jump-start his work. He believed he would once again draw inspiration from the people and landscapes of the Don region.

By the time he handed over the chapters for publication, it was clear to him that the momentum of the war had decisively shifted. Weeks earlier Soviet authorities permitted a detailed map of the front lines to be published.[12] Shaded sections on the map highlighted the 480,000 square kilometers of territory that had been liberated in recent months. References to specific railroad lines that had been recovered or repaired provided an even more glaring sign of Stalin's confidence. The new buzzword was *advance*.

In early summer 1943, while Sholokhov was in Moscow on publishing business, he received an urgent summons to come to the building of the Soviet organization in charge of cultural ties with foreign countries. He initially declined. After several insistent follow-up calls, he finally relented.[13] An American delegation had delivered a major shipment of medicines for the Soviet war effort.[14] He was expected to take part in a reception for the delegation. He reluctantly went, though in hindsight it probably would have been better not to attend.

He must have been in a bad mood that day, and alcohol was clearly involved. He lamented that no American writers of reputation had been sent on such an important mission and wondered whether it was a waste of his time to be there, since he did not see any Steinbecks or Hemingways in attendance. At the reception he provoked a loud, public argument with another Soviet writer, Ilya Erenburg. Sholokhov chided his colleague for focusing attention on Jewish casualties in one of his descriptions of the western front.[15] The latter proudly and publicly refused to be seated at the same table as Sholokhov. Sholokhov abruptly downed a glass of vodka and hastily departed. One of the bureaucrats pursued him in an attempt to convince him to return, but he waved him off dismissively. He returned to his hotel.

The next morning there was a knock at the door. Two NKVD officers were waiting outside. "Comrade, come with us!" they ordered. They accompanied him to a waiting car. It drove straight to the Kremlin and stopped in front of the corner office. He was taken upstairs to Stalin's waiting room.[16] Poskrebyshev greeted him with silence. After several minutes Poskrybeshev finally whispered, "You won't be able to weasel your way out of this one." As he opened the door Sholokhov noticed that

Stalin was standing with his back to him. The Boss continued to gaze out the window. After a painful period of silence, Stalin turned around and approached him. For the first time, he did not extend his hand to the writer. Looking directly into the writer's eyes, Stalin coldly inquired, "Where is your family, Comrade Sholokhov?" As Sholokhov started to explain, fear engulfed him. Was this a friendly inquiry or a dire warning?

After upbraiding the writer for his excessive drinking, Stalin adopted a softer tone and inquired about Sholkhov's progress on the war epic. Sholokhov must have emphasized how it would be devoted to "our people and the sources of their heroism," claiming that he was hard at work writing a novel that was worthy of the "historical significance of the struggle." When Stalin had enough, he concluded, "Well, Comrade Sholokhov, take care of yourself. The party needs you. The people need you as well." Sholokhov later recalled this encounter as an act of devilish toying by Stalin. The dictator's carefully orchestrated power play combined both concern and cunning. As if to say . . . *Don't forget.*

Hours later Sholokhov received word that he was once again expected at the scene of his earlier indiscretion. He was told to give an interview expressing gratitude to the Americans for their assistance. This was clearly his chance to make up for the previous evening. He complied.[17] He mentioned that he was writing a new novel about the heroic struggle of the Soviet people. In emphasizing how the war had caused misfortune to every Soviet citizen, he nearly broke down while recounting the death of his own mother. Although he expressed gratitude for all the Fords, aviators, and medical supplies that Americans were sending, he repeatedly criticized the Americans for not opening up a second front. He even proclaimed that true military friendship can never be based on one person fighting alone in battle while his friend throws him more ammunition and applauds, saying, "Bravo, you're fighting so well."

He was instructed to follow up the meeting by writing an open letter to Americans in which he described his personal experiences of the war and thanked them for their assistance. He also received advice that the tone of the letter needed to be less accusatory. It needed to emphasize the unprecedented cruelty of the common enemy while expressing amicable hopes for a second front. He complied. The letter he wrote struck a more appropriate tone by praising the multiple ways in which the United States was supporting the Soviet war effort. The letter was not published. Stalin had subjected him to obedience training.

In fall 1943 he decided to relocate his family from western Kazakhstan to a city on the Volga. He did not want to be perceived as waiting too long to return, and he could reasonably expect that accommodation would now be available. By late 1943 they were established in Kamyshin.[18] Sholokhov had hoped to survey the situation in Vioshki in early March 1944, but an early spring thaw forced him to turn back. The trip enabled him to claim that he had visited key areas where the defense of Stalingrad unfolded.

In early 1944 Sholokhov also traveled to Moscow on a delicate mission. While taking part in a session of the Supreme Soviet, he resolved to secure additional resources for rebuilding and reviving the areas around Vioshki.[19] In those months the government was spending 16 billion rubles on rebuilding nine regions that had been liberated thus far from the Germans. Sholokhov's goal was to tap into those funds. Materials to repair half a million homes were being distributed. Over two million head of cattle and 500,000 chickens were being transported from other areas to revive agriculture. More than 12,000 tractors were being allocated to collective farms. Whole forests were being cleared so that one million cubic meters of wood could be sent to construct barns, fences, and pens. Every district had a long wish list of items it needed—everything from medical equipment to lubricants for engines—to get its economy going again. Only one district had Sholokhov.

In a meeting in Moscow with Boris Dvinskii, the head of the regional party committee, he learned about the heroic recovery efforts in the Don region.[20] The restoration of railways, electric stations, and food processing industries was nearing completion. The regional government was trying quickly to construct cement factories in order to facilitate the rebuilding of cities and factories. Most schools and hospitals were functioning again, although their quality still left much to be desired. In rural areas the situation was still extremely dire. Though cattle, sheep, and goats had been sent in large numbers from other areas, there were few buildings to house them and a desperate shortage of winter fodder.

The local population had spent the late fall cutting grass along roads and railroads, gathering and drying the stalks and leaves of fall crops, collecting acorns and cutting edible branches from trees to use as fodder. Due to fuel shortages and military requisitions of horses, fall planting and plowing were completed through the extraordinary physical exertion of women. Local governments were facing numerous bureaucratic headaches. They had to produce detailed inventories of every single item of economic value that was destroyed or taken by the Germans. They also had to account for hundreds of thousands of head of cattle that were transferred to the region from Ukraine in 1941 and 1942. Time that could have been spent on rebuilding was spent accounting for missing items taken by the Germans, requisitioned by the Red Army, or distributed to locals during the dark days of invasion.

In Moscow Sholokhov managed to secure a meeting with Andrei Andreev, the chairman of the Supreme Soviet. Andreev was one of a handful of officials whom Stalin had placed in charge of rebuilding the country's economy. Since every important ministry responded to his phone calls, he had the unique ability to instantly cut through red tape. Sholokhov described the situation in his region and pleaded for immediate additional assistance.[21] Phone lines to Vioshki had not been restored yet, so he was only able to make a general request with the understanding that Lugovoi would be in touch with all the specifics. He met with success. He telegraphed Lugovoi to report that help had been promised.[22] In a matter of minutes Vioshki moved to the front of a priority line that was otherwise reserved for coal-producing districts and economic powerhouses.

While Sholokhov was in Moscow the first anniversary of the victory at Stalingrad was being widely commemorated. There was nothing unusual about the fact that generals wrote articles about heroic battles and lauded Stalin's "genius plan" to encircle the Germans there in the same manner that the Carthaginian general Hannibal encircled the Romans. It was more interesting to observe how propaganda officials mobilized memories of the battle for inspiring the epic task of reconstruction. Pledging to turn all of their energies towards recovery and reconstruction, 546,348 residents of Stalingrad signed a letter to Stalin crediting him with the miracle of the victory.[23] The new battle to be waged was with economic devastation.

In March 1944 Sholokhov read an article that he couldn't stop thinking about.[24] In a periodical published in Russian by the British government for its Soviet allies, he saw a small notice about Soviet POWs who had been liberated by British soldiers and were now fighting together with the allies. It revived his hopes that Vas'ka had somehow survived. Though he realized that this was a pipe dream, he nonetheless sent a copy of the article to Vas'ka's wife and shared his hopes that Vas'ka would soon return.

In May 1944, after the school year ended, he moved his family back to Vioshki. His hopes that returning to the Don region would quickly renew and reinvigorate him were soon dashed. On one of his first hunting trips after returning home he stumbled onto a sight he would never forget.[25] Years later it still tormented him in the middle of the night and sometimes appeared to him even when his eyes were open. A dark image became so deeply seared in his mind that he could never shake it. No matter how much reason and logic he applied, he could not untangle the nightmarish realities.

While hunting in a wooded area on the other side of the Don, he split off from the members of his party. After a while he noticed odd indentations in the ground. These aroused his curiosity. He resolved to follow the trail for as far as he could. As the faint traces became more defined he continued to track them. These were definitely not the footprints of a rare elk or a large deer. Rather his quarry was a German tank, and he was following the marks made by its caterpillar tracks. In the distance he saw a burned-out tank, which was beginning to rust. As he approached closer to get a look at the "caterpillar," he recoiled in horror. A sudden flash of heat gripped his body. "Oh my God!" he gasped. It was thirty centimeters long. "The horror!" he exclaimed. A grayish strand of a woman's hair was tangled up within the tracks of the tank. The puzzle of this unthinkable tragedy would continue to distress him for years. Did the woman fall in front of the tank? Or did the driver of the tank hunt her down? What kind of bastard could do such a horrible thing? Didn't he have a mother? How was a tank suddenly destroyed while grinding up a person? Try as he might, neither the memory nor the mystery could ever be expunged from his mind.

In early summer 1944 he handed over additional chapters of the war novel.[26] Almost as if by command, one of his protagonists had finally been wounded in battle. The chapter began with him suddenly regaining consciousness. He came to with a mouth full of dirt and pants wet with blood clinging to legs riddled with shrapnel wounds. In a powerful scene, he regained and lost consciousness three times as he struggled to get away from the raging battle. In between he was dragged from the battlefield by a teenage nurse and revived with vodka from an aluminum flask. The scene concluded in a field hospital, where the protagonist worried more about his boots than his wounds. Although Sholokhov had recently complained to a friend that his war muse was an old cavalry nag rather than a mechanized force to be reckoned with, he was starting to produce impressive results.

Without the intense pressure to finish before the end of the war, he might have completed a Soviet equivalent to *The Red Badge of Courage*. Instead, he fretted that nothing would content Stalin other than a heroic epic. The daily reports of Soviet forces advancing into Belarus', the Baltic Republics, and east Prussia only further stoked his creative anxieties. Of course he joyously celebrated these Soviet victories. But each one brought him closer to his own day of reckoning. An attempt to escape his anxieties for only a day nearly resulted in disaster.

Taking off with two friends and a large glass container of alcohol in a small boat, he attempted to cross a branch of the Don River in April 1945.[27] The fast-running current near some rapids caused the boat to swiftly rock and careen uncontrollably. In seconds it turned over. Sholokhov found himself being pulled under by the heavy boots he was wearing. Ice cold water encircled him. He could imagine international headlines proclaiming: "Treasured Soviet writer dies in foolish accident." No, the party would make sure that never happened. Headlines would read: "Treasured Soviet writer dies valiantly at the front." He managed to duck underwater and pull one of the boots off. This eased the drag, and he was able to keep himself afloat. In the distance he saw the top of a poplar tree rising amid the raging river. He swam for it and clung to it for dear life. In the distance he heard several shots. One of his comrades made it to a small island and was trying to draw attention to their predicament. A fisherman in a nearby boat came to his rescue. His skin was already turning blue. They took him to a nearby settlement to warm up. He would spend some of the final, decisive weeks of the war as a convalescent.

Like most Russians, his experience of the war's conclusion came while listening to a confident, assertive radio announcement on May 9, 1945.[28] In deep bass tones, the broadcaster Yurii Levitan delivered the long-awaited news. Levitan's stern, military diction emphasized the weight and gravity of each syllable he was speaking. It seemed as if he was purposefully elongating and enunciating in order for his weighty message to sink in. "Moscow speaking!" he began. "Act of Military Capitulation." He paused. "Signing of the act of capitulation . . . of German Military forces." He paused again. "We, who have signed below, acting in the name of the German Supreme Command"—short pause—"have agreed to an unconditional capitulation of all of our military forces . . ." The Sholokhov family broke out in jubilation, along with all the residents of Vioshki. There was singing, dancing, and carousing in the streets.

A few days later Sholokhov received an invitation to a grand gala and victory parade in Moscow.[29] He would witness one of the greatest military spectacles ever staged. The Soviet military commander Grigorii Zhukov rode into Red Square on a white horse, Marshal Stalin stood at attention on the mausoleum of Lenin, and thousands of soldiers, sailors, and airmen marched in massive, orderly columns. An endless succession of tanks and trucks pulling rocket launchers, antiaircraft guns, and cannons advanced with grace and perfect precision through Red Square. An exclusive gala dinner was held in the Kremlin for high-ranking officers. While other guests feasted on roasted meats, game birds, caviar, and smoked delicacies, Sholokhov seethed. That evening Stalin pronounced a toast to soldiers, to the simple, ordinary, modest "screws" who held together the great mechanisms of war and state. In celebrating these respected comrades, the dictator nonchalantly added, "No one writes anything about them." Either he hadn't bothered to read Sholokhov's recent chapters, or he now considered the writer a nobody.

TWENTY

U pon the conclusion of the war, Sholokhov came under intense pressure to deliver the novel he had promised to Stalin. He boasted to journalists in Moscow in September 1945 that he would soon travel to Stalingrad to acquire crucial information for narrating the historical battles that took place there in 1942. But instead of conducting extensive research in Stalingrad, he journeyed to the steppes of Kazakhstan to hunt.[1] Since Stalin kept tabs on the writer, such behavior risked alienation. Sooner or later the dictator's patience was bound to run out.

Why did Sholokhov lose his first battle with the war novel Stalin craved? Personal tragedy once again derailed political expediency. On a visit to Moscow soon after the end of the war he received news that shook him to the core. He found out that Vas'ka's fate had taken a dramatic turn.[2] Matilda Kudasheva had received a letter with a strange military postmark. The letter revealed that Vas'ka had not died in 1941. Captured by the Germans, he had been transported to a concentration camp in German territory, where he became acquainted with the letter's author. They had evidently made some sort of pact to memorize the other's address to send word to the other's family. The letter provided frustratingly few facts due to military censorship. Sholokhov could only imagine the hell his friend had endured. He knew from interviews with POWs during the war that starvation, disease, humiliation, and torture awaited them. Tormented by thoughts about captivity, which remained a taboo topic in the postwar era, he could not write about the war in a heroic mode.

Stalin was losing patience. Concerned about Sholokhov's lack of tangible progress on the war novel, Stalin tried to manipulate the writer's competitive spirit. In fall 1945, a leading Soviet journal published an article by an American critic who speculated about a novel that would become the *War and Peace* of World War II.[3] The article pronounced Sholokhov to be the writer who was most likely to rise to that level of greatness. Remarkably, this article was unknown in the United States. Most likely it was a special commission to spur Sholokhov into action. However, it had the opposite effect.

Sholokhov began to buckle under the pressure of great expectations. The burden of producing a second masterpiece from scratch was crippling. The stakes were too high, the task too daunting. Even if he somehow stumbled onto a cache of sources, there was no recovering the audacity of youth or retrieving the boundless ambition that once propelled him. Now everything seemed risky. To write risked exposure. To wait risked Stalin's wrath. His only remaining strategy was to obfuscate and avoid. He would promise progress on the novel, only to put it aside for unexplained reasons. He could not admit that unexpected news and personal tragedy made it painful for him to contemplate the heroic war.

Throughout 1946 Sholokhov could blame the novel's delays on the bombing of his house by the Germans. The damages it sustained and the hasty repairs in 1944 deprived him of optimal working conditions. But this excuse for his lack of results was not a lasting one.[4] Stalin decided to build the writer a new home. In October of 1945 the Central Committee approved funds for the construction of summer "cottages" for members of the Academy of Sciences, but Sholokhov did not desire a spacious holiday home near Moscow. He negotiated in early 1946 to have the funds directed towards the construction of a new house in Vioshki. This grand, two-story house with extensive balconies looked more like a 19th-century aristocratic mansion than the residence of a Soviet citizen.

At the end of the year Sholokhov received surprising news. He learned of his nomination for the Nobel Prize for Literature by a leftist Swedish poet.[5] He also found out that socialist circles were actively promoting his candidacy in the Swedish press. Believing that there was a campaign to promote his candidacy, he was eager to travel to Sweden to assess his chances.

Driven by ambition, on July 29, 1947, Sholokhov wrote a letter to Stalin that he would quickly regret sending.[6] He did not provide any details about his progress on the war novel. Instead he requested permission to travel abroad to collect foreign royalties for translations of his books. Mentioning that a prominent official had cautioned him a few months earlier against a trip to England and the United States, which were believed by Soviet leaders to be fomenting hostility against their former ally, the USSR, Sholokhov requested permission to travel with his wife to Sweden for a short period of time. He reminded Stalin that he had not been out of the country since 1935 and that several of his colleagues, including Fadeev, Simonov, and Erenburg had traveled abroad since the war. By rattling off the names of other writers, he appeared envious and pathetic.

He committed additional mistakes by attempting to deceive the dictator. He claimed to have been working diligently on *They Fought for the Motherland* for the past few years. Stalin had no doubt received reports to the contrary. Sholokhov claimed to be "on the eve of finishing the book." This was inaccurate. He insisted that he "didn't dare to request that You meet with me in person about such a trifle of an issue." Those were words of a scared lackey rather than a favored friend. The letter went unanswered.

Sholokhov's timing was terrible. He should have been more alert to political signals. In July 1947 the Central Committee had issued a confidential letter to party committees explaining that two Soviet professors had collaborated with an American spy to transfer an important discovery, a medicine for curing cancer, to the United States.[7] The two scientists "were motivated by considerations of personal glory and cheap popularity abroad." They had "embarked upon a path of direct lies and deception," and in desiring to please foreigners they had forgotten their sense of self-worth and duties as Soviet citizens. The Central Committee labeled this a widespread condition among the intelligentsia and revived the contagion rhetoric of the terror years while warning of the "dangerous disease of kowtowing to the rest of the world."

Stalin's receipt of Sholokhov's request to travel abroad coincided with the start of a wide-ranging ideological campaign against all things foreign. The writer was now on record as having recently desired to travel to the very two countries that the dictator believed were engaged in an all-encompassing struggle against the Soviet Union. Instead of simply informing Stalin that he wanted to find out more about his Nobel Prize nomination, he had resorted to deception. Perhaps his real goal was to seek the attention of foreigners. Was he no longer content with being an inaugural recipient of the Stalin Prize? By emphasizing translations of his works, was he seeking "cheap popularity abroad"? Moreover, no significant portions of the war novel had been handed over for publication in recent years.

By mentioning no more compelling motive for the trip than money, Sholokhov committed an even bigger transgression. A few months earlier, Stalin had received a petition from a group of playwrights complaining that they were being excessively taxed on their royalties.[8] The complaint alleged that their important intellectual and ideological endeavors were being taxed no differently than the labors of individual craftsmen such as watch-repairmen. Indignant that "engineers of human souls" were being mistreated by financial authorities, they appealed to Stalin. Intrigued, Stalin decided to launch an investigation. After all, Lenin had made progressive taxation of income one of the central tenets of his vision of communism. He ordered Fadeev and the head of the State Planning Agency to conduct a thorough review of compensation for intellectual labor.

The financial officials opened Stalin's eyes to the fact that the Writers' Union had not only a theater sector and prose sector but also a millionaire's sector. Tax records indicated that dozens of Soviet writers hauled in six-figure incomes in certain years, and a few even approached seven figures. On average writers were making ten times more than ordinary workers, but the highest-salaried writers were occasionally earning twenty-five times more than the lowest-paid workers in spite of the fact that Lenin was on record proposing that highly qualified specialists be paid up to four or five times more than ordinary workers. In their zeal to defend their tax policies, the bureaucrats also compiled lists of the Soviet Union's highest-earning writers. Near the top of one of those lists was Mikhail Sholokhov, who collected an Academician's salary of over 120,000 rubles plus income from royalties that in certain years exceeded six figures. In view of this information, Sholokhov's request looked even more inappropriate and self-serving. The overwhelming majority of Soviet citizens managed to get by with sixty times less than just the minimum annual income that Sholokhov was guaranteed by the Soviet state.

After weeks of uncomfortable silence from Stalin, Sholokhov must have realized the gravity of his mistakes. He made new overtures to the Kremlin. He was soon permitted to travel, but not to Sweden as he had hoped. Instead he was sent as a delegate to a socialist, anti-American peace conference in Soviet-occupied Poland in late August 1948. He was added at the last minute and sent by plane rather than train. He delivered a speech that was likely prepared by the secretaries of the Central Committee.[9]

In Poland a curious meeting with Fadeev proved that Stalin's favor was always precarious.[10] Fadeev was the head of the Soviet delegation. He was rewriting his Stalin Prize–winning novel devoted to a group of youths who became partisan fighters during the German occupation. Out of the blue, critical response abruptly shifted from praise to excoriation. A wave of scathing criticism faulted him for failing to properly portray the leadership role of the party in directing partisan warfare. He spent several months completely rewriting the novel. He knew that Stalin was behind the criticism, because the dictator had expressed similar thoughts to the director of a film based on Fadeev's book. Little did Sholokhov know that he soon would be following in Fadeev's footsteps in spite of the fact that he lent his name to one of the most vicious pieces of rhetoric produced during the early stages of the Cold War.[11] Sholokhov's article even compared Harry Truman to Nazi ideologues and perpetrators of wartime atrocities. He ratcheted up his fawning rhetoric in praise of the dictator, calling Stalin the embodiment of "peace, democracy, and liberty for all peoples" and the "hope of progressive humanity."

Curiously, a few months later Sholokhov got an alarming call from a friend in Moscow. The twelfth volume of Stalin's collected works had appeared in bookstores there.[12] The friend warned him that one of Stalin's previously unpublished letters from 1929 criticized Sholokhov and appeared to make an example of him. To Feliks Kon, a Polish communist, Stalin wrote:

> The famous author of our time Comrade Sholokhov made a number of egregious errors and [included] downright incorrect information regarding Syrtsov, Podtelkov, Krivoshlykov, etc., but does it follow then that *Quiet Don*—is a completely useless thing, which deserves to be taken out of circulation?

The letter provided no answer to this dangerous rhetorical question. The phrase "egregious errors" during the terror could often mean that someone was finished. What was the significance of the letter's publication in 1949? Did Stalin decide to publish it in order to send Sholokhov and others a message?

Sholokhov immediately sat down to pen a letter to Stalin.[13] He wrote:

> Dear Comrade Stalin!
>
> In the twelfth volume of Your works Your letter to Comrade Feliks Kon was published. In that letter it is stated that I permitted myself to commit in the novel *Quiet Don* "a series of the crudest mistakes and demonstrably untrue information about Syrtsov, Podtelkov, and Krivoshlykov and others."
>
> Comrade Stalin! You know that the novel is read by many readers and is studied in the high school classes and by students of the literature departments of universities and

pedagogical institutes. It is only natural that after publication of your letter to Comrade Kon, for readers, students, and teachers of literature questions arise about the nature of my mistakes and how to correctly understand the events described in the novel, the role of Podtelkov, Krivoshlykov, and others. They are contacting me for explanation, but I remain silent awaiting Your words.

I very much request, dear Comrade Stalin, that you explain to me the substance of the mistakes that I committed.

I would take your directives into account during the reworking of the novel for future publications.

With deep respect towards You,
M. Sholokhov

In lieu of a reply he received reminders that he still owed 300,000 rubles to the government for the construction of his new house.[14] This turned up the pressure. He would not be able to publish anything until he recovered his favor with Stalin. The pressure intensified when he found out that Vasilii Grossman was completing a novel about the battle for Stalingrad and was trying to publish it in the leading journal *Novyi Mir*.[15] The new *War and Peace* was being written, but by another author. Though Sholokhov deployed his considerable clout to delay its publication, he could not prevent the inevitable. Another man was succeeding where he had failed. The situation threatened to hurl him back to the uncertainties of 1922, except now he had a huge debt, a family, and an international image.

In the meantime, Stalin's secretary, Poskrebyshev, queried Sholokhov about the war novel and told him to keep the Central Committee abreast of his progress.[16] Sholokhov continued to stall. He insisted he needed archival documents. He wrote a letter requesting materials but left Moscow before any decision could be reached. Stalin must have realized that Sholokhov was deceiving him about his work on the novel. In 1947 in a published interview Sholokhov claimed he had enough materials, he only needed the overall vision; now he claimed to have the overall vision but not the materials. Though he was called back to Moscow to meet with an official to assess his needs, Sholokhov did not show up for the meeting. The process of Stalin writing him off had begun in earnest.

Stalin's silence was disturbing. Sholokhov had no idea of how best to approach a leader who at the same time was becoming more reclusive. When Stalin was in the public eye, it was possible to at least guess what he was thinking.[17] In recent months he spoke from the rostrum less frequently and published only rarely. To Sholokhov he became inscrutable and mysterious. By 1951 Sholokhov became impatient. He finally beseeched Stalin's secretary for a meeting.[18] He was told to be patient.

After several months of waiting Sholokhov again looked for a path towards reconciliation with Stalin. His best opportunity came with the grand opening of the Volga-Don canal in late July 1952.[19] This grandiose engineering project had been carried out at tremendous cost. Rumors insisted that thousands of prisoners had perished while digging the canals and building the locks. The canal even spawned a biting anagram-anecdote. Two acquaintances shouted at each other from windows of trains heading in opposite directions. One claimed to be heading for the Volga-Don [na Volga-Don], the other claims to be heading nadolgo von—far, far away for a long, long time. There would be no room for such humor in Sholokhov's long and flattering article devoted to the canal.

He glorified Stalin for achieving an immortal goal once dreamed of by Peter the Great. He referred to the colossal statue of the dictator, which now towered over the Volga as a "majestic monument of Stalin, whose genius united the waters of two great Russian rivers." In pouring out praise for the engineers and builders who constructed the canal, he was also profusely praising the leader, whom he addressed directly: "Dear Comrade Stalin! Look at what a people you have brought up!" He insisted that all of the gigantic constructions of the "Stalin epoch" were solely for the benefit of the people and never could have been carried out in a capitalist country.

Continuing his efforts to wheedle his way back into Stalin's good graces, he even did research in an archive for the first time in decades. He was not there in search of materials for the war novel. Rather he was there in an effort to discern what was wrong with *Quiet Don* way back in 1929. He was hoping that archivists could point out additional sources on the two Cossack revolutionaries who were lynched in 1918. By September 1952 he had located materials that would help him "correct" the novel. [20]

But this was not sufficient. He racked his brains trying to recall everything Stalin had ever said about the novel. He shared these thoughts with an editor, who sedulously set about excising anything remotely similar to any of his recollections. [21] *Quiet Don* was subjected to hundreds of lacerations and a handful of latter-day additions. He even introduced Stalin into two passages of the novel. Readers now learned that Stalin created the plan which led to the rout of a whole counterrevolutionary army.

Sholokhov also gave General Kornilov a radical makeover. [22] While at their fateful meeting in 1931, Sholokhov audaciously defended his portrayal of the general; now he gutted and blackened it. In the new version of *Quiet Don*, Kornilov colluded with representatives of Anglo-French imperialism, who were "hurrying him to commence with his actions against the revolutionary populace." He was backed by opportunists, bankers, black-hundredists, incorrigible monarchists, and scavenger bastards, who wanted to "rip open the veins of the country." He and his reactionary supporters desired to "clamp in iron claws the revolutionary working class, which was led by Lenin and Stalin, in order to decapitate and strangle the forces of revolution." In spite of such drastic changes, editors were still reluctant to accept it for publication without some assurance that Stalin had endorsed the edits. Because of his enormous debts to the government, Sholokhov faced a grave crisis—he was in danger of losing his home. A Kremlin insider cautioned him, "Call the Boss! Until you straighten out things with him, no one will publish you. You don't want to be evicted from your home!"[23]

By 1952 Sholokhov was at his wit's end. In fall 1952 he finally called Poskrebyshev to beseech a meeting with Stalin. [24] This time the secretary was uncharacteristically obliging. After a brief perusal of the dictator's calendar, an appointment was scheduled for 1:00 P.M. the next day. For the first time since the war, Sholokhov would come face-to-face with Stalin. He became noticeably nervous and edgy and could not concentrate. Unpredictability and uncertainty were eating away at him.

What would he face tomorrow? It's what you don't know that torments you. How do you prepare acrobatics for an audience that is inscrutable and potentially hostile? That afternoon Poskrebyshev stopped by Sholokhov's apartment to prepare him for the next day. He took the writer's assistant aside and warned him that Sholokhov was not to leave the premises, not to have any guests, and not under any circumstances to drink liquor. He emphasized to Sholokhov the serious nature of what he anticipated to be a long and difficult meeting. "The Boss is waiting for you," he stressed. His words signaled both a sense of anticipation and mystery. "We'll send a car for you." He continued, "I hope you'll be a good lad. The Boss is not in the best condition at the moment." "Is he offended at me?" Sholokhov inquired. "Don't exaggerate your individual role in history!" Poskrebyshev retorted, "I suggest that you get some rest." When Poskrebyshev departed, Sholokhov awkwardly joked to his assistant that this was their chance to make a run for it. But then they noticed a government car parked in the courtyard. Two men in identical overcoats were posted downstairs.

The next morning Sholokhov could barely stand the wait. Struggling to find outlets for his nervous energy, he repeatedly trimmed his mustache. He put on an outfit similar to the one he wore during his first meetings with Stalin: a military long shirt and boots. The car arrived early. The men in trench coats were replaced by a new pair in similar attire. At the appointed time Sholokhov and his assistant got in the car. As it approached Red Square, Sholokhov implored the driver to stop. He requested a detour to the Grand Hotel and bolstered it with compelling logic: "I can't show up empty-handed." One of the suits signaled that this would be okay, and the driver stopped. "We'll only be a minute," Sholokhov declared.

They made their way to the restaurant, and Sholokhov greeted the maitre d' by name. He ordered two bottles of the most expensive cognac from the Republic of Georgia. The bottles miraculously appeared from a side stash. When the assistant gave the writer a concerned look, Sholokhov reiterated that one was a present for Stalin. He demanded a table and, sitting down, ordered the maitre d' to open one of the bottles and bring three glasses. "For a successful endeavor," he toasted and

An artistic rendering of an undated photograph of Sholokhov from the 1920s. This and similar images were important for Sholokhov's revolutionary self-fashioning (see page 7). *Artwork by Wendy Zumpano.*

An artistic rendering of Sholokhov's meeting with Stalin and Gorky to discuss *Quiet Don* in 1931 (see page viii). *Artwork by Eric Jimenez.*

An artistic rendering of a Viktor Ruikovich photo that provoked the ire of Kremlin officials in 1958 (see pages 247–8). *Artwork by Wendy Zumpano.*

An artistic rendering of a Viktor Ruikovich photo depicting Sholokhov in the spirt of Vasilii Perov's painting *Hunters at Rest* (1871). *Artwork by Eric Jimenez.*

An unattributed image from *Literaturnaia Gazeta*, February 6, 1934. Georgian film director N. Shengeleia "convinces" Sholokhov to finish the screenplay of *Virgin Soil* (see page 79).

ABOVE: Sholokhov reads aloud from *Quiet Don*, ca. 1928 (see page 16). *Courtesy of Getty images.* BELOW: Sholokhov at a command post during World War II, fall 1941 (see pages 177–179). *Courtesy of Getty images.*

Khrushchev's visit to Sholokhov's home in 1959 (see page 252). *Courtesy of Getty Images.*

Sholokhov among the Nobel Prize winners for 1965 (see page 296). *Courtesy of Getty Images.*

downed a shot. Two more doses of liquid courage later, his assistant began to worry and started pointing to the clock. "There's plenty of time," Sholokhov insisted.

Somewhat later the pair in trench coats reappeared. They were not alone. Poskrebyshev was with them. He rapidly approached and angrily confronted the writer.

"Mikhail, do you imagine that you have a spare head?" he inquired.

"We've all got just one," Sholokhov replied.

Motioning to the maitre d' to bring another glass, Sholokhov indicated that he should pour one for Poskrebyshev. "Go ahead and pour," Poskrebyshev replied. As the others drank, Poskrebyshev demonstratively poured his on the floor. "Let's go," he insisted. "I've moved your meeting back by an hour. The Boss won't wait after that."

"I waited for over a year," Sholokhov muttered.

Poskrebyshev's face became expressionless. He stared at Sholokhov for a few seconds and departed in haste, followed by the suits.

Sholokhov demonstratively placed the second bottle on the table and motioned for the maitre d' to open it. After he and his assistant finished it, they staggered to the door. The car that was supposed to take the writer to the Kremlin wasn't there. When Sholokhov called the Central Committee's dispatcher to request another one, he was told that none would be available. He tried calling his main contact in the Kremlin, but the underling who answered the phone curtly informed him that no one was around. Sholokhov's instinct told him to head home. He left Moscow on the first train out. He would never learn why the dictator agreed to meet him again.

TWENTY-ONE

A new, uncertain era in Sholokhov's life began on March 4, 1953. That morning he received shocking and ominous news: Comrade Stalin had lost consciousness and fallen into a state of paralysis. Disconcertingly, the first reports declared that twenty-four hours had already elapsed since the onset of dangerous symptoms. The invincible demigod of propaganda had suddenly succumbed to a series of mortal afflictions to his brain and heart. In an officially atheist state there could be no sanction for the saying of prayers, so instead thousands of loudspeakers in thousands of locations commanded millions of Soviet citizens to show resoluteness of spirit, be vigilant, and redouble their energies in the building of communism. The medical bulletins recalled those when Gorky died.[1] They seemed to be preparing the populace for a fatal outcome by doling out pessimism in ever larger doses. The subsequent reports included readings of the dictator's gradually weakening vital signs.

The reports brought a rush of strange emotions to Sholokhov. Relief and regret simultaneously intermixed with sadness, emptiness, and hopelessness. Anxiety and uncertainty weighed on him. Would Stalin's demise create new opportunities or new problems? Who would now rule the Soviet Union? How could he remain relevant? By what means could he stay in favor?

On March 6 an official announcement proclaimed: "At 21:50 hours, with cardiac failure growing and insufficiency of breathing, J. V. Stalin died." So testified several academicians and professors of medicine.[2] The early announcements insisted that Stalin was in his Kremlin apartment during his illness, but for some unexplained reason the later reports unexpectedly omitted a location. Nor was there any indication of who was at his bedside. Such information was likely withheld on purpose in order to prevent speculations about who would succeed him. In a surprising turn of events, Nikita Khrushchev headed the commission to organize the funeral. Sholokhov had crossed paths with this mid-level member of the Politburo on various occasions, but he'd had no serious face time with him. By the next day things became less opaque. Georgii Malenkov would head the Council of Ministers. Evidently he was now in control.

The suddenness of this turn of events conspired with the extreme road conditions in early spring to keep Sholokhov away from Stalin's funeral. Working against one of the tightest deadlines of his career, he penned a tribute and telegraphed it to *Pravda*.[3] It started: "Farewell father! Farewell dear and to the last of our breaths beloved father!" Sholokhov attempted to speak for millions who would only be able to pass before Stalin's coffin in their own imagination. "We bow low as we kiss you in the manner of a son sending off his father on his final journey." Of the eulogies printed in the days after Stalin's death, Sholokhov's was the only major one to directly address the dictator. He continued: "We hear your voice in the rhythmic hum of the turbines of the mightiest of hydroelectric stations, in the crash of waves of new seas created by your will . . ." He boldly proclaimed that Stalin would forever remain dear to the Soviet people.

On the day of the memorial gathering in Vioshki, Sholokhov could hardly contain his emotions and hurriedly departed after briefly listening to one of the speeches.[4] Every certainty he had known for two decades had suddenly been thrown into question. From the coverage of Stalin's funeral, Sholokhov could discern that Malenkov, Beria, and Molotov had formed a triumvirate upon his death. When *Pravda* announced on March 16 that the ministries of State Security and Internal Affairs would be merged into a single institution headed by Beria, it seemed pretty certain that his influence was rising. There was little mention of Nikita Khrushchev. Only the fact that he was occasionally called upon to deliver important speeches hinted at his continuing influence. Then on April 6, Beria's position teetered. The secret police were accused of falsifying plots, and several officers were arrested. Nevertheless, Beria somehow managed to survive. Judging by the photos published on May 1, the triumvirate was still in power. Two months later Malenkov stunned the world. On July 10, 1953, he delivered a report dedicated to the "criminal, antiparty, anti-state activities of L. P. Beria."

Resurrecting for a final time one of the central tropes of the Great Terror, Malenkov insisted that Beria had been "unmasked" as a foreign agent. Reading between the lines, Sholokhov could discern signals that Beria had made some sort of aggressive move. This move, perhaps a bid for power, had threatened the other members of the triumvirate. They'd taken swift action. Malenkov insisted that for years the head of the secret police masterfully managed to hide the fact that Beria was carrying out the disruption of the Soviet state in the interests of foreign capital. His goal was to seize power, and to this end he'd manipulated the Ministry of Internal Affairs. He had tried to disrupt collective agriculture in order to bring about food shortages. He had made some kind overtures for support among the non-Russian nationalities. As a result, Beria was excluded from the party as an enemy of the people, and his case was handed over to the supreme court. After praising collective leadership in various ways, the report introduced an opaque quote from Karl Marx about his aversion to any kind of "cult of personality." This mysterious phrase would initiate a new era in Soviet politics. Was this a reference to Beria? Or an aspersion directed against Stalin?

Sensing a tectonic shift in the Soviet political landscape, Sholokhov sprung into action. He telegraphed a condemnation of Beria to Moscow for immediate publication.[5] His Soviet sixth sense told him that Beria was finished. Malenkov would now move to forestall possible actions by Beria's supporters in the secret police. The writer decided to get on the right side of the Soviet Union's new leader. Adopting a folksy tone, he wrote, "Beria has sat down in it so deep that the next time he will be able to stand upright is to stand before a judicial tribunal. One can only hope that he won't have to stand for a long time." He was suggesting that Beria was entitled to the same swift punishment he enacted upon others. Proclaiming that treason has always been considered the "blackest, the dirtiest, and the most despised" of human activities, Sholokhov reminded his readers that in the army it was punishable by death. He demanded a verdict against Beria of the "harshest, most merciless, and therefore of the fairest kind." When Sholokhov's article was published the next day, his was the only one to demand the death penalty. Several more days passed, but he was still the only major figure to openly and publicly call for such retribution.

Just when Sholokhov started to second-guess his decision to take the lead in the campaign against Beria, he received a message of reassurance. It came in the form of an invitation to write an important article for *Pravda*.[6] Weeks after he had proclaimed that Stalin would be dear to the Soviet people forever, the new leadership called upon him to assist in the first attempt to partially dismantle the Stalin dictatorship. The collective leadership decided to revive an anniversary that had not been widely celebrated since 1933. It was the date of the founding of the Bolshevik party. This anniversary was gradually downgraded during Stalin's reign because he was in exile when the party was founded and played no active role in its creation.[7] During the Great Terror, railroad transport day was even celebrated instead of this important party date.

Sholokhov was among the first in the Soviet Union to find out about Stalin's impending demotion. He was one of only two writers to receive some advance talking points from a brochure that was being prepared to explain the sudden, renewed relevance of the party anniversary.[8] It was jarring to read for the first time in nearly two decades a key party document in which Stalin was only mentioned in passing. The writer had become so immune to excessive multiplication of the dictator's lofty epithets that to see Stalin merely mentioned as Lenin's pupil seemed almost surreal. As he read, he could comprehend that the days of the Stalin cult were numbered. The document never directly stated so, but several signals were there. Gone were any words uttered by the late dictator. Instead they were replaced by the constant refrains of "Lenin" and "collective." The victory in the war and the economic recovery were now completely recast as the result of "collective experience and collective wisdom." Several statements explained inadequacies in how the party's history had previously been portrayed. As everyone knew, Stalin had personally approved the short course on the party's history.

Sholokhov agreed to prepare a statement for publication on the day of the anniversary. It repeated the standard propaganda lines about the Soviet people's tremendous love for the party and emphasized that recent triumphs had resulted from mutual affection. He emphasized that despite imperialist scoffing, the party had facilitated recovery after the war and carried out successful rebuilding. More importantly he embraced the new line. He avoided any mention whatsoever of Stalin. He even floated a neologism—the "collective supreme leader"—to describe the new political era. It did not take hold.

As Sholokhov correctly anticipated, Beria's name promptly disappeared from Soviet official memory. It was excised from plaques in libraries, factories, and schools that had once proudly borne it. The writer was unable to predict the crude lengths to which the subsequent campaign of *damnatio memoriae* would go. Subscribers of the Great Soviet Encyclopedia were even sent instructions to use a razor or scissors to remove the specific pages on which the article about Beria had appeared.[9] They were provided with replacement pages with additional information about the Bering Sea to glue in. In popular culture memories of Beria's sudden fall persisted for several years. A little ditty rhymed:

"Beria . . . oh . . . Beria,
is no longer in a trusted area,
Malenkov our dear comrade,
Kicked him really, really bad."[10]

News of Beria's execution soon appeared in the Soviet press.

In subsequent months, Sholokhov returned to work on the second volume of his novel *Virgin Soil*. Because parts of the manuscript were lost during the war, he was forced to reconstruct several sections from memory and pen other sections anew. He was sorely disappointed when Malenkov showed little interest in the new chapters and instead suggested in September 1953 that he forward them to Nikita Khrushchev. At that time Khrushchev was too busy with political intrigue to directly involve himself in literature. Instead, Khrushchev relied on the verdict of Mikhail Suslov, a fastidious teetotaler and former regional official whom Stalin had elevated after the war.[11] The excessively stern, bespectacled ideologue informed Sholokhov that he would not permit the chapters to be published in *Pravda*. At best he only considered small sections acceptable for publication. At the time the Soviet government was attempting to raise the status of directors of collective farms, but many of Sholokhov's selections depicted a farm director who spent more time pursuing erotic adventures than supervising workers in the fields. Sholokhov's demands for more space in the newspaper were met with stiff refusals.

In early 1954 Sholokhov faced outright rejection for the first time in over twenty years. The editorial board of a major literary journal also declined to publish his new chapters. Its editor even went so far as to proclaim some sections to be "unworthy" of the great writer's pen.[12] The death of the Supreme Censor had unleashed a legion of lesser censors who would not be kind to the dead dictator's favorite.

During those dejecting months, he suffered injury to his reputation. Thousands of copies of the "improved" version of *Quiet Don* hit the shelves of Soviet bookstores. Changes that had seemed wise to Sholokhov only months earlier now served as blatant indictments of his willingness to compromise. Though hailed in Soviet reviews as a "new version" that perfected the novel, even ordinary readers could not help but notice that many of Sholokhov's characters had lost their folksy local color and bawdy edginess. More politically attentive readers noticed statements in the editor's preface about Stalin's role in correcting Sholokhov's "mistakes" and traced them to a new section of the text, which lauded Stalin for rejecting Trotsky's "defeatist plan" and reproduced in full Stalin's letter to Lenin about the southern front.[13] The letter had played a major role in promoting the Stalin cult in 1929. Now it appeared grossly outmoded.

In early 1954 a literary opportunity created a political dilemma for Soviet leaders. The Swedish Academy contacted the aging Stalinist writer Sergeev-Tsenskii about nominating a candidate for the Nobel Prize in Literature.[14] The Soviet Writers' Union was divided about whether or not any invitation should be accepted from a "reactionary instrument of war-mongering." It believed that the Nobel committee had discredited itself by awarding the prize to Winston Churchill. The chief ideologue Suslov referred the question to a group of officials responsible for science and culture. They recommended nominating a "progressive" Soviet or foreign writer. Over a month passed before the Writers' Union got around to proposing a candidate. It nominated Sholokhov and penned a draft letter presenting his case to the Swedish Academy.[15] It took a few additional days for Suslov and the secretaries of the Central Committee to approve the nomination. By the time a carefully vetted letter was mailed to the Swedish Academy, the deadline had already passed. By March of 1954 it was clear that Sholokhov's nomination could only be discussed the next year.

The news that his nomination for the Nobel Prize had been held up by bureaucratic deliberation fueled his anger and frustration. In subsequent months Sholokhov's increasingly erratic behavior became a major concern for both ideological officials and the Writers' Union.[16] Some of its leading members lamented that he "systematically drinks, has seriously undermined his health, and for a long time has not written new works."

There was even a move to deny him a speaking role at the first Soviet Writers' Congress to be conducted since the death of Gorky. Sholokhov's supporters successfully petitioned Khrushchev to intervene in what they considered a concerted effort to exclude him. As a result he was assigned a major speaking slot near the end of the congress.[17] Over fifty foreign writers were expected to be in attendance, and even eight authors from "bourgeois capitalist" countries were expected to participate.

Sholokhov criticized the congress for its placid atmosphere and condemned a gray stream of bland, mediocre literature that was destined for recycling. He lashed out at a literary establishment accustomed to meaningless prizes and medals that suffocated youth and talent. He warned that thaws bring about slush as well as rust, lambasted Konstantin

Simonov as a naked emperor impressed with his new clothes and unde-
served awards, and excoriated Erenburg for excessive sensitivity.

The speech in general, and the personal attacks against Erenburg
and Simonov in particular, were poorly received by a number of visiting
foreign writers.[18] Informers quickly reported to Soviet authorities their
disparaging comments. One pronounced Sholokhov to be a carnival
jester looking for cheap applause. Another wondered how someone who
hadn't written a book in twenty years could even dare to take on the
moral mantle of criticizing others.

By early 1955 clear signs of disagreement within the collective leadership started to appear. Cryptic press declarations about "rightist deviations" and misguided efforts to promote light industry at the expense of
heavy industry signaled that Malenkov's position had become less secure.
Speeches by Nikita Khrushchev became longer and more frequent. Then
on February 8, 1955, Malenkov resigned as chairman of the USSR
Council of Ministers and was replaced by Nikolai Bulganin. Khrushchev
remained First Secretary of the Communist Party but assumed a public
role as the Soviet Union's leader.

Throughout 1955 Sholokhov confronted Stalin's legacy. As he struggled to stay sober, hundreds of letters poured in from across the Soviet
Union soliciting his assistance.[19] The government had quietly initiated
the process of releasing and rehabilitating victims of repression and terror.
People shared their personal tragedies with Sholokhov in hopes that one
word from him could dramatically speed up the processing of their cases
or ease their transition to freedom. He faced a barrage of letters from
intellectuals, common convicts, and former party officials who had spent
decades behind barbed wire. Their tragic stories were enough to drive
anyone to drink.

Among the piles of letters one in particular piqued his interest. It was
from an individual who claimed to be an important character in volume
three of *Quiet Don*.[20] Pavel Kudinov featured prominently in that part of the
novel, where he was depicted as a leader of the Cossack uprising that convulsed Sholokhov's home region in 1919. Kudinov's story was as incredible
as it was heart-wrenching. At the end of the civil war he escaped across
the Black Sea to Turkey. Rather than face forced resettlement in a refugee

camp, he struck out on his own and did odd jobs and backbreaking labor in Istanbul. After saving a little money, he headed to Greece and then on to Bulgaria. There he established a residence and engaged in petty trade, beekeeping, and photography. His participation in Cossack émigré politics earned him a series of arrests and temporary exiles to Romania and then Czechoslovakia in the 1930s. When Soviet troops marched through Bulgaria in 1944, he warmly welcomed them to his village and eagerly greeted them. He proudly announced to a Soviet officer that he was a character in *Quiet Don*. This statement doomed him. A commissar who had read the book recognized him as an anti-Soviet character and led him away. For months he languished in prison while officials tried to find a crime to charge him with. Since being a literary character in a novel was not a crime, archival files on the civil war had to be dredged up in order to prosecute him. After nearly three years in legal limbo he was sent to the Gulag. There the sixty-year-old endured eleven years of hard labor, felling lumber in forest camps. As a foreign citizen he was amnestied during the first wave of releases after Stalin's death, and he wrote to Sholokhov looking for assistance in returning to the Don region. Unfortunately, by the time Sholokhov unearthed his letter, Kudinov had already been sent back to Bulgaria.

On his good days Sholokhov drank champagne and edited the screenplay for a planned feature-length color film based on *Quiet Don*. On his bad days he imbibed cognac and avoided visitors. Local party officials and members of his family zealously shielded him from guests who might endanger his sobriety. [21] He tried to be on his best behavior when envoys from Moscow arrived. For these efforts he was rewarded with official attention.

In late May 1955 an official celebration of his fiftieth birthday took place in Moscow with a gala evening in the Chaikovsky concert hall. Khrushchev decided not to attend the event. Instead the Central Committee marked the occasion by awarding Sholokhov the Order of Lenin. A flood of congratulatory letters and telegrams did little to bolster his mood. The more Soviet citizens proclaimed that they were eagerly awaiting his new works and wished him luck in finishing the war novel, the more acutely his literary paralysis haunted him.

In June 1955 Soviet diplomats in Stockholm learned that the Nobel committee was again seriously considering Sholokhov's nomination for the prize in literature. In response to these signals, cultural bureaucrats began commissioning new translations and urged Sholokhov to raise his international profile. In late July 1955 Sholokhov floated the idea of an international writer's roundtable in an article published in the second issue of a new journal dedicated to foreign literature.[22] He advocated a renewal of cultural ties ruptured "after the war." In particular he invited the participation of American, English, West German, and Japanese writers and proclaimed his hopes of finding common language with them. Whether these efforts were sincere or just a ploy to get his name in the news in advance of Nobel deliberations, they sparked considerable interest in Soviet circles. As it became apparent that no Western writer of note was willing to cosponsor his call, Sholokhov again turned to the bottle.

In early September 1955 an official from Moscow delivered the news that Sholokhov was expected in the capital. This time it was for hospitalization.[23] The Central Committee expressed alarm that his drinking was now completely out of control. He had increased his daily dose to three bottles of cognac, and his binges had started to last for several days at a time. Officials from two ministries organized consultations with the country's leading doctors. The Kremlin hospital made arrangements for a serious detox regime. When Sholokhov attempted to protest, a document was produced. Signed by Suslov, it "obligated Comrade Sholokhov as a member of the party to strictly adhere to the [medical] regime" that doctors were developing for his treatment.

Sholokhov could not refuse hospitalization. He traveled to Moscow and presented himself for evaluation to the Kremlin doctors. After hours of consultation, they diagnosed him with chronic alcoholism and added additional maladies to his medical chart: cirrhosis of the liver, high blood pressure, arteriosclerosis, and heart disease. They decided to keep him there for more than a month. For those in Sholokhov's condition, the standard treatment started with generous doses of bed rest and copious amounts of fruit juices to replenish vitamin intake. Patients were expected to sleep for twelve to fifteen hours a day. Various intravenous concoctions were pumped into their arms with unnerving frequency. What came next largely depended on how cooperative each individual patient proved to be. Visitors were strictly limited. A parade of doctors and professors of medicine visited Sholokhov's bedside, including the one who had literally written the book on the Soviet Union's battle against alcoholism.

Dr. Ivan Strel'chuk had established himself as the Soviet Union's foremost authority on the treatment of alcoholism.[24] A burly man with large hands, his face was slightly off center. One side sloped downward at an angle, causing his right eyebrow to appear to be raised in disapproval. In profile there was something sinister about him. His voice was that of a train station dispatcher. He believed alcoholism to be a "harmful vestige of capitalism" and classified drunks as individuals who showed blatant disregard for socialist morality and productivity. He was trained by followers of Russia's first Nobel Laureate, the scientist Ivan Pavlov, whose famous experiments on dogs had included bowls of milk laced with liquor as well as bells and tasty treats.

Strel'chuk had experimented with a drug called antabuse.[25] In combination with even the smallest doses of alcohol it unleashed a chain of revolting bodily reactions. It caused the heartbeat to become exceedingly rapid. The patient soon began to feel a deficit of oxygen and experienced a sensation of viewing the world from a height of four thousand yards. These symptoms were followed by acute pain and copious vomiting. After five such sessions, even the smell of trace amounts of alcohol would induce the same negative physical reactions in his patients. Unfortunately Sholokhov's stomach and intestinal tract were deemed far too fragile to prescribe this aggressive method.

When Strel'chuk appeared at Sholokhov's bedside with his disapproving eye, he began to exhort the writer to change his ways. The professor adeptly characterized alcohol's effects on the body and the internal organs by quoting from the findings of gruesome autopsies conducted on dead alcoholics. He scared his patients with vivid details of the foul-smelling, slimy, mucous-like, half-digested contents of their stomachs. His descriptions of enlarged livers were intricate and grotesque. Additionally he would try to inculcate a sense of shame and societal harm. He could even quote Lenin's words to the German socialist Klara

Tsetkin that "the proletariat as a rising class has no need of intoxication." If that didn't work, he was ever ready to warn about the next stages of degradation and the onset of demonic hallucinations.

But Sholokhov had no tolerance for being harangued. He immediately proclaimed, "I'm a resilient guy with a positive attitude, a little drinking from time to time won't do me any harm." Strel'chuk's efforts to convince him otherwise were only met with more denial. "We're only talking about a daily dietary supplement," Sholokhov insisted. "I'll be fine."[26]

Strel'chuk believed that an appeal to the latest, most progressive scientific methods might work. His recent experiments had demonstrated the effectiveness of hypnosis and the potential of anti-alcohol suggestion.[27] He had succeeded in hypnotizing patients from all walks of life. Once they were in a hypnotic state, in a rhythmic cadence he would forcefully repeat: "In your state of health alcohol is a poison for you. A poison . . . A poison . . . A poison . . ." Then he planted hypnotic suggestions that even the faintest smell of alcohol would make his subjects instantly suffer from nausea. In many experiments with patients he provoked strong physical reactions such as wincing, grimacing, nose scrunching, and even violent jerking when he confronted them with empty shot glasses. In some sessions he and his associates were even able to induce vomiting in multiple patients at the mere mention of drinking.

The professor was promising Sholokhov a life free from alcohol. But in order to secure this liberty, he had to trust his mind to a stranger. Having served a dictator for decades, he feared his own subconscious. His answer was decidedly no. He would have none of it. He became annoyed and refused to cooperate any further. He shunned treatments and constantly demanded discharge. He returned to Vioshki and attempted to stay sober while anxiously awaiting news from Stockholm and the Nobel Prize committee.

The Nobel deliberations had taken place in Stockholm while he was hospitalized. His candidacy advanced past the first round of eliminations.[28] His name was included among a small group of finalists whose works were closely read and actively discussed by the committee. An expert evaluation prepared for the committee by a Swedish scholar concluded that Sholokhov had written almost nothing of merit in recent years. His recent works were dismissed as purely political. The writer had made too many compromises in the name of loyalty to the regime. More than a thousand changes had been made to the newest edition of *Quiet Don*. Moreover, no progress had been made on the long-promised war novel. The recently published chapters of *Virgin Soil* were devoid of both the lyricism and naturalism of his earlier prose. Sholokhov's name was all too often associated with scandal, and at the Writers' Congress he had unleashed personal attacks upon Simonov and Erenburg. These pronouncements were decisive. The Nobel committee concluded that "for the last fifteen years he has published very little work of good quality" and moved on to considering other candidates.

By late 1955 Sholokhov realized that there would be no Nobel Prize for him that year. The award went to a writer from Iceland whose most recent works were not available in Russian. Sholokhov had to content himself with reading the latest publication by the 1954 recipient, Ernest Hemingway.[29] While he was in detox, *The Old Man and the Sea* had been translated and published in a Soviet journal devoted to foreign literature. Ideological officials branded it as "apolitical." Reading it brought tears to Sholokhov's eyes. Why did it affect him so greatly? It was a story about an old fisherman down on his luck in pursuit of a huge fish, moving ever farther from land with dogged determination to stay with it or die. This was a story of tenacity and triumph over adversity, of a man who, in the words of Hemingway's protagonist, "can be destroyed but not defeated." Sholokhov relished the challenge and dreamed of writing a tale of Russian resilience that would rival and surpass Hemingway's story.

TWENTY-TWO

Nineteen fifty-six was a year of returns, revelations, and revising of history.[1] Thousands of former labor camp inmates poured into Soviet cities. A constant stream of revelations about arrests, terror, and repression came in their wake. Stalinism began to be openly criticized in the Soviet press. For the first time ordinary people publicly discussed the horrors of Stalin's reign. Even the Soviet past started to look very different after a series of revelations by Khrushchev at the Party Congress that year.

For Sholokhov the process of dismantling Stalin's legacy presented a peculiar set of problems. How could he relaunch a career that was so intertwined with Stalin's favor? Should he join the chorus of voices condemning the dead dictator, or would he side with those who urged caution instead of candor? Were the promises he made in the waning years of Stalin's reign still binding? First he rewrote the story of his own relationship to Stalin, then he exploited the revelations of a returnee and a shift in policy to endear himself to Khrushchev.

A new edition of his collected works provided a golden opportunity to revise his personal history as an apologist for Stalinism.[2] Sholokhov made a number of deletions to his articles and speeches from the '30s, '40s, and early '50s. He started by excising sections from his 1939 speech to the Party Congress. Without those sections it read as if he never praised the purges or endorsed the view that fellow writers had helped to murder Gorky. The grateful blacksmith who had survived the famine due to the dictator's generosity disappeared, together with the rest of the article he wrote for Stalin's birthday in 1939. References to Stalin as the embodiment of peace, democracy, and liberty for all peoples were removed from his speech at a peace conference in 1949. Several fawning paragraphs were erased from his remarks about the Volga-Don canal. Such revisions made it appear as if he never called Stalin Supreme Leader, never endorsed the theory of dictatorial genius, and always refrained from joining the "Long Live Comrade Stalin" chorus. Simultaneously, he actively restored hundreds of original readings to *Quiet Don*.

In early 1956 he traveled to Moscow to speak to a young writers' conference. Those meetings were entirely forgettable, save for an unforgettable encounter.[3] After one of the sessions, he was approached by a pale, emaciated man.[4] The man's features were those of the sallow hermits depicted on old icons. His sunken-in eyes had seen horrors. His hands shook uncontrollably. Trying to suppress a grimace, he greeted the writer as if they were old acquaintances. He claimed to have just returned from the "place from which no one ever returns." There was indeed a resemblance to someone Sholokhov had known in another time, a different place. Perhaps this was an old Bolshevik whom he had once encountered at Gorky's house. The stranger, who appeared to be in his eighties, introduced himself: "The broken and maimed old man [you see before you] is Van'ka Makar'ev." Sholokhov was shocked. He had heard nothing of Ivan Makar'ev's fate since 1937. This was the man who'd saved his writing career in 1929 by scuttling the charges that he had sided with the *kulaks*.

Sholokhov invited Makar'ev to visit his Moscow apartment for tea. He also invited a younger writer named Shkerin to witness the meeting. Makar'ev began to tell of his ordeal in a soft, barely audible voice.[5]

Arrested as a Trotskyite saboteur early in the terror, he managed to make it through the NKVD meat grinder by never signing a confession. After months of agonizing torture, he was sent to one of the coldest places on earth. Located hundreds of miles above the Arctic Circle, it was a land of enduring darkness. He was imprisoned in a labor camp with ordinary criminals. The inmates were tasked with turning open tundra into one of the world's largest nickel-smelting operations. Among the thousands of prisoners who subsequently arrived during the terror, he frequently recognized the faces of fellow writers and delegates to important party conferences. The city of Norilsk rose before his very eyes. From a few clusters of log cabins it became a Stalinist city of thousands.

During the Second World War, a group of inmates attempted to secure weapons and stage a rebellion. Makar'ev warned a nearby guard, who was able to barricade himself in a building and sound the alarm. For this Makar'ev was savagely attacked by the inmates with iron tools and sustained multiple lacerations and contusions. For his loyalty, the camp commandant promised to shorten his sentence. He was released but not allowed to leave Norilsk. He found a job as a dispatcher in a construction company and helped to found a newspaper. After Stalin's death, his case was reviewed. He had just been permitted to return to Moscow.

Sholokhov listened to Makar'ev with bated breath. This man had been to hell and back, yet he still remained true to his communist ideals. What an amazing resilience! He suddenly felt discomfort about his own actions. He insisted to Makar'ev that when he heard of his colleague's arrest in 1937 he went to see Yezhov to inquire about his release. Yezhov insisted, "Don't panic, I'll get to the bottom of this." Sholokhov lamented that only now—nineteen years later—had they gotten around to getting to the bottom of things.

Sensing Sholokhov's discomfort, Shkerin changed the subject. He inquired whether Makar'ev had been able to write in Siberia. The latter explained that for many years writing was an impossible dream. From the camps he even wrote brief missives to Fadeev, begging to be sent some sharpened pencils and the cheapest writing paper. No response ever arrived. Makar'ev continued, "Days after returning [to Moscow] I went to see Sasha [Fadeev]. I had imagined in my mind that we would heartily embrace like nothing ever happened. Instead I just shook his hand. I asked him, 'Did you get my letters?' 'I did,' he replied. 'Forgive me, I behaved like a coward.'"

Makar'ev was on a mission to settle scores with Fadeev. Sholokhov was one of the last living witnesses to their close friendship before the terror. Months before his release, Makar'ev's wife begged Fadeev for help in obtaining a new apartment.[6] Four members of Makar'ev's family were already living in a single room in a communal apartment, and the Gulag returnee would be the fifth. After Fadeev made some assurances of support, she gathered all sorts of official paperwork about their terrible living conditions and handed them over to Fadeev's assistant. Upon arrival, Makar'ev learned that Fadeev's promises had been broken. Instead of helping, he sent a letter containing a litany of excuses. Some unspecified illness and the "necessity of traveling to the various metallurgical areas of the country for work on a new novel" had prevented him from doing anything. He even complained about his own difficulties in securing even a small plot of land for his own cottage. Sholokhov concluded that Fadeev's shame knew no boundaries. It was no secret in literary circles that Fadeev's summer cottage was a mansion by Soviet standards.

Makar'ev then revealed to Sholokhov a crucial piece of information that he had saved for last. While reviewing his petition for release, one of the investigators had allowed him to peruse his arrest file. Leafing through those materials, he encountered a familiar hand and a familiar signature. Fadeev had been a coward in matters both big and small. He had signed a denunciation of his closest friend. Makar'ev decided then to confront Fadeev about his role in the arrest. However, he first needed Fadeev's support for reinstatement to the Communist Party. Only then did he spring his revelation. Fadeev could not muster any words other than "Forgive me, I was a coward . . . Spit in my face."

Upon hearing this, Sholokhov intensely desired to put Fadeev in his place. The meeting ended with pleasantries and plans for future meetings. Sholokhov could not stop thinking about Fadeev's treachery. The thought of him signing off on the arrest of one of his best friends was incomprehensible. But now it all seemed to make sense. He recalled that once when he appealed for Fadeev's help during the terror, Fadeev had displayed the same noncommittal attitude. Could he have actually been working behind the scenes against Sholokhov too? Recently there had been much talk about all the faces that were missing at the second Writers' Congress. Did Fadeev play a role in their disappearances? While engrossed in such thoughts, a clarion call to action presented itself. Sholokhov was invited to deliver the key literary speech at the upcoming party conference.

The Twentieth Party Congress in February 1956 would long be remembered as the event that shocked the Soviet system.[7] In a secret speech to the delegates, Khrushchev exposed Stalin's crimes. For hours, the First Secretary provided example after example. He mentioned Lenin's fears about Stalin coming to power, the dictator's trampling on collective principles of rule, and the cult of personality. Long sections of the speech blamed the terror on the dictator and highlighted his mistakes on the eve of and during the Second World War. The transcript, which was later read aloud to party members, was not published in the USSR.

For Sholokhov, many of the revelations merely confirmed what he already knew. It did not surprise him to hear that cases were fabricated against innocent people during the terror. He knew enough about the inner workings of the Kremlin to doubt Khrushchev's portrait of a Politburo that had been completely cowed into submission solely by fear. The picture of Stalin that emerged from the speech did not quite reflect his own experiences. It was a dark image of a cruel and capricious despot. It portrayed Stalin as playing a driving role in his own glorification.

The revelations about the war were among the most difficult to stomach because Khrushchev insinuated that millions of casualties might have been prevented. Stalin ignored multiple credible warnings about the impending German attack. Dismissing them as provocations, he stubbornly clung to the hope that Hitler would not betray him. The decimation of the military leadership on the eve of the war greatly contributed to the disastrous losses and retreats during the early weeks. The dictator ensconced himself in the Kremlin and did not visit the fronts. Instead, he directed the war by looking at a globe rather than consulting strategic maps. Stalin's view of himself as a genius who was never wrong caused him to frequently override the decisions of his generals and advisors. Sholokhov's visit to the front in 1941 made these allegations seem credible.

When the time for his speech arrived, Sholokhov started with a scathing indictment of the state of Soviet literature.[8] He insisted that all of the statistics cited by literary bureaucrats were hollow. Many of the Soviet Union's 3,773 writers were "dead souls." Though they were listed on the membership rolls of the Writers' Union, in reality they produced nothing. Correspondingly much of the literature published in the USSR was mediocre and unreadable. Reprints of classics comprised a large portion of the books that didn't languish unsold on the shelves of bookshops. Unlike prerevolutionary writers, who spent considerable time traversing Russia and getting to know its people, the current generation of writers was trapped in a vicious, triangular circuit: Moscow-summer cottage-health resort, health resort-summer cottage-Moscow. Most writers had ensconced themselves in large cities "where not even a tractor could pull them away from their cozy, habitual places." Nothing new could be expected from writers who were blind to the life of the people and had grown accustomed to receiving huge honoraria for slapdash work. Since the death of Gorky the Writers' Union had excelled in holding meetings and proliferating bureaucratic paperwork rather than producing treasured books. So who was to blame for all this? Fadeev!

Sholokhov looked out into the cavernous hall, but he couldn't see Fadeev, who had been relegated to an unprestigious balcony seat in the back fringes of the building.[9] Echoing a central theme of the congress, he highlighted the flaws of one-man rule and called for the dismantling of a dictatorship, in this case a literary one. "Fadeev turned out to be quite a power-loving GenSec," he thundered, "and he did not wish to acknowledge the principle of collegiality." Despite years in power he had not succeeded as either a dictator or as a writer. He wasn't even a real dictator, since few writers either respected him or followed his marching orders. Lost to literature, he spent his years "giving reports and allocating apartments" and rarely was able to find time for such a "trifle" as writing books. Sholokhov challenged Fadeev to "journey for three or four small years to Magnitogorsk, Sverdlovsk, Cheliabinsk, or Zaporozh'e and write a good novel about the working class." Only then would he finally be able to write something equal in significance to his first novel.

These comments were designed to both publicly humiliate Fadeev and deliver a decisive blow to his self-image. Coded insinuations were intended for Fadeev and his allies. Sholokhov chided him for finding apartments for others in order to remind him of Makar'ev, the friend he betrayed. He ridiculed the excuses about constant travel by drawing public attention to the fact that Fadeev hadn't actually managed to either finish or publish his planned metallurgy novel. The most creative years of his life had been wasted.

The delegates' reaction to the speech was positive. Laughter and generous applause greeted several of Sholokhov's lines. But writers were livid. He had attacked their privileges and aired their dirty laundry. It didn't take long for the Writers' Union to strike back. The attack came disguised as a letter to the editor supposedly penned by an ordinary party member.[10] Published in the *Literary Gazette* within a few days of Sholokhov's speech, it accused him of demagoguery. Having done nothing to provide leadership or take part in the union's activities, Sholokhov was criticizing others without being self-critical. While the letter defended Soviet writers by declaring that there is no shame in owning cottages or visiting resorts, oddly there was no attempt to defend Fadeev. Turning the tables on Sholokhov, the letter inquired why Sholokhov, who lived in the countryside in close contact with the people on a regular basis and who clearly wasn't languishing in a communal apartment, was producing less and less each year. Shouldn't the Soviet populace demand new works from him too? "In sixteen years he has produced a dozen or so chapters of *Virgin Soil* and a small amount of chapters of *They Fought*. Isn't that far too little?" For the first and only time Sholokhov was criticized in the Soviet press for being a writer who had all but stopped writing. While Sholokhov's supporters directed their ire at the editorial board and penned spirited responses, he quietly resolved to start writing again. He aspired to write something that would speak to the new post-Stalin era.

On May 14, 1956, disturbing news began to make the rounds in Moscow. Fadeev was found dead. The details were few and unreliable. The sudden death of his former nemesis disturbed Sholokhov. Not least because he couldn't help but wonder about whether his own speech at the congress had driven a desperate man over the edge. He decided to suspend judgement until the official announcement came. There would no doubt be a glowing tribute to Fadeev's role in the creation of Soviet literature.

The next day *Pravda* published an announcement on the death of Fadeev from the Central Committee and a memorial article from the Writers' Union.[11] In addition to all the appropriate words about his biography, literary achievements, and dedication to the party, both articles went out of their way to emphasize that in recent years alcoholism had impaired Fadeev's ability to write. Sholokhov was incensed. Was this any way to treat a man who had dedicated his life to Soviet literature? How could the party and his fellow writers place an asterisk for all time on a man's legacy by branding him an alcoholic? It was as if he was staring into his own future and sensing posterity's appraisal of his own legacy.

Looking for an explanation, his eye could not help but notice a small text in the middle of the page. The text was entitled "Medical Conclusion on the Disease and Death of Comrade Aleksandr Aleksandrovich Fadeev."[12] It was cold, it was clinical, and it angered Sholokhov beyond measure. It read: "A. A. Fadeev for many years suffered from a severe and progressive ailment—alcoholism. Over the course of the last three years episodes of the disease became more frequent and brought about complications such as the dystrophy of the muscles of the heart and liver. He was hospitalized and treated in sanatoriums on several occasions (in 1954 for four months, in 1955 for five and a half, and in 1956 for two and a half). On May 13 in a state of depression, brought about by the latest onset of this ailment, A. A. Fadeev ended his life by means of suicide." Sholokhov continued reading. The next words leaped off the page. "Doctor of Medical Sciences, Professor I. V. Strel'chuk . . ." There were other names, but they mattered little next to this one. It was right there in black and white. The hypnotist had gotten hold of Sasha Fadeev and held him in captivity. Could he have driven him mad with drugs and hypnotic suggestions? Something seemed fishy about this whole business.

Sholokhov tried for days to confirm the actual circumstances of Fadeev's death. In the end the news brought no comfort. Fadeev's eleven-year-old son found him dead at his summer cottage. He was lying naked on the bed with a self-inflicted gunshot wound to his aorta. Next to him there was a revolver. On an adjacent table there was another object. Some said it was a portrait of Stalin, others claimed that it was an angry letter to the Central Committee.

Sholokhov called Voroshilov to complain about the party's ill treatment of Fadeev.[13] Agitated, he screamed, "How is it that a hero of the civil war, a man who was wounded while storming Kronstadt, can be treated so poorly? He was one of our most talented writers!" Voroshilov tersely responded, "He left a suicide note. In it he assailed several members of the Central Committee. If you knew what it said, you would not be asking such questions." Though Sholokhov decided not to press the matter, he could never forget it. Fadeev was the last living member of the plagiarism inquiry in 1929. Could he really have revealed some secrets?

TWENTY-THREE

In the months after the congress, millions of Soviet citizens debated whether Khrushchev had gone too far in his condemnation of the late dictator or whether he had in fact said far too little. Sholokhov resisted the temptation to take a public position. Khrushchev's statements were too contradictory to discern a clear strategy. This made any utterance unwise. Moreover, Sholokhov was waiting to see how the leadership would handle the question of complicity. He only joined Khrushchev when signs appeared that the leader would rehabilitate a whole category of second-class Soviet citizens.

The same political figures who were now criticizing Stalin had once publicly stood in his presence and flattered him. The same ideologues who were eagerly exposing the dictator's flaws had publicly praised his merits beyond any measure. Their subsequent attempts at clarification only generated oddly impersonal statements about how the Stalin cult "was formed and cultivated in our country for many years" or how it had "assumed ugly forms."[1] Khrushchev's secret speech and subsequent attempts to clarify it failed to explain why those who created and abetted the cult had been afraid to speak out against it. Nor was there any explanation of why it took three years after Stalin's death to reveal the truth. Sholokhov feared that the secret speech would lead to the repudiation of a whole epoch.[2] Reports indicated that portraits of Stalin were already being torn down in various parts of the USSR. Many observers feared that the leader had unleashed forces that could neither be contained nor controlled.

A major test of Khrushchev's candor about the Soviet past came in June 1956. The twentieth anniversary of Gorky's death provided an opportunity for the leader to tell the truth about one of Stalin's most enduring mysteries. Khrushchev's handling of the anniversary would provide hints about how far he was actually willing to go in the name of truth. Would he reveal more of Stalin's secrets? Would he acknowledge the murder? The anniversary publications were sorely disappointing. Even the lead article was written by a hack author who said nothing about the cause of Gorky's death.[3]

It turned out that Khrushchev was moving in a different direction. In summer 1956 Sholokhov learned of an impending shift in Soviet policy towards former prisoners of war.[4] After the Party Congress, Marshal Zhukov convened a secret committee to rehabilitate nearly two million Soviet soldiers who had been captured by the Germans through no fault of their own. Those around Stalin had stubbornly insisted that no true Soviet soldier would ever allow himself to be captured alive. After the war the dictator mandated that returning prisoners of war be treated with suspicion and derision. They were denied housing, barred from party membership, and not permitted to work in various professions. Their children were often deprived of a post-secondary education. More importantly, these veterans were stripped of medals and commendations that they had earned during the war and were not entitled to either veteran's status or benefits. The Zhukov committee recommended that all such Stalin-era restrictions be abolished. Furthermore, it called for an ideological campaign to give recognition to the heroism of Soviet soldiers in captivity.

Sholokhov was among the first to respond to this call. He quickly penned a short story that hewed closely, but brilliantly, to the formulas developed by Zhukov's committee. The story was loosely based on the life of a man he met on the road after the war. It was dedicated to a Soviet soldier named Andrei Sokolov, whose imagined biography paralleled Zhukov's emphasis on soldiers who "bravely and stoically endured the hardships of captivity and the cruel humiliations of Hitlerites." The plot centered around the kind of "heroic escape from captivity" and "crossing of the front line" outlined by the Zhukov commission. The hero conformed to several additional formulas: he "behaved with integrity and dignity towards comrades in captivity" and "rejected all attempts by the adversary to use him against the Motherland." Written in an accessible, popular style—the kind of voice one would hear in a barroom or barracks—Sholokhov's story was a panegyric to the resilience of ordinary Russians.

Captured in the early months of the war, Andrei endured the indignities of life behind barbed wire, only to confront the death of his entire family, the destruction of his home, and the indifference of Soviet society to his plight after the war. He got back on his feet with help from fellow veterans and adopted an abandoned, orphaned, beggar boy. A man who has extended kindness to another man's progeny must forever conceal the truth from the world in order to forge a better future for both.

Almost immediately editors expressed doubts that the story could be published in the USSR. The Communist Party was largely absent from its pages. The narrative contained no positive arc about society's increasing happiness and prosperity. It raised the uncomfortable issue of enduring trauma, which had been taboo since the war. Andrei alternately couldn't sleep or suffered nightmares of being separated from his family by barbed wire. He was a rough-hewn Russian who ironically owed his survival to his blatant disregard for death. His prowess in drinking vodka had so amused a Nazi camp commandant that he commuted Andrei's death sentence on the spot.

Several months passed without a decision about publication. If the story landed on Suslov's desk, there was no way it would ever see the light of day in a Soviet publication. Sholokhov decided to try again after a hunting trip to Kazakhstan. In fall 1956 he launched an appeal to a higher censor.[5] He asked a contact in the Kremlin to bring the matter to Khrushchev's attention.

In the last weeks of 1956, an invitation was tendered to visit the General Secretary's cottage outside Moscow.[6] Though apprehensive at first, Sholokhov soon found common language with Khrushchev. One on one, the Soviet leader turned out to be far more congenial than Sholokhov expected. He discovered that Khrushchev shared his interest in hunting and his fondness for Russian proverbs and coarse, folksy humor. Neither had a high opinion of the Soviet Writers' Union or a fondness for exercises in erudite intellectual abstraction.

Khrushchev was eager to discuss his theory that Hungarian writers played a major role in fomenting the uprising that had recently been suppressed by the Red Army. He believed that their public criticism of the Hungarian government in summer 1956 had culminated in an armed uprising. By undermining the prestige of the government and demanding "complete freedom" for the arts, they contributed to a wave of anarchy. Even as events spiraled out of control, many writers failed to condemn the violence. Khrushchev concluded from this that the party needed to tighten control over culture in the USSR, and he solicited Sholokhov's advice and support. Sholokhov had to rely on the little he knew about Hungary from Soviet press reports, which portrayed the uprising as a carefully planned operation by imperialist instigators who first fomented dissatisfaction with socialism, then unleashed a wave of terror on communists and innocent citizens of Budapest in October 1956. He concurred with Khrushchev that the party should strengthen its directing role in culture. He readily agreed to pen a few words about the situation in Hungary for domestic and international distribution.[7]

As they walked along a series of narrow garden paths, which had recently been cleared of snow, Sholokhov broached the subject of publishing *Fate of a Man*. Almost immediately after hearing about the resilience of an ordinary Russian who overcame every imaginable obstacle that fate could throw in his path, Khrushchev interrupted Sholokhov to declare the story would be published. He kept his promise. It was serialized in the first issues of *Pravda* for 1957.[8] Sholokhov also remained true to his word. He issued a statement to a Hungarian journalist both chastising Hungarian writers for not raising their voices against "reactionary forces" in the past and expressing optimism that the majority of them could still become useful builders of socialism. This exchange of favors was the beginning of an important relationship.

In early 1957 Sholokhov's battle with alcoholism continued. Little did he know that ideological officials were debating whether to deprive him of liberty for several months. After receiving multiple reports that the writer had resumed drinking and his health was getting worse, three Kremlin doctors were called in to discuss aggressive treatment options. A stenographer was sent to record their deliberations for the Central Committee.[9] Chief among them was the hypnotist Ivan Strel'chuk.

He proposed that Sholokhov be subjected to "appropriate supervision" in order to deal with his alcoholism. Standard treatments would be to no avail with this patient. Only isolation and complete control of access could ensure that no contraband alcohol reached Sholokhov. Strel'chuk was confident that complete isolation would enable him to induce the kind of hypnotic suggestions that would forever cure the writer. He argued that Sholokhov had to be kept in his care for no less than half a year to make sure that all his cravings for alcohol could be vanquished. The other doctors debated whether such a strict regime could in fact be organized in a hospital, or if it would be better to isolate the writer in a cottage at a state sanatorium. One of the other doctors proposed seeking an order from higher political authorities that would force Sholokhov to accept the treatment and "would smash his opposition." Subsequently the doctors' recommendations were discussed by one of Khrushchev's assistants and several top officials. A document was issued that obligated Comrade Sholokhov to undergo a "long-duration, special, strict hospital regime."

As word of the decision started to circulate within the Kremlin, one of Sholokhov's supporters called in a favor. Implementation of the order was delayed while Sholokhov could be alerted to the danger and instructed to urgently seek Khrushchev's intervention.[10] If he didn't act fast, he would be delivered into the clutches of the hypnotist Strel'chuk. Fearing that hospitalization would doom him to Fadeev's fate, he searched for the right way to approach the leader.

He recalled that Khrushchev had spoken fondly of reading the first book of *Virgin Soil* and that his favorite character was the foolish, folkish

Shukar'. Sholokhov arranged to have *Pravda* publish new excerpts featuring this character and his comical escapades.[11] One narrated how his efforts to relieve himself in a hayloft were interrupted by an angry goat. Another exploited for comic effect his aspirations to manufacture and market dog fur leggings as a cure for rheumatism. Sholokhov followed up with a warm letter congratulating Khrushchev on his upcoming birthday and his being named a hero of socialist labor.

This calculated act of flattery worked like a charm. One of Sholokhov's contacts in the Kremlin informed him that rather than six months of isolation, drugs, and hypnosis, he would now embark on his first trip to the capitalist world since the mid-1930s. He was being sent on a monthlong publicity tour of Scandinavia, and he was expected to charm officials into awarding him the Nobel Prize for Literature. Although Khrushchev had personally vouched for him, he was warned in no uncertain terms that any drunken episodes abroad would give his detractors in the Kremlin such as Suslov the upper hand.[12] Any drunken scenes would also seriously damage his chances of winning the prize. On the other hand, positive behavior would be rewarded with continued support. Sholokhov swore to stay sober during the trip. He had narrowly escaped the clutches of Strel'chuk and vowed not to return.

Soviet officials arranged a grueling schedule of public events, publicity outings, and meetings with Scandinavian writers. His itinerary was carefully structured to form a Nobel coalition. Diplomatic handlers managed to shield him from provocative questions.[13] They prepped him and fed him talking points about writers he needed to mention and praise in each Scandinavian country.

During the trip Sholokhov wrote to a contact in the Kremlin emphasizing his abstemious behavior. "Neither an excess word, nor an excess sip of [liquor]," he boasted. Proudly he reported that at official receptions he succeeded in limiting himself to only one shot of cognac. In his view the Nobel campaign was proceeding successfully.[14] All the newspapers, even those hostile to the USSR, were proclaiming him to be the likely recipient of the Nobel Prize. He was already starting to imagine how he would click his heels in the presence of the Swedish king and in a generous, socialist gesture turn the prize money over to the Communist Party.

While he was in Denmark in late June 1957, rumors began spreading that something unusual was afoot in the USSR.[15] A high-ranking official delegation expected in Leningrad for its scheduled anniversary festivities failed to arrive. Vacationing Soviet officials were suddenly recalled back to Moscow. An unscheduled, extraordinary plenum of the Central Committee was convened in the capital on very short notice. There was talk of some kind of move against Khrushchev. Sholokhov and the embassy staff anxiously awaited news. By early July a few unusually forceful, but frustratingly vague, appeals to party unity arrived by cable. These indicated that something major had transpired. Then on July 4 an official announcement reported that an "anti-party group" headed by Malenkov, Kaganovich, and Molotov had formed inside the party presidium. A plenum had been convened to discuss the faction's attempt to "change the composition of the leadership organs of the party." This cryptic wording confirmed that Khrushchev had survived an attempt to oust him. The plenum's condemnation of the faction was by the book. What happened next, however, was incredible. Rather than send his rivals to their deaths or cast them into dungeons, Khrushchev exiled them to minor government posts. He took over as Chairman of the Council of Ministers and started to title himself as Premier.

A few weeks after his return from Scandinavia, Sholokhov received a most prestigious invitation. He was summoned to visit Khrushchev at his summer residence in Crimea. Recent press coverage highlighted meetings there with foreign dignitaries such as Ho Chi Minh and Eleanor Roosevelt, so it was clear that his visit was considered a high priority.

Khrushchev had recently unveiled ambitious goals to overtake the United States in per capita production of milk and meat.[16] Each Soviet cow would now be expected to deliver 15 percent more milk. Cows that didn't comply would be expected to contribute to increasing the meat side of the ledger. In order to feed cattle, Khrushchev was using every available opportunity to encourage Soviet farmers to grow more corn. He hoped to quadruple production in many areas and expand its range even into the Arctic. His irrational exuberance about corn was in part spurred by his own experiences in Ukraine and his encounters with a farmer from Iowa who visited the USSR. To feed the Soviet population, he hoped to tap new sources of grain. His Virgin Lands campaign was opening up millions of new acres for cultivation in Kazakhstan, the Urals, and Siberia. His view of Soviet agriculture was largely an optimistic one. With the right crops, the right technologies, and the right incentives, he fervently believed that collectivized agriculture could succeed.

In contrast Sholokhov's view of Soviet agriculture was more measured and less optimistic.[17] Decades of haughty treatment and exploitation had made rural people deeply distrustful of the government. The young and the talented were fleeing from the farms at every available opportunity. During his most recent visits to hunt in Kazakhstan, he had seen that Krushchev's Virgin Lands campaign was not really the triumph trumpeted in the Soviet press. While regional officials were announcing impressive results and commending each other, much of the grain had rotted away due to the fact that there simply wasn't an infrastructure for storing and transporting it. In some areas it was left in the fields too long and dried up. In others it was harvested hastily and improperly, leading to all sorts of rot and mildew. On paper everything was a great success. In actuality the party was repeating the mistakes of the past. The campaign to promote corn had become so all encompassing that Sholokhov even joked that an ear of corn would be the hero of his next novel.

Their conversations frequently turned to politics. When he was in a talkative mood, Khrushchev liked to reveal how he had emerged as the final man standing and how he had outmaneuvered the triumvirate that took power upon Stalin's death. In Stalin's last years, Beria held all the initial advantages due to his ability to manipulate Stalin's increasing isolation and paranoia. Upon Stalin's death, Beria quickly moved to concentrate power in his own hands, but Khrushchev—in his own retelling—clearly foresaw this and prevented it. He convinced the weak-willed Malenkov to abandon Beria. Later he moved against Malenkov for his incompetent handling of agriculture and consumer goods. There had been many moments when Khrushchev went to bed at night not knowing whether his political fate would change before the next morning.

One morning Sholokhov and Khrushchev went for a walk along the sea. Khrushchev suddenly stopped and began what seemed like a confession.[18] "I'd like to tell you a fairy tale. It's going to surprise you. It's the one about how the mice buried the cat." They sat down on a boulder. Khrushchev continued, "That evening he was healthy and in joyous spirits, he left in a good mood. He went to sleep at the usual time, but in the morning he did not leave his bedroom. He was always punctual, so those who worked at the Nearer Cottage became concerned." From the words "nearer cottage" Sholokhov comprehended that this was a story about Stalin. Khrushchev went on: "Hours and hours passed and there was not the slightest sound from beyond the door, which was barred from the inside by a steel bar. You know Stalin did not entrust his life to any locks." Sholokhov had not visited Stalin in his last years, so he could only imagine the suspicious dictator frantically barricading the door of his bedroom each night.

"It was impossible to open the door, and none of the staff were brave enough to knock, fearing that they might disturb his sleep. So the head of security finally called Malenkov. He called us, and the whole kahal went out there to check on him." Now it was clear to Sholokhov that this story was about the moment when the collective leadership had emerged. "On our tiptoes we creeped around, trying making as little noise as possible. We each went up to the door and listened." Sholokhov was in suspense, waiting to hear what had happened. "Someone needed to knock, but no one was brave enough. We whispered to each other but could not make a decision for eighteen hours." Khrushchev was confiding in Sholokhov. He needed to confess to someone that the same prominent individuals who had publicly proclaimed their love for Stalin were too paralyzed by fear to save him during his critical hour of need. "Then all of a sudden there was a thud in the bedroom. At that point we unanimously decided to open the door. A joiner and a locksmith had been waiting there with their tools for quite a while. They were given the order to open the door, and we found Stalin laying on the carpet all contorted, his face up but his eyes closed. His breathing was very labored. The doctor was the first to approach him. Taking his pulse, the doctor said, 'It's very grave,' and his hand gestures signaled to us that there was no hope." Sholokhov sensed that Khrushchev's tale was about to take a dramatic turn.

"The first to approach him was Beria. Giving a look to all of us, he loudly proclaimed, 'The tyrant has fallen. He's croaked!' From these loud words, Stalin appeared to awaken. He opened his left eye. In an instant it became fixed on Beria. It surveyed the room, then it returned to Beria. Everyone saw that his gaze was normal, sentient. What a nightmare!" Sholokhov sensed Khrushchev's palpable agitation four years later. No one in the room had either upbraided Beria or intervened to stop him. They demonstrated to Stalin their indifference to his fate. "At once Beria fell on his knees before Stalin and started to sob. 'Dear Comrade Stalin, forgive this fool, have mercy.' Molotov took him by the collar and pushed him aside. Stalin closed his eyes and there were no more signs of life."

Sholokhov marveled at this rare moment of candor. He was now one of only a handful of people in the world who knew the truth about Stalin's death. Khrushchev entrusted him with his private fears about his own behavior that day. Those revelations became their bonding moment.

TWENTY-FOUR

I n spring 1958 Soviet diplomats in Stockholm received a dire warning. A sympathetic Swedish writer reported that the Nobel Prize committee was preparing an exceedingly unpleasant surprise for the USSR. According to highly informed sources, several members were advocating awarding the prize for literature to Boris Pasternak, a controversial Soviet writer whose most recent novel had been smuggled abroad and published in Italy.[1] In response, Soviet ideologues attempted to thwart the Pasternak candidacy by promoting Sholokhov as a politically palatable alternative. Their efforts to maneuver Sholokhov as a cultural pawn in a Cold War prestige contest would harm his candidacy in 1958 but help him in the long run. Sholokhov benefited from the Pasternak affair in ways that were both unusual and unpredictable.

The secret report from Stockholm actualized fears that had been brewing for nearly two years.[2] In summer 1956, Pasternak had given a copy of his manuscript to an Italian visitor to Moscow after his efforts to publish it in the USSR had failed. Ideological officials had categorized

Dr. Zhivago as a "hostile outburst against the ideology of Marxism," which slanderously portrayed the revolution as a thoughtless and cruel jacquerie consisting of only chaos and degradation. When efforts to have the manuscript returned to the USSR failed in early 1957, Soviet officials tried unsuccessfully to pressure foreign publishers into not releasing it. The Italian publisher Feltrinelli decided to go ahead with publication in fall 1957 in spite of the fact that Pasternak, under pressure, withdrew his permission and proclaimed that publication would be a "direct and crude violation" of his rights. English and French translations were hastily prepared, not without the help of the CIA.

Soviet ideologues decided to simultaneously promote Sholokhov's candidacy and exert pressure on the Swedish Academy to reject Pasternak. They miscalculated by intertwining the two writers. By being too assertive, they further mishandled the situation. Soviet diplomats in Sweden were ordered to communicate to various audiences that an award for Pasternak would be treated as an unfriendly act against the Soviet public. In trying too hard to influence the confidential discussions of the Nobel committee, they displayed blatant disregard for Swedish neutrality.[3] Their highly unsubtle crisis mitigation produced only backlash.

Though Sholokhov was aware of efforts to promote his candidacy, he refused to facilitate the official campaign. He exacerbated his position by permitting a talented Soviet photographer to document his daily activities. Over the span of a twenty-year career, Viktor Ruikovich had established himself as one of the country's best photojournalists. While following Sholokhov around Vioshki, Ruikovich captured images of Sholokhov fishing, hunting, regaling locals with tall tales, and being affectionate with his dogs. Missing were any carefully staged pictures of the great writer sitting behind his desk creating a new masterpiece. Sholokhov grew so accustomed to Ruikovich that he even consented to being photographed while inebriated and in unguarded moments.

When several of the pictures were published in a Soviet illustrated magazine in summer 1958, ideological officials feared that the portrait of Sholokhov was too down to earth and too common.[4] Depicted in a tattered, cotton insulated jacket, he could easily be mistaken for a rustic yokel rather than a great writer. Foreign dissemination of pictures of a disheveled Sholokhov could also harm the well-orchestrated Nobel campaign and reveal to the world the secret of his incurable alcoholism. A decree from the Central Committee thundered against a series of photographs that presented Sholokhov unshaven, with unkempt hair, swollen eyes, and bulging veins on his forehead. The photographer received a browbeating and a stern warning. Sholokhov was warned against a repetition of lax image control.

In late October, as the date of a possible Nobel decision approached, ideological officials contacted Sholokhov. They issued instructions about how he was expected to behave in the event that the Nobel committee or foreign journalists contacted him. They gave him permission to accept the award if he was named the sole laureate for 1958. But further instructions hinted that they were in possession of some kind of secret information. They were clearly anticipating that the Nobel Prize might be divided between him and Pasternak.[5] If this happened, they ordered him to defiantly reject the award and declare to the press that he refused to be a recipient of any award that was being manipulated for anti-Soviet objectives.

On October 25, the Soviet press announced that the Nobel Prize had been awarded to Boris Pasternak, the author of a novel that had "grievously slandered the USSR." The *Literary Gazette* paired the Nobel announcement with a publication of the rejection letter sent to Pasternak by the journal *Novyi Mir*.[6] An editorial about the first foreign reactions to the decision called the award a provocation directed against the Soviet Union. The Soviet response also continued the pre-award strategy of intertwining Pasternak and Sholokhov. It lamented that the prize was not awarded to a "worthy continuer of great traditions of Russian literature" and did not go to a "truly people's writer . . . loved by millions." These were standard talking points about Sholokhov in official propaganda. The article also quoted K. Vennberg, a Swedish writer, that the committee passed over the candidacy of Mikhail Sholokhov due to political motivations. Taking a cue from these signals, a few days later the Moscow branch of the Writers' Union invoked Sholokhov in its unanimous decision to expel Pasternak from its ranks. It proclaimed that "the Nobel committee did not recognize the world-renowned artistic treasures created by Leo Tolstoy, Chekhov, Gorky, Maiakovskii, and Sholokhov." It was impossible not to notice that Sholokhov was the only living writer included in the list. Subsequent publications unleashed a wave of vicious condemnation of *Doctor Zhivago* and its author by ordinary Soviet citizens. This wave even created a late Soviet aphorism: "I haven't read it, but I wholeheartedly condemn it."

Sensing that the Pasternak affair would be detrimental to his Nobel prospects in the future, Sholokhov refrained from participating in the vitriolic condemnations of Pasternak.[7] Sholokhov held Pasternak's poetry in high regard but found his skills as a novelist to be deficient. He was conspicuously absent from the extraordinary meeting of the Writers' Union that condemned Pasternak and expelled him from its ranks. He remained aloof from the series of dramatic public condemnations that unfolded in rapid succession. Amid vociferous public statements calling for Pasternak to be kicked out of the country and labeling him a creature worse than a pig, which defecates in the same place where it sleeps and dines, he remained silent.

During those tense, dramatic days when the literary world was intensely focused on the fate of Pasternak, few paid attention to a troubling piece of news that was making the rounds. Ivan Makar'ev had slit his own wrists.[8] They found him alone and bleeding to death on the floor of his apartment. He could not successfully rebuild his life after returning from the camps. Old wounds continued to torment him until the day he took his own life. For Sholokhov this loss meant that all of the comrades who played a major role in his early successes were now gone.

Contacts in the Soviet diplomatic service reported that Sholokhov's unfulfilled promises to finish *Virgin Soil* probably harmed his candidacy in 1958. Therefore he set his sights on finishing the novel during the first weeks of 1959. Only a few chapters remained to be written. The rest were sent to *Neva*, a new literary journal in Leningrad. He wrote to Khrushchev in January 1959 requesting permission to travel to Italy, England, Denmark, and Sweden to negotiate with publishers about the novel. He emphasized in good fashion that none of these foreign publications would appear before the Soviet publication of the novel—a loyal hint in the aftermath of the Pasternak publications.[9] He also requested permission to bring several relatives along and to lodge in Soviet embassies in order to avoid any undesirable encounters. Khrushchev approved the request. An intermediate stop in France was added to the official itinerary in order to facilitate the journey from Italy to England. This late addition would become a bone of contention between Sholokhov and ideological officials.

While in France, Sholokhov ignored the advice of his handlers and openly engaged with journalists at a press conference devoted to a range of topics.[10] Though on multiple occasions an embassy official attempted to intervene, insisting that they were out of time and had to stop, Sholokhov continued to veer dangerously off script. He calculated that this was his best opportunity to comment on the Pasternak affair, and he was determined to capitalize on it. He made it clear that he was not involved in any way with the decision not to publish *Dr. Zhivago* in the USSR. Nonetheless he emphasized that he did not think very highly of the novel. It remained half-baked because Pasternak had rejected the advice of his colleagues and refused to revise it. He insisted that the Writers' Union got a "little hot headed" and "lost its nerve" in its reaction to the awarding of the Nobel Prize to Pasternak. He suggested that Pasternak should have been allowed to publish *Dr. Zhivago* in the USSR. Such a decision would have resulted in the novel being quickly forgotten by Soviet readers. "Like Khrushchev, I think that a big mistake was made in making so much noise as a result of a book that didn't deserve it."

By Soviet standards, this was an act of defiance. The official position at the time was that no attention whatsoever should be devoted to Pasternak. By even answering questions, Sholokhov was courting trouble. To make a bad situation worse, he avoided all of the official talking points about *Dr. Zhivago*. He did not call it a distortion of Soviet reality, a pasquill of the revolution, or a slander of the Soviet intelligentsia. He did not content himself with merely questioning the competence of Soviet ideological officials and the Writers' Union. He even claimed to speak for Khrushchev and in some reports was quoted as calling him a friend.

News of the French interviews quickly reached ideological officials in Moscow. They ordered the Soviet ambassador in Paris to verify whether

Sholokhov had in fact uttered such careless statements.[11] Upon confirmation, the ambassador issued Sholokhov a stern rebuke. In London Sholokhov again addressed the subject of *Dr. Zhivago*.[12] This time, in an attempt at damage control, he insisted that his remarks in Paris had been distorted by the French press. Once again questions about Pasternak dominated the press conference. Sholokhov insisted that he could not take it upon himself to decide the fate of another author's work and doubted that Pasternak would still want to publish the novel in the Soviet Union. In a halfhearted effort to toe the party line, he argued that Soviet intellectuals had a right to be indignant about a work that had slandered them. When a journalist retorted, "How can someone be indignant about something he has not read?" Sholokhov conceded that they were indignant about the passages quoted in the official rejection letter published in the *Literary Gazette*. Only after a substantial grilling did the discussion return to perfunctory questions about his own work. When asked about rumors that censorship was the reason for the long delay in completing the war novel, he acknowledged that such rumors had been widespread but claimed that there were difficulties in writing about the war at the time.

At subsequent meetings he was accompanied by a secret police officer, who closely watched over him and even attended dinners and small gatherings with him.[13] As a result, Sholokhov was often forced to hold his tongue. One British intellectual who encountered him at a dinner in his honor insisted he had the "bearing of a morose taxi driver annoyed/dissatisfied with his tip." The dinner was hosted by Charles Percy Snow, a British scientist, politician, and novelist, who had recently been knighted by Queen Elizabeth. He was particularly interested in communication across boundaries. Though he soon became famous for his musings about the breach of communication between humanities and the sciences, he also feared that the Cold War could lead to similar breaches.

For the rest of the trip Sholokhov adhered to script by avoiding political topics and uttering uncontroversial banalities. Nonetheless the subject of Pasternak kept coming up. He also remained uncharacteristically tight-lipped during the Third Writers' Congress in May.

When he learned in June 1959 that Khrushchev was planning a trip to Scandinavia later that summer, he conceived of a publicity stunt to reinvigorate his Nobel prospects.[14] He reminded Khrushchev about his acceptance of an invitation to visit Vioshki. In order to create a sense of urgency, he announced that he was finishing *Virgin Soil* and claimed that the biggest honor after working on the novel for thirty years would be to have Khrushchev congratulate him in person. The long letter he wrote to Khrushchev did not explicitly mention the Nobel Prize, but it mentioned Scandinavia and alluded to the need to "demonstrate the unity of the party and literature." For the first time he expressed in writing a love for Khrushchev, which he qualified as a "somewhat crude, but stern, manly soldier's [kind of] love."

Khrushchev quickly accepted the invitation. The local party committee began preparations for a grand reception. It made plans to bus in thousands of collective farmers from the surrounding area and neighboring provinces to greet Khrushchev and line the path from a tiny airfield to Sholokhov's home. A grand meeting was planned and a series of photo-ops with locals in colorful Cossack costumes was organized.

Before the Premier's planned trip to Vioshki, events took a dramatic turn. The Premier suddenly cancelled his tour to Scandinavia. Allegedly, anti-Soviet statements in the Danish and Swedish press were to blame for the "postponing" of the trip. He prolonged his vacation in Crimea instead. There were fears that he would also postpone his visit to Sholokhov. It turned out that the Scandinavia trip was cancelled due to President Eisenhower's invitation of Khrushchev to a high-level summit.

Sholokhov would have to settle for a short visit. There would be no hunting, no serious fishing, and precious little face time. There were even disappointing reports that Khrushchev would stay in a guarded rail car rather than in the writer's house. Security officials arrived days in advance to scour the entire vicinity for any sign of trouble.

On August 30, Khrushchev arrived as planned.[15] With journalists in tow he met with Sholokhov, took a boat tour of the Don River, listened to a Cossack ensemble, and posed for hundreds of pictures. Sholokhov played his part by publicly calling Khrushchev not a guest but a friend, and praising his upcoming historical visit with the American president.

That afternoon Khrushchev delivered a long and tedious speech in praise of Sholokhov and his works. Beyond boilerplate praises and phrases, there was little in the speech that was memorable. But near the end of it, Khrushchev publicly announced the surprise that he had planned for Sholokhov. He was inviting Sholokhov on his upcoming trip to America.

Almost simultaneously with Khrushchev's visit, an American journalist in Moscow published a scandalous article.[16] Writing for the *New York Times* and citing "Moscow literary circles," a journalist named Harrison Salisbury declared that the purpose of Khrushchev's visit to Vioshki was to settle a dispute over the ending of *Virgin Soil*. Salisbury speculated that Sholokhov had originally delayed completion of the novel because there was a danger that Stalin would be dissatisfied with the results. When he completed it in summer 1958, chiefs of the Communist Party pronounced the ending to be unsuitable because the novel's chief communist hero, Davydov, was arrested and committed suicide in prison. Unwilling to rewrite the ending, Sholokhov then threatened to follow Pasternak's example and find a foreign publisher. "The Sholokhov case had the makings of another Boris Pasternak case," Salisbury hypothesized. Allegedly only Khrushchev's timely intervention prevented this.

The story was wildly inaccurate. It was based on only a small kernel of demonstrably true information—Sholokhov's invitation to Khrushchev indeed coincided with his completion of the novel. The authority of the *New York Times* gave dubious Moscow literary rumors instant international credibility. On his trip to the United States a few weeks later, Sholokhov was understandably surprised by the fact that serious people gave credence to absurd, unsubstantiated rumors. He used his only press conference to label Salisbury's article a "mad fantasy." The incident fueled his suspicion of the West, which in his view was only interested in cheap, superficial controversy.

Sholokhov responded to the controversy by publishing a satirical article about the honest, respectable Little Boy Harry, who grew up to be the disreputable journalist Mr. Salisbury.[17] A "malicious and stupid fantasy led him a long way on the road to sensation and the earnings he received were dirty and dishonorable." He excoriated the journalist for never attempting to contact him about the ending of the book and relying on rumors. He blustered that Salisbury deserved to be flogged like a character in a Dickens story for his ignoble behavior.

Though the visit to the United States was considered a political success, for Sholokhov it was a frustrating experience.[18] At every turn Khrushchev was greeted by huge, enthusiastic crowds of ordinary Americans. They were so eager to see the Soviet leader that they pushed through barricades and police security cordons. The leader's every move became a grand occasion covered by dozens of journalists. In contrast, Sholokhov was barely noticed. He was bothered that almost no one seemed to know who he was. This anonymity disturbed him. He was unquestionably one of the most famous people in the communist world, yet here he was constantly defined by his connection to Khrushchev.

Only when Khrushchev went out of his way to direct attention to the presence of a great Russian writer did anyone briefly pretend to care. The few intellectually inclined people he met all too often wanted to talk about Pasternak rather than his own works.[19] Nonetheless, he resolved to retain his sense of humor. When at a Hollywood gathering Charlton Heston recognized his name and proudly announced that he had once read excerpts from one of Sholokhov's novels, Sholokhov expressed his gratitude and promised to watch excerpts of Heston's next movie.

Sholokhov returned with mixed impressions. Like many Soviet visitors, he came away convinced that America was both a bastion of technological progress and a cultural wasteland. He was acutely attentive to extreme disparities of wealth and privilege. He likely shared the widespread sentiment of Soviet diplomats that the American organizers of several events had orchestrated them to embarrass Khrushchev. The mayor of Los Angeles had indecorously permitted himself to preach to a head of state. Hollywood officials organized a cancan dance to provoke a reaction. A meeting with labor union leaders in San Francisco was hijacked by token labor leaders, whom he suspected of being loyal lapdogs of capitalism. All of these occasions took advantage of the Premier's openness and informality to dishonor him. He refused to write an article for a book about the visit being edited by Khrushchev's son-in-law.[20] The leader's assistants hounded him for months, but he stuck to his guns.

TWENTY-FIVE

n the early '60s Sholokhov started to have concerns about Khrushchev's leadership. Six years after he came to power, the Premier attempted to bolster his political position by rewriting history, attacking vanquished enemies, and discarding the dead dictator's corpse. While Khrushchev railed against the Stalin cult, his allies were busy promoting a new one to replace it. Both Khrushchev and Sholokhov struggled to keep their promises to the Soviet people. The writer reneged on pledges to finish the war novel. The Premier was unable to deliver more meat and milk to consumers. By summer 1962 an unwise policy decision brought them to the brink of conflict.

After years of promising progress on the war novel, Sholokhov found that the time for tangible results had arrived. For months he stared at blank pages out of a sense of duty. The results were so meager that he actively tried to lower public expectations.[1] He claimed that he was writing slowly in order to get it right. He opined that he was facing the dual problems of how to begin and how to end the novel. He insisted that he was awaiting the publication of memoirs of key military figures. However, the time for general phrases and vague platitudes about the heroism of ordinary Soviet soldiers had long passed.

He had repeatedly claimed that the novel would have a whole section devoted to the battle for Stalingrad. Now those promises came back to haunt him. To even mention the battle in the early '60s would set him on a collision course with Khrushchev. A new official history was seeking to replace one myth with another.[2] The victories at Stalingrad were now being attributed to Khrushchev rather than Stalin.

In early 1961 Marshal A. I. Yeremenko became one of the first Soviet generals to publicly mythologize Khrushchev's leadership during the war.[3] A few years earlier this general had made several clumsy efforts to ingratiate himself to Sholokhov. The writer immediately dismissed the Marshal's heroic war stories as the inventions of an officer who had rarely ventured far from heavily guarded, concrete command bunkers far from the front lines. But in the intervening years this windbag and his malleable memories of the war became valuable to Khrushchev.

As Khrushchev's economic reforms sputtered and his promises about massive increases in milk and meat production remained unfulfilled, he looked for other ways to enhance his political position. He began to take credit for the victory at Stalingrad. As the chief witness to Khrushchev's creatively enhanced role in the defense of the city, Marshal Yeremenko played a willing part in the creation of the myth of Khrushchev as a great military man. Reimagined as a gifted strategist, talented organizer, and popular leader, Khrushchev conveniently emerged as a star of the marshal's memoir. Peppered with pictures of Khrushchev during the war, the book linked his arrival in Stalingrad to the beginning of the end of Hitler's war machine. The marshal proudly insisted that he had worked "together with Nikita Sergeevich" to turn the tide at Stalingrad.

This was the first significant attempt to mythologize Khrushchev. Almost simultaneously, an official, multivolume history of the Second World War started to be published.[4] It mentioned Khrushchev more times than any other Soviet figure and in several sections assigned him twice as much space as any of the leading generals. Khrushchev's supporters also systematically erased Stalin from the narrative of the Soviet victory. The dictator's name was usually mentioned in connection with mistakes that had resulted in massive casualties, though occasionally his positive role in mobilizing the population was begrudgingly acknowledged. Often Stalin's leadership was hidden behind euphemisms such as "headquarters" or "supreme command." Several sections of the new official history were clearly written to support the premier's controversial assertions about Stalin's military incompetence. Sholokhov was highly skeptical of this new narrative.

Though he was still benefitting from the alliance with Khrushchev—the premier had approved his trip with several family members to England and Italy—the emerging new view of the war complicated matters. Inevitably one day Khrushchev would inquire about the Stalingrad chapters, and Sholokhov would have to either prevaricate or risk a confrontation.

When Yurii Gagarin became the first person to "conquer the cosmos" in April 1961 to the thunderous excitement of the world, Sholokhov was called upon to provide an apt expression of Soviet pride.[5] As soon as news of the first successful manned flight into space and return to earth was made public late on April 12, Sholokhov became one of a handful of Soviet figures contacted to provide a first reaction for a special extra edition of *Pravda*. Going for a folksy economy of words, he exclaimed, "*Vot eto da!*" This can be translated as 'Yes, that's it' or the kind of enthusiastic "Oh Yeaaah!" one shouts when impressed by a feat of prowess or skill. Two days later at a government reception for Gagarin in the Kremlin, Khrushchev ended his official remarks by reflecting upon how hard it is to find words for expressing the pride felt by Soviet citizens. He declared, "Sholokhov managed to find the most adroit way out of the situation by simply writing, '*Vot eto da!*' And now each one of us has already repeated that hundreds of times . . ."[6]

Not long after this triumph, Khrushchev unexpectedly called a Party Congress to once again denounce the "cult of personality" and to excoriate party rivals he had vanquished back in 1957.[7] Several speakers insinuated that Viacheslav Molotov had recently sent a secret letter to the Central Committee that criticized the Premier and his policies. This effort to "splinter" the party ostensibly provided the pretext for dredging up the

Stalinist past and ferociously condemning factionalism. Many keynote speeches also lashed out at tiny communist Albania and its leaders, who remained stubbornly committed to Stalinist policies and methods. This was an effort to criticize China by proxy. Khrushchev's allies affirmed that his triumph in 1957 saved the Soviet Union from a new wave of purges and repressions that the "anti-party group" consisting of Molotov, Malenkov, and Kaganovich wanted to unleash. In contrast to the hopelessly old and conservative ideas of his vanquished rivals, Khrushchev's allies claimed that he brought progressive and innovative leadership to the country.

Khrushchev assigned Sholokhov an important speaking slot at the Twenty-Second Party Congress. The writer was more than willing to condemn the Premier's vanquished rivals, but he could not endorse Khrushchev's efforts to rewrite history. Unlike most of the other speakers, whose talking points and surprises from secret archives stretched all the way back to the 1930s in order to claim that the "anti-party group" was responsible for the Great Terror, Sholokhov completely avoided advancing specific allegations about repressions of the Stalin era.

The shadow of the Great Terror hung heavily over the congress. Various speakers accused the "anti-party group" of personal responsibility for mass arrests of innocent people. Malenkov, Kaganovich, and Molotov were portrayed as heartless hypocrites who sent thousands of honest communists to their doom. Khrushchev insisted that even after the secret speech, "they wanted a return to those exceedingly difficult times for our party and country, when no one was insured against arbitrary violations and repressions."[8] To the shock of his audience, he claimed that a new investigation of Kirov's murder was uncovering all sorts of strange and unresolved questions. The "anti-party group" had allegedly been waiting for such a pretext to unleash repression upon the population.

Though Khrushchev unveiled many new facts about the attempted coup against him in 1957, he suppressed the most significant fact of all. Without the support of Marshal Zhukov, whom he subsequently dismissed and sent into retirement, he would not have prevailed over his rivals. One of the speakers at the congress even suggested that Zhukov had tried to create his own "cult of personality" in the army.[9] It was ironic that a leader who was exaggerating his own war leadership would resort to such charges.

In his speech to the congress Sholokhov supported Khrushchev but sidestepped the "cult of personality."[10] He praised Khrushchev's new party program, expressed "masculine love" for Nikita Sergeevich, and confidently announced that communism would be attained in twenty years. Then he briefly addressed the major theme of the congress: condemnation of the factionalists. Mobilizing quotes from Gogol's *Taras Bul'ba* on the sacred bonds of comradeship and mentioning a short story about bandits by O. Henry, he had his audience laughing and applauding. Taking a serious turn, he thundered, "Aren't we being excessively tolerant towards those upon whose consciences [weigh] the deaths of thousands of true sons of the Motherland and party and the destroyed lives of thousands of their near and dear ones. The congress is the supreme organ of the party, let it pronounce its harsh, but just, decision." Many in the audience probably recalled that he had uttered similar words not long before Beria was executed.

While other speakers dredged up the past, Sholokhov devoted a prominent section of his speech to humiliating a current official. Mobilizing a potent combination of misogyny and sarcasm, he addressed a report to the congress by Ekaterina Furtseva, the only female minister in Khrushchev's government. A few years earlier she had ignored the writer's appeals and refused to permit the publication of one of Hemingway's stories in the USSR.[11] This personal literary slight was ultimately less important than a political one. Khrushchev's team found out that she had made disparaging remarks about the leader to another official. They, it would seem, urged Sholokhov to go after her with full force.[12]

Praising her charming appearance and feminine politeness, he paid her a backhanded compliment by claiming that she manages pretty well with her ministerial job. He ridiculed her for citing statistics about culture in her talk. "Your numbers and percentages are a cunning thing, Comrade Furtseva, before you know it they'll let you down," he declared. In his view, most of the 780 new plays she boasted about had already been forgotten and were not worthy of being ever performed again. "It is better for those numbers to dwell somewhere in the Central Statistical

Administration," he sarcastically admonished. "They will be considerably more comfortable there than in the realm of art." He then mocked her proposal that young artists should be encouraged to visit communist construction sites. "Let Comrade Furtseva take her lumps and bruises in carrying out such a noble endeavor," he joked. In his view the plan would never work because after a week they would start to miss their heated bathrooms and head home.

Public mockery was a prelude to her political demotion and his elevation. Days later she was not reelected to the Politburo. Not long after that she attempted to commit suicide.[13] Khrushchev was so disturbed by her actions that he permitted her to retain her post as Minister of Culture. Sholokhov, on the other hand, was elected to membership in the Central Committee. This made him a privileged member of the party elite who could vote in occasional plenums that decided important matters of policy.

Sholokhov played no role in the crowning achievement of the congress. Khrushchev and his assistants decided to press the congress for a decision to remove Stalin's embalmed body from Lenin's mausoleum. Rumors insisted that a Chinese delegation tried to lay a wreath inscribed with words attacking Khrushchev near Stalin's corpse and that this pushed the Premier over the edge. Others proclaimed that the move was planned in advance and that his assistants were lining up support as soon as important delegations arrived in the capital from the republics. Only hours after a motion to remove the dead dictator from public display was introduced by the Leningrad delegation and supported by the congress, the deed was carried out in the dead of night.[14] Stalin's body was reburied near the Kremlin walls near less prominent leaders of the party.

After the congress Sholokhov decided to capitalize on his mercenary performance. He petitioned Khrushchev for permission to travel to Sweden and Finland in early 1962.[15] Probably aware that he was once again under consideration for the Nobel Prize, he did not mention this in his request. Instead he insisted that the imminent completion of the war novel necessitated negotiations with publishers in those countries. To make his request appear altruistic, he promised to advocate on behalf of young Soviet writers to have their works published abroad. The Politburo viewed Sholokhov's request with suspicion, not for its deception or self-serving ends but due to the political risks of his destructive vice. Fearing that the writer's alcoholism was once again becoming a problem, on behalf of the Central Committee Khrushchev rejected the request.

In order to demonstrate that this rejection portended no lasting political disfavor, another unusual request from Sholokhov was carefully considered by Khrushchev and the entire Politburo around the same time.[16] A publishing house controlled by an ally of Sholokhov was planning to publish his collected works, including *Quiet Don*, in an edition of over 300,000 copies. Due to an arcane technicality in Soviet copyright law, Sholokhov stood to lose nearly 45,000 rubles if the publication was treated as a supplement available to subscribers of a journal rather than as a stand-alone publication. He petitioned for a onetime exception to Soviet tax regulations. Khrushchev and the Politburo granted it. As a result, in one day he earned more than twenty times the annual salary of a Soviet teacher.

In the months after the congress Sholokhov started to receive overtures from conservative intellectuals.[17] Emboldened by a brief, vague reference about "protecting youths from alien influences" in his speech at the congress, they sought to cultivate his support for a new struggle against "moral degradation" and "bowing down before the West." They valued order, patriotism, and protecting the wholesomeness of Soviet youth. Though they paid obligatory lip service to Marxism, they professed a love for motherland and a cultural program that was decidedly Russian. Sholokhov used his influence on more than one occasion to help them secure access to publishing outlets.

A different kind of recognition came in April 1962 when he was invited to receive an honorary doctorate from the University of St. Andrews in Scotland.[18] The invitation came from the rotund Englishman with the double chin and thick black-rimmed glasses who had hosted a dinner in his honor in London in 1959. Charles Percy Snow had been recently elected rector of the university. As one of his first actions he decided to award Sholokhov its highest honor. This time Khrushchev gave his approval after extracting promises of good conduct and sober behavior from the writer.

Sholokhov enjoyed the pomp and circumstance of the ceremony. He had to dress up in a medieval-style cap and robe and give a speech. At a dinner in his honor, he regaled his British hosts with bawdy stories and made his translator blush from laughter. This time he and Snow hit it off. For an Englishman Snow could hold his drink like a Russian. His quiet demeanor and unhurried, deliberate mode of speaking concealed an ascerbic wit. He knew his Russian literature and proved to be quite an aficionado of *Quiet Don*, proclaiming it to be the best Russian novel since the revolution.

Weeks after returning from Great Britain, Sholokhov became embroiled in one of the most tragic and controversial events of the Khrushchev era. A bad policy decision by the Premier provoked popular anger.[19] Overnight the government increased the price of meat by more than 30 percent. In Novocherkassk, the former Cossack capital turned industrial city, the ensuing crisis reached a boiling point in only a few hours. A series of frantic phone calls in early June 1962 warned Sholokhov that a bloodbath was about to unfold.

Callers reported that an angry crowd had assembled in Novocherkassk to protest the "necessary" and "temporary" measures announced by the government on June 1. Beyond those basic facts the details were uncertain and contradictory. Some claimed that the workers of the Electro-locomotive factory had gone on strike to protest the fact that the dramatic rise in prices had coincided with a systematic drop in wages. They were demanding a meeting with someone from the government. Others insisted that provocateurs and agitators had fanned hostility against the government and that under their malicious influence the protesters began chanting antigovernment slogans and threatened to storm local government buildings. Conditions were ripe for a riot, and the military was mobilizing. Without decisive intervention, there would be violence.

Some of the callers begged Sholokhov to fly to Novocherkassk to use his authority to convince the crowd to disperse before it was too late. Though he initially contemplated making the journey, the more he pondered the issue, the more he feared the risks. His friends warned him that if he traveled to Novocherkassk, he would be taking ownership of the crisis. He would be staking his reputation on a policy that he did not endorse. Khrushchev must have understood that the price hike would be both controversial and unpopular. He nonetheless implemented it without wide consultation with the Central Committee, and he made sure that his own name was not mentioned anywhere in the initial announcement.

After weighing the risks, Sholokhov decided to wait and see how events would unfold the next day. There was no point in listening to the regional news broadcasts that evening. They ignored the protests and featured upbeat stories. More phone calls the next day confirmed his worst fears. The protests had moved from the factory district to the center of the city. [20] The military had taken up positions in the vicinity of key government buildings. What happened next would remain highly disputed. Some insisted that instigators worked the crowd into a mad frenzy and that it attempted to storm the city police headquarters and unleashed attacks on figures of authority. Others insisted that the crowd became unruly but not riotous when not a single representative of the government would come out and hear its demands. One thing was clear: a bloody massacre ensued. Volleys of machine gun fire strafed the crowd. Witnesses saw dozens of bodies being carried away. There was talk of hundreds injured. The Soviet media remained completely silent about the events in Novocherkassk.

The news that Red Army troops had fired on Soviet civilians outraged Sholokhov. The fact that such a crisis was completely unnecessary was even more troubling. Why couldn't prices be raised gradually? Didn't anyone in the Central Committee realize that young families were already spending almost their entire wages on food and housing? The propaganda apparatus had completely botched the unveiling of the policy. Rather than speak honestly and directly to the populace, Khrushchev ordered his assistants to couch the key announcement in reams of statistics and ideological platitudes. [21] Didn't the Premier realize that his own unfulfilled promises about massive increases in meat production fueled popular anger?

When he heard that six members of the Politburo had traveled to the region to deal with the aftermath of the tragedy, Sholokhov decided to fly to Rostov to take part in their hastily scheduled meeting with regional party leaders. On the ground in Rostov, additional facts began to emerge.

The director of the factory had insulted workers who expressed to him their concerns about the price hike. Allegedly he told them if they could no longer afford meat, they should just make do with liver pies instead. Talk of such disrespectful and haughty behavior instantly spread from workshop to workshop, causing hundreds of workers to abruptly stop work. The local government was paralyzed with inaction while waiting for instructions from the Kremlin. Lack of engagement caused further frustration among the crowd. Hundreds on the streets swelled to thousands. The two highest-ranking officials sent from Moscow to deal with the mounting crisis were divided about what to do. Anastas Mikoian wanted to defuse the crisis by talking with the protestors, while Frol Kozlov, Khrushchev's right-hand man, favored the use of force.[22] In the aftermath of the massacre, Kozlov was blaming local officials and lashing out at them for their alleged cowardice.

In front of hundreds of regional party officials, Sholokhov confronted Khrushchev's deputy. He challenged Kozlov to cite a single party document that granted district or regional party committees the authority to order military troops to fire on civilians. He chastised Kozlov for trying to shift the blame away from central authorities, who had implemented the price hikes. Realizing that Sholokhov could not be bullied, the regional party elite supported him. Kozlov was unable to pass his resolution firing several local officials. Sholokhov could take solace in the fact that his intervention had saved the careers of several regional officials. The Novocherkassk massacre left lingering doubts about Khrushchev's team.

The massacre would never be acknowledged in print. Though *Pravda* reported on the regional party meeting, readers would form the impression that nothing extraordinary had occurred.[23] The regional party leadership had merely convened a meeting to discuss how to better achieve goals for producing meat, butter, and milk. Some unspecified party organizations were chided for having weakened their ties to the masses and for lapses in their ideological work. Frol Kozlov had once again given a big and important speech. It seemed as if under his direction the regional party leadership resolved to put an end to disparaging attitudes towards the needs and demands of laborers.

TWENTY-SIX

n late 1962 all of Moscow was talking about three topics: abstract art, labor camps, and Khrushchev's unpredictable behavior. The most pressing and engrossing topic was the third, but any assessment of the Premier's behavior hinged on opinions about the first two. In a remarkably short period of time, Khrushchev managed to upset both conservative "old guard" ideologues and young reformers. He careened towards one extreme, only to turn on a dime and careen in another. Sholokhov had no idea of what to expect next.

By choosing a hunting trip over responding to a new imperative outlined at the Party Congress, Sholokhov skipped an opportunity to publicly support Khrushchev, who called for more attention to be devoted to telling the truth about Stalin's victims. Another writer appeared out of nowhere to answer this call. Aleksandr Solzhenitsyn was a math teacher from Riazan', a provincial town south of Moscow. He had written a short story about a day in the life of an inmate in a Stalinist labor camp. It was a portrait of resilience rather than a catalogue of relentless horrors.

It highlighted humor and humanity in even the most savage of situations. In that respect it was similar to Sholokhov's *Fate of a Man*. But Solzhenitsyn wrote with an intimate understanding of repression that came from firsthand experience. His story exposed Soviet citizens to a strange and terrible parallel world that had existed in their country for decades—a penal space with its own rules, hierarchies, and culture.

It was no secret that such a story could only have been published with permission from the highest authorities. There was talk that one of Khrushchev's assistants read every word aloud to him for approval. Though Sholokhov was not one of the writers asked to provide an official prepublication evaluation of the story, he did not use his considerable clout to stand in the way of its publication either. He even sent a gesture of goodwill to Solzhenitsyn by asking the editor of *Novyi Mir* to communicate his approval and to pass on a congratulatory kiss to the author.

The publication was timed to coincide with a gathering of the entire party elite in Moscow.[1] Special copies were distributed to party officials, and a major article in *Pravda* on November 23, 1962, summarized the story. It was lauded as a model literary work inspired by the Twentieth and Twenty-Second Congresses. Khrushchev deployed the story as a cudgel against unnamed internal adversaries in the party who were objecting to de-Stalinization. The story was said to contribute to a struggle against "heirs of Stalin" who were still trying to interfere with the building of communism. All of these actions portended a move towards liberalization.

Weeks later, however, Khrushchev sent completely different signals.[2] He appeared at an art exhibition at the Manezh, a large exhibition space in central Moscow. When he saw abstract works of art, he became unhinged and made several angry outbursts.[3] Conservative circles insisted that he rightly put the abstract artists in their place by insisting that the government would not waste money subsidizing works that no one could understand and provided no inspiration for the building of socialism. To the conservatives, abstractionism represented nothing more than vain self-indulgence and aping of the decadent West. Nonetheless, the Premier's behavior at the exhibition became a major cause for concern. Bordering on buffoonery, it violated the restraint and decorum expected from a leader. The liberals interpreted Khrushchev's antics—such as calling the abstractionists pederasts and labeling their work dog shit—as a signal that the hardliners had his ear and were urging him to crack down on artistic expression and ties to the West. The Moscow rumor mill overflowed with differing versions of the event, but all agreed that something extraordinary had happened.

Sholokhov received direct confirmation of this when he was summoned to an assembly of the leadership of the Communist Party of the Soviet Union and the creative intelligentsia on December 17, 1962.[4] The selection of a location—the enormous House of Official Receptions in the Lenin Hills on the outskirts of Moscow—indicated that this would be a big and important gathering. Formal dress was required. The choice of a large venue testified to the scale of the controversy. When Sholokhov arrived he discovered that hundreds of artists, writers, composers, and cinematographers had also been summoned from various corners of Russia and the republics. As he was ushered into a large foyer with parquet floors, ample natural light, and gigantic crystal chandeliers, Sholokhov could see that the offending exhibition, or at least parts of it, had migrated from the Manezh. Surprisingly, Politburo members entered through the same doors as everyone else. Khrushchev mixed freely with the intellectuals and casually moved about the room without bodyguards. His assistants circulated around as well in order to sign up those wishing to speak. Everything suggested that this would be an unprecedented two-way dialogue and exchange of perspectives.

An announcement directed guests to proceed to the next hall. As Sholokhov made his way to the door, he noticed that Khrushchev was heading in his direction. He was accompanied by Tvardovskii, the editor of the journal *Novyi Mir*, and an awkward red-haired man in a somewhat shabby provincial suit. Seeing Sholokhov at the door, the trio stopped to say hello.[5] A brief exchange of pleasantries revealed that this was Aleksandr Solzhenitsyn, the author of the celebrated short story about the day in the life of a labor camp inmate. Solzhenitsyn greeted Sholokhov and immediately mentioned to him that he also grew up in the Don region. "A fellow countryman!" Sholokhov proclaimed. Before the conversation could develop further, Khrushchev motioned to some photographers and a film camera operator, directing them to head with him and Solzhenitsyn into the next room. Sholokhov was left behind. Competitive jealousy reared its ugly head. He had become so comfortable with his status as a Kremlin favorite that he was shocked to find himself unceremoniously edged out of the limelight. Concerns that Khrushchev had found a new favorite grew into fears minutes later. Khrushchev introduced Solzhenitsyn to the assembled audience as "the new generation" in Soviet literature.

A cavernous hall with even more impressive chandeliers was laid out for a banquet. Several long tables, which were covered in starched white tablecloths, stretched from one end of the room to the other. There was a head table, reserved for high officials and members of the Politburo, but save for its perpendicular placement, it was not distinguishable from the other tables. Sholokhov noticed that there were neither shot glasses nor bottles of vodka on any of the tables. This signaled that serious business was about to transpire. Khrushchev quickly confirmed this. He approached a microphone at the head table and announced that first they would eat—a generous spread of various delectable dishes of fish and game fowl would be served—before turning to very serious matters.

After the feast, an ideologue named Il'ichiev rose to deliver what promised to be a series of dry and carefully vetted remarks about Leninism, abstract art, and party controls over culture.[6] A balding, burly, middle-aged man in thick-rimmed glasses, everything about him indicated he had built a career on blandness and caution. If the afternoon and evening had continued in this vein, it would have been forgotten quickly. But things did not go quite as planned.

Il'ichiev planned to emphasize that permissible criticism of the Stalin cult should never be exploited to raise doubts about communist ideology. As he tried to deliver this message, Khrushchev garrulously interrupted him with erratic outbursts.[7] Khrushchev was fixated on the sculptor Ernst Neizvestnyi, who had been assigned a seat in the front of the room within view of the Politburo. At several points Khrushchev interrupted Il'ichiev to comment on the sculptures or to direct snide comments at the sculptor. His verbal incontinence could not be controlled. He spouted crude comments about accurate representation of female anatomy. He insinuated that the sculptor had pilfered the bronze. He boasted that he knew what it is like to be a miner digging metal ore underground. He recalled things he said at the Manezh and proudly blurted out that he was completely sober when he uttered them. Il'ichiev struggled to continue his remarks and wisely decided to shorten them. This would clearly be the Premier's show.

Khrushchev was angry about a letter signed by several prominent cultural figures, chief among them Ilya Erenburg.[8] The signatories of the letter expressed fears that Khrushchev's criticism of the art exhibition would be interpreted as a revival of the conditions "which flourished under Stalin" and begged him to put an end to "a return to methods from the past." He was outraged that after he exposed the cult of personality, revealed Stalin's crimes, and lessened ideological controls, intellectuals could still paint him as a closet Stalinist.

And yet throughout the assembly, his contradictory struggle to come to terms with his own role in Stalin's regime was on full view. He condemned Stalin's repressive methods while asserting that the party was in unison with Stalin on the question of art. He thundered against those who dared to question Stalin's wholehearted commitment to Marxism, while confidently asserting that Stalin had been mentally ill. At one point he threw out the rhetorical question, Am I a Stalinist or not a Stalinist? No one was bold or rash enough to answer. He even told an anecdote about an incident when Stalin defended him against Yezhov's dangerous allegations that he was a Polish nationalist merely hiding under the name Khrushchev.

Though forty intellectuals had signed up to speak that evening, only a fraction of them actually made it up to the podium. In addition to the Premier's outbursts and the fawning comments of his supporters, a dramatic confrontation unfolded between Ilya Erenburg and Galina Serebriakova, a writer who had survived the Gulag.[9] Serebriakova accused Erenburg of hypocrisy. How could someone who had benefited from Stalin's favor for so many years present himself in his memoirs as if he had been a victim? She intimated that Poskrebyshev had recently spoken to her of how Stalin loved and defended Erenburg.[10] The very mention of Poskrebyshev must have sent chills down the spine of many in the audience. He had mysteriously disappeared around 1953.[11] She signaled that the only man alive who knew the bulk of Stalin's secrets might finally break his silence. If he was writing memoirs, Sholokhov would not get off lightly either. Erenburg's response raised the uncomfortable issue of silence in the highest circles of power during the terror.[12]

Realizing that the assembly had exceeded its allotted time, Khrushchev promised to hold a second gathering in the near future. He adjourned the assembly. A few days later Sholokhov received an apologetic message. It was from Solzhenitsyn.[13] Recalling the brief encounter in Khrushchev's presence, he expressed his regrets about the unusual circumstances of the unplanned encounter. Those circumstances had prevented him from properly paying homage to the great writer. He wrote to express "how highly I value the author of the immortal book *Quiet Don*." This communication allayed Sholokhov's concerns that Solzhenitsyn was out to steal the spotlight and capture Khrushchev's favor.

For weeks Khrushchev mulled over the assembly. One phrase in particular continued to eat at him.[14] Erenburg raised the vexing question of complicity. "We were saying [to each other during the terror]: Can it truly be that no one will tell the truth to Stalin?" Erenburg was pointing fingers at Stalin's inner circle. Of those who surrounded Stalin at the height of the terror, only Khrushchev and Mikoian still occupied important positions of power.

Such insinuations reminded Khrushchev of his own complicity.[15] His own fears had hindered him from speaking truth to Stalin. His was one of the loudest voices endorsing the terror and praising the dictator during the terror. Now Khrushchev prided himself upon the fact that he revealed the truth to the party and the Soviet populace in 1956. Nonetheless he continued to deceive himself into believing that he only learned of the true scale of arrests and repressions after Stalin's death. Could Erenburg be correct? Did anyone ever try to confront Stalin with the truth? How did the dictator react? Khrushchev sent his aides to the archives in search of answers, and he reached out to the one person he believed could help him—Sholokhov.

Khrushchev invited Sholokhov to his cottage outside Moscow on Saturday February 16.[16] After days of preparing for the second assembly with Soviet intellectuals, he was racked with anxieties and tormented by contradictory impulses. His fear of losing control over the Politburo was only matched by his anxieties about whether he could keep Moscow from becoming a scene of mass uprisings like Budapest in 1956. By invoking the idea of "mutual coexistence" in the cultural sphere, Erenburg had activated one of Khrushchev's deepest fears—that intellectual disunity could plunge the country into anarchy.

Sholokhov had never seen Khrushchev quite so unhinged. He readily agreed that Erenburg's insinuations had crossed a line. One can almost hear Sholokhov's voice in Khrushchev's subsequent dictation to one of his assistants about Erenburg—"He needs a thorough whipping"—and in a series of ramblings about Erenburg's "Zionist" leanings.[17] These were originally included in Khrushchev's speech but subsequently deleted.

While Khrushchev continued to fume about Erenburg's remark about silence in the highest circles of power during the terror, Sholokhov was disturbed by Erenburg's disavowal of Stalin's favor. Was this intended as a dig against him? By publicly proclaiming that he didn't write to Stalin or call him, was Erenburg pointing fingers at him? Didn't he understand that such contacts could be used for beneficial purposes? After all, his letters to Stalin had helped his district.

For Sholokhov, one exchange from the assembly particularly stood out. The young poet Evgenii Yevtushenko had tried to assume the role of mediator. Vouching for Neizvestnyi, he insisted that the sculptor would recognize his mistakes and correct them. To this Khrushchev thundered back a Russian proverb: "The hunchback can only be corrected by the grave!" Yevtushenko quickly fired back, "I nonetheless think that in these times corrections are no longer made by means of graves."[18] Applause ensued. Uncharacteristically Khrushchev refrained from response.

Sholokhov could not comprehend why the Premier would permit such an insolent remark to remain unchallenged. When he inquired about this, Khrushchev became dismayed. He insisted that he did not hear the poet's retort. The poet's ambiguous words were disconcerting to say the least. Was he insinuating that Khrushchev didn't have the guts to unleash a new wave of arrests in order to restore order? Or was he praising the Premier for his calculated restraint and conscious rejection of Stalinist methods? Nonetheless how could a poet dare to talk back in public to a head of state? Didn't such intellectual audacity lead to an uprising in Hungary? Khrushchev fumed about Yevtushenko's witty retort for days.

The two protégés of Stalin pondered the rise of a new generation without sufficient faith in the regime or fear of it. The dismantling of the Stalin cult had deprived the younger generation of blind faith in the Soviet leadership. The emptying of labor camps and Khrushchev's acts of mercy towards his vanquished enemies had also diminished the levels of fear in society. To many optimistic intellectuals of the early '60s, the Premier's own rhetoric about socialist legality and restoration of Leninist norms made repression seem like an artifact of a bygone era.[19]

TWENTY-SEVEN

S holokhov left the cottage with a nagging feeling that he would have to say something at the second assembly. Khrushchev hinted that only someone with Sholokhov's stature could put Erenburg in his place, but he stopped short of directly imploring the writer to deliver a speech.[1] Sholokhov would have to exercise caution. He could not endorse either Khrushchev's recent recklessness or his particular vision of the Stalin era. For Sholokhov the decision boiled down to an assessment of Khrushchev's political future. Should he continue to invest in a relationship with a leader who had of late made so many mistakes? While the writer wavered about whether to support the Premier, Khrushchev plotted to put Sholokhov center stage in the discussion about silence, candor, and Stalin.

The Cuban missile crisis had greatly damaged Khrushchev's political reputation within the party elite. Soviet leaders emphasized that Washington brought the world to the brink of thermonuclear war. Propaganda tried to make Khrushchev into the calm leader who searched for a wise solution while Kennedy continued to issue hot-headed threats and plan for an invasion of Cuba. While most Soviet citizens believed that their government saved the world from catastrophe by not giving into provocations and averting an invasion of Cuba, Soviet leaders were becoming more concerned about Khrushchev's judgement.

In response, in late January 1963 Marshal Yeremenko once again tried to tout Khrushchev's military prowess in a lead article in *Pravda*.[2] The article downplayed Stalin's contribution to the victory in the battle of Volgograd (known as Stalingrad until 1961). This retroactive renaming of the decisive battle raised many eyebrows. He once again insisted that the Premier had played a major role in history. He claimed that the recent aversion of thermonuclear war with the United States over Cuba had coincided with the twentieth anniversary of the start of Khrushchev's planning for an offensive against the Germans. Khrushchev's backing down was further spun as a victory for "peace-loving forces" that was historically equivalent to a major turning point in the war.

Sholokhov agreed to speak at the second assembly, but he wavered about what to say. Conservative party circles were starting to question Khrushchev's judgement. What could be strategically gained from hectoring a bunch of intellectuals if the leader wasn't willing to back up his words with decisive, corrective intervention? Meanwhile liberal circles were predicting a swift move against the intelligentsia. Moscow was rife with rumors that Sholokhov would denounce Solzhenitsyn.[3] Many believed that Sholokhov would throw the weight of his authority behind a group of "hatchet men" who in recent weeks had bitterly denounced Erenburg's "science of silence" during the Great Terror.

The second assembly on March 7 and 8, 1963, was all about hierarchy. It was held inside the Kremlin in the ornate, columned Sverdlov hall. Guests had to obtain special access passes and clear security before entering. The atmosphere was official. This time there would be no casual intermingling. Ten high-ranking officials and members of the Politburo were seated on an elevated tribune, which towered over the podium for speakers. They appeared to be sitting in judgement over the proceedings.

With such stage management Khrushchev tried to signal that he was firmly in charge. He started the assembly by demanding that all foreign agents immediately leave the room. No one budged. He then warned that if his comments were quickly leaked to the foreign press, as they had been in December, the law on state secrets would be decisively deployed.[4] Clearly vexed that the expression "thaw" coined by Erenburg was widely used to characterize his policies, he insisted that severe frosts awaited anyone who put themselves in opposition to his government.

With this introduction he set the stage for contentious proceedings. Il'ichiev (the ideologue who spoke at the previous assembly) then raked Erenburg over the coals for hypocrisy. He quoted obsequious poems Erenburg had published about Stalin's love for ordinary people. Whereas others sincerely believed in the Stalin cult while they were praising him because they did not know about his role in the terror, Erenburg in his recent memoirs claimed to have comprehended Stalin's role in the terror as early as 1937 and yet he continued to praise the dictator without believing in him.

The Politburo watched as Khrushchev struggled with the conundrum of complicity. He told anecdotes that revealed his close proximity to Stalin, yet he denied knowing about the scope and scale of the terror until after Beria was unmasked in 1953. Again he frequently departed from his prepared comments and spouted improvised remarks. These exposed his own anxieties: "So a writer sits in an outhouse smelling its stench and says that abstractionism has appeared in our country because agriculture is failing, industry is failing. He has no right to determine policies!"[5] Angry one minute, he seemed pensive the next. His threats and exhortations came across as unconvincing.

Khrushchev's improvisations threw Sholokhov into a tumult. In a matter of minutes his turn to speak would arrive. The old acrobat had to perform a new balancing act. An endorsement of Khrushchev's remarks could be interpreted as an endorsement of his leadership style. He had to find a way to appear loyal and maintain a distance at the same time.

Signaling that he would depart from his prepared comments, Sholokhov looked out over the audience.[6] It waited with bated breath. Looking in the direction of Erenburg, he began, "Erenburg said that Stalin's love for him was not mutual. Of course love that's not mutual isn't love. We love our present government, and very much hope that love is mutual." Khrushchev interpreted this as a sign of support and interrupted him to proudly declare on behalf of the government that such love was indeed mutual. Sholokhov continued, "For some reason love isn't working out for Erenburg with the present government either. That's all I wanted to say." He was finished in less than a minute. The audience was stunned.

He could have unequivocally expressed his unwavering support for Nikita Sergeevich, but he didn't. He could have endorsed any of Khrushchev's talking points about Stalin, but he demurred. He could have lashed out at Solzhenitsyn and the other writers who focused on labor camps and other "dark and depressing" aspects of Soviet history, but he preferred not to. He did the minimum that the situation demanded of him. He stuck to a key point of the official script and added nothing more.

Khrushchev's rejoinder to Sholokhov would come the next day. Unbeknown to the writer, the Premier's team made a discovery that would return the writer to center stage in the debate about Stalin. Archivists dug up the letter that Sholokhov had written to Stalin during the famine and the dictator's response to it.[7] Khrushchev decided to make the two letters central to his argument that Stalin remained deaf "to the signals of Sholokhov as well as many other courageous communists."

Even though Sholokhov declined to give a long speech, his words would still define the assembly. Khrushchev began:

> Our esteemed Mikhail Aleksandrovich Sholokhov in spring 1933 raised his voice of protest against the arbitrary violations which were taking place at that time in the Don [region]. Recently in the archives two letters from Mikhail Aleksandrovich to Stalin and Stalin's answers to those letters were discovered. One cannot read without experiencing a rush of emotions those letters which were written with the blood of the heart and Sholokhov's words about the outrageous actions of people, who carried out criminal affairs in Vioshenskaia and other districts of the Don. Mikhail Aleksandrovich wrote to Stalin in his letter of April 16, 1933: "Such examples could be countlessly multiplied. These were

not some isolated examples of distortions, this was a 'method' of carrying out the grain requisitions which had been legalized on a district scale. I either heard about these facts from communists, or from collective farmers who experienced these 'methods' upon themselves and who afterwards came to me with requests to 'write about that in the newspaper.'

Thus far Khrushchev's excerpts avoided the dramatic examples of medieval tortures or excessive cruelty in Sholokhov's letter. He said nothing about starvation, which was a main concern at the time. Perhaps that was yet to come.

Khrushchev continued to quote Sholokhov:

Do you remember Joseph Vissarionovich, Korolenko's sketch "In the pacified village"? In this case such a "disappearance" was not carried out against three peasants who were suspected of stealing from a *kulak*, but against thousands of collective farmers. Moreover as you can see, it was carried out with a wider range of technical methods and with more cunning sophistication.

Khrushchev then went on to stress that Sholokhov asked Stalin to look into what was going on in the districts: "One should investigate the case files of not only those who tortured and humiliated the collective farmers and made a mockery of Soviet power, but also the case of those whose hand directed them . . . If everything I described deserves the attention of the Central Committee, then send to Vioshenskaia district true communists who have enough courage to expose all, regardless of their position, whose fault it is that collective agriculture in the district has been compromised. [Send those] who will truly investigate and reveal not only all of those who deployed disgusting 'methods' of torture, beating, and other humiliations against collective farmers, but also those who inspired them to take such actions."

Khrushchev was twisting the facts. He said nothing about the Shkiriatov commission that had actually investigated. The Premier implied that

Stalin failed to act upon Sholokhov's request. As usual, Khrushchev left key questions unanswered. Were any officials ever punished? Who had actually inspired such methods? What about grain requisitions in other districts? Ironically, the Premier had rehabilitated the very person whom Sholokhov believed was most to blame for the atrocities of 1932–33. Boris Sheboldaev had unleashed violence in connection with grain requisitions first in the lower Volga and northern Don regions in 1929 and then on a wider scale throughout southern Russia in 1932–33. In the late '50s Sheboldaev was rehabilitated and his biography was recently restored to an honored place in a Soviet encyclopedia. [8]

Next Khrushchev emphasized that Sholokhov had never published his honest and courageous letter to Stalin. [9] This was a rebuke of Erenburg. Unlike Erenburg, Sholokhov did not remain silent. Unlike Erenburg, Sholokhov had not rushed to signal his virtue and publish memoirs after Stalin died.

Building a case against Stalin, Khrushchev quoted almost the entire text of the dictator's response to Sholokhov in May 1933. Since Stalin's collected works had ceased publication in the early '50s, it was the first and only unpublished letter by Stalin to be unveiled in the Khrushchev era. The Premier homed in on Stalin's contention that Sholokhov's "letters create a somewhat one-sided impression," yet at the same time he eliminated the crucial statements at the beginning of the letter about forthcoming food aid and official investigation of Sholokhov's allegations. He continued:

"So you see it turns out that the writer Mikhail Aleksandrovich Sholokhov who signaled to Stalin about sheer lawlessness, [in Stalin's view] observed these events in such a manner 'as it might appear from a distance.' And this was said to a writer who was [firmly embedded] in the midst of the people and who created the best, most truthful, party-minded work about collectivization, *Virgin Soil*."

Sholokhov could understand why Khrushchev would use his correspondence with Stalin for political purposes. But why did he have to distort the contents?

Khrushchev then came to his final talking point regarding Sholokhov.

"As a true writer-Bolshevik, Mikhail Sholokhov did not reconcile himself to appalling injustice but rose up against the ongoing lawlessness at that time, though Stalin remained deaf to those signals of Sholokhov, as [he did] to the many similar signals from other courageous communists."

Khrushchev's Stalin was a dictator who remained deaf to reason. By manipulating memory, the Premier could console himself that had he ever tried to speak out, it would not have mattered. Yet again, he insisted that he only found out about Stalin's abuses of power after Beria was defeated. Oddly, Khrushchev felt a need to confess that his own tears at Stalin's funeral were sincere while stressing that Beria could not hide his joy upon Stalin's death. He would never cease wrestling with his personal guilt.

In the weeks after the assembly Sholokhov mulled over whether he should have supported Khrushchev more vigorously in his remarks. Though he could not enthusiastically endorse how his letters had been used, the widespread dissemination of Khrushchev's speech in the Soviet press offered him an opportunity. He could correct some of Khrushchev's omissions and help gain recognition for two old friends who had partnered to save his life during the Great Terror. Two years earlier Petr Lugovoi had written a memoir about his experiences during the 1930s, which he had not yet been able to publish. Similarly, Ivan Pogorelov had written up his recollections of the NKVD's machinations against Sholokhov and the meeting with Stalin in 1938. Plans to publish his account in Moscow had not panned out. Sholokhov now gave them the green light to go public with their accounts.[10]

He hoped to transmit to posterity a more accurate version of his correspondence with Stalin. The situation was not black and white; there were many shades of gray. He offered answers to a series of awkward questions that arose from Khrushchev's selective paraphrase of his letters. Who was to blame for the grain requisitions crisis? The regional leadership at that time. What specifically did Sholokhov ask for? Both an investigation and food assistance for his district. Did Stalin do anything for the people of Vioshki? Yes. In arranging for his associates to share their testimonies with the Soviet public, Sholokhov was indirectly providing his own corrective to Khrushchev's view of Stalin. It was true that the dictator upbraided him in a letter, but he also responded with help. In his own way Sholokhov was pushing back against Khrushchev under the loyal guise of expounding upon the Premier's recent praise for his civic bravery. As a fixture of the establishment, he now spoke truth to power through proxies.

Deciding that it would be wise to renew overtures to Khrushchev, in May 1963 he invited the Premier on a bird hunting trip to Vioshki. He had negotiated with local officials to keep a special area off limits to ordinary citizens in anticipation that the Premier might come for a hunt. Khrushchev, who was planning important talks with Fidel Castro, immediately declined. Declaring, "The doors of our homes and our hearts are always wide open for you, dear Nikita Sergeevich," Sholokhov issued a second invitation later that summer.[11] It too was rejected.

TWENTY-EIGHT

One day in summer 1963 as Sholokhov was emerging from a drunken stupor, Aksiniia Astakhova appeared in his hotel suite.[1] As he lifted his head a little, the room began to spin. The heroine of *Quiet Don* flickered buxomly before his red, bloodshot eyes. "Why is she in Leningrad?" he thought. On the table next to him there was an unsightly assemblage of empty bottles, overturned plates of half-eaten food, and heaps of cigarette butts. Strangers slumped in contorted poses all around him. "What's happening? Could this be a dream?" he thought. Aksiniia looked as if she had stepped out of an illustrated magazine. She stood there, gazing in his direction. Her clothes were those of an emancipated city woman. "Mikhail Aleksandrovich," she called. That voice! It startled him. He needed to get back to the literary symposium. It would be extremely embarrassing and highly scandalous if he didn't show up. They must all be sitting there by now, talking about that schizoid Kafka and those other decadents. The voice exclaimed, "How dare you? What are you doing to Sholokhov the writer?" It was undoubtedly Aksiniia's voice. He wanted to explain everything. The novel was dead now. They had said as much at the congress. "Shut up! Shut up!" he heard his voice answering. A painful sensation overtook him. The last thing he remembered saying was, "Do you think I don't know that I never wrote anything greater than *Quiet Don*?"

After the hangover fog receded, Sholokhov determined that this lamentable encounter was not a product of his impaired imagination. Others had seen her too. The actress Elina Bystritskaia had actually visited his hotel room. Sholokhov had selected her to play Aksiniia in the blockbuster 1957 film adaptation of *Quiet Don*. There was something about her dark black hair and confident, defiant gaze that made her stand out in a pile of photographs. Her performance in the film brought him to tears. Now his performance had a reciprocal effect. Luckily none of the visiting foreigners had heard his confession. He could go back to the symposium and pretend to be a writer.

He delivered a few brief, superficial words of welcome on the opening day of the international symposium on the future of the novel.[2] The European delegates were praising experimental French novels and extolling writers such as Proust and Joyce, who were barely known in the USSR. The defense of realism offered by the Soviet delegates smacked of the 19th century. It produced snickers among some in the audience. While the delegates continued to talk past each other, he receded into the background. None of the delegates had highlighted *Quiet Don* in their presentations. Though he claimed to be working on the war novel, he could not bring himself to admit that his recent output had been very meager. There were whole months in which more paper went into the wastebasket than in the finished drawer.

After the symposium concluded, Mini-cult surprised everyone. Soviet citizens had jokingly started to refer to Khrushchev as Mini-cult due to the way he fumed about the "cult of personality" every time the Chinese or Albanians criticized him. Out of the blue Khrushchev invited several delegates, including Sholokhov, to his government vacation home in the Black Sea region. They were put on a waiting plane and flown to Sochi. From there they were driven to a tropical resort in Abkhazia. The guests were taken on a tour of the resort complex.[3] Khrushchev seemed eager to show off his swimming pool pavilion and the special button that commanded a wide, glass-paneled curtain to go up and down on rollers. Surely he hadn't brought them all that far just to see this?

They were soon led to a conference room and seated around a table. After warm words of greeting from Sholokhov and the other writers, Khrushchev began to speak. As usual he permitted himself to range from topic to topic.[4] It was a peculiar potpourri of free associations and ideological evaluations. One minute he was justifying the invasion of Hungary, the next he was wondering aloud why American workers voted for wealthy politicians like the Kennedys. He recalled an article he read in a newspaper back in 1911 about a beggar and a twenty kopeck coin, noted that suicides were on the rise in the West but not in the USSR, where individuals were valued, and proudly declared that the Cuban missile crisis had made a treaty on nuclear arms possible. He criticized the Chinese for assuming that a person who owns two pairs of pants must be a bad Marxist. He explained his decision to abolish the phrase "dictatorship of the proletariat" and to call the Soviet Union "a state of the whole people." Speaking of the Stalin cult, he strangely recalled an elephant that everyone flocked to see in the small village where he grew up as a child. Sholokhov already knew from long experience that Khrushchev's remarks would be rewritten by his capable assistants. When printed in the press in the coming days, they would become both coherent and structured.

The guests were invited for a lunch on the terrace. The language barrier made it difficult for the writers to interact with each other. Khrushchev ate and drank reluctantly. The doctors must have gotten on his case again. When the guests finished their salmon, smoked trout, caviar, and glasses of Georgian wine, Aleksandr Tvardovskii read aloud his satiric poem *Terkin in the Other World*. There appeared to be some kind of behind-the-scenes maneuvering going on. Khrushchev had bitterly denounced the poem a few years earlier, yet now he appeared delighted by it. Tvardovskii read aloud for fifty minutes, but no translators were present. Jean-Paul Sartre and the other foreign writers had to watch the expressions on the faces of Khrushchev and Sholokhov to tentatively decipher which moments were humorous. Hours later the guests were flown back to Moscow. They were there to serve as witnesses. But of what?

Upon returning home, Sholokhov attempted to write again. He was annoyed that he had been treated like a footnote in the history of world literature. Words came to him for the first time in months. He wrote a scene for the war novel featuring Stalin. It described a visit by Stalin to the front west of Moscow to award ceremonial banners to a heroic division defending the city.[5] This act of creative defiance initiated his emancipation from Khrushchev. The Premier had alleged in his secret speech that Stalin did not visit the fronts during the war. Sholokhov knew this to be incorrect. Though recent military memoirs were censored to omit the dictator, Sholokhov was aware of publications dating back to the late '40s that mentioned such visits.

Before leaving for a touristic trip to western Europe with several members of his family, Sholokhov made arrangements to host Charles Snow and Pamela Hansford Johnson and their son in Vioshki.[6] He had arranged for the British writer to receive an honorary doctorate from Rostov University. The guests arrived in October 1963. He impressed his visitors with his acerbic wit and generous hospitality. He took them on a boat tour of the Don River and introduced them to picturesque locals who looked like they could have stepped out of his novels. The spreads of alcohol, wild game, and fish were so extensive that they reminded Snow's son of Valhalla. Elaborate breakfasts were prepared each morning for dozens of people. On at least one occasion Sholokhov arrived at the breakfast table already tipsy. The words *feudal style* came most readily to mind when they described their visit.

On his way home, Snow stopped in Moscow to conspire with several scholars at the Gorky Institute of World Literature. There he hatched a plan to revitalize Sholokhov's candidacy for the Nobel Prize in literature.[7] He pledged to use his authority in the West to raise Sholokhov's profile while secretly coaching the Soviet expert Ivan Anisimov about how to present Sholokhov's case to the Swedish Academy. Anisimov needed to avoid the statistical appraisals that were so beloved by the Soviet bureaucracy. The committee would not be impressed by the fact that Sholokhov's works had been translated into all major languages of the USSR or that nearly twenty million copies of *Quiet Don* had been distributed to Soviet readers. After all, the government controlled all publishing. The Writers' Union could send that kind of letter, since government bureaucrats would need to sign off on it. Anisimov's letter needed to be different.

The short nomination letter sent by Anisimov and three members of the Academy of Sciences was written in English.[8] It tried to speak directly from the heart. It characterized Sholokhov as an "outstanding master of the literary art." Ideology took a backseat. A key phrase was eye-catching: "The mighty uncompromised truthfulness of his skill is inspired by the noble ideas of creation and peace, deep respect and love for the Man." The letter emphasized truthfulness to resonate with Khrushchev's remarks in March 1963 and a letter that Snow was sending.

Snow and Hansford wrote to the Swedish Academy in January 1964.[9] They urged the committee to give Sholokhov's candidacy "another look." Recognizing that they had no official right to advance a nomination, they nonetheless put forward three compelling reasons to resurrect his candidacy. Snow articulated what was best left unsaid by Anisimov—a widespread feeling of grievance that the most universally esteemed Russian writers did not receive international recognition from the Nobel foundation. The second identified Sholokhov as the most widely admired writer inside Russia and as a man who "made protests to Stalin which no other writer would have the courage or standing to do." The third emphasized the enduring value of Sholokhov's novels and compared *Quiet Don* with *War and Peace* by Tolstoy.

While others advocated for his Nobel candidacy, in early 1964 Sholokhov attempted to resuscitate the moribund war novel. He arranged to interview M. F. Lukin, a prominent general who was involved in the defense of Moscow and was subsequently captured by Germans.[10] Sholokhov briefly interacted with Lukin at the front in fall 1941. Recently Lukin had solicited advice about writing his memoirs. Thrilled at the opportunity to acquire raw materials for his novel, Sholokhov wrote to an acquaintance, "Writers need to have requisite contact with such heroes, otherwise the material will end up in the hands of literary beetles or even fly-by-night operators." He arranged for Lukin to stay at a resort near Rostov and hired a stenographer to record their conversations over the course of several days. In the available excerpts, Sholokhov comes across as a passive interviewer whose inquiries about the war rarely rose above the level of generalities. He occasionally had to reassure the general that he was actually listening. After the meeting he proclaimed on multiple occasions that Lukin would serve as a prototype for one of the characters in his novel. The meeting also provided an additional benefit. It now served as an excuse for the delay in publishing any new chapters.

Sholokhov never revealed why the meeting led to so few tangible results. The onset of serious neurological problems resulting from a minor stroke could account for the fact he wrote infrequently in the early '60s. On more than one occasion he voiced concerns that he could not write poorly about the war. On other occasions he lamented that the novel still had no beginning and no main plotline. He never stopped deceiving himself and others that he would write again. There is no doubt that he continued to actively read and critically appraise memoirs about the war. The evidence that he actually put pen to paper is very slim. Almost all testimonies that he wrote any prose after the Lukin meeting originate with his friends and apologists.

At the very moment when Sholokhov began to comprehend that his well of creativity was running dry, he became a front-runner for the Nobel Prize in Literature at last.[11] Of the seventy-six nominations received for 1964, the Swedish Academy seriously considered only a handful. Sholokhov was among them. Nothing that he wrote after *Quiet Don* contributed one iota to his candidacy. For the committee his recent work smacked of party directives. The discussion focused on the merits of *Quiet Don* as an epic. His own drunken appraisal of his career to the actress Bystritskaia in Leningrad was fully shared by the prize committee.

While he was on a hunting trip to Kazakhstan in early fall 1964 officials urgently tried to summon him to Moscow. He ignored their telegrams and continued to relax. Several days later he learned why Moscow had been calling. A terse announcement in the Soviet media signaled a tectonic shift in political alignments: "Due to his advanced age and the worsening of his health the Plenum of the CC CPSU has approved the request of Comrade Khrushchev to release him from his obligations as First Secretary." It continued: "The Plenum has elected L. I. [Leonid Il'ich] Brezhnev First Secretary of the CC CPSU."[12] Sholokhov knew

Brezhnev from the war. The two had even slept under the same blanket one night near the front. He knew Brezhnev's capabilities and his limitations. He was sincere and good natured, but he was no genius. His reaction was blunt: "Il'ich is in charge, but he's the wrong Il'ich."[13] He couldn't stack up to Lenin.

It took only a few inquiries to find out what happened to Khrushchev. A group of Politburo members took advantage of Khrushchev's vacation to hatch a plot against him. While he was away enjoying his swimming pavilion in Abkhazia, they moved to depose him in early October. By the time they summoned him back to Moscow, they had enough votes in the Central Committee to deploy his own talk of socialist democracy against him.[14] For two days he was subjected to a litany of criticism. Almost no one said anything in his favor. In the end he was allowed to speak, but he did not fight the decision to stage a vote on deposing him. He was said by some to have almost broken down in tears while pleading for some kind of useful assignment in the party. The members of the Central Committee were allowed to peruse a document accusing Khrushchev of concentrating power in his own hands, deciding important issues without consulting other leaders, being rude, and making major mistakes in implementing party decisions. Sholokhov was one of only 16 members (out of 169) of the Central Committee who was absent for the vote. No one voted against the resolution.

The sudden fall of Khrushchev did not shock Sholokhov. There had been grumblings in higher party circles for many months about his ego and his unpredictable behavior. It also didn't take long for Sholokhov to forget how he had actively courted the disgraced leader.[15] In the weeks after Khrushchev's dismissal and exile to his cottage outside Moscow, Sholokhov radically restructured his memories of their relationship. Khrushchev had invited himself to Vioshki. Khrushchev had proclaimed himself to be Sholokhov's friend rather than vice versa. Khrushchev courted Sholokhov for a decade because he wanted to appear in the war novel. They would never speak again.

Only days after Khrushchev's name completely disappeared from the Soviet media, a sensational piece of news stunned the literary world. Jean-Paul Sartre became the first person to ever turn down the Nobel

Prize for Literature. He offered several reasons for his refusal.[16] Among these he outlined socialist political sympathies, which made him unable to accept the award. Naturally Soviet coverage seized on these. Sartre declared, "The Nobel Prize stands objectively as a distinction reserved for the writers of the West or the rebels of the East." He went on to note, "It is regrettable that the prize was given to Pasternak and not to Sholokhov, and that the only Soviet work thus honored should be one published abroad and banned in its own country." In Sholokhov's retelling, Sartre had refused the prize because it had not been awarded to him.[17] He conveniently forgot about the last few words.

Sartre's decision also stemmed from his personal choice not to be associated with any institution and his aversion to being transformed into an institution by either fame or prize money. Such concerns were alien to Sholokhov. He was accustomed to receiving hundreds of letters a month from fans and Soviet citizens pleading for his assistance. He regularly contacted ministers and government officials to intercede for individuals whom he had never met and would never meet. In some years Soviet citizens sent him requests for money totaling more than a million rubles. He had long become accustomed to privileges reserved for the party elite. The list of items he regularly brought back from restricted stores in Moscow reserved for the party hierarchy reads like an inventory for the store Principle in a popular late Soviet anecdote. A tired Soviet citizen repeatedly asks in vain a shop assistant if a delicious item is available. The assistant stands in front of sparsely stocked shelves and consistently keeps telling him, "In principle that is for sale, but we don't have it today." The citizen finally breaks down and demands, "I want to know where the store Principle is because that's where all the good stuff goes." Sholokhov's shopping list included smoked fish, sturgeon, salmon, black caviar, eel, herring, sausages, other encased meats, candies, chocolates, lemons, mandarins, hothouse vegetables, tea, coffee, spices, export quality vodka, cognacs, and wines.[18] None of these items could be easily purchased by ordinary Soviet citizens.

Since he had failed to participate in the October plenum, Sholokhov needed to find a way to signal his active support for Brezhnev. When he learned that Brezhnev was planning to install an ally to head the regional party committee, he decided to show his demonstrative support. He flew to Rostov in December 1964 and actively worked the room to drum up a consensus for Brezhnev's preferred candidates.[19] His efforts were gratefully acknowledged in a phone call between Brezhnev and the regional party leadership.

Next he sought to test the waters by asking Brezhnev's "blessing" for a trip abroad. His request was befittingly modest for a suitor's first approach.[20] He wanted to travel to Finland with his wife for a few days to meet with a writer he had known for several years and to issue him an invitation to his sixtieth birthday celebration. Brezhnev responded favorably. He even sent a gift for Sholokhov's birthday: a new hunting rifle with an optic scope. It came with a leather gun-case and an inscription: "To My Friend M. A. Sholokhov From L. Brezhnev. March 1965."

Brezhnev was charting a guarded, conservative political course that Sholokhov could support.[21] The new leadership claimed to be restoring Leninist principles and doing away with the "subjectivism" of his immediate predecessor. Hardliners who were urging Brezhnev to articulate a clear position on Stalin and the party's criticisms of him in the recent past were disappointed by his silence.

While Sholokhov was traveling to Finland, visiting Hungary as a personal guest of socialist strongman Janos Kadar, marking his sixtieth birthday in a series of official celebrations in Moscow and Rostov, and preparing for a family trip to the Urals region, a local journalist was preparing an irritating surprise for him.[22] Vladimir Molozhavenko, a forty-year-old war veteran from the Don region, had stumbled upon the story of Fedor Kriukov. Molozhavenko's mysterious article would in time become one of the most important publications in Sholokhov's biography. Even today it is still not clear whether Molozhavenko was incredibly naïve or remarkably cunning.

The article, which was published in Rostov in August 1965, introduced Kriukov as a talented Don Cossack writer whom Gorky had praised for his penchant for truth. He was highly popular in the Don region before the revolution and was still remembered by older residents even though literary scholars had ignored him for decades. On the eve of the revolution, Kriukov started working on a big novel devoted to the

Cossacks. While suffering from typhoid fever during the ill-fated retreat of the White Armies in 1920, Kriukov would occasionally regain his senses and grab for a small metal trunk filled with manuscripts. As he lay dying among strangers, he curiously heard the very same song that Grigorii Melekhov heard while incapacitated during evacuation from his home territory. By employing a quote from *Quiet Don* without attributing it to Sholokhov or mentioning where it was from, Molozhavenko invited his readers to read between the lines. Anyone who tried to expose the article as an attack on Sholokhov would have to explain how their unhealthy suspicions were aroused in the first place. This made it difficult for Sholokhov's allies to find a proper response.[23]

For Sholokhov the publication of an ambiguous article by a political nonentity was only a minor problem. He had a more pressing concern. He learned that one of the officials of the Swedish Academy had visited Moscow.[24] In conversations with members of the Soviet Writers' Union, the Swede was hinting that Sholokhov was a favorite for the Nobel Prize. This news, which should have delighted him, created a major concern. Would Brezhnev actually allow him to accept the prize if he won it? Because the award had been such a matter of controversy in 1958, how should he react? He sent a letter to Brezhnev, inquiring, "Just in case if the prize will (contrary to the class convictions of the Swedish committee) be awarded to me, what does my CC [Central Committee] advise?"[25]

Because he was planning to leave for another hunting trip to Kazakhstan in late August, he requested an expedited response. Brezhnev promptly took up the issue with the Politburo.[26] It decided—apparently unanimously—that Sholokhov could accept the award, but it delegated the Cultural Department with crafting the wording of a response to Sholokhov. The department dawdled for nearly two weeks before informing him. Something in the wording of the decision did not sit well with Sholokhov. If it resembled the uninspired phrasing in the department's report to the Politburo, it was both bureaucratic and non-affirmative: "The department does not see any grounds for refusing the prize if it will be awarded." Sholokhov got on a plane and flew to Moscow for further instructions. The most important award in the world was no opportunity for improvisation. He had recently claimed to be a good soldier of the party, and he needed his marching orders.

Months later a Swedish journalist called Sholokhov's home with important news. He was calling to inform the writer that his quest for the Nobel Prize was finally over.[27] Unfortunately, the news could not be delivered. Sholokhov could not be reached by phone because he was hunting in a remote area of the Kazakh steppe, which was more than fifty miles from the nearest working telephone. The Central Committee got in touch with local officials and ordered them to search for the writer. They found him the next morning. He was camping in a tent near a lake frequented by wild geese. In the middle of nowhere a local official delivered the news from the Swedish Academy.

The official drove Sholokhov to the nearest airstrip. Soon a small, two-passenger plane landed. It flew him roughly a hundred miles to a party headquarters building, which was known to have a reliable telephone connection. He took a call from *Pravda*. Impressed that he could hear almost every word, he dictated the text of a telegram to Stockholm accepting the award, and he granted *Pravda* the right to an exclusive interview. Then he called a high-ranking Moscow official in charge of culture. An assistant claimed that the official was busy. Sholokhov became angry: "I only need two minutes!" he thundered. Seconds later the embarrassed official came on the line to congratulate him. They briefly discussed the logistics of accepting the award. When he hung up, Sholokhov fumed that it was easier to schedule a meeting with either Stalin or Khrushchev than to meet face-to-face with some of those self-important Central Committee functionaries.

TWENTY-NINE

Minutes before Sholokhov and the other Nobel Laureates entered a festively decorated reception room to meet the king of Sweden, Sholokhov became anxious. Words from a distant childhood suddenly welled up from deep inside him. He nervously sang to relieve his tension.[1] He sang a rhyming ditty about a cat brought home by grandfather, which soon experienced a blunt force trauma from grandmother. He also sang a lullaby about a raven who sat on an oak branch and played a gilded silver trumpet. As he was preparing to receive the world's most coveted literary award, his thoughts for some reason turned to cruelty and a creature known in many cultures as a trickster. Did he imagine himself as the cat who somehow evaded death, or as the raven who cunningly overcame his lack of beautiful song and adornment? Or was he just recalling pleasing rhythms a mother once recited to animate a shy and bashful child? Upon his Nobel triumph in Stockholm, other literary blackbirds would come tapping at his chamber door. Doubters would equate him with Aesop's jackdaw, which was ridiculed for its borrowed plumes, and there would be a dissident visitation reminiscent of Edgar Allan Poe's ominous bird of yore and its constant croaking of "nevermore."

Just getting to that moment in Stockholm required weeks of negotiation with multiple Soviet bureaucracies.[2] After returning from Kazakhstan, he immediately began making preparations for the trip to Sweden. He secured official permission to take along his wife and family. He negotiated to travel with a translator and a film camera operator. He petitioned the Writers' Union to delegate a specialist who could help him prepare remarks about Soviet literature. It approved the request, but the Ministry of Finances declined to pay, insisting that Sholokhov would have to cover the expenses from his own funds. The Cultural Department gained approval to issue Sholokhov a cash advance of three thousand American dollars to be repaid from the Nobel Prize award money, which was estimated to be around fifty thousand dollars. Several secretaries of the Central Committee, among them the all-powerful Suslov, deliberated on whether or not to approve his planned stopover in Finland en route to Stockholm. The Nobel committee required a special formal suit, a black tailcoat with silk facings, which could not be sewed in the USSR in time for the ceremony. Only days before Sholokhov's scheduled departure, high-ranking Kremlin officials approved the decision to obtain it in Helsinki.

While he was in Moscow, he found out about a sensitive emerging situation. Two writers had been arrested for publishing anti-Soviet works abroad. They were individuals he had never heard of. Yuli Daniel was a freelance translator, and Andrei Siniavskii was a scholar from the Gorky Institute of World Literature. The arrests portended major controversy. The Central Committee was still uncertain about what to do with them. Because no official Kremlin position on the arrests had been announced, it was very important that Sholokhov avoid any discussion of the matter in his upcoming interviews with Western correspondents. Soviet officials were expecting various provocateurs to try to exploit the arrests in order to discredit Soviet culture in the Western press.

In fact, at that very moment two Polish intellectuals in exile in France and Italy were ingeniously strategizing about how to gain maximum publicity for the jailed writers by capitalizing on Sholokhov's Nobel Prize.[3] In the process of defending Siniavskii and Daniel, whose works they had helped to publish, they planned to remind the world of the Pasternak affair and link Sholokhov's name to both cases. Sholokhov unwittingly played into their hands when he gave an interview to foreign correspondents in late November.[4] Amid a series of terse and generally uninformative answers to a range of questions, he expressed his pride in being the first Soviet winner of the Nobel Prize. When journalists reminded him of Pasternak and pushed for a clarification, he labeled Pasternak an "internal émigré" and declared that he hadn't changed his opinion of him. He said nothing about the two jailed writers.

His silence led to a prominent appeal from François Mauriac, the French winner of the Nobel Prize in Literature for 1952. He asked Sholokhov to use his influence to avert a second Pasternak affair and implored him to serve as an intermediary between the brotherhood of Nobel Laureates and the Soviet government in seeking a favorable outcome for Siniavskii and Daniel. Mauriac was working in coordination with one of the Polish exiles. For weeks telegrams addressed to Sholokhov flooded into the headquarters of the Soviet Writers' Union and the Ministry of Culture.[5] In one form or another they pleaded with him to intercede on behalf of the two jailed writers. Hundreds of writers from France, Italy, England, Denmark, the United States, Japan, India, Mexico, Australia, and other nations signed collective appeals.

In a rare breach of Nobel etiquette, Swedish newspapers published leaks on the eve of the award ceremony suggesting that Sholokhov was not a consensus choice.[6] There were indeed dissenting voices on the prize committee. A year earlier the prize committee had recalled Sholokhov's "regrettable behavior during the Pasternak affair" but decided to exclude that as a factor in their deliberations. The politicization of his candidacy by Khrushchev, who went out of his way to promote Sholokhov during a trip to Scandinavia only weeks before he was unceremoniously deposed in 1964, also did not help. Sholokhov became the riskier of two equivalent candidacies, so the prize went to Sartre. In 1965 Sholokhov's age and the possibility of a perceived slight against Russian literature were the main new factors weighed by the committee. Curiously these factors were not mentioned in the nominating letters for 1965 but were emphasized in the letter sent by Snow and Sholohov's in 1964. Several configurations in which two authors shared the prize were even given cursory consideration. In one of these Sholokhov would have shared the prize with the Russian poetess Anna Akhmatova.

Sholokhov and his entourage arrived in Helsinki and acquired their tailored formal wear without a hitch. From there they traveled to Stockholm. The day before the Nobel Prize ceremony Sholokhov made international headlines for not answering his telephone and being absent from the hotel suite that was reserved in his name. A representative of the British publisher Collins showed up in Stockholm and staged a publicity stunt in which he demonstratively knocked on the door of Sholokhov's hotel room to discuss the fate of the jailed writers with him.[7] After the door failed to open, a press conference was organized. Copies of the various telegrams and appeals sent to Sholokhov were distributed to the international press corps. The publisher challenged Sholokhov to speak up for Siniavskii and Daniel in Stockholm, threatening that otherwise his Nobel Prize would be tainted by tacit support for the persecution of two fellow writers.

Since Sholokhov was staying at the Soviet embassy, he likely only learned of the stunt the next day, on the very morning of the awards ceremony. He already had complicated feelings about the award. After years of pondering what it would be like to win, he expected to feel relief when that piece of unfinished business with Stalin was finally over. Now, on a gray, snowy day, rather than savor his greatest moment of recognition, he was livid that two "splinterers" were taking attention away from him and that their supporters were trying to steal the spotlight.

The morning of the ceremony he participated in a rehearsal at the Stockholm concert hall. There he and the other laureates mastered the protocol. They would have to wait behind the stage while an anthem played. Then they would be led into a large hall and escorted to seats on stage by official ushers. They received detailed instructions about how to bow in the presence of the Swedish king and how to ascend and descend from the stage to accept the award while having their pictures taken.

Following an afternoon reception at the Soviet embassy, he and his family arrived at the Stockholm concert hall. Cameras flashed as he passed through a special entrance. Then he was taken to a restricted waiting area. Since other laureates could not be expected to speak Russian and he did not speak any foreign languages fluently, he was accompanied by a Soviet diplomat. His nervous anxiety came and went. Humming childhood ditties seemed to help.

As the ceremony commenced, the laureates entered from backstage with great pomp.[8] Bugles blared. The hall was decorated with flags and wreaths. Hundreds of men in black formal wear and women in lavish evening gowns stood up to applaud as they entered. There were a handful of special seats in the front of the hall. These were set aside for the Swedish royal family, but they were not thrones in any conventional sense. Contrary to all Sholokhov's stereotypes about royalty, the king was not wearing a crown. Since his award was not among the first, he was forced to sit through speeches in several languages he didn't understand. At times he appeared uneasy and sat in his chair like a pupil who is uncomfortable in a classroom.

When they announced his name, he descended from the stage to the right and approached King Gustavus from the left.[9] Simultaneously a page came from the king's right side and handed the award diploma and medal to the monarch. As Sholokhov came closer, he noticed that the king was a rather ordinary-looking man wearing small round spectacles. Only a colored sash, a prominent medal topped by a crown worn on a chain around his neck, and two shining, star-shaped honors on his chest distinguished him. Sholokhov bowed as instructed. The king shook his hand and said something. Sholokhov delivered a brief phrase of gratitude in English as he had rehearsed and smiled when he received the award diploma. Photographers standing behind the king unleashed a blinding flurry of lightbulb flashes. Then Sholokhov ascended to the stage from the left and bowed again in the direction of the king. After returning to his seat, he studied the award diploma, which featured hand-painted images of Cossacks on the left and his name and some words in Swedish on the right. The ceremony adjourned after additional declamations and the singing of a hymn.

That evening he and his family attended a lavish banquet in the golden hall of the Stockholm city hall building.[10] It was a grandiose and towering room. It glittered with millions of gold mosaic pieces on all sides. Tables were set for hundreds of guests and decorated with elaborate centerpieces, candles, and flowers. They were served several dishes with French names he could barely pronounce, but these were similar to fancier things he had tried at the Hotel National in Moscow. There were little pastries filled with fish, a chicken breast stuffed with some kind of minced meat and nuts, and a sweet, fatty goose liver paté. They were also served those long, green, pointy vegetables that made his urine reek. To his delight, fine French cognac was served at the end of the meal. It was more smooth, subtle, and complex than any Soviet brand. It packed hints of heat without the burn in the back of the throat. If only Stalin could have seen him sitting there at the table of the king of Sweden, savoring a glass of cognac. When Stalin once asked him what he thought about the Central Committee serving cognac to it guests, he replied, "It's an honest to goodness C[entral] C[ommittee]."[11] So now he could say that Gustavus was an honest to goodness monarch as well.

The Nobel ritual required that both Sholokhov and the head of the prize committee give speeches.[12] The Swedish writer Anders Österling provided a perceptive appraisal of Sholokhov's career, noting that it took him fourteen years to finish *Quiet Don*. He spoke of Soviet critics who did not welcome an objective treatment of a tragic Cossack rebellion. One phrase even hinted at an understanding of Sholokhov's moral dilemmas: "In view of the controversial aspects of his theme, there can surely be no doubt that in starting out upon the writing of this novel Sholokhov was taking a daring step, a step which, at that point in his career, also meant the settling of a conflict with his own conscience." He provided a lyrical description of *Quiet Don* and proclaimed that it would, "on its own, thoroughly merit the present award . . ." He said nothing about Sholokhov's recent work.

In contrast Sholokhov's speech did not contain a single word about *Quiet Don*. He said very little about the writer's craft. Portions of the speech provided a conservative defense of the realistic novel. Other sections offered softened socialist rhetoric that could have been penned by a Comintern intern in the time of Gorky. Allusions to the devastations of the Second World War and the destructive potential of thermonuclear warfare gave the speech more contemporary currents. Claiming to be a writer for workers, builders, and heroes, Sholokhov left both victims and perpetrators off his list. Only one passage spoke directly to his personal mythology: "To be honest with the reader, to tell people the truth—which may sometimes be unpleasant but is always fearless." Though he had long since succumbed to the lure of privilege and ambition, his words were a sincere reflection of how he had behaved once upon a time.

Upon his return from Stockholm, Sholokhov guarded his thoughts about two burning issues that were being actively discussed by Soviet intellectuals.[13] He said nothing about the trial of Daniel and Siniavskii, whose conviction and sentence to several years of incarceration shocked observers in the West and disheartened liberals in the USSR. He also avoided weighing in on the other controversial issue that was being vigorously debated in private in early 1966—the rehabilitation of Stalin. It was widely believed at the time that Brezhnev was contemplating changes to previous party declarations about the "cult of personality." Both liberals and conservatives considered the issue to be of vital importance to the future of the USSR. Sergei Pavlov, the leader of the Communist Youth League, argued that one-sided, negative, and overwhelmingly dark portrayals of the Stalin years had harmed the cause of Soviet patriotism. He believed that Soviet youth were displaying nihilism, distrust of authorities, and disregard for past generations precisely because of such criticisms. A group of intellectuals and cultural figures who sent Brezhnev a letter against the rehabilitation of Stalin argued precisely the opposite. They affirmed that no clarifications or pronouncements of any kind could make Soviet youth believe in Stalin again, and any attempts to whiten his image could lead to dangerous rifts in society and even provoke political "complications." Sholokhov kept a respectable distance from both sides. His choice proved to be prescient.

Brezhnev decided not to reopen the issue of Stalin at the Twenty-Third Party Congress in April 1966. Contrary to the expectations of many, he and his allies affirmed earlier party statements and advanced oblique criticisms of the "subjectivism" that obstructed them. When

Sholokhov asked Brezhnev about Stalin, the Soviet leader raised his famous bushy eyebrows and declared, "When I merely mentioned Stalin's name in my speech [a year earlier] the whole audience responded with enthusiastic ovations. From that response, we [in the Politburo] understood that Stalin's name should only be used with extreme caution."[14]

Sholokhov spent several weeks preparing his speech to the Party Congress.[15] The section that was most dear to him was near the end. If he had passionately delivered this part as originally planned, it might have become the catalyst for a powerful ecological movement within the USSR. He worked for nearly a week preparing a harsh indictment of the poor state of environmental protection. He lamented the felling of protected trees in the Crimea and the Caucasus and the irrational harvesting of timber in Ukraine and Siberia for short-term economic gains. He gathered testimonies about the disappearance of fish from the Volga, the Don, and several Siberian rivers. He planned harsh words of criticism for leaders at all levels. Then he started to second-guess his phrasing. How would it look through the eyes of the enemy? Would a tough approach backfire? Would officials get offended? Could his words could be twisted to discredit the government in the eyes of the people?

On the eve of the congress he received word that Brezhnev wanted to meet with him. They discussed his speech and came to an arrangement about what the writer would and would not say. Brezhnev was cautious and protective of the prestige of the party apparatus that had spawned him. The names of certain ministers disappeared from the speech. Harsh comments were toned down. Environmental problems that had not yet been openly discussed in the national press were avoided. Though Sholokhov made promises to Brezhnev, he was not happy about the changes. He even alluded in his speech to "friends from the front" to whom he gave his word that he would soften the speech.[16]

He began the speech with a lighthearted introduction:

> I don't share the optimism of the Tula party secretary from the anecdote, the one who when asked about the development of literary cadres answered, "[Everthing is] normal, even good! If earlier in the Tula governorship [under the tsar] we only had

one writer, Leo Tolstoy, today we have twenty-three members
of the Tula branch of the Writers' Union."

His audience laughed heartily in response to this absurd and glaring
imbalance between quantity and quality. He probably did not realize, however, that a newer, and darkly funnier version of the anecdote was making
the rounds in literary circles after the arrests of Siniavskii and Daniel. The
new version concluded "today we have twenty-three writers on file."
The expression hinted at the operative files that the KGB kept on both its
secret informants and the subjects of investigations. In the new version
the local official was boasting that twenty-three writers were either collaborating with the KGB or under surveillance.

The remaining environmental portions of the speech still packed a
few punches. He accused an unnamed factory of criminal indifference to
poisoning the Volga River and killing between 11 and 22 million fish.
He claimed that the "glorious sea, sacred Baikal" was in danger from the
felling of forests and the construction of cellulose paper industries along
its pristine shores. He cited statistics about the dumping of waste water
into the Don River and condemned the tenfold decline in the number
of fish. In spite of key deletions, he still skewered the Fisheries Minister
for bringing the Azov sea basin to "the edge of catastrophe." Sholokhov
was the only keynote speaker at the congress who spoke of nature as
something more than a resource for immediate economic exploitation.
Dozens of other speeches emphasized the conquering of nature for
industrial growth, but his was the only one to even mention the problem
of industrial waste.

Instead of being remembered as the bold statement that galvanized a
burgeoning environmental movement, his compromised speech became
the ugly coda to the prosecution of Siniavskii and Daniel. His talking
points about the literary controversy mainly derived from the KGB's pre-
trial appraisal of their works.[17] He unapologetically joined the camp of "I
haven't read it, but I wholeheartedly condemn it." His original contributions came mainly in the form of vicious attacks on the two dissidents and
their defenders within the USSR and abroad. His rhetoric purposefully
harked back to the 1930s.

Recent developments reactivated his deep Stalinist programming about the responsibilities of a Soviet writer. Moscow colleagues insisted that Siniavskii had defamed Gorky in works smuggled and published abroad while praising the classic in Soviet publications.[18] Not only was this a classic example of treacherous double-dealing but it also violated the central unwritten rule about Gorky. He could be creatively quoted, regarded as a curious museum artifact, or even ignored, but he could not be defamed. In appealing for leniency in the name of humane ideals, the Soviet supporters of the two dissidents only confirmed to Sholokhov that they had forgotten the lessons of the 1930s. No one had ever annulled the customary laws that all Soviet writers were expected to abide by.

He alluded to a letter sent to the Politburo by sixty-two writers on the eve of the congress.[19] The signatories expressed doubts that Siniavskii and Daniel pursued an anti-Soviet agenda and questioned the outcome of the trial, suggesting that the defendants' guilt was never proven and the sentence was too harsh. They insisted that the circumstances of the times demanded an expansion of freedoms for artistic and intellectual experimentation rather than contraction. They contended that the two writers should be given an opportunity to make up for their mistakes. It would be in the best interests of the country and the international communist movement to release them, with the implied assurances that those who pledged surety would keep them in line. The most prominent signatory of the letter was Erenburg.

Sholokhov's speech provided a curt answer to the sixty-two signatories. He thundered, "I am doubly ashamed of those who offer their services and appeal with requests for convicted splinterers to be handed over to be released on their pledges of surety." There is good reason to believe that his remarks were approved by Brezhnev, whose comments in the opening speech of the congress were similar in spirit but far more measured and cautious. Sholokhov also lashed out against the writers and intellectuals who had crashed his Nobel party: "I would also like to say to the bourgeios defenders of the pasquilleists: don't worry about the condition of criticism in our country. We will support and develop criticism, it will be sharply voiced at this congress. But slander is not criticism, and muck from a mudhole is not the palette of an artist."

Sholokhov decided to remind everyone of Gorky's article entitled "Who Are You with Masters of Culture?"[20] It was the culmination of a series of articles in which Gorky argued that Western intellectuals constantly applied a double standard to the USSR. They habitually ignored appalling violations of human rights elsewhere in the world, particularly in their own colonies, but raised an outcry whenever criminals were justly punished in the USSR. Gorky ridiculed foreign writers and intellectuals who signed petitions. He disparaged the sighs of "professional humanists" who were blind to all the injustices of capitalism. He claimed that "proletarian humanism" was dedicated to freeing the world's working masses from oppression. It is in this context that Sholokhov spoke of "revolutionary humanism" and declared, "Humanism is by no means sniveling softness."

The most jarring phrase of his speech would be remembered for years. It reads: "If these delinquents with their black consciences pulled the same stunt back in the twenties when people were judged not in accordance with strictly delineated articles of the Criminal Code but instead operated with a 'revolutionary understanding of what is right,' oh how these turncoats would have received an altogether different form of punishment!" He then ridiculed those who were still talking about the "harshness" of the verdict, and he followed up with demagoguery about swift justice meted out to traitors in wartime.

Soon after the speech, Aleksandr Tvardovskii recorded in his diary his private appraisal:

> Sholokhov is now a former writer, who only is capable of supporting his official prosperity by means of his shameful self-isolation from the fate of art and literature today. Sholokhov's speech was horrible . . . He is a depraved old man, but how much good he could do for literature and everything in general, if only he acted without fear, if only he were a little more independent, more free and more humane. It is both bitter and shameful.[21]

Such views would remain the standard view of Sholokhov in liberal circles. Conservatives would continue to view him as a pillar of Soviet order.

Shortly after the congress Sholokhov headed off for a multi-week trip to Japan with his family. By the time he returned, piles of critical letters about his speech had arrived. The most important of these was by Lidiia Chukovskaia. She was the daughter of an intellectual whom Sholokhov had helped in the early 1940s. She became a writer and a talented editor. For several years she had tried to publish a shocking story she wrote about a mother struggling to come to terms with the arrest of her only son during the Great Terror. It was too frank even for Khrushchev at the height of his de-Stalinization drive.

Her open letter to Sholokhov was an indictment of him in the name of Russian literature.[22] Chukovskaia proclaimed that his speech was the only occasion in the history of Russian literature when a writer publicly expressed regrets that a verdict against a fellow intellectual was not harsh enough. He had betrayed a long-standing literary tradition of intercession and had opted for persecution instead. She juxtaposed the Sholokhov of 1966 with the man who wrote the epic novel, declaring, "It was surprising to hear such rude, un-nuanced declarations from the author of *Quiet Don*, which extends empathy even to individuals who committed crimes against the revolution." She defended literature as a higher ideal that would always prevail: "Literature cannot be judged by courts, ideas can only be combated with ideas, not camps and jails."

In a series of direct addresses to Sholokhov, she issued a prophecy and pronounced a moral verdict. "History will not forget your shameful speech," she warned. Here she was invoking a higher, more universal history than the officially controlled version practiced in Soviet academies. She continued, "Literature will avenge itself as it metes out vengeance upon all who retreat from the difficult obligations that come with it. It will sentence you to the highest form of punishment there is for an artist—creative sterility. No kinds of honors, money, or awards, either domestic or international, can prevent this verdict from landing upon your head."

There were now enough typewriters and copy machines in large Soviet cities to foster unofficial publishing networks, referred to as *samizdat*. Chukovskaia's open letter became a *samizdat* sensation, and her verdict would be shared by thousands of like-minded readers. Individuals and small informal groups churned out hundreds of copies of her letter even though they risked arrest for doing so. Sholokhov inadvertently gave a boost to the first efforts to challenge the government's monopoly on the circulation of information.

Meanwhile literature was plotting one more ordeal for him. The dormant authorship controversy was reawakening.[23] In the West aging Cossacks who had emigrated from Russia at the end of the civil war labeled Sholokhov a fraud. They pointed to a publication from 1920 that mourned the death of Fedor Kriukov and lamented that he took with him to the grave a Cossack novel on the scale of *War and Peace*. In the USSR young intellectuals started questioning whether the court jester they saw in recent speeches could have ever written anything as glorious as *Quiet Don*. Most consequentially of all, Aleksandr Solzhenitsyn started to have doubts about Sholokhov's authorship and initiated a search for Kriukov's manuscripts.

THIRTY

T hough at first Sholokhov paid no attention to his detractors, he
increasingly desired to prove them wrong. The mere suggestion that
he would never write again incensed him. He resumed working on
the war novel yet again. He was highly apprehensive that he would write
poorly, but his fears of being written off by the entire Soviet establishment
were even more compelling. Like the horizon, his anticipated completion date for the war novel was ever present and always receding. For a
while he even claimed that if not for the Nobel Prize and all the fuss it
involved, he would have already finished.

In Sholokhov's official biography, the most important event of 1967
was his meeting with the only Soviet citizen who was undeniably more
famous than he was.[1] The cosmonaut Yurii Gagarin paid a brief visit to
Sholokhov that June. By all accounts they enjoyed a pleasant meeting,
which was subsequently immortalized in a pretentious poem by a second-
rate poet. Having successfully weathered the perils of Soviet celebrity,
they might have swapped stories about star-struck temptresses, eager

toastmasters bearing bottles of strong spirits, and inane gatherings hosted by insistent party officials, but there is no evidence they did. Instead, the poem proclaimed that Sholokhov experienced a premonition of Gagarin's impending death in an aviation accident. Given his grossly inaccurate predictions about his own literary progress, Sholokhov's prowess as a prophet must be disregarded. One thing is certain. Two famous sons of Russia's turbulent 20th century savored a few hours away from fawning admirers and jostling photographers.

Sholokhov had decided to mentor a group of young writers and invited several of them to his home to coincide with Gagarin's visit. The writers he favored with his attention had shown conservative tendencies or sympathies for Russian national culture. Their careers could still be shaped, but for some reason his thoughts were pervaded by the past. On the second day of their visit, Sholokhov invited a select group for brunch at his home. For no apparent reason he started to reminisce about the plagiarism commission in 1929. After all those years the tribunal still haunted him. A shadow still hung over him. In the middle of the conversation he made an utterly baffling declaration: "Guys, I really am a good writer!"[2]

His visitors struggled to make sense of such a strange proclamation. Nobody at the table had hinted in the remotest possible manner of anything to the contrary. The dialogue of doubt was entirely in his own head. No person of their generation could have encountered anything in print from after 1940 that either questioned or disparaged him. The young writers attempted to convince him that of course they appreciated his talent. "No, you don't understand," Sholokhov lamented. "I really wrote *Crimson Steppe*." Once again they did not know how to interpret this remark.

There was no way to make them understand. He was recalling the point in his career just before he took on *Quiet Don*. He was pondering the life he lost when fame and celebrity arrived. He would never know how his career might have developed. *Crimson Steppe* was an artful and well-crafted short story.[3] Now it was forgotten. He cryptically lamented that he betrayed himself back in the mid-1920s. He could have honed his craft over time rather than hurrying. But that was not an option. He could no longer picture his life without the twin burdens of borrowed glory, political favor, as well as the ambition that fueled both.[4]

He also opined that the present government would not permit him to write the truth about the war. In connection with this declaration he unburdened himself of recollections of his encounters with Stalin. He spoke of their meeting in 1942 and the conversation in which he promised to write the war novel. Stalin had challenged him to finish the novel in three years. Now, three decades later, that original number seemed almost mystical to him: "I don't know if it was a coincidence that he named that particular number or whether he insightfully foretold when the war would end." In his mind Stalin had issued him an almost mythical challenge. In his retelling, he had met the deadline. A variant of the novel existed by 1945.

Alarmed by such confessions, Maria Petrovna kept moving the bottle away from him. He was not ready to admit it, but he had collapsed under the weight of his promise to Stalin, now decades old. The war novel was business that would never be finished. Staring at the finality of failure, he desired to give it one more try. After the departure of the young writers, he got out the manuscripts of some chapters he'd written in 1964. He knew they needed serious work based on a candid evaluation he received from a competent editor. He scribbled for months before he was willing to let anyone have a look.

In August 1967 the Writers' Union sent him a reassuring sign of his continuing relevance. It solicited his evaluation of two works by Aleksandr Solzhenitsyn. The leadership of the union wanted to revoke Solzhenitsyn's membership. Sholokhov had paid little attention to Solzhenitsyn in recent years. His Moscow friends occasionally informed him of curious developments.[5] In early 1964 there was a push by liberal writers to award Solzhenitsyn the Lenin Prize for his story about Ivan Denisovich, but conservative forces thwarted these plans. Solzhenitsyn took offense and became less cooperative with literary authorities. As he got hung up on the darker sides of the Soviet experience, he encountered major difficulties in publishing. In May 1967 he attempted to hijack the literary congress with an open letter calling for the abolition of censorship and reforms to the Writers' Union. All attempts to reason with him failed.

He insisted on circulating his writings in *samizdat* copies and continued to seek attention from the West.

For Sholokhov it mattered little that Solzhenitsyn had not tried to publish the play *Banquet of Victors* or that the novel *First Circle* existed in multiple versions. Nor was it relevant to him that both works were incomplete when the KGB confiscated them from their author. Sholokhov categorized the characters in these works as either complete bastards or men without a cause. He viewed Solzhenitsyn as a troublemaker who was only posing as a seeker of truth. He "points with malice and bitchy obsession to all mistakes, all oversights committed by the party and Soviet government since the 1930s."

Sholokhov shared with the leadership of the Writers' Union his suspicions that Solzhenitsyn was suffering from a mental illness and delusions of grandeur. He called Solzhenitsyn a "malicious lunatic, who has lost control of his reason, and become fixated on the tragic events of 1937 and following years and therefore represents a huge danger for all readers, especially young ones." He concluded that whether the dissident was ill or merely anti-Soviet, he did not belong in the Writers' Union and could not be trusted with a pen. In spite of such a strong statement, the leadership of the union decided to try to bring Solzhenitsyn back into the fold.

While he was lambasting the dissident, Sholokhov was also attempting to answer him.[6] He tried to demonstrate that a writer loyal to the regime could address the topic of repressions from a Soviet position. He introduced some brief allusions to life in labor camps into the chapters of the war novel he was working on. To individuals who had actually experienced Soviet labor camps they appeared lame, inconsequential, and improbable.

By that point Solzhenitsyn had developed an almost pathological hatred of Sholokhov as well.[7] When Jean-Paul Sartre visited the Soviet Union in 1966, Solzhenitsyn refused to meet with him on the grounds that the French philosopher "had successfully lobbied" for the Nobel Prize to be awarded to Sholokhov. Sholokhov's actions in the affair of Daniel and Siniavskii made him a "hangman" in Solzhenitsyn's eyes. The dissident even began to openly voice his vague suspicions of plagiarism.

Sholokhov sent two chapters of the war novel to publishers in 1968. None were willing to publish them, allegedly not even the journal *Don*, which was a mouthpiece for Sholokhov's supporters and ran regular columns on the writer. The literary world secretly whispered about how bad the selections were.[8] An anecdote making the rounds in Moscow insisted that they were so terrible that even *samizdat* had rejected them. He found himself in the uncomfortable position of being denied publication. Because of his reputation, editors were unwilling to offer him sharp and direct appraisals. This caused him to imagine that the refusals were due to his boldness.

In late October 1968 he wrote to Brezhnev to request that in accordance with tradition, his "chapters" be published in *Pravda*.[9] The editorial board claimed that they had languished on the Soviet leader's desk for over three weeks without a decision. Brezhnev had abruptly cancelled a meeting with the writer around that time. Cautioned by his assistants that Sholokhov's loosely connected scenes were of unacceptable quality for publication, Brezhnev sidestepped the issue and claimed to be busy preparing for the upcoming party Plenum. Sholokhov's letter smacked of both desperation and frustration. In three different ways he pleaded for an expedited decision. He begged for only two minutes of the leader's time. He offered to talk to whomever Brezhnev would delegate to settle the question. He invoked both comradeship and basic politeness. In the end none of these proved to be compelling enough to overcome caution.[10]

In an effort to nudge the matter forward, Sholokhov's allies published articles designed to stoke public anticipation for the new "chapters."[11] Even this failed to provoke a reaction from the Central Committee. Sholokhov fumed for two more months before writing to Brezhnev again. This time he issued a veiled threat. Citing persistent rumors in Moscow that "[now] even Sholokhov is not being published," he hinted that the *New York Times* might soon publish an article comparing him to Solzhenitsyn and naming him among the ranks of opposition writers.[12] Pretending that this would add insult to the injury caused by waiting for so many months, he implored Brezhnev for a reply or the name of a Kremlin official with whom he could discuss "corrections."

Sholokhov was preparing to back up his threats with action. He penned a letter to his old nemesis Harrison Salisbury of the *New York Times*. His choice was far from accidental. He knew from 1959 that Salisbury was interested in sensational stories about Soviet leaders and censorship. He planned to initiate a correspondence about Hemingway.[13] If Salisbury took the bait, he was planning to plead his case in a subsequent letter. Sholokhov could regale the American journalist with curious tales about how Hemingway had been prohibited in the USSR. He knew secrets of Fidel Castro's involvement in trying to lift the ban, and he could reveal details about Suslov's role in maintaining it. This discussion could provide a natural segue to his own current situation. He seemed to have relied on the certainty that postal surveillance would pick up on the triangle *New York Times*-Sholokhov-Hemingway and immediately report to the top.

Sholokhov made a grave error in selecting a capitalist correspondent. Harrison Salisbury was completely on the side of the dissidents. He was an admirer of Solzhenitsyn and was becoming interested in the biography of Chukovskaia. He had never forgotten that in 1959–60 Sholokhov had suggested that he be horsewhipped or dragged across the steppe for his articles about *Virgin Soil*. More crucially, Salisbury was one of the few Western correspondents who was well acquainted with the authorship controversy.

The members of the Politburo faced a difficult decision. If they didn't approve publication of Sholokhov's "chapters," they would be contributing to the Chukovskaia prophecy coming true. If they did publish the excerpts, they would reveal to the world that the Soviet classic had lost his ability to develop a plot. The gerontocracy endorsed what appeared to be the most cautious and sensible option. They waited. When the writer demonstrated that he was willing to act upon his veiled threats, several moderately redacted and partially abridged selections appeared in *Pravda*. Brezhnev both published him and censored him.

Sholokhov's last word in literature was an odd patchwork quilt.[14] He presented a disjointed series of fireside conversations, which meandered from marital estrangement to fishing to Stalin. The fishing sections were patterned on an episode of *Quiet Don*. The general tendency was to insist that in spite of repressions the protagonists remained loyal to the Soviet system. Their personal tragedies were only hinted at in passing in order to demonstrate that they were able to put their suffering behind them and did not lose faith in the party.

Sholokhov thought he was being provocative by discussing the taboo topic of Stalin in connection with the ninetieth anniversary of the dictator's birth. The Stalin section started with a strangely cobbled together paraphrase of the writer's own first meeting with Stalin:

> In the evening the conversation turned to the civil war and one of the military leaders accidentally let slip the following phrase about Kornilov: 'He was subjectively an honest person.' Stalin's yellow eyes narrowed, like a tiger preparing to pounce, but he said in a rather restrained manner: 'A subjectively honest person is one who is together with the people, who fights for the cause of the people, but Kornilov went against the people, fought against the army created by the people, how does that make him an honest person. Everyone who was honest from the intelligentsia and even the nobility followed the Bolsheviks, the people and Soviet power.'

The protagonist immediately agreed with Stalin. There was no compelling logical connection to the surrounding narrative. Another direct reference to Stalin seemed to convey a facet of Sholokhov's personal struggles:

> I am offended at Stalin. How could he allow something like that [the arrests during the terror]? I am trying to objectively understand what makes him tick and feel like I just can't. One thing gets in the away, if my attitude to him is hostile, then it doesn't matter a damn to him, he's neither cold nor hot as a result of that. But if his attitude towards me involves hostility, then I would be cold, and hot, and even something much worse.

His personal psychological struggle to understand Stalin had reached an impasse. In explaining the Great Terror he returned to a widely promoted propaganda cliché from 1939. The chapter repeated the fiction that slanderers were primarily to blame for the fact that the majority of people who suffered were innocent. He lost all credibility by blaming Beria rather than revealing the role of the NKVD. As one prominent Soviet writer noted, almost everything had been said before, and in better prose, by other writers.[15]

By November 1969 the Writers' Union finally decided to expel Solzhenitsyn from its ranks unless he denounced the publication of his works in the West and apologized for various literary and political mistakes. When he refused, the *Literary Gazette* published an article proposing that the dissident could receive an exit visa and should emigrate from the USSR. Sholokhov threw his weight behind the harassment campaign in a speech delivered to several thousand collective farm officials.[16] He remarked, "While you [in agriculture] have done away with pests, we [in literature] still have Colorado beetles, people who want to eat Soviet bread but who want to serve Western bourgeois masters and send their works there through secret channels. Soviet [men of letters] want to get rid of them too." He compared Solzhenitsyn to one of the biggest problems confronting ordinary Soviet citizens. An infestation of stripy, brown beetles was devastating the garden plots upon which millions depended for supplementing their meager salaries. Widespread rumors alleged that the CIA had unleashed the beetles to devastate the Soviet economy.

Contrary to Sholokhov's expectations, Solzhenitsyn did not emigrate. He remained in the Soviet Union. For his boldness and candor the Swedish Academy awarded him the Nobel Prize for Literature in 1970. Thereafter he became more committed to his secret quest to expose Sholokhov as plagiarist.[17] He began corresponding with Irina Medvedeva-Tomashevskaia, the author of several historical studies devoted to literature and history of the early 19th century. When he shared with her his suspicions about *Quiet Don*, it turned out that she had been harboring similar doubts for decades. They decided to collaborate on an experiment to identify which sections of the novel had been plagiarized.

For Sholokhov there were various signs that his political influence was waning.[18] In 1970 he asked Brezhnev and the Politburo to approve a celebration of the four hundredth anniversary of the Don Cossacks. It rejected his proposal after consulting with historians from Rostov and Moscow. In 1971, for the first time since the Stalin era, Sholokhov was not invited to deliver a keynote speech at a Party Congress. In 1972 he could not prevent changes to the editorial board of *Molodaia Gvardiia*, which diminished its "patriotic" focus. On the positive side, Brezhnev still took his calls and approved his request for permission to once again travel to Scandinavia.

By 1973 the director of the Cultural Department of the Central Committee grew so tired of dealing with Sholokhov's demands that he permitted himself a rare flippant remark.[19] Sholokhov had repeatedly tried to lobby for official recognition of a book about him by one of his most avid supporters, the local literary scholar Konstantin Priima. After several calls in which Sholokhov requested that the book be placed on Brezhnev's desk and emphasized that it was worthy of favorable coverage in the national media, the frustrated functionary decided to play along. He proclaimed the local scholar's book to be "the most important literary event of the year" and hinted that it might even be nominated for the Nobel Prize. Sholokhov, not sensing the sarcasm, was delighted.

THIRTY-ONE

n early fall 1974 Sholokhov contacted a high-ranking officer in the Fifth Directorate of the KGB. This secret department was created in the late '60s to monitor dissidents and to combat psychological warfare operations against the USSR by foreign governments. The writer's request was highly extraordinary. He urgently needed to obtain a photograph of a document from 1926 in a KGB archive. Of what relevance was a half-century-old piece of paper to the current struggle against internal and external enemies? Why did the writer believe that the secret police would grant his request? Because *Quiet Don* was in danger. "Enemy voices" were using shortwave radio broadcasts to slander him and the USSR. For the first and only time in history, a recipient of the Nobel Prize publicly accused another laureate of plagiarism. Sholokhov had contributed to making Solzhenitsyn a non-person in the Soviet Union; now the dissident would have his revenge by assailing Sholokhov from abroad.

The last Sholokhov had heard, the irascible Solzhenitsyn had been stripped of his citizenship and kicked out of the country for his virulent hatred of the Soviet government and socialism.[1] Since there was no way to guess the kinds of testimonies or evidence that the dissident had gathered, Sholokhov needed a more reliable defense strategy. The document in the KGB archive would become a cornerstone.

Solzhenitsyn was expelled from the USSR on February 13, 1974. One of the first people he contacted upon arriving in the West was Harrison Salisbury of the *New York Times*.[2] Salisbury played an important role in finding a translator for *The Gulag Archipelago*, Solzhenitsyn's extensive literary-historical exposé of the Soviet labor camp system. The dissident was in a bad mood. He blamed his expulsion from the USSR on his allies. He believed that unreasonable delays in getting *Gulag* in the hands of "millions of American readers" emboldened the Soviet authorities. Salisbury managed to win back his confidence with wartime analogies based on Solzhenitsyn's military service and a clear explication of the technological and bureaucratic obstacles that hindered a quick mass publication in the West. He succeeded in convincing Solzhenitsyn that the *New York Times* could become a very important medium for advancing his cause. Although Salisbury had retired from the *New York Times*, he continued to have a strong network of contacts there.

Sholokhov had expected that the year 1974 would initiate a series of important celebrations. They would commence in January with his fiftieth wedding anniversary, which he would celebrate both in Moscow and Vioshki. The thirtieth anniversary of the victory in the war would then be widely commemorated in early May of the next year. After that his seventieth birthday would be on the horizon.

For his wedding anniversary he had planned to invite around two dozen friends over to his Moscow apartment. When he arrived in the capital in early January, a high-ranking official intimated that the guest list needed to be expanded.[3] Leonid Il'ich was expecting an invitation. It was a common cliché in Russia that a general invited to a wedding would enhance its prestige but a General Secretary at a golden anniversary was not so common. In response to Sholokhov's suggestion that Brezhnev might not feel comfortable among the writer's small circle of friends and family, the official hinted that everyone would feel highly uncomfortable if no invitation were extended. Sholokhov arranged a call to Brezhnev to issue the invitation. Brezhnev tentatively agreed to come but claimed he still needed to consult with his doctors. He was having problems with insomnia and his nervous system and was obliged to adhere to a strict medical regime. He advised the writer to hold the event in a banquet hall in a Moscow hotel. Instantly all of the plans for the celebration had to be revised. A hall had to be booked, menus needed to be selected, and guests had to be contacted about the change of venue. On the day of the anniversary, as the appointed hour for the festivities approached, Sholokhov became edgy. At exactly 7:00 P.M., one of Brezhnev's assistants arrived with flowers, gifts, and apologies. The doctors had allegedly not granted him permission to attend.

For Sholokhov the biggest event that spring was a trip to Stockholm to spend the remaining portion of the Nobel Prize money. While he was making arrangements for delivering his newly purchased Mercedes to Vioshki, Solzhenitsyn was finalizing the text of his attack on Sholokhov.[4] In early July he contacted Salisbury, proposing that as a connoisseur of Russia, the journalist would want to be among the first to provide a response to a book that would be published in a matter of weeks. It would be a literary detective story rather than a legal accusation of plagiarism. He lamented that it remained unfinished due to the untimely death of its author, who uncovered contradictions and peculiarities in *Quiet Don* and identified two distinct authorial voices. He offered to provide the journalist a prepublication copy of the book, which would have "enormous importance for Russia." Salisbury responded with enthusiasm and even proposed that a subsidiary of the *Times* might be interested in publishing an English edition.

The KGB appears to have gotten wind of Solzhenitsyn's plans through confidential informers among émigré communities in Geneva or Paris.[5] It tried to warn Sholokhov. An official of the Cultural Department paid a visit to Vioshki. Ostensibly he was there to talk about the planning for the celebration of Sholokhov's upcoming seventieth birthday, which was several months away. Unofficially he was there to find out how Sholokhov would handle the news that his authorship of *Quiet Don* was again being challenged. No record of that meeting has ever been published. Even the writer's assistant was sworn to utmost secrecy. In literary circles a rumor soon appeared that Sholokhov had angrily refused to cooperate. He purportedly screamed at the Moscow official, "It was my job to write *Quiet Don* and now it's your job to defend me."[6] The Central Committee was particularly concerned that Solzhenitsyn's attack was being timed to cast a shadow over the celebrations of Sholokhov's birthday.

Their assessment was incorrect. Solzhenitsyn rushed the publication forward for his own reasons. He wanted to discredit the regime, draw attention to himself in exile, and change the news cycle. He was expecting the imminent publication of a series of compromising letters and revelations by his ex-wife, Natalia Reshetovskaia.[7] These would depict him as selfish, egotistical, and ready to profit from the suffering of others. He needed an altruistic change of message. Honoring dead comrades would help dispel such charges. He hoped to honor the man whom he believed to be the true author of *Quiet Don*, Fedor Kriukov, and Medvedeva-Tomashevskaia, the deceased researcher who vindicated him.

Acting in coordination with Solzhenitsyn, Salisbury published a major article in the *New York Times* on September 1, 1974, a day after brief reports about the plagiarism allegations first appeared in Scandinavian news outlets.[8] Salisbury managed to secure prominent space for the story on the second page with the headline SOLZHENITSYN QUESTIONS AUTHORSHIP OF CLASSIC NOVEL BY SHOLOKHOV, A FELLOW WINNER OF THE NOBEL PRIZE. He provided a preview of a book that would soon be published in Paris. A deceased literary scholar known as "D" would argue that Sholokhov's novel was based on a text written by Fedor Kriukov. While providing little discussion of the specific evidence and arguments advanced in the book, Salisbury noted that controversy had surrounded Sholokhov's name on various occasions since 1928. The *Times* publication ensured that the story would be picked up by international press services. In the days following his article, Salisbury eagerly awaited a cable from the *Times*'s Moscow correspondent about Sholokhov's reaction. A week passed before the correspondent cabled: ". . . cannot believe that Soviets would let it pass by. But nothing yet."

When Soviet agents succeeded in obtaining a copy of the Paris publication, they discovered that it read like a rough draft of a literary study.[9] Parts of it consisted of only preparatory notes and preliminary conclusions.[10] There were no sensations. Fears that Solzhenitsyn had stumbled onto some kind of bombshell manuscript evidence were dispelled immediately. The book contained precious little evidence. The strongest parts of the study raised provocative questions about the evolution of characters and plotlines in *Quiet Don*. "D" provided numerous examples of how the novel appeared to veer off in unanticipated directions that did not seem to adhere to the original vision offered in the first book. "D" cast Sholokhov as a mediocre, ideologically motivated, communist coauthor who introduced numerous false notes and inconsistencies. The sections about Kriukov were brief, vague, and unconvincing. "D" allegedly died before completing a reconstruction of the "original" text of the novel, so only a series of vague and confusing tables summarized the extent of Kriukov's alleged contributions.[11] Solzhenitsyn's preface appeared slanderous, but it derived almost entirely from Soviet published sources and well-known rumors. He republished the article by local journalist Molozhavenko from 1965. He also published a curious excerpt from a Soviet article about the Cossack Iakov Lagutin.[12] Solzhenitsyn found it odd that Sholokhov did not clearly recall borrowing from Lagutin's memoirs and gave "vacuously empty" answers to a local researcher.[13] The most serious charge, however, was that no manuscripts of *Quiet Don* existed.

Soviet officials faced a conundrum. On the one hand, widespread international media reports about the plagiarism controversy tarnished Sholokhov's reputation. From the slanted coverage, it appeared as if "D" had indeed proven that Sholokhov had written only 5 percent of the first two volumes and around 30 percent of the third and fourth volumes. On the other hand, it was difficult to assess how much lasting damage might be done by an incomplete and anonymous book.

Although Soviet officials initially appeared to be ignoring the controversy, they solicited a letter of indignation from Vladimir Molozhavenko, the local journalist who nearly a decade earlier had published the small article about Kriukov and his small trunk full of missing manuscripts. Solzhenitsyn had republished that article as an appendix to the Paris book. Calling Sholokhov a "literary giant," the journalist disingenuously claimed that there had never been a ban on Kriukov's works in the USSR and tried to distance himself from the scandal stirred up by Solzhenitsyn. Soviet embassies in Washington and London distributed copies of an English translation of the letter to major publications.[14]

Intriguingly, in the first version, which was sent from Washington, the Rostov journalist declared, "Let it be known to Mr. Solzhenitsyn that I have never doubted the author's rights of Mr. Sholokhov to the novel *And Quiet Flows the Don*, and he will not find a like-minded person in me." The ambiguity of the original wording left lingering suspicions about whether the journalist in fact believed that all parts of the novel had been written by Sholokhov. A second, redacted version, which was sent after early publications about the plagiarism controversy, introduced significant alterations. The London version declares, "For the record, may I say categorically that I have never at any time doubted the authenticity of Sholokhov's authorship of the *Quiet Don*, nor will Solzhenitsyn find in me an even remotely like-minded person." The latter version became an unequivocal statement of belief in Sholokhov.

For weeks, there was no further official comment from anyone in the Soviet Union. This silence distressed Sholokhov and surprised his distant, dissident adversary.[15] Solzhenitsyn was expecting a flurry of rage from the Soviet propaganda machine. After weeks without official comment, he was perplexed. He projected his own state of bewilderment back onto Soviet officials, believing them to be so taken aback that they were at a loss as to how to respond. In order to further provoke them, he decided to advance additional allegations at a press conference in Geneva.

Two thousand miles away, Sholokhov was also questioning the silence. Why didn't his dear party vigorously spring to his defense? Could it be that someone in the Kremlin harbored doubts about him? He had on multiple occasions denied ever reading anything by Kriukov. To properly defend himself, Sholokhov would have to fully reveal the secret of his sources and prove that no author who died in 1920 could have written the novel. Instead, he petitioned the KGB.

He decided to fight on the terrain that was most favorable to him. Because the sections of *Quiet Don* devoted to the Vioshki rebellion were almost entirely his own creation, they demonstrated his authorship more forcefully than other sections. His letter to Harlampii Yermakov would prove that he was working on the novel in 1926 and was interviewing key participants of the rebellion, whom Kriukov could not have known. To his chagrin, the regional KGB office proved to be less than cooperative. It did not grant his request for a copy of his own letter. So he went as high up the chain of command as he could. [16]

By late October 1974 a copy of the letter was in his hands. The letter did not quite turn out to be the trump card he envisioned. To Yermakov, Sholokhov had written, "I need to receive from you some additional information pertaining to the epoch of 1919. I hope that you will not refuse me the courtesy of providing me those facts when I arrive from Moscow." [17] It demonstrated that he knew one of the most prominent leaders of the rebellion, but it did not mention *Quiet Don* or outline the specific purpose of the inquiry.

Word soon spread that Konstantin Simonov had given an interview to a West German correspondent about the plagiarism controversy. Soviet writers did not normally issue such statements without authorization from above. Given their past friction, this news troubled Sholokhov. He contacted a high-ranking ideological official and demanded to know what Simonov had said. The official came in person to his Moscow apartment. This did not seem to bode well.

The official read him a translation of Simonov's interview, which defended Sholokhov and emphasized Solzhenitsyn's hatred for everything Soviet. [18] Artfully dodging a question about whether Sholokhov could have used the manuscripts of another author, Simonov attributed the controversy to long-standing envy of Sholokhov. He praised a few of the Don stories without actually naming any one in particular, and called them the beginning of a long and productive literary career.

Sholokhov was profoundly grateful for Simonov's decision to rise above personal grievances. He pushed for a full publication of the interview in the *Literary Gazette*. Since "enemy voices" were blasting about the controversy via shortwave radio, such an article would shut up anyone who continued to make noise.

His request was forwarded to the Kremlin. Suslov quickly vetoed his idea. Since ordinary Soviet citizens did not harbor any doubts about Sholokhov's authorship, there was no need to prove anything to them. The information blackout would be total. Even scholars were prohibited from directly mentioning the controversy in their obscure academic articles devoted to his birthday and the fiftieth anniversary of the novel's publication.

Suslov's masterful, quiet move completely caught Solzhenitsyn off guard. The lack of a rabid Soviet reaction deflated his enthusiasm for the plagiarism crusade. As the controversy quickly retreated from the headlines, the dissident lost interest.[19] He turned his attention to working on his novels and filing lawsuits against some of the Western intermediaries who had once tried to help him publish his works. However, he still had one more surprise in store for Sholokhov.

Sholokhov turned his attention to the official preparations for his upcoming seventieth birthday in May 1975. These were starting to become both onerous and unsettling. The government was going to extraordinary lengths to plan celebrations in Moscow, Rostov, and Vioshki. Even though there were still several months to go before any actual events were staged, his phone was constantly ringing. The anticipated number of ceremonies, visiting delegations, and official receptions was snowballing. He could picture congratulatory backslappers converging upon him from all directions. For weeks on end he would be forced to shake the hands of eager, grinning strangers and pose for countless, pointless pictures. Swarms of journalists would descend upon him with invasive questions he had already answered many times.

More than anything he desired to be left alone.[20] But he also realized that in the Soviet system, "round dates," or major anniversaries, provided rare, one-of-a-kind opportunities to petition the government for extraordinary funds. Local officials were eager to take maximum advantage of this opportunity. They planned to milk the government for a new monument to Lenin, a new airport, a capacious restaurant building, funds for the general sprucing up of the area in anticipation of thousands of visitors, and the repainting and restoration of the writer's house. Sholokhov reluctantly agreed to cooperate on two conditions. They would permit him to skip events in Rostov, and they would construct a higher and sturdier fence around his house.

A few weeks before the birthday festivities in Moscow, his demeanor noticeably changed.[21] He became distant and silent. Something appeared to be bothering him. He spent unusual amounts of time alone and could not bring himself to talk about his woes. His thoughts turned to something that had occurred around fifty years earlier. He struggled to find the right words for the speech that he would deliver. He announced that he was writing it for history.

Soon after arriving in Moscow he received a high-ranking visitor from the Writers' Union. The official brought him a porcelain tea set and bad tidings. Solzhenitsyn had published some kind of memoirs in Paris. Once again there were some kind of allegations about Sholokhov.

The resurgence of controversy spurred Sholokhov to make changes to his speech. He spent the next day writing. For the first and only time he planned to publicly address the plagiarism charges. He selected as a leitmotif an old Arabic saying. The common version of it reads, "Dogs bark, the caravan goes on its way." It is an exhortation to get on with your business without paying attention to howling critics. In his version it became "Dogs bark, the rider goes on his way."[22] In his imagination he alone was confronting a mob of persistent curs and vicious bloodhounds.

The day before the ceremony, he welcomed an old friend. Andrei Plotkin stopped by to congratulate him. They hadn't seen each other in years. The visit brought back a rush of memories and emotions about Stalin, collectivization, the famine, and comrades such as Lugovoi, who had died in intervening years. As Sholokhov made his way to the bedroom for a midday rest, he lost his balance.[23] With extreme difficulty he lowered himself towards a bed. His speech started to slur. His right arm and right leg weakened and would no longer obey his commands. His frightened family called an ambulance. The medics determined that he had suffered a stroke and began injecting him with medicines. They rushed him to the Kremlin hospital. He insisted on taking the text of his speech along with him. All but the first page subsequently disappeared.[24]

THIRTY-TWO

The official celebration of his seventieth birthday at the Bolshoi Theater went on without him.[1] The speeches were predictably full of praise, pride, and references to humanism, socialist realism, and the didactic value of his prose. Several moments bordered on surreal. A military commander called the enfeebled, hospitalized Sholokhov "a moral example for youth [today]." A literary expert conveniently forgot about Stalinism and labeled *Virgin Soil* an unsurpassed depiction of Lenin's "scientific" program for solving the peasant question. A collective farmer from the Moscow region of all places stood up to thank Brezhnev of all people and proclaimed that "every day life is getting better and more joyous." Did he not realize that Stalin had uttered very similar words on the eve of the terror? Was he oblivious to the fact that millions of Soviet citizens were complaining about empty shelves, deficit items, and long lines? Save for a few forward-looking phrases such as, "Sholokhov has never stood, nor can he stand to the side of literary movement" or "we wish him new achievements in his multifaceted activities," many of the speeches could easily have doubled as obituaries.

The most important official guest was also absent that evening. Brezhnev was in the Kremlin hospital at the same time as Sholokhov. Because the leader's health was a highly secret matter of national security, no explanation was given for his absence. Though there was some relief that everyone would be spared a multi-hour oration, guests were left wondering why Suslov headed the government delegation to congratulate the writer. Brezhnev's slurred speech in a recent television appearance sparked concerns that he'd suffered a stroke as well.[2] It turned out that he was only in need of dental surgery.

Sholokhov faced a long recovery. The stroke hospitalized him for several weeks. He soon recovered his ability to speak. It took longer for physical therapy to return his mobility and make him less unsteady on his feet. His diminished mobility made it harder for him to hunt or travel. He was still capable of brief periods of sustained intellectual activity, though fatigue was always a concern.

He kept a copy of Marshal Grigorii Zhukov's war memoir close at hand in case he some day decided to start working on the war novel again.[3] He was vaguely aware of Zhukov's struggle to publish the book around the same time that his own chapters were censored. Unlike many memoirists of that era, Zhukov included passages about Stalin's leadership during the war. Though many of these were subsequently censored upon publication, Sholokhov admired the fact that the marshal was willing to stand up to Brezhnev and buck a major trend. He remarked to his assistant, "Stalin led the country for thirty years, and eliminating him from the history of the state is a sacrilege."

In 1977 Sholokhov experienced a first in the history of world literature. He came face-to-face with a scholar who used a computer to vindicate his authorship.[4] A young Norwegian named Geir Kjetsaa felt that the widespread international press coverage of Solzhenitsyn's plagiarism allegations was politically motivated. He assembled a team to create an "objective" means of testing Sholokhov's authorship of *Quiet Don*. For the first time a computer was asked to decisively arbitrate a human intellectual dispute involving a living author. Though such studies were still in their infancy, computers had already been programmed to analyze works attributed to the prophet Isaiah, Saint Paul, Shakespeare, and various British and American authors of earlier centuries.

In autumn 1975 Kjetsaa teamed with three other Scandinavian scholars to initiate a study to test three thousand sentences.[5] The sentences were taken in equal proportions from *Quiet Don*, from indisputable works authored by Kriukov, and from works authored by Sholokhov. Lines of text had to be entered as upper case letters on punched cards, which could then be fed through a card reader for the computer to perform a statistical analysis of sentence length and distribution of parts of speech. A detailed analysis of patterns, charts, and percentages led to a bold conclusion: "Kriukov is markedly dissimilar from Sholokhov in his writing, and that Sholokhov writes remarkably like the author of the *Quiet Don*."[6] Kjetsaa sent his article to Sholokhov and several Russian literary scholars. Sholokhov sent a telegram inviting the scholar for a visit.

In 1977 Kjetsaa gave a lecture on his findings to a group of literary scholars in Moscow. On the eve of his planned flight to Rostov, a phone call from an official notified him that Sholokhov was very ill and would not be able to meet him. The local scholar who had been arranging his visit to Sholokhov had for some mysterious reason suddenly been admitted to the hospital. Kjetsaa was savvy enough about Soviet realities to realize that meeting cancellation syndrome could be a convenient way for the authorities to avoid the hassle of surveilling foreigners in areas that rarely received international visitors. Why fill out forms, write meticulous reports, and send multiple agents to the field when it was easier to just ward them off? A late-night conspiratorial phone call arranged by an intermediary in Moscow confirmed that the visit to Sholokhov was still on.

As he traveled for six hours by car across bumpy roads pockmarked with potholes caused by a brief thaw, Kjetsaa pondered his upcoming meeting. Would Sholokhov be interested in the computer that vindicated him? How could he describe a computer to a Soviet citizen who had probably never seen one? It looked like a modernistic version of a draftman's table with a metal cabinet below. On the left side there was something that looked like a typewriter. On the right there was a panel of buttons and blinking lights. At the top there was a panel that displayed two sequences of up to thirty numbers, along with a dancing array of red, green, and orange blinking indicator lights. It was connected by cables to a series of tall metal cabinets, which were full of circuits and memory disks. Would Sholokhov ask him about the kinds of literary problems that computers were solving? If so, he would have to admit that most scholars were using them to create concordances and word indexes, since these mainly involved the relatively simple tasks of sorting and arranging. Simple of course was an understatement, because everything had to be coded and entered in a machine-readable form. The more ambitious projects, like his own, were now finding patterns, calculating frequency of words and grammar, and even analyzing style. The attribution of anonymous works was still the holy grail. For that one needed to input, or feed, as many as a million words into the computer's memory. His own project had only involved a tiny fraction of that.

Sholokhov hosted the Norwegian scholar and the local scholar, Priima, for a late lunch. He walked slowly, deliberately, and cautiously to greet his visitors. "Velkommen!" he exclaimed, having learned the word for 'welcome' on one of his various trips to Norway. He immediately noticed that the Norwegian didn't match his impression of a professor. His guess that his guest was from a farm family was spot on. Kjetsaa was of average build and seemed vigorous and energetic. He had a very high forehead, wore thick glasses, and spoke fluent Russian. After some small talk conducted in a parlor below the mounted head of a large black elk, Sholokhov motioned his guests to the table. A large bottle of vodka bearing a black label and the image of an 18th-century diplomatic dandy in a red European frock coat appeared on the table.

Sholokhov was in a good mood. Kjetsaa passed on a greeting from one of his female students, who asked the professor to tell the writer that she loved *Quiet Don* more than any other work. To this Sholokhov replied, "I would wish that she was willing to convey something else to me." Maria Petrovna quipped, "But she doesn't know anything whatsoever about your present capabilities." Her cutting double entendre hinted at sexual and creative impotence.

The most intriguing part of their conversation was entirely omitted from subsequent Soviet publications about the meeting. In response to a question about Kriukov, Sholokhov became indignant: "But Kriukov lived in Glazunovskaia, which is one hundred kilometers from here. How could he have knowledge about events that occurred in the vicinity of Vioshenskaia where the actions of *Quiet Don* take place?" Kjetsaa conceded and asked a follow-up question about Kriukov's status as a well-known author in the region. "Did you really never read anything by him?" he asked. Sholokhov flared up in agitation. "You may not believe it, but I never read Kriukov." He quickly calmed down and reiterated that the plagiarism rumors originated with fellow writers. "Envy. Organized envy," he thundered.

In their wide-ranging conversation, the computer was barely mentioned. When Kjetsaa tried to explain that the computer had demonstrated the richness of Sholokhov's vocabulary and the unconventional way in which he ended sentences, the writer showed only minor interest. A local scholar had already made a summary translation for him of Kjetsaa's article. He was amused, however, that the Norwegian had uncovered curious patterns in his prose, such as omissions of the word *and*, which he had never noticed before. The meeting ended cordially, and Sholokhov even invited Kjetsaa to come back the next day. The next morning the meeting was cancelled. Sholokhov had "taken ill."

In March 1978 Sholokhov lent his name to a long letter to Brezhnev lamenting that Russian culture was becoming degraded in the USSR.[7] It insisted that Russians were an endangered nation rather than a dominant one. Given that he wrote almost nothing in those years and that at least one Moscow intellectual claimed some credit for its contents, the letter should be viewed as a platform that he endorsed rather than his own rhetoric.[8] Nonetheless, it demonstrated that he alone was willing to attach his name and authority to a program dedicated to the "defense" of the Russian nation. A dozen years later, a little-known politician named Boris Yeltsin would capitalize on similar sentiments of grievance.

Rhetoric about the perceived victimization of Russia would have an exceptionally long shelf life. The letter charged that enemies in general, and Zionists in particular, were contributing to the intellectual degradation of the Russian nation by denying the progressiveness, creativity, originality, and distinctiveness of Russian culture. Anti-Russian ideas were being disseminated through film, television, and the press. Several specific points addressed the future of socialism. The evidence mentioned in the letter was sparse: a recent Soviet film about the era of Peter the Great in which Peter was not portrayed as fully heroic was one of the few specifics. The letter claimed that it was practically impossible under present circumstances to "organize an exhibition of a Russian painter of patriotic orientation, who works in the traditions of the school of Russian realism," while at the same time "exhibitions of the so-called 'avant-garde' are organized one after another." The letter also insisted that Russian architectural monuments were imperiled. The letter proposed three important actions for defending Russian culture: creating a journal of Russian culture, a museum of Russian life, and an authoritative committee to create a multi-year plan of action. It closed by praising Brezhnev's attention to economic improvements in central Russia and insisting that Russian cultural figures and the entire Soviet people would be thankful for his constructive efforts.

An offended Brezhnev eschewed a direct response. Instead he deployed the time-honored tactic of death by task force.[9] The Politburo designated a special seven-member committee to produce a report on the issues outlined in Sholokhov's letter. It took only three months to generate a detailed response. The fact that the task force took its obligations seriously is a testament to the respect attached to Sholokhov's name in higher party circles. It gathered statistics, assessed attitudes, and examined the role of recent anti-Soviet diversions carried out by such hostile forces as the Voice of America. Like most special committees, it arrived at the foregone conclusions it was expected to reach while at the same time expanding its charge in interesting and unexpected ways. It determined that there was no objective evidence for claiming that Russian culture had been neglected and that such slanderous claims were the result of anti-Soviet propaganda from abroad. It did find considerable evidence of predominance of Moscow-based intellectuals in all areas of Soviet culture. Intellectuals from the Russian provinces had far less access to print media, television, and performance venues than their counterparts from either the capital or the republics. The committee also obliquely acknowledged that certain periods of Russian history were not receiving "sufficient attention" and that scholars were now capable of more actively engaging the influence of the church upon Russian culture and other formerly controversial topics. In the end it concluded that it would be "inadvisable to adopt a special resolution regarding the questions posed in the letter of M. A. Sholokhov."

In summer 1978 the Politburo delegated a secretary of the Central Committee with the task of communicating a response to Sholokhov. His instructions were concise: "Explain to Comrade Sholokhov the actual situation with the development of culture in our country [in general] and in the Russian Federation, and the necessity of a deeper and more precise approach to the questions he raised in the name of the higher interests of the Russian and entire Soviet nation. No open discussions will be initiated regarding the issues of Russian culture, which he raised." The fact that neither Brezhnev nor any of his closest associates were involved in delivering the response sent a strong signal to the writer about his relative place in the Soviet hierarchy.

A few months later there was a minor concession to Sholokhov. It slightly sweetened the bitterness of being dismissed by Brezhnev and Suslov on the matter of Russian culture. His allies were permitted to publish a book containing some of the materials they had prepared in 1974 as a rebuff to Solzhenitsyn's plagiarism charges.[10] Sholokhov's 1926 letter to Yermakov was published. An article drew attention to several scenes in *Quiet Don* that derived directly from Sholokhov's background and local events that he witnessed. Priima, the favored local scholar, promoted his pet theories about Trotskyist enemies who worked to hinder Sholokhov in the 1920s. Most importantly, an abridged translation of Kjetsaa's 1976 article introduced Soviet readers to the computer's conclusions and the plagiarism controversy that had raged four years earlier.

A year later Sholokhov endured the most bitter insult that a writer can receive. A publishing house in Moscow requested permission to publish an edition of his complete works. He fumed for several days: "When a writer is still alive, there's no conceivable way to publish his 'complete' writings."[11] Another insult came when Brezhnev was awarded a Lenin Prize for his "authorship" of the war trilogy *Malaia Zemlia*, which as many suspected had been written by a team of ghostwriters.[12] A vicious anecdote insisted that when Brezhnev was told about his book's epic scope rivaling *Quiet Don*, emulation of the style of the Russian classics, and inspiring examples of party leadership, he quipped, "If it's really so good, maybe I ought to read it some time."

As Sholokhov's health continued to decline, his family became preoccupied with his legacy. They attempted to locate the lost manuscripts of *Quiet Don*.[13] The last hopes of finding them were dashed when they contacted the widow of Sholokhov's old friend Vasilii Kudashev. Some believed that Kudashev kept the manuscripts after the conclusion of the plagiarism tribunal in 1929. His widow claimed to have lost them during a move.

While they continued their search, Sholokhov managed to outlive two Soviet leaders.[14] In spring 1982 Brezhnev disappeared from public view for several weeks after a trip to Central Asia. The leader's departure from Moscow was widely covered on Soviet television, but the disturbing absence of any footage of his return to the capital immediately sparked speculations about his health. After several weeks he reappeared, looking frail and easily confused. He soldiered on in poor condition for a few months and expired immediately after the November 7 anniversary of the revolution. His successor was Yurii Andropov, who had served as head of the KGB since 1967. Fifteen months later Andropov also expired.

In September 1983 Sholokhov engaged *Quiet Don* for the final time.[15] He made a series of decisions about a new edition. He agreed to reintroduce multiple passages that had been excised by various censors. The last major decision of his literary career was to restore Trotsky's name to the novel after nearly five decades of absence. The name that had caused him so much trouble during the Great Terror was now, much like himself, a relic of a bygone era.

In late December 1983 Sholokhov was hospitalized with advanced, inoperable throat cancer. His greatest fear was that he would die in Moscow. In late January 1984 the doctors gave him permission to forego radiation therapy. He returned home to die. He rejected painkillers and spent his last days in agony. In spite of constant breathing problems and severe coughing fits, he tried to find warm words for his family and issued instructions about his burial. His last words, mumbled several times in rapid succession, were "Where is my CC [Central

Committee]? Where is my CC [Central Committee]?" Even in death he sought the Kremlin's intercession.[16]

The Soviet government immediately began making plans for an elaborate state funeral in Vioshki. The new seventy-two-year-old General Secretary Konstantin Chernenko, who had assumed power only days earlier, could not attend. His own health was not in serviceable shape. He seemed short of breath at times as he pronounced a brief speech at the funeral of his predecessor. Even on Soviet television, which showed only a few carefully vetted selections of footage, he appeared to be unsteady on his feet. The Kremlin instead sent the same secretary of the Central Committee who had been in charge of lacerating Sholokhov's excerpts in 1969 and evaluating the 1978 letter on Russian culture. The first eulogy was delivered by the only Soviet official who suspected in 1978 that Sholokhov was "under some kind of, most certainly not positive, influence."[17] The official proved to be true to his apparatchik stripes. In his closing remarks at the funeral he even managed to slip in an ideological admonition to all the mourners to "honestly and selflessly labor to implement the historical decisions of the Twenty-Sixth Party Congress and the decisions of the February Plenum of the Communist Party."

The ceremony turned out to be excessively official.[18] The theater of state took precedence over the needs of a grieving family and local community. Soldiers carried Sholokhov's casket from the House of Culture and placed it on an artillery carriage pulled by an armored personnel carrier. Guns saluted as the casket made its way to the central square of Vioshki, where thousands waited. A procession of mourners and soldiers carried special pillows adorned with his various Soviet medals. After several speeches, Sholokhov was laid to rest on a hill overlooking the Don River.

When his family was eventually able to face the task of going through his papers after his death, they entered his office.[19] They had taken precautions to leave everything as it was. They even stopped the clock so that the hands would permanently point to the hour and minute of his death. After several minutes of inspection, they discovered to their great astonishment that the drawers of his desk were completely empty. Sholokhov had destroyed every page of the war novel and had burned the remaining traces of his life as Stalin's scribe.

AFTERWORD

This book originated in a series of unusual conversations I had while living in Russia in 1999. When the locals found out that I was an American scholar and a fluent speaker of Russian, they eagerly wanted to discuss three topics. Was Putin balding? Would Cruz take Eden back? And would Sholokhov's manuscripts quietly flow abroad?

The "American" question confronted me first: "How does *Santa Barbara* end?" Russian television had for the first time started to show episodes of an American soap opera. Many Russians were enthralled by its passions, emotions, and narratives of conspiracy and betrayal. I had to disappoint them. I knew nothing about Cruz, Eden, or any of the other characters that vitally interested them. When Russian television abruptly stopped airing *Santa Barbara* in spring 1999 for financial reasons, pensioners complained to anyone who would listen that they had not worried so much about the unresolved fate of two star-crossed lovers since Grigorii and Aksiniia. Who were they I wondered? I had taken various courses on Russian history and literature in the United States and never encountered them.

A second, more sensitive, question often probed patterns of history and hair loss. There was already talk that the newly appointed prime minister, Vladimir Putin, was being auditioned for the role of Boris Yeltsin's successor. To my surprise many Russians intensely scrutinized his forehead for clues to their future. The Soviet epoch, they insisted, had followed a peculiar, but persistent, pattern. Bald reformers were inevitably followed by hairy hard-liners. Had Yeltsin flipped the pattern? Many of us thought we saw signs of balding in Putin but we couldn't quite be sure of what it meant. A year later, when allies of the new Russian president pressured a major Russian TV network to withdraw a puppet of Putin from a popular satirical show, old timers saw the writing on the wall.[1] Conversations became less candid. Colleagues became more cautious. The boundaries between satire and slander were becoming blurry again.

The third question often turned to Sholokhov. I learned that in parts of Russia Sholokhov was frequently the focus of passions no less intense than any melodrama. How come in the late 1960s the American government—or was it the CIA?—offered $5000 to anyone who could prove that Sholokhov didn't write his famous epic? What did I think about Sholokhov's letter to Stalin about the famine? Why did the NKVD try to frame him? Was he worthy of the Nobel Prize? How come the Israelis (an allegation I still do not know the origin of) desired to obtain the manuscripts of *Quiet Don*?[2] As those conversations unfolded it became clear that to some Russians he was a dastardly villain who savagely attacked dissidents and lent his authority to any message the regime desired to communicate. To others he was a hero who had saved thousands during the Stalin era, celebrated Russian resilience, and retrieved an entire people, the Cossacks, from the brink of extinction. In anticipation of such conversations, which were a litmus test of my view of the Soviet legacy and the Stalin years, I started to confront the problems of Sholokhov's biography.

While I was only starting to discover Sholokhov, a behind-the-scenes battle was unfolding about his own his legacy. A savvy Moscow journalist named Lev Kolodnyi discovered that the missing manuscripts of early parts of *Quiet Don* were in the hands of Vasilii Kudashev's heirs.[3] He located them and started to publish tantalizing articles in a Moscow newspaper. In a time of widespread lawlessness and banditry, he wisely withheld the location of those manuscripts in order to protect their caretakers. Following such publications, Sholokhov's heirs began to assert that the manuscripts were rightfully theirs. Skeptics chimed in and began to publish articles claiming that the manuscripts were not actually the manuscripts. An article published in *Izvestiia* in February 1998 raised the alarm that the precious relics were about to be sold abroad for half a million dollars.[4] A national treasure was about to disappear forever. In late 1999 Vladimir Putin stepped in. He authorized his government to negotiate the purchase of the manuscripts for around 50,000 dollars in order to donate them to the Gorky Institute of World Literature.[5] The Sholokhov family agreed to this arrangement and anointed Putin the savior of *Quiet Don*.

Putin also turned out to be quite a connoisseur of *Virgin Soil*. In 2000 in one of the earliest and most candid interviews about his decision to break with the KGB in favor of a new Russia, he suddenly and unexpectedly quoted Sholokhov.[6] "Kondrat Maidannikov only with great difficulty severed the umbilical cord," he declared. From somewhere deep in the recesses of his Soviet upbringing he recalled a significant scene in *Virgin Soil*. A farmer endures a restless night before joining the collective farm. Sholokhov wrote: "Even in his sleep things were complicated and difficult. It wasn't easy to reconcile himself to the collective farm! With a tear and with blood, Kondrat severed the umbilical chord which connected him to [private] property, to his oxen, to his dear parcel of land . . ." The next morning Sholokhov's character embarked on a new and necessary life. When it came time for Putin to talk about the most difficult moment of his biography he turned to Sholokhov! Unnoticed by Kremlinologists, what happened next should have attracted more attention. When the interview was subsequently reprinted as a book a few weeks later, the Sholokhov quote and other candid revelations were gone.

After returning to the States I put my thoughts of Sholokhov aside for a few years until a post-doctoral fellowship at the Harriman Institute for Russian Studies at Columbia University in 2004. There,

I closely analyzed Sholokhov's entire correspondence with Stalin for the first time. Stunned by his candor, I struggled to reconcile the sympathetic, even noble, Sholokhov who emerged in the letters with the vindictive, vitriolic man described in so many dissident accounts of late Soviet history. My struggles went on in vain until I met Ivan Bezugloff, a Cossack émigré in Cleveland, a few months later. His relative Sergei Korolkoff had illustrated *Quiet Don* in the 1930s. Korolkoff was convinced that Sholokhov changed as a result of his harrowing experiences during the Terror. This was the clue that I needed to write this book. An individual who survived, and even prospered, in Stalin's time could not emerge from the Terror whole. He remained forever captive to his fears of those years.

As I began to conceive of this book, I came across a small article devoted to an intriguing event. President Vladimir Putin had traveled to Vioshki to lay flowers at Sholokhov's grave in commemoration of the one hundredth anniversary of the writer's birth in 2005. During his visit he was also taken to see the very "fireplace in which Sholokhov burned the third part of *They Fought for the Motherland*."[7] Both "facts" were intriguing. By then I had already encountered claims that Sholokhov had altered his year of birth in order to avoid a harsh sentence after his arrest in 1922. This made me curious. What had actually happened to the unfinished war novel?

Soon into my search for an answer I stumbled onto a testimony that the writer burned the manuscript two decades before he was thought to have burned the manuscript. A Russian émigré in 1981 reported having a conversation with a famous Soviet poet and editor, Aleksandr Tvardovskii, who died in 1971.[8] Tvardovskii claimed that in a drunken fit Sholokhov burned the manuscript of his last novel and that it was lost forever. The émigré decoded this act as symbolically similar to Nikolai Gogol's burning of the second book of *Dead Souls* shortly before his death. If Sholokhov burned the manuscript around 1970 then all the testimonies about him working on it after that were false. The fireplace that Putin saw was indeed important, but not for the reason he thought. That fireplace was a smokescreen. Could Sholokhov have collaborated with his family to concoct a story that would give his life a "classic" end?

Could he have even plagiarized the tale that marked the coda to his literary career? If the two facts which book-ended Sholokhov's biography were both suspicious, what about the rest of it?

Thanks to the opening of Russian archives, in subsequent years I discovered that Mikhail Sholokhov's official Soviet biography is a tissue of legends, half-truths, and a tangled web of contradictions. I was only able to solve a number of puzzles by dismantling his official story and starting from scratch with a critical approach. It was well worth the effort. The fog turned out to be as interesting as the facts. His compromises were as fascinating as his candor.

In the course of writing this book I changed my mind about Sholokhov.[9] I was preconditioned to revile Sholokhov the plagiarist. As the chair of the Academic Integrity Board at a large university, the very thought that he got away with it—and even prospered from it—angered me. However, as I reread the novel and scrutinized the plagiarism charges, I realized that they oversimplified a complicated person and a contradictory epoch. In my eyes he became less of a literary marauder and more of a successful surrogate parent. Even if characters and plotlines originated with another author, it took Sholokhov, with his own talents, to give them life in a new era. He had to find a way to make the narrative palatable to Stalinist censors and meaningful to Soviet readers. He had to keep the characters growing and moving forward. As it got more and more difficult, he stuck to his guns. Had he been willing to compromise there would have been fewer delays in finishing the final installments. He could have avoided ten tortured years by simply turning Grigorii into a Red Army hero and making Aksiniia a decorated Stalinist milk maid. Instead he stayed true to his vision. Even if the tales he told about his sources were too tall to be noble, his talents earned him the Nobel Prize. *Quiet Don* was not saved in 1999 by Putin. It was saved by Sholokhov in 1926, Stalin in 1931, and Pogorelov in 1938.

The moral and ethical compromises that Sholokhov made both in his life and in his work were attuned towards survival. He was not the only person in the Soviet Union in the 1920s whose ambitions initially exceeded his abilities. He was one of millions trying to make it in a country rebuilding after an unfathomably devastating war, civil strife, famine, and revolution. Stalin's Russia was full of self-promoting nobodies, reckless con-men with audacious invented personas, false specialists, and talented imposters who for a time succeeded in both faking it and making it.[10] Even the highest party officials were revolutionary improvisers lacking either the experience or training to do what history demanded of them.

Sholokhov could, in some sense, be viewed as the most successful of them all. He impersonated a great writer long enough to truly become one. By the time his skills developed to match his ambition, the purges were approaching. It took all of his talents to survive and free his friends. His confident self-promotion and stubborn self-defense strategies worked. He played his role so successfully that he was never exposed. He gamed the most important mark in the Soviet Union. Or was it perhaps the other way around?

It is my hope that this more nuanced portrait of the man and more empathetic portrayal of the difficult choices he faced will stimulate new interest in both Sholokhov's era and his literary legacy. Though some of his secrets no doubt remain buried deep in closed archives, his contributions to Soviet history can now be recognized.[11] Sholokhov's life was as complicated and contradictory as the Soviet experience itself, encompassing as it did ideology and absurdity, candor and conformism, generosity and servility, good and evil. His stories are valuable for decoding the puzzle of Stalinism as an episode in the *longue durée* of Russian history. Pupils in the Russian Federation today read both *Dr. Zhivago* and *Quiet Don*. Sholokhov's heroes are remarkably relevant again in Putin's Russia. Explaining this will require us to admit that while western eyes were focused on urban Russians who thought like us, Russia's flyover regions continued to treasure the humbly stoic, remarkably resilient, and un-repentantly Russian characters brought to life by Stalin's scribe.

ACKNOWLEDGMENTS

I owe a debt of gratitude to many individuals who contributed to the shaping of this book. Ivan Bezugloff, who passed away in 2011, provided some key information about Sholokhov and Pavel Kudinov. Ben Hayes offered some important and much appreciated early editorial advice in 2013. Laura Springman and Joe Esposito read the first drafts of key chapters in 2015. They both asked particularly insightful questions and made valuable suggestions for structuring the narrative. Glenn Peers, Liz Lillehoj, Roman and Mary Ann Szporluk, Maria Georgopoulou, Christian Raffensperger, and Valentina Tikoff provided generous hospitality and warm occasions for discussing ideas over delicious dinners. Herman Ermolaev kindly imparted a small portion of his vast knowledge of Sholokhov's literary career to me during a visit to Princeton in spring 2015. At DePaul University Tom Foster, Lucy Rinehart, Guillermo Vasquez de Velasco, and Martin L. denBoer understood the importance of the book and facilitated time away from the classroom to complete it. Olivier Hekster, Danielle Slootjes, and the Excellence Initiative at

Radboud University made possible a stimulating, productive and life-enriching stay in the Netherlands, where the final chapters of this book were completed in 2018. My agent Don Fehr patiently and expertly guided me through the long process from query to comprehensive proposal. His involvement made this a better book. My editor and publisher Jessica Case enthusiastically embraced the project, made a number of excellent suggestions, and allayed my concerns about a book that kept getting bigger.

This book would not exist without the timely, sagely interventions of my wife, Elena. She graciously welcomed the intrusion of Sholokhov into our lives and intellectual itineraries. She made a number of prescient observations about Sholokhov and the text of *Quiet Don*, which were often confirmed by further research and manuscript evidence. She improved every chapter with suggestions, deletions, and queries. On long, blissful walks amidst towering oaks she often shared with me insightful observations about laughter, resistance, and intellectual autonomy under an arbitrary and all-pervasive dictatorship. In between marvelous bike rides through Cuypian landscapes we reflected on ambition, resilience, and the consequences of speaking truth to power. Her care and patience kept this book on track. I admire her more than words can express.

ENDNOTES

PREFACE

1 Multiple researchers, including those loyal to Sholokhov, have discovered passages in *Quiet Don* that consist of whole chunks of narrative taken almost verbatim from texts published by others. While from a strictly technical standpoint Sholokhov without a doubt plagiarized from others, he often deployed his purloined passages in ingenious ways. V. V. Gura, *Kak sozdavalsia "Tikhii Don": tvorcheskaia istoriia roman M. Sholokhova*, 2nd ed. (Moscow: Sovetskii Pisatel', 1989), 241, 290–91, 305–08, 340–44; Herman Ermolaev, *Mikhail Sholokhov and His Art* (Princeton, N.J.: Princeton University Press, 1982), 215–263. For insightful analysis of what such passages can reveal about Sholokhov's skills and objectives, see A. G. Makarov and S. E. Makarova, "K istokam 'Tikhogo Dona'," in *Zagadki i tainy "Tikhogo Dona,"* ed. G. Porfir'ev (Samara: P.S. Press, 1996), 229–292.

2 David Daley, "Rushdie: Mo Yan is a 'patsy of the regime'," *Salon*, December 7, 2012, https://www.salon.com/2012/12/07/rushdie_mo_yan_is_a_patsy_of_the_regime/

3 On Putin's official visit to Sholokhov's home and grave, see http://kremlin.ru/events /president/news/33426/ (last accessed June 2018).

ONE

1 None of the texts of those plays survive. Viktor Petelin, ed., *Mikhail Sholokhov v vospominaniiakh, dnevnikakh, pis'makh i stat'akh sovremennikov* (Moscow: Sholokhovskii Tsentr MGOPU im. M. A. Sholokhova, 2005), 1: 173–176, 473; 2: 506.

2   Gosudarstvennyi arkhiv rostovskoi oblasti, Shakhtinskii filial, f. 760, op. 1, d. 209, ll. 13–14; A. Palshkov, "Molodoi Sholokhov," *Don*, no. 8 (1964): 160–171.

3   Murat Mezentsev, "Molodoi Sholokhov," *Vechernyi Rostov*, October 11, 1991.

4   One of the few first-hand statements from Sholokhov about awaiting execution can be found in A. Sofronov, "Bessmertnik," *Ogoniok*, July 26, 1964, 10.

5   Here and throughout I derive probable inferences about affect from testimonies recorded after the fact. Sholokhov's emotional world remained a black box even to individuals who were very close to him. Evgeniia Levitskaia, who helped launch Sholokhov's career and spent considerable time in his company, recorded in 1930 her frustration with trying to figure out what was going on in his mind: "He remains a mystery even after my stay in Vioshenskaia. He guards his internal world [*vnutro*] behind [the proverbial] seven locks and [adds] one more on top of that." Evgeniia Levitskaia's reminiscences entitled "Stanitsa Veshenskaia 19. XVII-6.VIII 1930 goda," were published by Lev Kolodnyi, "Na rodine 'Tikhogo Dona': Zapiski E. G. Levitskoi," *Ogoniok*, no. 17, April 1987, 6–8. The quote is from page 7.

6   Mezentsev, "Molodoi Sholokhov."

7   Sholokhov's life began anew in 1922. His move to Moscow brought about important changes in both his self-presentation and self-understanding. Because of this, I decided not to begin this biography in the traditional manner. Almost all accounts of his childhood are either saccharine or selective. The circumstances of his birth remain uncertain. His mother, who was of Ukrainian background, grew up as a domestic worker in a manor house. By all accounts she doted on her son. He was raised by Aleksandr Mikhailovich Sholokhov, who apparently adopted him after the death of the father listed on his birth certificate. A. M. Sholokhov worked as an administrator for trading firms (some owned by well-to-do relatives) and had the means to pay for tutors and to send his son to private secondary schools outside the region. As non-Cossacks, the family would have been viewed as outsiders by many of their neighbors. As a boy, Sholokhov would have grown up as an "insider-outsider." He would have been surrounded by Cossack culture but separated from the Cossack community by juridical and caste boundaries. He could observe Cossack culture from a close vantage point but could never participate in it fully as an equal. This simultaneous proximity and distance served him well while working on *Quiet Don*.

8   On Sholokhov in Moscow, see Lev Kolodnyi, *Kto napisal 'Tikhii Don': khronika odnogo poiska* (Moscow: Golos, 1995), 9–65.

9   Petelin, *Mikhail Sholokhov v vospominaniiakh*, 1: 235–250.

10   Viktor Shklovskii, "O pisatele," *Novyi LEF*, January 1927, 29. Bulgakov's short story "No. 13–Dom El'pit-Rabkommuna," vividly depicts such an environment.

11   Petelin, *Mikhail Sholokhov v vospominaniiakh*, 1: 250–260; Lev Kolodnyi, *Kto napisal*, 65–78.

12   Where English editions of key publications of Sholokhov's stories are available, I cite them here. Because of the complicated publishing history of Sholokhov's works, few of the English translations precisely reflect the texts as originally published. Nonetheless, they provide a sense of how his career unfolded. See Mikhail Sholokhov, *One Man's Destiny and other Stories, Articles and Sketches 1923–1963*, trans. H. C. Stevens (London: Putnam, 1967), 49–51.

13   Petelin, *Mikhail Sholokhov v vospominaniiakh*, 1: 220, 227–233.

14   *Ekstrennyi vypusk gazet: Pravda i Izvestiia* (Moscow), January 22, 1924.

15   Kolodnyi, *Kto napisal*, 43. The story is "Nakhalenok," trans. H. C. Stevens as "The Shame-Child," in Mikhail Sholokhov, *Tales from the Don* (London: Putnam, 1961), 74–103.

16   For documentary film footage, see "Siuzhety proshchanie s V. I. Leninym," *Kinodokument No. 55340*, available at https://www.net-film.ru/film-55340/ (last accessed June 2018).

17   Letter from Sholokhov to Maria (aka Marusia), early November 1924. Viktor Petelin, ed., *Mikhail Sholokhov, Pis'ma 1924–1984* (Moscow: Sovetskii Pisatel', 2003), 80–82. For finances, see Petelin, *Pis'ma*, 78–79.

18   When Sholokhov visited publishers with the manuscript of *Quiet Don* in 1927, he was wearing a leather jacket and fur cap like the one in illustration 1. Lev Kolodnyi, *Dve tetradi Evgenii Levitskoi* (Moscow: Golos-Press, 2005), 214. On the cover of early editions of the novel he was also depicted in such a cap. See the cover of Mikhail Sholokhov, *Tikhii Don: kniga pervaia* (Moscow: Gos. Izd. Khudozhestvenoi literatury, 1931).

19   See Mikhail Sholokhov, *Tales from the Don*, trans. H. C. Stevens (London: Putnam, 1961).

20   Petelin, *Mikhail Sholokhov v vospominaniiakh*, 1: 223. On Serafimovich as a mentor, see L. Iakimenko, *'Tikhii Don' M. Sholokhova: O masterstve pisatelia* (Moscow: Sovetskii pisatel,' 1958), 21–22.

21   The concluding paragraphs of this chapter are based on a series of letters that Sholokhov sent to Maria in 1926. See Petelin, *Pis'ma*, 88–106.

22   Letter to Maria August 17, 1928, Petelin, *Pis'ma*, 97.

23   Tarasov-Rodionov's letter to Sholokhov, June 1927, Petelin, *Pis'ma*, 109.

TWO

1   Several scholars have raised serious doubts about Sholokhov's sole authorship of *Quiet Don*. There is at present no scholarly consensus regarding the extent to which Sholokhov drew upon existing stories and sketches created by others. My own position is that the skeptics have grossly underestimated Sholokhov's contributions to the creation of the epic. On the manifold challenges of attempting to finish an incomplete novel, see Camilla Ulleland Hoel, "The Completion of Edwin Drood: Endings and Authority in Finished and Unfinished Narratives" (PhD diss., University of Edinburgh, 2012), 76–77, 82, 107, 109–110, 125, 129–130, 149, 153, 159, 165, 170, 173, 179, 192, 202, 204.

2   His belief that he would be able to complete the novel within nine months and also write as many as ten new short stories suggests to me that he underestimated the challenges of working with his sources. Letter to Maria, August 1926, Petelin, *Pis'ma*, 103.

3   Andrei Zimovnov, *Sholokhov v zhizni* (Rostov: Rostizdat, 2005), 255.

4   A. V. Venkov, *"Tikhii Don": Istochnikovaia baza I problema avtorstva* (Moscow: Airo-XXI, 2010).

5   Andrei Chernov, a skeptic, has drawn attention to cases that appear to be transcription errors from old orthography in the manuscript of the first volume of *Quiet Don*. Intriguingly, Sholokhov's other works do not appear to contain such errors. A. Chernov, "Striamia 'Tikhogo Dona,'" in *Zagadki i tainy 'Tikhogo Dona': Dvenadtsat' let poiskov i nakhodok*, ed. A. G. Makarov and S. E. Makarova (Moscow: AIRO-XX, 2010), 78–108.

6   I concur with the skeptics that Sholokhov's sole authorship of the first volume of *Quiet Don* is highly improbable. At the same time, I would agree with Sholokhov's supporters that the skeptics have gravely erred in portraying Sholokhov as a mediocre writer and inattentive copyist. My own view is that Sholokhov's successful transformation of a mélange of sources into a publishable Soviet epic remains an unparalleled literary achievement regardless of his motives. The proponents of Sholokhov's sole authorship have systematically ignored key evidence and arguments provided by the skeptics. Scholars who doubt sole authorship also sharply disagree about who began the unfinished novel that became *Quiet Don*. Often the skeptics do not even agree about the forms of evidence and lines of argumentation that are most significant for challenging Sholokhov's authorship claims. As I make clear in the text, Soviet law at the time of the novel's publication gave Sholokhov unambiguous rights to the epic.

7   In early April 1926 he wrote from Moscow to his wife: "Upon arrival I will right away sit down with the novel [sazhus' za romanom]." This is the first secure reference to *Quiet Don*, but the phrasing is highly ambiguous as to the nature of the work he anticipated doing. The context of the phrase, which was framed as one of several matters of greater interest to Maria, suggests that he was responding to an inquiry in Maria's letter to him, which apparently no longer exists. It is highly intriguing that he was unwilling to admit to A. S. Serafimovich that he was working on a novel in winter 1927. These facts suggest that he had not yet decided on a course of action. Petelin, *Pis'ma*, 92, 106, 110. His appraisal of his early stories as naïve and juvenile, see Iakimenko, '*Tikhii Don' M. Sholokhova*, 27.

8   "O kazachestve," *Pravda* (Moscow), May 15, 1925; "Po voprosu o kazachestve: rezoliutsiia aprel'skogo (1925 g.) plenuma TsK RKP(b)," in *KPSS v rezoliutsiiakh i resheniiakh s"ezdov, konferentsii i plenumov TsK*, Part 1, 1898–1925 (Moscow: Izd. Politicheskoi literatury, 1953), 932–934.

9   In a letter from Moscow to Maria in October 1927 he refers to the "pile of money" he was expecting from the novel's publication. See M. Iu. Garnets, *Sholokhovskii vek* (Rostov: Omega, 2005), 91.

10   See Feliks Kuznetsov, *Tikhii Don: Sud'ba i pravda velikogo romana* (Moscow: IMLI, 2005), 276–282. [Henceforth referred to as Kuznetsov, *Sud'ba i pravda*.]

11   Letter to Godlevskaia, September 1928, in Petelin, *Pis'ma*, 118.

12   Tsentral'nyi ispolnitel'nyi komitet SSSR, *Postanovlenie ot 30 ianvaria 1925 goda ob osnovakh avtorksogo prava*: http://istmat.info/node/30729 The quote is from section 4b (last accessed June 2018).

13   *Dekrety Sovetskoi vlasti*, volume 2, March 17–July 10, 1918 (Moscow: Izdatel'stvo Politicheskoi literatury, 1959), http://museumreforms.ru/node/13947 (last accessed June 2018). See also V. A. Riasentsev, *Ocherki istorii nasledstvennogo prava* (Voronezh: Voronezh University, 1979).

14   On this, see N. V. Kornienko, "*Skazano russkim iazykom*": *Andrei Platonov i Mikhail Sholokhov vstrechi v russkoi literature* (Moscow: IMLI RAN, 2003).

15   We know of multiple Cossack exhortations during the civil war about gathering materials for posterity. See A. V. Venkov, "*Tikhii Don*": *Istochnikovaia baza*, 568–9, 576.

16   Sholokhov almost never spoke about his experiences growing up as a non-Cossack among Cossacks. The fact that he suffered from derision would appear to follow from a candid,

but cryptic, comment to Evgeniia Levitskaia that his short story "Nakhalenok" was partly autobiographical. Levitskaia, "Stanitsa Veshenksaia," 6.

THREE

1   S. Tret'iakov, "Novyi Lev Tolstoi," *Novyi LEF*, no. 1, January 1927, 33–34.

2   Petelin, *Mikhail Sholokhov v vospominaniiakh*, 1: 243.

3   Kuznetsov, *Sud'ba i pravda*, 418–423.

4   A. Serafimovich, "Tikhii Don," *Pravda*, April 19, 1928.

5   One of the earliest and most enthusiastic editors to support Sholokhov was Evgeniia Levitskaia (née Frenkel) of the press "Moskovskii Rabochii." She had joined the party in 1903. They formed a friendship and he often visited her when he traveled to Moscow. She often sent him news and publications of interest from Moscow and he sometimes affectionately referred to her as "mother." His letters to her provide some of the most important insights into his biography. For the first full publication of his letters to her, see Lev Kolodnyi "Istoriia odnogo posviashcheniia," in [n.a.] *S kroviu i potom: neizvestnye stranitsy iz zhizni M. A. Sholokhova* (Rostov: Rostov Knizhnoe Izdatel'stvo, 1991).

6   Letters to Maria, May 1928, December 1928, in Garnets, *Sholokhovskii vek*, 94–96.

7   Lev Kolodnyi, *Dve tetradi*, 221.

8   Kuznetsov, *Sud'ba i pravda*, 129–190.

9   On Yermakov, see A. I. Kozlov, *M. A. Sholokhov vremena i tvorchestvo: po arkhivam FSB* (Rostov: Rostovskii Gosudarstvennyi Universitet, 2005), 9–138.

10 The intriguing recent appearance on the Internet of a letter, typed report, and photographs linking Sholokhov to a secret police official named Stepan Bolotov in the late '20s caused a minor sensation in Sholokhov studies. The report specifically mentions Sholokhov's request for sources about the rebellion. For a traditional appraisal, see Feliks Kuznetsov, "Polynno gor'kaia Pravda: Sholokhov-110," *Literaturnaia gazeta* (Moscow), May 20, 2015. For skeptical commentary and the text of the report, see Andrei Chernov, "Krepka, krepka pokoinitsa Sof'ia Vlas'evna (O chekiste Mikhaile Sholokhove)," https://nestoriana .wordpress.com/2016/01/22/ (last accessed June 2018).

11 For testimony that he received materials from the secret police, see Levitskaia, "Stanitsa Veshenskaia," 7.

12 In volume 2, part five, chapters 26, 27, 28, 30, Sholokhov borrowed extensively from A. A. Frenkel, *Orly Revoliutsii* (Rostov: Tsentropechat', 1920), 19–24, 27, 28, 30. In volume 2, part five, chapter 10, he created a composite text by alternating between borrowings from F. G. Kosov, "Podtelkov v Novocherkasske," *Donskaia Volna* (Rostov), December 16, 1918, reprinted in Donskaia Istoricheskaia Komissiia, *Donskaia letopis': sbornik materialov po noveishei istorii Donskogo Kazachestva so vremeni Russkoi revoliutsii 1917 goda* (Belgrade: Donskaia Istoricheskaia Komissiia, 1923–4), vol. 2: 307–315, and Lagutin's memoir, see below. On Lagutin, see Kuznetsov, *Sud'ba i pravda*, 396.

13 Kuzentsov, *Sud'ba i pravda*, 451–2.

14 Syrtsov had written his own account about the revolutionaries shortly after the events. See Sergei Syrtsov, "Na Donu: Geroi proletarskoi revoliutsii," *Izvestiia* (Moscow), May 30, 1918.

15 Lev Kolodnyi, *Dve tetradi*, 221; Iu. B. Lukin, "Iz knigi 'Vospominaniia'," in *Sholokhov na izlome vremeni: Stat'I i issledovaniia. Materialy k biografii pisatelia. Istoricheskie istochniki "Tikhogo Dona." Pis'ma i telegrammy*, ed. V. V. Petelin (Moscow: Nasledie, 1995), 143.

16 The main source for the paragraphs on the plagiarism tribunal is Letter to Maria, March 1929, published in A. A. Kozlovskii, F. F. Kuznetsov, and A. M. Sholokhov, eds., *M. A. Sholokhov, Pis'ma* (Moscow: IMLI RAN, 2003), 28–31.

17 See N. M. Gordeeva, *Literaturnyi Rostov 20-kh godov* (Rostov: Izdatel'stvo Rostovskogo Gosudarstvennogo Universiteta, 1967).

18 Mikhail Obukhov, "Vstrechi s Sholokhovym (20–30-e) gody," in *Tvorchestvo Mikhaila Sholokhova. Stat'i, soobshcheniia, bibliografiia*, ed., V. A. Kovaleva and A. I. Khvatova (Leningrad: Nauka, 1975), 286–92. Neither Lev Kolodnyi, *Kto napisal*, 305, nor Feliks Kuznetsov, *Sud'ba i pravda*, 66, 385, noticed the problem with Sholokhov's assertion.

19 Ironically Sholokhov's plagiarism from Iakov Lagutin's 1925 memoir proves that no author who died during the civil war could have written that portion of the novel. Bar-Sella completely ignores this evidence in his fascinating, but unconvincing, effort to prove that Sholokhov was merely a mediocre copyist. Zeev Bar-Sella, *Literaturnyi kotlovan: Proekt "Pisatel' Sholokhov"* (Moscow: Rossiiskii gumanitarnyi universitet, 2005). On Lagutin, see additional notes below.

20 Kuznetsov, *Sud'ba i pravda*, 53–64.

21 A. Serafimovich, V. Kirshon, A. Fadeev, V. Stavskii, "Pis'mo v redaktsiiu," *Pravda*, March 29, 1929.

FOUR

1 For archival documents on the districts north of Sholokhov's home, see I. V. Kotova, ed., *Kollektivizatsiia na territorii Volgogradskoi oblasti, 1928–1932 gg.: dokumenty* (Volgograd: Kruton, 2011), 139–210. I also consulted the documents in V. Danilov, R. Manning, L. Viola, eds., *Tragediia sovetskoi derevni: kollektivizatsiia i raskulachivanie. Dokumenty i materialy v 5 tomakh, 1927–1939* (Moscow: Rossiskaia Politicheskaia Entsiklopediia, 1999–2006).

2 Letter to Levitskaia, June 1929, Kolodnyi "Istoriia odnogo posviashcheniia," 154.

3 Ibid.

4 On these events see James Hughes, *Stalinism in a Russian Province: A Study of Collectivization and Dekulakization in Siberia* (New York: St. Martin's in association with Centre for Russian and East European Studies, University of Birmingham, 1996).

5 Letter to Levitskaia, June 1929, Kolodnyi "Istoriia odnogo posviashcheniia," 153.

6 M. Kotomkin, "Priemnaia t. Kalinina," *Krestianskaia gazeta*, March 29, 1929. The entire issue is devoted to praise of Kalinin.

7 Letter to Levitskaia, June 1929, Kolodnyi "Istoriia odnogo posviashcheniia," 153–5.

8 See Hughes, *Stalinism*, 79–83. I. V. Stalin, "Letter to Frumkin," in his *Sochineniia*, vol. 11, (Moscow: OGIZ, 1949), 116–126.

9 N. Prokof'ev, "Tvortsy chistoi literatury," *Bol'shevistskaia smena* (Rostov), September 8, 1929. Gordeeva, *Literaturnyi Rostov*, 150. Republished in Kozlovskii, Kuznetsov, and Sholokhov, *M. A. Sholokhov Pis'ma*, 44. Letter to Levitskaia, October 1929, Kolodnyi "Istoriia odnogo posviashcheniia," 158–9.

10   See the coverage in *Molot* (Rostov), for early October 1929.

11   Ibid.

12   Gordeeva, *Literaturnyi Rostov*, 151.

13   Ibid.

14   Ibid.

15   Ibid., 153–4.

16   See Mikhail Sholokhov, *Quiet Flows the Don*, trans. Robert Daglish, rev. ed. Brian
     Murphy (London: J.M. Dent, 1996), 767–68.

FIVE

1   Tovah Yedlin, *Maxim Gorky A Political Biography* (Westport, Conn.: Praeger, 1999).

2   For the text of the poem see https://ru.wikisource.org/wiki/Письмо_писателя
     _Владимира_Владимировича_Маяковского_писателю_Алексею_Максимовичу
     Горькому(Маяковский) (last accessed June 2018).

3   Gura, *Kak sozdavalsia "Tikhii Don,"* 34; F. A. Abramov, V. V. Gura, *M. A. Sholokhov.
     Seminarii* (Leningrad: Ministerstvo Prosveshcheniia RSFSR, 1958), 140.

4   M. Gorky, "Rabochii klass dolzhen vospityvat' svoikh masterov kul'tury," *Literaturnaia
     gazeta*, July 25, 1929.

5   A. Kurs ed., "Pochemu 'Tikhii Don' ponravilsia belogvardeitsam," *Nastoiashchee*
     (Novosibirsk), no. 8 (1929), 5.

6   Andrei Artizov and Oleg Naumov, *Vlast' i khudozhestvennaia intelligentsia: Dokumenty
     TsK RKP(b)–VKP(b), VChK-OGPU-NKVD o kul'turnoi politike 1917–1953 gg.* (Moscow:
     Fond 'Demokratiia' 1999), 123–25; letter to Levitskaia, January 1930, Kolodnyi "Istoriia
     odnogo posviashcheniia," 160–161.

7   Benedikt Sarnov, *Stalin i Pisateli* (Moscow: ESKMO, 2009), 1: 11.

8   B. Beliaev, *Stranitsy zhizni: A. Fadeev v 20-e i 30e gody* (Moscow: Sovetskii Pisatel',
     1980), 56–80.

9   Letter to Levitskaia, April 1930, in Kolodnyi "Istoriia odnogo posviashcheniia," 161–163.

10   Ibid., 161.

11   Petelin, *Mikhail Sholokhov v vospominaniiakh*, 1: 269–70.

12   Artizov and Naumov, *Vlast' i khudozhestvennaia intelligentsia*, 130, 138.

13   Kolodnyi, *Kto napisal*, 92–93; Petelin, *Mikhail Sholokhov v vospominaniiakh*, 1: 352–55.

14   Peter Dorp, "Goebbels' Kampf gegen Remarque," *Erich Maria Remarque Jahrbuch* 3
     (1993): 45–72.

15   Iurii Murin, *Pisatel' i vozhd': perepiska M. A. Sholokhova s I. V. Stalinym 1931–1950 gody:
     Sbornik dokumentov iz lichnogo arhiva I. V. Stalina* (Moscow: Raritet, 1997), 22–26.

16   Murin, *Pisatel' i vozhd'*, 22–26.

17   Letter to Gorky, June 1931, in Petelin, *Pis'ma*, 155–158.

18   There has been some debate about the location of the meeting. The mansion seems a more
     likely location.

SIX

1   The most extensive version of Sholokhov's reminiscences about the meeting was recorded
     by the local scholar Konstantin Priima in 1973. Konstantin Priima, *S vekom naravne:*

stat'i o tvorchestve M. A. Sholokhova (Rostov: Rostov knizh. Izdatel'stvo, 1981), 147–149; Konstantin Priima, *S vekom naravne: stat'i o tvorchestve M. A. Sholokhova*, 2nd ed. (Rostov: Rostov knizh. Izdatel'stvo, 1985), 148–150. I have reconstructed the dialogue from Priima's account. My interventions will be footnoted separately below.

2   Gura, *Kak sozdavalsia*, 2nd ed., 304; Ermolaev, *Mikhail Sholokhov and His Art*, 222.

3   I agree with Gura here. Ermolaev, *Mikhail Sholokhov and His Art*, 223; Gura, *Kak sozdavalsia*, 2nd ed., 305–8.

4   I conjecture that Sholokhov introduced the subjective/objective distinction in an effort to counter a major criticism of his novel. A prominent critic had accused him of having a penchant for "objectivism." The same critic drew attention to the fact that Sholokhov "does not deprive many White Guard personalities of attributes of subjective honorableness." He correctly decoded Stalin's reference to a particular line of "proletarian" criticism of the novel. Iu. Selivanovskii, "Predislovie," in Mikhail Sholokhov, *Tikhii Don: kniga pervaia* (Moscow: Gos. Izd. Khudozhestvenoi literatury, 1931), 14.

5   For the criticisms advanced by S. Dinamov in 1931, see Kuznetsov, *Sud'ba i pravda*, 668.

6   For a stimulating study of this issue, see David Brandenberger, *National Bolshevism: Stalinist Mass Culture and the Formation of Modern Russian National Identity* (Cambridge, Mass.: Harvard University, 2002).

7   Artizov and Naumov, *Vlast' i khudozhestvennaia intelligentsia*, 81–100.

8   Ibid., 101.

9   See the articles cited in E. Mikhailova, "Litfront," [1932] in vol. 6 of *Literaturnaia entsiklopedia*, ed. A. V. Lunacharskii (Moscow: Izdatel'stvo Kommunisticheskoi Akademii, 1932), 501–513, and A. Mikhailov, "Pereverzev," in vol. 8 of *Literaturnaia entsiklopedia*, ed. A. V. Lunacharskii (Moscow: Izdatel'stvo Kommunisticheskoi Akademii, 1934), 501–512.

10   Andrei Zimovnov, *Sholokhov v zhizni* (Rostov: Rostizdat, 2005), 128.

11   A. L. Nosovich (A. Chernomortsev), *Krasnyi tsaritsyn vzgliad iznutri: Zapiski belogo razvedshika* (Moscow: AIRO-XX, 2010); originally published in the issues of *Donskaia Volna* for late 1918 and 1919.

12   K. Voroshilov, *Stalin i Krasnaia Armiia* (Moscow: Partizdat TsK VKP(b), 1937), 44–65. [n.a.] *Stalin: Sbornik statei k piatidesiatiletiiu so dnia rozhdeniia* (Moscow: Gosizdat, 1929).

13   Fedor Shakhmagonov, "Bremia 'Tikhogo Dona,'" *Molodaia Gvardiia* 1997, no. 5, 50.

14   Andrei Zimovnov, *Sholokhov v zhizni* (Rostov: Rostizdat, 2005), 129.

15   Letter to Gorky, June 1931, in Petelin, *Pis'ma*, 155–158.

16   Artizov and Naumov, *Vlast' i khudozhestvennaia intelligentsia*, 105.

17   Literary historians have debated for two decades whether or not there was a quid pro quo between the dictator and the writer. The idea was first advanced by Sergei Semanov, who visited Sholokhov in the late '70s. See S. N. Semanov "O nekotorykh obstoiatel'stvakh publikatsii 'Tikhogo Dona,'" *Novyi Mir* no. 9 (1988), 265–69. In my opinion, the fact that the publication of *Quiet Don* only resumed after the submission of the collectivization novel supports Semanov's contention. In a 1937 speech, Sholokhov publicly acknowledged Stalin's role in reviving the publication of *Quiet Don* after a delay of over a year. See [n.a.] "Rech' doblestnogo patriota," *Komsomol'skaia Pravda* (Moscow), December 1, 1937.

18   Zimovnov, *Sholokhov v zhizni*, 129.

SEVEN

1 Letter to Levitskaia, November 1931, Kolodnyi "Istoriia odnogo posviashcheniia," 167.

2 Lugovoi's memoir is one of the most interesting sources for Sholokhov's biography. It was published in 1991 in a volume with other material. [n.a.] *S kroviu i potom: Neizvestnye stranitsy iz zhizni M. A. Sholokhova* (Rostov: Rostov knizhnoe izdatel'stvo, 1991) [hereafter Lugovoi, *S kroviu i potom*]. The publishers neglected to acknowledge assistance Lugovoi received from local journalists. He began working on the memoir in 1961. For his arrival in Vioshki, see Lugovoi, *S kroviu i potom*, 4–9.

3 L. G. Iakimenko, *Tvorchestvo M. A. Sholokhova: idei i obrazy, tvorcheskii metod, zhanry, stil,' masterstvo, poetika* (Moscow: Sovetskii pisatel', 1964), 145–146.

4 Lugovoi, *S kroviu i potom*, 14–15, 17, 22, 25, 31.

5 Ibid., 10, 59.

6 Ibid., 13–14.

7 Petelin, *Mikhail Sholokhov v vospominaniiakh*, 2:522.

8 This account is designed to provide a sense of how collectivization generally unfolded in the areas near Sholokhov's home. P. G. Chernopitskii, "kollekvizatsiia na Donu," *Donskoi Vremennik* 10 (2001): 40–49.

9 Petelin, *Mikhail Sholokhov v vospominaniiakh*, 1: 479–480.

10 See Andrei Platonov, *Vprok: Proza* (Moscow: Khudozehstvennaia literatura, 1990), 376–436.

11 I. V. Stalina, "Otvet tovarishcham kolkhoznikam," *Pravda*, April 8, 1930.

12 For Moscow rumors, see Aleksei Varlamov, *Andrei Platonov* (Moscow: Molodaia Gvardiia, 2011), 223–224.

13 Fadeev, "Ob odnoi kulatskoi khronike," *Izvestiia*, June 3, 1931; Makar'ev, "Kleveta," *Na literaturnom postu*, no. 18 (1931), 22–29.

14 D. Khanin and V. Diatlov, "Paskvil' na kholkhoznuiu derevniu," *Za kommunisticheskoe prosveshchenie* (Moscow), June 12, 1931.

15 A. V. Luncharskii, *O massovykh prazndestvakh, estrade i ts*irke (Moscow: Iskusstvo, 1981), 152–153; reprinted from "Kinematograficheskaia komediia i satira," in *Proletarskoe kino*, no. 9 (1931): 4–15.

16 On the Senin case, see A. V. Venkov, *'Delo Senina' ili operatsiia 'Trest' na Verkhnem Donu* (Moscow: AIRO-XXI, 2016).

17 Letter to Levitskaia, November 1931, Kolodnyi "Istoriia odnogo posviashcheniia," 168.

18 Viacheslav Polonskii, "Moia bor'ba na literaturnom fronte: dnevnik Mai 1920-ianvar' 1932," ed. S. V. Shumikhin, *Novyi Mir*, no. 6 (2008), 144–163.

19 Murin, *Pisatel' i vozhd'*, 157.

20 K. I. Priima, "Sholokhov v Vioshkakh," *Sovetskii Kazakhstan*, 1955, no. 5, 81–2.

21 Stalin had emphasized the importance of "breaking resistance" and "depriving it [*kulakdom*] of productive resources for existence and development." I. V. Stalin, "Kvoprosu o politike likvidatsii kulachestva, kak klassa," *Krasnaia Zvezda* (Moscow), Jan. 21, 1930.

22 For the text in English, see Mikhail Sholokhov, *Virgin Soil Upturned*, trans. Robert Daglish (Moscow: Foreign Languages Publishing House, 1957).

23 I. V. Stalin, "Rech' na konferentsii agrarnikov-marksistov," *Pravda*, December 29, 1929. Stalin argued that collective farms would increase sown areas by 30, 40, or even 50 percent. He called this a head-dizzying effect and asserted that collective labor and

ENDNOTES

tractors would make it possible to farm lands that were fallow under individual capitalist farming.

EIGHT

1   This and subsequent paragraphs about the Yagoda meeting are based on Sholokhov's letter to Fadeev in late January 1932. See Kozlovskii, Kuznetsov, Ushakov, and Sholokhov, *M. A. Sholokhov, Pis'ma*, 76–77.

2   See the inventory of Yagoda's possessions recorded upon his arrest in [n.a.] *Genrikh Iagoda. Narkom vnutrennykh del SSSR, General'nyi kommisar gosudarstvennoi bezopasnosti. Sbornik dokumentov* (Kazan': Krista, 1997), 89–93.

3   A. N. Ostrovskii, "Zapiski zamoskvoretskogo zhitelia," in *Khudozhestvennye proizvedeniia. Kritika, dnevniki. Slovar' 1843–1886*, vol. XIII, A. N. Ostrovskii, *Polnoe Sobranie sochinenii*, ed. A. I. Reviakin (Moscow: Izdatel'stvo Khudozhestvennoi literatury, 1952), 14–26.

4   *"Shirokie natury"* is the term used by Ivan Gorbunov. S. V. Maksimov, ed., *Sochineniia I. F. Gorbunova* (Saint Petersburg: Imperatorskoe obshchestvo liubitelei drevnei pis'mennosti, 1904), 1: 48–58. See also his "Ocherki o staroi Moskve," (originally written 1881), reprinted in *Iumoristicheskie rasskazy i ocherki* (Moscow: Moskovskii rabochii, 1962).

5   For these and other facets of political criticism of journal editors, see L. V. Maksimenkov, ed., *Bol'shaia tsenzura: pisateli i zhurnalisty v strane Sovetov 1917–1956* (Moscow: Fond 'Demokratiia', 2005), 211–226.

6   [n.a.] in Maksimenkov, *Bolshaia tsenzura*, 200–201.

7   Stalin was clearly aware of Sholokhov's involvement. Letter from Kaganovich to Stalin, RGANI, f. 3, op. 34, d. 186, ll. 266–67, published in Viacheslav Ogryzko, "Neizvestnye dokumenty ob Aleksandre Fadeeve," *Literaturnaia Rossia* (Moscow), September 16, 2015.

8   Denis Babichenko, "Kak partiia rukovodila literaturoi: odno desiatiletie," *Voprosy literatury*, no. 5 (1997), http://magazines.russ.ru/voplit/1997/5/publikac-pr.html (last accessed June 2018).

9   See Gorky, "O deistvitel'nosti," *Izvestiia*, March 9, 1931. Gorky, "Otvet intelligentu," *Izvestiia*, May 21–22, 1931.

10 Sholokhov's letter apparently no longer exists. It is mentioned among a list of similarly withdrawn statements. These were known to Stalin and Kaganovich. RTsKhDNI, f. 17, op. 163, d. 941, l.75. See Babichenko, "Kak partiia rukovodila literaturoi."

11 *Literaturnaia gazeta*, May 17, 1932. See also A. B. Zakharov, "K voprosu o vozniknovenii termina 'sotsialicheskii realizm'," *Vestnik Sankt-Peterburgskogo Universiteta*, seriia 2, vol. 1 (2006): 107–118.

12 Lugovoi, *S kroviu i potom*, 32–34.

13 Murin, *Pisatel' i vozhd'*, 32–33.

14 Lugovoi, *S kroviu i potom*, 46–7.

15 Murin, *Pisatel' i vozhd'*, 35–37.

16 Letter to Levitskaia, August 1932, Kolodnyi "Istoriia odnogo posviashcheniia," 177.

17 Petelin, *Mikhail Sholokhov v vospominaniiakh*, 1: 441.

18 Ibid., 1: 445.

19 The paragraphs about the meeting are based on the only extensive record of the meeting. It can be found in K. L. Zelinskii, "Odna vstrecha u M. Gor'kogo," *Voprosy literatury*, no. 5 (1991): 144–170. For a related account which contains interesting variations, see V. Ia. Kirpotin, *Rovesnik zheleznogo veka: memuarnaia kniga* (Moscow: Zakharov, 2006), 193–206.

20 M. Gorky, "Esli vrag ne sdaetsia—ego unichtozhaiut," *Pravda*, November 15, 1930.

21 M. Gorky, "Ob anekdotakh i—eshche koe o chem," *Pravda*, December 19, 1931.

22 "O chistke partii: Postanovlenie Tsk i TsKK VKP(b)," *Pravda*, April 29, 1933; "O chistke partii: Rech' tov. Kaganovicha," *Pravda*, May 21, 1933; "Pravitel'stvennoe soobshchenie ot Tsentral'nogo Komiteta," *Pravda*, June 2, 1933.

NINE

1 The paragraphs devoted to the period from November 1932 to April 1933 are based on Sholokhov's Letter to Stalin, dated April 4, 1933. APRF, f. 45, op.1, l.7–22, published in Murin, *Pisatel' I vozhd'*, 28–58.

2 Ibid., 38–44.

3 TsDNIRO, f. 36, op. 1, d. 44, excerpts published in Aleksandr Zhbannikov, *Mikhail Sholokhov–bol'she, chem pisatel'* (Rostov: ZAO Kniga, 2006), 83.

4 Independent confirmation of Ovchinnikov's actions can be found in a report to Sheboldaev filed in December 1932. Its author questioned the legality of several of Ovchinnikov's actions. See V. V. Kondrashin, ed., *Golod v SSSR 1929–1934*, Volume 2, *Iul' 1932-Iul' 1933* (Moscow: Fond 'Demokraiia', 2012), 203–205.

5 Lugovoi, *S kroviu i potom*, 37.

6 Ibid., 38.

7 Similar "medieval" phrasing and examples occur in a report from the Vioshki machine tractor station written in mid-April 1933. Kondrashin, *Golod v SSSR*, 2:468–69.

8 Murin, *Pisatel' i vozhd'*, 58.

9 Petelin, *Mikhail Sholokhov v vospominaniiakh*, 1: 274; Murin, *Pisatel' i vozhd'*, 59–66.

10 Stalin, *Sochineniia*, new series (Tver': Soiuz, 2006), 18: 46–47.

11 Danilov, Manning, and Viola, *Tragediia sovetskoi derevni*, 3: 717.

12 APRF, f. 3, op. 61, d. 549, l. 194, published in Murin, *Pisatel' i vozhd'*, 68–69.

13 On these events as a "strike" in which peasants refused to work, see the admirably balanced treatment in D'Ann Penner, "Stalin and the Ital'ianka of 1932–33 in the Don Region," *Cahiers du Monde Russe* 39, no. 1–2, (1998): 27–68.

14 Murin, *Pisatel' i vozhd'*, 157.

15 Kondrashin, *Golod v SSSR*, 2: 203–205.

16 Given the outcome of the meeting, Ovchinnikov must have capably defended himself. For his participation in the Kaganovich meetings, see Danilov, Manning, Viola, *Tragediia sovetskoi derevni*, 3: 549–5. He also claimed to local officials that he had Molotov's backing. See Murin, *Pisatel' i vozhd'*, 44. This could suggest that he knew about the Khataevich letter to Molotov and Molotov's answer, which prioritized the needs of the proletarian state over legality. See *Tragediia sovetskoi derevni*, 3: 555–556.

17 Kondrashin, *Golod v SSSR*, 2: 203–204.

18 I suspect that Sholokhov coached Plotkin on how to perform for Stalin. Though he complained about Plotkin in his letter to Stalin, he might have had ulterior motives for

bringing Plotkin to Stalin's attention. By introducing Stalin to a real-life prototype of Davydov, Sholokhov was reminding Stalin of *Virgin Soil*.

19 I provide this example as indicative of the stories Plotkin liked to narrate. A. Plotkin, "Na ogenek k Sholokhovu," *Vechernaia Moskva*, May 21, 1965. Reprinted in Petelin, *Mikhail Sholokhov v vospominaniiakh*, 1: 273.

20 The dialogue is derived from Vladimir Petroplavskii, a Voronezh journalist who corresponded with and met Plotkin in the late 1970s. See Vladimir Petroplavskii, "K 100-letiiu so dnia rozhdeniia M. A. Sholokhova. Moi Davydov," (2004), http://communa.ru /kultura/k_100-letiyu_so_dnya_rozhdeniya_m-a-sholokhova-_moy_davydov/ (last accessed June 2018).

21 See Andrei Plotkin, "Tridtsatye nezabyvaemye," *Tikhii Don* (Vioshenskaia), May 1, 1977.

22 RGASPI, f. 17, op. 3, d. 2040, l. 5–6; Danilov, Manning, Viola, *Tragediia sovetskoi derevni*, 3: 720–21.

23 TsDNIRO, f. 36, op. 1, d. 44; excerpts published in Zhbannikov, *Mikhail Sholokhov*, 82.

24 Lugovoi, *S kroviu i potom*, 50. Plotkin letter, in Petelin, *Pis'ma*, 215.

TEN

1 Petelin, *Mikhail Sholokhov v vospominaniiakh*, 1: 458–465. Letter to Levitskaia, January 1934, Kolodnyi "Istoriia odnogo posviashcheniia," 178.

2 M. Sholokhov, "Pis'mo v redaktsiiu," *Literaturnaia gazeta*, February 8, 1934.

3 The examples in this paragraph are merely indicative of the kinds of topics that were being discussed at the time. There was no way to predict which questions would be asked.

4 Murin, *Pisatel' i vozhd'*, 80.

5 Petelin, *Mikhail Sholokhov v vospominaniiakh*, 1: 465, 468, 480, 484, 486, 509. As late as 1937 he claimed to still be working on play. See Artizov and Naumov, *Vlast' i khudozhestvennaia intelligentsia*, 364.

6 TsDNIRO, f. 36, op. 1, d. 44; excerpts published in Zhbannikov, *Mikhail Sholokhov*, 83. Petelin, *Mikhail Sholokhov v vospominaniiakh*, 1: 509.

7 For the classic account, see V. Kravchenko, *I Chose Freedom, The Personal and Political Life of a Soviet Official* (New York: Charles Scribner's Sons, 1946), 132–147.

8 Letter to A. Soldatov, January 1933. Petelin, *Pis'ma*, 182–184. Although Soldatov wrote to Sholokhov first, it is clear that they had not been in contact for ten years. The writer could have chosen not to respond.

9 This account of the purge session is a composite text created through comparison and analysis of three similar accounts of the same event with occasionally significant variations. See [n.a.] "Na partiinoi proverke—pisatel' Mikhail Sholokhov," *Pravda*, July 31, 1934; "Na proverke–Mikhail Sholokhov," *Molot*, July 29, 1934; Ia. Altukhov, "Pisatel' M. Sholokhov na tribune chistki," *Bol'shevistskii Put'* (Millerovo), July 30, 1934, reprinted in Petelin, *Mikhail Sholokhov v vospominaniiakh*, 1: 474–476.

10 For the unexpected arrival of Sheboldaev and his silence, Lugovoi, *S kroviu i potom*, 52.

11 I. V. Stalin "O nekotorykh voprosakh istorii bol'shevizma," *Proletarskaia revoliutsiia*, no. 6, (1931), republished in Stalin, *Sochineniia* (Moscow: OGIZ, 1951), 13: 84–102.

12 Lugovoi, *S kroviu i potom*, 53.

13 TsDNIRO, f. 36, op. 1, d. 44; excerpt published in Zhbannikov, *Mikhail Sholokhov*, 83.

14   *Pervyi vsesoiuznyi s"ezd sovetskikh pisatelei, 1934: stenograficheskii otchet* (Moscow: Khudozhestvennaia literatura, 1934).

15   *Pervyi vsesoiuznyi s"ezd sovetskikh pisatelei*, 226–228. The first to speak was Comrade Chaban (no first name provided) from the Moscow region. The second was Comrade Smirnova, whose quote is on page 228.

16   *Pervyi vsesoiuznyi s"ezd sovetskikh pisatelei*, 5–19.

17   On Elankin, see Kozlov, *M. A. Sholokhov vremena i tvorchestvo*, 179–189.

18   It is intriguing that Elankin knew the name of Sholokhov's first attempt at a novel, *Donshchina*, long before this name was mentioned in print. Sholokhov indeed had a distant relative named Georgii Borisov. For the little that is known about Borisov, see Klara Korepova and Natal'ia Kirsanova, "Novye stranitsy rodoslovnoi M. A. Sholokhova: sem'ia I. S. Liovochkina," *Veshenskii Vestnik*, vol. 11 (2011): 140–152. For a letter to Borisov, see Petelin, *Pis'ma*, 261.

19   In a letter to Stalin Sholokhov alludes to local investigation into his "stealing" *Quiet Don* from Elankin. Murin, *Pisatel' i vozhd'*, 80.

20   TsDNIRO, f. 36, op. 1, d. 44; excerpt published in Zhbannikov, *Mikhail Sholokhov*, page 16.

21   His request was considered and granted by a vote of the Politburo. See Maksimenkov, *Bol'shaia tsenzura*, 385.

22   TASS, "Soobshchenie ob obstoiatel'stvakh smerti tovarishcha Kirova," *Pravda*, December 4, 1934. For press coverage, see Petelin, *Mikhail Sholokhov v vospominaniiakh*, 1: 500–505.

23   I. M. Maiskii, *Dnevnik diplomata. London 1934–1943 v dvukh knigakh* (Moscow: Nauka, 2006–2009), 1: 48, 57–69, 69–70.

ELEVEN

1   Murin, *Pisatel' i vozhd'*, 81–82.

2   The meeting took place on May 15, 1935, in Stalin's Kremlin office. Murin, *Pisatel' i vozhd'*, 158.

3   I infer this from Lugovoi, *S kroviu i potom*, 53, and the fact that Sholokhov did not behave as if it were necessary to introduce Lugovoi in his subsequent letters to Stalin.

4   See the coverage in *Pravda*, in the weeks leading up to the official opening ceremony.

5   [n.a.]"Vstrecha s vozhdem: rasskaz rabochikh zavoda imenie Ordzhonikidze," *Rabochaia Moskva*, April 28, 1935.

6   The quotes/cues are from I. V. Stalin, "Triumf strany sotsializma," *Rabochaia Moskva*, May 15, 1935. See also [n.a.] "Torzhestvennoe zasedanie po pusku metropolitena im. L. M. Kaganovicha," *Pravda*, May 15, 1935. For an earlier example see A. Avdeenko, "Vstrecha," *Pravda*, January 29, 1935.

7   On May 15 Stalin informed officials of his decision to accept Sholokhov's request not to travel to Paris. See Boris Frezinskii, *Pisateli i sovetskie vozhdi: izbrannye siuzhety 1919–1960 godov* (Moscow: Ellis Lak, 2008), 318. The Politburo approved the request on May 21, 1935. Maksimenkov, *Bol'shaia tsenzura*, 384. Sholokhov was included in the Paris delegation on April 19, 1935. Artizov and Naumov, *Vlast' i khudozhestvennaia intelligentsia*, 254.

8   I deduce a discussion about legal restrictions from the fact that Sholokhov mentioned
     restrictions that were still in place.

9   Andrei Zimovnov, *Sholokhov v zhizni*, 102, 132. Years later Sholokhov dated the meeting
     to 1934, but there is no evidence that Voroshilov was involved in dealing with either the
     question of Cossack clothing or service that year. There is abundant evidence that in late
     1935 such a campaign was being initiated.

10   Sholokhov's reference to the banning of Don Cossack red-striped trousers (*lampasy*) strikes
     me as reminiscent of a specific event in spring 1919 in which Lenin personally intervened
     to annul directives against Cossack clothing issued by Trotsky's subordinates. See Kazachii
     otdel Vserossiiskogo tsentral'nogo ispolnitel'nogo komiteta, *Kratkii istoricheskii ocherk i otchet
     Kazach'ego otdela VTsIK po oktiabr' 1919 g.* (Moscow: Gos. Izd-vo, 1919), 40–41.

11   M. M. Sholokhov, *Ob ottse: ocherki-vospominaniia raznykh let* (Moscow: Sovetskii Pisatel',
     2004), 135. The conversation is undated in the reminiscences of Sholokhov's son. When
     Sholokhov told of the meeting to a Soviet intelligence officer in Norway at some point in
     either 1957 or 1969, he added two elements that are crucial for dating. He had taken his
     first ever ride on the Moscow metro and had seen the Kirov station. V. F. Grushko, *Sud'ba
     razvedchika: kniga vospominanii* (Moscow: Mezhdunarodnye otnosheniia, 1997), 46.

12   V. I. Lenin, *Pis'ma noiabr' 1910-iuil' 1914*, vol. 48 of *Polnoe sobranie sochinenii* (Moscow:
     Gos. Izd-vo Polit. Literatury, 1964), 226–233.

13   See the coverage in *New York Times* for May 19 and May 20, 1935.

14   "Witness Describes Crash," *New York Times*, May 19, 1935.

15   See the coverage in *Pravda*, May 19, 20, 21, 1935.

16   See coverage in *Pravda*, May 21, 1935.

17   Gorky sent a telegram instead, "Telegramma M. Gor'kogo," *Pravda*, May 22, 1935.

18   Lugovoi, *S kroviu i potom*, 57–58; Murin, *Pisatel' i vozhd'*, 83–85.

19   [n.a.] "Geroicheskaia epopeiia khutora Podkushchevskogo," *Molot*, July 20, 1935; [n.a.] "V
     gostiiakh u Sholokhova," *Molot*, August 4, 1935.

20   On the zigzags in policies regarding the Red Partisans, see S. A. Khubulova, *Deiatel'nost
     komissii po okazaniiu pomoshchi byvshim krasnym partizanam Osetii 1920–1930-e g.g.:
     Sbornik dokumentov i materialov* (Vladikavkaz: 2016) available at http://izvestia-soigsi.ru
     /ru/archive/-23–62–2017/483-hubulova23 (last accessed June 2018).

21   [n.a.] "V gostiiakh u Sholokhova," *Molot*, August 4, 1935.

22   Khubulova, *Deiatel'nost komissii*, op. cit.

23   Petelin, *Mikhail Sholokhov v vospominaniiakh*, 1: 521–4.

24   The fact that the official propaganda campaign started with a letter to Stalin from the
     Cossacks of Vioshki can be no coincidence. See "Kazaki-kolkhozniki veshenskogo Raiona
     tovarishchu Stalinu," *Pravda*, February 24, 1936.

25   On the implementation of the policy shift, see A. P. Skorik, *Mnogolikost' kazachestva
     Iuga Rossii v 1930-e gody: Ocherki istorii* (Rostov: Izd. SKNTs VSh, 2008); A. P. Skorik,
     Kazachii iug v 1930–3 gody: grani istoricheskikh sudeb sotsial'noi obshchnosti (Rostov: Izd.
     SKNTs VSh, 2009).

26   [n.a.] *Kazachestvo pod bol'shevistskim znamenem* (Piatigorsk: Sevkavgiz, 1936), 45.

27   For reprints of the bulletins, see L. N. Spiridonova, *Taina smerti Gor'kogo: dokumenty,
     fakty, versii* (Moscow: OOO AST, 2017), 7–13.

28　There is still debate about whether Gorky was murdered. See Spiridonova, *Taina smerti Gor'kogo*; Pavel Basinskii, *Strasti po Maksimu: Gorkii, 9 dnei posle smerti* (Moscow: AST, 2011).

29　This view was propounded by Viacheslav Ivanov in "Pochemu Stalin ubil Gor'kogo," *Voprosy literatury*, no. 1 (1993): 91–134.

30　M. A. Sholokhov, "Telegramma," *Pravda*, June 21, 1936.

TWELVE

1　Herman Ermolaev, *'Tikhii Don' i politicheskaia tsenzura. 1928–1991* (Moscow: IMLI RAN, 2005), 48–50.

2　Included on the list of books that will appear in 1936 that was sent to Stalin. Artizov and Naumov, *Vlast' i khudozhestvennaia intelligentsia*, 285.

3　Murin, *Pisatel' i vozhd'*, 127.

4　J. A. Getty, *The Road to Terror: Stalin and the Self-Destruction of the Bolsheviks, 1932–1939* (New Haven, Conn.: Yale University Press, 1999), 247–57, 272.

5　TsDNIRO, f. 36, op. 1, d. 44; excerpts published in Zhbannikov, *Mikhail Sholokhov*, 15.

6　Getty, *Road to Terror*, 250–255.

7　On Makar'ev as a Trotskyist, see [n.a.] "Khudozhestvennaia literatura pobedivshego sotsializma," *Pravda*, April 23, 1937. Sholokhov's portrait was published next to P. Iudin, "Pochemu RAPP nado bylo likvidirovat'," in the same issue.

8　TsDNIRO, f. 36, op. 1, d. 44; excerpt published in Zhbannikov, *Mikhail Sholokhov*, 9, 39. Alternate quote TsDNIRO, f. 36, op. 1, d. 44, partially published in Zhbannikov, *Mikhail Sholokhov*, 12.

9　TsDNIRO, f. 36, op. 1, d. 44; excerpt published in Zhbannikov, *Mikhail Sholokhov*, 34, 41, 44, 170. Alternate quote TsDNIRO, f. 36, op. 1, d. 44; excerpt published in Zhbannikov, *Mikhail Sholokhov*, 39.

10　TsDNIRO, f. 36, op. 1, d. 44; excerpt published in Zhbannikov, *Mikhail Sholokhov*, 44. Lugovoi, *S kroviu i potom*, 59.

11　Murin, *Pisatel' i vozhd'*, 86–87.

12　TsDNIRO, f. 36, op. 1, d. 44; partially published in Zhbannikov, *Mikhail Sholokhov*, 13, 42.

13　For Sheboldaev's fall see, Getty, *Road to Terror*, 333–352. For Sheboldaev's confessions, see Getty, *Road to Terror*, 341–344. See also A. V. Venkov, "Soiuz trotskistov i belykh kazakov, ili razgrom partiino-sovetskoi verkhushki v Azovo-Chernomorskom krae v 1937 g.," *Nauka iuga Rossii*, vol. 13, no. 2 (2017): 79–90.

14　S. Babenysheva, "Iz vospominanii Very Panovoi," in *SSSR, vnutrennie protivorechiia*, no. 3 (1983), 287. Ovchinnikov's suicide appears to be confirmed by the absence of his name among a list of regional officials and party secretaries who were arrested after being exposed as Trotskyists. See L. P. Kosheleva, O. . Naumov, and L. A. Rogova, "Materialy fevralo-martovskogo plenuma TsK VKP(b) 1937 goda," *Voprosy istorii*, no. 8 (1995): 3–13.

15　TsDNIRO, f. 36, op. 1, d. 44; excerpt published in Zhbannikov, *Mikhail Sholokhov*, 12–18, 36–43. Murin, *Pisatel' i vozhd'*, 86–87.

16　TsDNIRO, f. 36, op. 1, d. 44; excerpt published in Zhbannikov, *Mikhail Sholokhov*, 166–7.

17　Ibid., 170.

18　Murin, *Pisatel' i vozhd'*, 88–89.

19　Ibid., 90.

ENDNOTES

20   Lugovoi, *S kroviu i potom*, 63–4.

21   Murin, *Pisatel' i vozhd'*, 91.

22   Ibid., 74.

23   "Griaznaia kleveta Andre Zhida," *Literaturnaia gazeta*, December 15, 1936. On the fall of Yagoda, see "Ob otreshenii ot dolzhnosti Narodnogo Kommissara Sviazi SSSR G. G. Iagody," *Pravda*, April 4, 1937; on the anniversary of Gorky's death, [n.a.] "Uchit'sia u Gor'kogo," *Literaturnaia gazeta*, June 18, 1937.

24   [Collective letter of Soviet writers], "Ne dadim zhit'ia vragam Sovetskogo Soliuza," *Literaturnaia gazeta*, June 15, 1937.

25   Ermolaev, *'Tikhii Don' i politicheskaia tsenzura*, 49. I have substituted "tsarist tools" for "Dudakov" (a tsarist general) in order to retain the rhyme of the original.

26   Murin, *Pisatel' i vozhd'*, 93.

27   The phrasing is reconstructed from Murin, *Pisatel' i vozhd'*, 92.

28   [n.a.] "Delo Kontsevicha," *Krasnodarskie Izvestiia*, November 19, 2013.

29   Murin, *Pisatel' i vozhd'*, 97–98.

30   Lugovoi, *S kroviu i potom*, 66.

31   Stavskii letter to Stalin, September 1937, in Murin, *Pisatel' i vozhd'*, 72.

THIRTEEN

1   Lugovoi, *S kroviu i potom*, 71–74.

2   Kozlov, *M. A. Sholokhov vremena i tvorchestvo*, 392–393.

3   Murin, *Pisatel' i vozhd'*, 100.

4   For these and other insights I am indebted to Sergei Korolkoff, who illustrated *Quiet Don* in the 1930s and met with Sholokhov on several occasions during the Great Terror before escaping to the west during the Second World War. Korolkoff was convinced that Sholokhov could not be understood apart from his harrowing experiences during the Terror. I was fortunate to meet Korolkoff's relative Ivan Bezugloff, a Cossack émigré living in Cleveland, in 2004.

5   V. Tonin, "Navesti Bol'shevistskii poriadok," *Literaturnaia Gazeta*, August 5, 1937.

6   V. Stavskii, "Rech'," *Literaturnaia gazeta*, July 15, 1937.

7   [n.a.] "S dvukh frontov: beseda s tov. Stavskim," *Literaturnaia gazeta*, July 26, 1937. On congress see Frezinskii, *Pisateli i sovetskie vozhdi*, 436–456.

8   Stavskii letter to Stalin, September 1937, in Murin, *Pisatel' i vozhd'*, 69–73. Also published in Artizov and Naumov, *Vlast' i khudozhestvennaia intelligentsia*, 380–383.

9   Stavskii letter to Stalin, September 1937, in Murin, *Pisatel' i vozhd'*, 71.

10   [n.a.] "Averbakhskie prispeshniki," *Literaturnaia gazeta*, May 20, 1937.

11   Lugovoi, *S kroviu i potom*, 74.

12   Ibid., 78–79.

13   Ibid., 84–85.

14   Ibid., 85–86.

15   Stavskii letter to Stalin, September 1937, in Murin, *Pisatel' i vozhd'*, 71.

16   Getty, *The Road to Terror*, 218, 321–22. On the suicide of Stalin's wife, see Simon Sebag Montefiore, *Stalin: The Court of the Red Tsar* (London: Weidenfeld and Nicolson, 2003), 94–99.

17   On lists see in Nikita Petrov and Mark Iansen, *"Stalinskii pitomets"—Nikolai Yezhov* (Moscow: ROSSPEN, 2008), 119.

18   Murin, *Pisatel' i vozhd'*, 158.

19   Ibid., 78.

20   This version of Yezhov's biography is derived from Petrov and Iansen, *"Stalinskii pitomets,"* 24–66.

21   M. Sholokhov, "Tikhii Don," *Pravda*, September 27, 1937. See book 4, part 7, chapter 24; in Mikhail Sholokhov, *Quiet Flows the Don*, trans. Robert Daglish, rev. ed. Brian Murphy, 1134–1143.

22   Murin, *Pisatel' i vozhd'*, 74.

23   For rhetoric involving troikas see Petrov and Iansen, *"Stalinskii pitomets,"* 131, 290.

24   Murin, *Pisatel' i vozhd'*, 104.

25   For Liushkov's involvement in the Krasiukov case, see TsDNIRO, f. 36, op. 1, d. 44; excerpt published in Zhbannikov, *Mikhail Sholokhov*, 32. He did personally interrogate Lugovoi, *S kroviu i potom*, 77–78.

26   Murin, *Pisatel' i vozhd'*, 74.

27   V. Goffenshefer, "Podlinnyi predstavitel' sovetskoi literatury," *Literaturnaia gazeta*, October 15, 1937.

28   Lugovoi, *S kroviu i potom*, 86–88.

29   Ibid., 91.

30   Murin, *Pisatel' i vozhd'*, 96–98.

31   Ibid., 100.

32   Ibid., 99.

33   V. V. Vasil'ev, "M. A. Sholokhov u studentov MVTU," in *Sholokhov na izlome vremeni*, 167.

34   Murin, *Pisatel' i vozhd'*, 91.

35   B. Chelyshev, "I torite dorozhki," *Molodaia gvardiia*, no. 5 (1965): 168–170.

36   See the coverage in *Izvestiia* for October 11 through December 12, 1937. Frequent articles stressed the uniqueness of the upcoming elections.

FOURTEEN

1   [Collective letter of workers from Tsymlianskaia], "Otdadim vse svoi golosa nashemu kandidatu," *Literaturnaia gazeta*, November 15, 1937.

2   APRF, f. 3, op. 61, d. 549, l. 165; published in Murin, *Pisatel' i vozhd'*, 148–9.

3   M. Frinovskii, "Na strazhe zavoevanii sotsializma," *Pravda*, December 20, 1937.

4   J. Arch Getty, "Pre-election Fever: The Origins of the 1937 Mass Operations," in *The Anatomy of Terror: Political Violence Under Stalin*, ed. James R. Harris (Oxford, U.K.: Oxford University Press, 2013): 216–35.

5   [n.a.], "Vstrecha tov. M. A. Sholokhova so svoimi izbirateliami," *Literaturnaia gazeta*, December 1, 1937. For a slightly longer version of the same speech see [n.a.], "Rech' doblestnogo patriota," *Komsomol'skaia Pravda* (Moscow), December 1, 1937.

6   Kuznetsov, *Sud'ba i pravda*, 270.

7   Murin, *Pisatel' i vozhd'*, 78, 102.

8   APRF, f. 45, op.1, l. 41–61; published in Murin, *Pisatel' i vozhd'*, 76–106.

9   Murin, *Pisatel' i vozhd'*, 103.

10   Ibid., 105.

11   Ibid.

12   Ibid., 110.

13   Ibid., 118.

14   Ibid., 106–108.

15   Ibid., 121–123.

16   Ibid., 119–120.

17   Ibid., 125–7.

18   Petrov and Iansen, *"Stalinskii pitomets,"* 170.

19   Ibid., 67, 75, 160.

20   On Liushkov and the decline of Yezhov, see Getty, *The Road to Terror,* 529.

21   The paragraphs about Liushkov's escape are derived from Alvin D. Coox, "L'Affaire Lyushkov: Anatomy of a Defector," *Soviet Studies* 19, no. 3 (1968): 405–420.

22   Petrov and Iansen, *"Stalinskii pitomets,"* 160–1.

23   Some scholars believe that Sholokhov engaged in a love affair with Yezhov's wife. See Montefiore, *Stalin: The Court of the Red Tsar,* 236, 249. On this issue I side with the Rostov historian Kozlov, who considered the documents about Sholokhov's involvement with Yezhov's wife to be an NKVD fabrication. Kozlov, *M. A. Sholokhov vremena i tvorchestvo,* 450–52.

24   Lugovoi, *S kroviu i potom,* 96–97.

25   Ibid., 102.

26   I rely on Pogorelov's narrative for the next two paragraphs: Pogorelov's letter to Sholokhov, published in *Mikhail Sholokhov: Pis'ma 1924–1984,* ed. V. Petelin (Moscow: Sovetskii Pisatel', 2003), 594–595. For a variant version see S. A. Kislitsyn and E. I. Dulimov, *Sholokhov v istorii Rossii* (Rostov: SKAGS, 2005), 217–219. For Lugovoi's version, see *S kroviu i potom,* 102–111.

27   Lugovoi, *S kroviu i potom,* 104; for traveling to an alternate station see F. Shakhmagonov, "Bremia 'Tikhogo Dona'," *Molodaia Gvardiia* no. 5 (1997), 72.

28   Pogorelov, letter to Sholokhov, published in *Mikhail Sholokhov: Pis'ma,* 604.

29   Ibid., 596–602.

30   Shakhmagonov, "Bremia 'Tikhogo Dona'," 71–76.

31   Ibid., 73–74.

32   The dialogue is reconstructed from the testimony in Lugovoi, *S kroviu i potom,* 109–110. See also Pogorelov, letter to Sholokhov, published in *Mikhail Sholokhov: Pis'ma,* 606.

33   Lugovoi, *S kroviu i potom,* 109.

34   The dialogue is reconstructed from the testimony in Pogorelov, letter to Sholokhov, published in *Mikhail Sholokhov: Pis'ma,* 596, 606. I have inferred Stalin's questions about handwriting and the apartment from the flow of the narrative. Otherwise, handwritten scribblings about a conspiratorial meeting place would be of little value.

35   The continuation of the dialogue is reconstructed from Lugovoi, *S kroviu i potom,* 109.

36   Lugovoi, *S kroviu i potom,* 109.

37   Pogorelov, letter to Sholokhov, published in *Mikhail Sholokhov: Pis'ma,* 592, 606. Frightening affidavits, K. I. Priima, "'Ia im veriu!'," in *Sholokhov na izlome vremeni,* 163.

38   Letter of Pogorelov to Sholokhov, published in *Mikhail Sholokhov: Pis'ma,* 607.

39   Priima, "'Ia im veriu!'," 163; Pogorelov, letter to Sholokhov, published in *Mikhail Sholokhov: Pis'ma*, 607, 608.

40   Lugovoi, *S kroviu i potom*, 110. Lugovoi's retelling clearly telescopes over the aspects of the proceedings that were central to Pogorelov and enhances the importance of his own words.

41   Priima, "'Ia im veriu!'," 163.

42   Letter of Pogorelov to Sholokhov, published in *Mikhail Sholokhov: Pis'ma*, 608.

FIFTEEN

1   See the coverage and stenographic reports of morning and afternoon sessions in *Pravda* under the heading, "Protsess antisovetskogo 'pravo-trotskistskogo bloka'" for March 3–13, 1938.

2   Revelations about Gorky and poisons came out the morning of March 9 and on March 11. For editorial outrage, see [n.a.] "Tsep' chudovishchnykh prestuplenii," *Pravda*, March 10, 1938.

3   For his visit see [n.a.], "Novye materialy Muzeia A. M. Gor'kogo," *Literaturnaia gazeta*, November 15, 1938.

4   This account relies on an early description of the museum's exhibitions. See Vsevolod Ivanov, "Muzei Maksima Gor'kogo," *Izvestiia*, September 27, 1937.

5   On the book, see Ioakhim Klein, "Belomorkanal: Literatura i propaganda v stalinskoe vremia," *Novoe literaturnoe obozrenie* 71 (2005): 231–262.

6   [n.a.] "Novye materialy Muzeia A. M. Gor'kogo," op cit.

7   Platonov's wife, Maria Aleksandrovna Platonova, mentioned Sholokhov's efforts to help to several individuals in later years. Aleksei Varlamov, *Andrei Platonov*, 401–402. V. Goncharova i V. Nekhotina, "Andrei Platonov v dokumentakh OGPU-NKVD-NKGB. 1930–1945," in *Strana filosofov' Andreiia Platonova: problemy tvorchestva*, ed. N. V. Kornienko (Moscow: Nasledie, Nauka, 2000), 4: 848–884.

8   Varlamov, *Andrei Platonov*, 404.

9   Goncharova and Nekhotina, "Andrei Platonov v dokumentakh," 864. Platonov's revisions to his letter to Stalin appear to have followed Sholokhov's instructions. He now emphasized his belief in the humaneness of the Soviet government and in Stalin. See Andrei Platonov, ". . . Ia prozhil zhizn": pis'ma (1920–1950gg)*, eds. Natal'ia Kornienko and Elena Shubina (Moscow: Astrel', 2013), 445–447. On faith as a strategy, see O. V. Khlevniuk, *Khoziain: Stalin i utverzhdenie stalinskoi diktatury* (Moscow: ROSSPEN, 2010), 329.

10   Varlamov, *Andrei Platonov*, 396–8, 405–410.

11   Letter to Levitskaia, November 1938, in Kolodnyi "Istoriia odnogo posviashcheniia," 184.

12   E. Iu. Litvin, ed.," 'Chto zhe s nami delaiut?' Pis'ma k A. N. Tolstomu—deputatu Verkhovnogo soveta SSSR," *Zven'ia. Istoricheskii al'manakh* 1 (1992): 505–528.

13   For the most extensive retelling of the memory, see Valentina Oberemko's interview with Svetlana Sholokhova, "Iz-za 'Tikhogo Dona' ottsa pytalis' ubit'," *Argumenty i fakty* (Moscow), January 31, 2008. See also Feliks Chuev, *Soldaty imperii: Besedy. Vospominaniia. Dokumenty* (Moscow: Kovcheg, 1998), 414.

14   I take no position on whether this was confabulation or delusion. Some real event could have been restructured in his memory as a result of the anxieties of the terror. For the rich

literature on false memories, see Michael D. Kopelman, "Varieties of confabulation and delusion," *Cognitive Neuropsychiatry* 15, no. 1–3 (2010): 14–37.

15 On Frunze's death and stories circulating in the literary world about it, see D. M. Fel'dman, "Grani skandala 'Povest' nepogashennoi luny' B. A. Pil'niaka v gazetno-zhurnal'nom kontekste 1920-kh gg.," *Vestnik Rossiiskogo gosudarstvennogo gumanitarnogo universiteta. Seriia 'Filologicheskie nauki. Zhurnalistika. Literaturnaia kritika'* 93, no. 13 (2012): 79–106.

16 This and subsequent paragraphs about the speech are based on "Rech' t. Sholokhova (Rostovskaia oblast')," *Pravda*, March 20, 1939.

17 Letter to Kniazev, September 1939, Petelin, *Pis'ma*, 310–311.

18 Letter to Levitskaia, July 1939, Kolodnyi "Istoriia odnogo posviashcheniia," 185.

19 Anatolii Kalinin, "Vstrechi," in *Literaturno-kriticheskii sbornik* (Rostov: Kn. Izd., 1940), 148.

SIXTEEN

1 Letter to Levitskaia, July 1939, in Kolodnyi, "Istoriia odnogo posviashcheniia," 185.

2 Sholokhov's son recalled that around that time he claimed to be "indestructible." M. M. Sholokhov, *Ob ottse*, 66.

3 Murin, *Pisatel' i vozhd'*, 127–129.

4 [n.a.] "Rech' po radio Predsedatelia Soveta Narodnyh Komissarov SSSR tov. V. M. Molotova," *Pravda*, November 29, 1939. See also the coverage on subsequent days, which appeared under the consistent heading "Operatsionnaia svodka shtaba Leningradskogo voennogo okruga."

5 A. Kalinin, "U avtora 'Tikhogo Dona'," *Komsomol'skaia Pravda*, January 9, 1940. Anatolii Kalinin, "Veshenskoe leto," *Ogonek*, October 14, 1962, 17; Anatolii Kalinin, "Vstrechi," in *Literaturno-kriticheskii sbornik* (Rostov: Kn. Izd., 1940), 152.

6 Murin, *Pisatel' i vozhd'*, 129.

7 The articles were published in *Pravda* over the course of several days around December 18, Stalin's birthday. Sholokhov's article "O prostom slove" appeared in *Pravda* on December 23, 1939. Articles by major political figures were also published in a separate volume. [n.a.] *Stalin: K shestidesiatletiiu so dnia rozhdeniia* (Moscow: Pravda, 1940). For Sholokhov's article, see 239–42.

8 [n.a.] "Postanovlenie SNK SSSR ob uchrezhdenii premii imeni Stalina," *Pravda*, December 21, 1939.

9 V. A. Aleksandrov, ed., "M. A. Sholokhov v dokumentakh Komiteta po Stalinskim premiiamm 1940–41 gg," in *Novoe o Mikhaile Sholokhove: Issledovaniia i materialy ed. F. F. Kuznetsov et al.* (Moscow: Institut Mirovoi Literatury, 2003), 494.

10 This account of Sholokhov's meeting with A. N. Tolstoi is based on the reminiscences of Liudmila Tolstoi as told to Iurii Oklianskii. See Iu. M. Oklianskii, *Besputnyi klassik i kentavr: A. N. Tolstoi i P. L. Kapitsa. Angliiskii sled* (Moscow: Pechatnye Traditsii, 2009), 294–99.

11 The paragraphs about the deliberations are based on Aleksandrov, "M. A. Sholokhov v dokumentakh Komiteta," 486–551.

12 Ibid., 500.

13 Ibid., 506–8.

14 Ibid., 505.

15 Ibid., 514–16.

16 V. Goffenshefer, "Pisatel'-bolshevik," *Izvestiia*, December 10, 1940.

17 Aleksandrov, "M. A. Sholokhov v dokumentakh Komiteta," 538–9.

18 See the front page of *Pravda*, March 15, 1941.

19 For his sparse, unenthusiastic remarks to a local audience, see TASS, "Vecher vstrechi s M. Sholokhovym," *Pravda*, March 29, 1941.

20 I have reconstructed the text of the letter from a version sent to another winner. A picture of the letter appeared on an old version of a family website devoted to Aleksei Novikov-Priboi http://novikov-priboy.ru/ (last accessed March 2015).

21 For this account of Sholokhov's activities between 1941 and early 1942, in places I rely upon the memoir of Stepan Vasil'evich Bondarenko which was written in 1977. It contains unique information acquired during the author's residence in Vioshki as a TASS correspondent and his interactions with Sholokhov. I have cross-verified several of the author's statements with other sources and have deemed them to be reliable. The memoirs [henceforth Bondarenko *Memoir*] are available at http://www.tetradimemory.narod.ru /Tetrad9_Veshki.htm/ (last accessed September 2015). [An attempt to access the site in summer 2018 was unsuccessful due to some type of malfunction or malware.]

SEVENTEEN

1 [n.a.] "Vystuplenie po radio Zamestitelia Predsedatelia Soveta Narodnykh Komissarov Soiuza SSR i Narodnogo Komissara Inostrannykh Del tov. V. M. Molotova," *Izvestiia*, June 24, 1941.

2 TASS, "Kazatskai pulia, kazatskaia sablia vsiudu nastignut vraga!," *Izvestiia*, June 26, 1941; M. Sholokhov, "Miting v stanitse Veshenskoi," *Pravda*, July 6, 1941.

3 We know that he was an active reader of the daily briefings about the war. See David Ortenberg, *Frontovye poezdki* (Moscow: "Sovetskaia Rossiia," 1983), 14.

4 On Sholokhov as a puzzled observer of these events, see S. M. Sholokhova, "K istorii nenapisannogo romana," in *Sholokhov na izlome vremeni*, 104.

5 These examples are drawn from patterns of coverage in *Pravda* during the first weeks of the war. Sholokhov was officially a special correspondent of the paper.

6 "Vystuplenie po radio Predsedatelia Gosudarstvennogo Komiteta Oborony I. V. Stalina," *Izvestiia*, July 3, 1941.

7 Kuznetsov, *Sud'ba i pravda*, 25.

8 According to the Bondarenko *Memoir*, Sholokhov initially doubted the atrocity stories and cited the Tolstoi/Goebbels exchange as an example. For A. N. Tolstoi, "Fashisty otvetiat za svoi zlodeniia," *Krasnaia Zvezda* (Moscow), August 20, 1941. Tolstoi's response to Goebbels, see A. N. Tolstoi, "Litso gitlerovskoi armii," *Izvestiia*, August 31, 1941.

9 For examples of such articles see TASS, "Sekretnoe soveshchanie u Gitlera," *Krasnaia Zvezda*, August 3, 1941; P. Vladimirov, "Rastlennaia moral' fashistskikh ubiits," *Izvestiia*, August 16, 1941; N. Leonidov, "Fashizm i zhenshchina," *Pravda*, August 21, 1941. For Soviet women's response, see [n.a.] "Edinyi front zhenshchin vsego mira protiv gitlerizma," *Izvestiia*, September 9, 1941.

10 Sovinformbiuro, "Dvukhmesiachnye itogi voiny mezhdu gitlerovskoi Germaniei i Sovetskim Soiuzom," *Izvestiia*, August 23, 1941.

11   Such rules can be deduced from a close reading of wartime coverage. For a general discussion, see G. A. Kurenkov, "Perekhod tsenzury na 'voennye rel'sy'. Glavlit 22 iunia 1941 g-dekabr' 1941 g.," at http://opentextnn.ru/censorship/russia/sov/libraries /books/?id=5367&txt=1 (last accessed June 2018). For documents on censorship, see A. Ia. Livshin, I. B. Orlov ed., *Sovetskaia propaganda v gody Velikoi Otechestvennoi voiny: "kommunikatsiia ubezhdeniia" i mobilizatsionnye mekhanizmy* (Moscow: ROSSPEN, 2007), 124–125, 596–602, and passim.

12   Livshin and Orlov, *Sovetskaia propaganda*, 126.

13   M. A. Sholokhov, "Na smolenskom napravlenii," *Krasnaia zvezda*, August 29, 1941. See also Evgenii Petrov, "Frontovye zametki," in Il'ia Il'f and Evgenii Petrov, *Sobranie sochinenii* (Moscow: Gosudarstvennoe izdatel'stvo khudozhestvennoi literatury, 1961), 5: 602–615.

14   This paragraph presents the kinds of information Sholokhov would have learned from the soldiers he encountered. Lev Lopukhovsky, *The Viaz'ma Catastrophe: 1941*, tr. Stuart Britton (Solihull: Helion and Co., 2013). See also [n.a.] *Kniga pamiati. Sibiriaki v bitve za Moskvu (1941–42)* (Moscow: Inform-Znanie, 2001), 153–84.

15   Bondarenko *Memoir*. Sholokhov's brief article "Gnusnost'," *Krasnaia zvezda*, September 6, 1941, would appear to contradict this aspect of Bondarenko's account. However, as Bar-Sella noted, the "article" is based on secondhand testimony for which Sholokhov merely provided captioning and commentary. See Bar-Sella, *Literaturnyi kotlovan*, 221.

16   Bondarenko *Memoir*. Only a systematic study could confirm Sholokhov's claim to Bondarenko that his report to propaganda officials caused the number of such stories to diminish.

17   M. A. Sholokhov, "Voennoplennye," *Pravda*, August 31, 1941.

18   Ortenberg, *Frontovye poezdki*, 28.

19   On this meeting see Bar-Sella, *Literaturnyi kotlovan*, 222–223.

20   A. Kogan and Z. Korzinkina, *Stroka, oborvannaia pulei: moskovskie pisateli, pavshie na frontakh Velikoi Otechestvennoi voiny* (Moscow: Moskovskii rabochii, 1976), 304–305; Petelin, *Pis'ma*, 322.

21   Murin, *Pisatel' i vozhd'*, 136; Petelin, *Pis'ma*, 321.

22   Lugovoi recalled hearing that Shcherbakov, the head of the information service, wanted Sholokhov to write an "inflammatory brochure" about the German occupiers, but that Sholokhov opined that he was having difficulty writing such a publication. Lugovoi, *S kroviu i potom*, 120.

23   Bondarenko *Memoir*.

EIGHTEEN

1   The reminiscences of Sholokhov's daughter Svetlana provide important details about this period and his family's two evacuations. See A. Kochetov, "Sholokhov v Pobedu veril vsegda: beseda s docher'iu velikogo pisatelia Svetlanoi Sholokhovoi," *Sovetskaia Rossiia* (Moscow), May 5, 2005.

2   M. F. Tulikov, *Mikhail Sholokhov v Nikolaevske* (Volgograd: Izdatel', 2008), 22–27.

3   Kuznetsov, *Sud'ba i pravda*, 28–29.

4   D. I. Ortenberg, *God 1942: rasskaz—khronika* (Moscow: Izdatel'stvo Politicheskoi Literatury, 1988), 268–9. I concur with Zeev Bar-Sella that the testimonies regarding

a head injury which Sholokhov allegedly sustained in a forced landing of an airplane in early 1942 are too contradictory to trust. See Bar-Sella, *Literaturnyi kotlovan*, 352–363. It seems suspicious that F. S. Kniazev, who closely interacted with Sholokhov in 1942, does not mention any accident or lasting health effects. He does mention Maria Petrovna's concerns about Sholokhov's coughing and her efforts to limit his drinking. See *Sholokhov na izlome vremeni*, 164–5. The relevant portions of Sholokhov's military records remain unavailable to researchers. The Bondarenko memoir mentions a "light trauma" but does not report the cause.

5   Ferdman is mentioned in a war notebook, which is preserved at Sholokhov's house-museum in Vioshki.

6   I. V. Stalin, "Prikaz narodnogo komissara oborony SSSR 1 Maia 1942 goda No. 130," *Pravda*, May 1, 1942.

7   Extracted from the speech, the Stalin quote also appeared on the masthead of Soviet newspapers. See the front page of *Pravda* for June 28, 1942.

8   Mikhail Sholokhov, "Lesson in Hatred," in *One Man's Destiny*, 186–204.

9   This account of the dinner is a composite reconstruction. I have generally relied on Vladlen Kotovskov based on Sholokhov's testimonies to him in 1967. See Vladlen Kotovskov, *Sholokhovskaia stroka: stat'i, stranitsy iz dnevnika* (Rostov: Knizhnoe izdatel'tsvo, 1988). The comment about Fadeev comes from Kniazev, *Sholokhov na izlome vremeni*, 164. The phrase, "Nonetheless, we'll arrange for you to have some time off from your duties as a correspondent," has been inferred from Kniazev's remark that "the Boss demanded this rest/time off to be organized." See also Valentin Osipov, *Tainaia zhizn' Mikhaila Sholokhova: dokumental'naia khronika bez legend* (Moscow: Izdatel'stvo Libereia, 1995), 234–235.

10 Bar-Sella, *Literaturnyi kotlovan*, 242.

11 Osipov, *Tainaia zhizn' Mikhaila Sholokhova*, 239.

12 Ibid., 239.

13 Kochetov, "Sholokhov v Pobedu veril."

14 Lugovoi, *S kroviu i potom*, 125–6.

15 Kochetov, "Sholokhov v Pobedu veril"; Lugovoi, *S kroviu i potom*, 121–122; also M. M. Sholokhov, *Ob ottse*, 58–62.

16 Kochetov, "Sholokhov v Pobedu veril."

17 First published in Petelin, *Pis'ma*, 324–26.

18 Bondarenko *Memoir*. Lugovoi, *S kroviu i potom*, 123–127; A. Sofronov, "Bessmertnik," *Ogoniok*, July 26, 1964, 11; Ermolaev, *Mikhail Sholokhov and his art*, 47–50.

NINETEEN

1   In a conversation with his assistant in 1965 Sholokhov recalled several intriguing details about the battle for the Stalingrad railroad station and the loss of a battalion there. See Zimovnov, *Sholokhov v zhizni*, 69. The specific information in Sholokhov's account does not appear to derive from the published memoirs or accounts of the battle up to that point.

2   See [n.a.] "Ostoiat' Stalingrad!" *Krasnaia zvezda*, September 11, 1942; [n.a.] "Geroi Stalingrada," *Krasnaia zvezda*, October 1, 1942; A. Chuianov, "Gorod-geroi," *Krasnaia zvezda*, October 1, 1942.

3   See A. I. Rodimtsev, *Na poslednem rubezhe; zapiski komandira divizii* (Volgograd: Nizhne-Volzhskoe knizhnoe izdatel'stvo, 1964), 27–54; V. I. Chuikov, *Nachalo puti* (Moscow: Voen. Izdatel'stvo, 1959), 96–160. See also A.I. Rodimtsev, *Gvardeitsy stoiali nasmert'* (Moscow: Dosaaf, 1969); N. G. Kuznetsov, "Voennye moriaki v Stalingradskoi bitve," in *Stalingradskaia epopeia*, ed. A. M. Samsonov (Moscow: Nauka, 1968), 403–419.

4   It seems likely that Sholokhov formed his view of the battle from testimonies of members of the Volga Military flotilla, which played a key role in ferrying troops and supplies across the Volga. We know that his itinerary included awarding medals to members of the river flotilla. See V. Mamontov, *Svet tekh vstrech: volzhskie stranitsy o M. A. Sholokhove* (Kamyshin, 1992); N. T. Kuznetsova, ed., *Mikhail Sholokhov: letopis' zhizni i tvorchestva (materialy k biografii)* (Moscow: Galeriia, 2005), 190–6.

5   For a recent account, see V. N. Drobotov, "Rekviem po pervomu batal'onu," *Otchii krai* (2017), no. 4, 51–70.

6   Sholokhov mentions the hospitalization from November to late December in a letter to Lugovoi but does not reveal the cause. Lugovoi, *S kroviu i potom*, 125; first complete publication Petelin, *Pis'ma*, 326–7.

7   See the daily briefings for January 16, 17, 19, and 20, 1943, published in *Krasnaia Zvezda* issues for those dates.

8   Lugovoi, *S kroviu i potom*, 125.

9   M. A. Sholokhov, "Oni srazhalis' za Rodinu," *Pravda*, May 5–8, 1943.

10   For an example of such a letter, see *Sholokhovskii vek*, 139; S. M. Sholokhova, "K istorii nenapisannogo romana," in *Sholokhov na izlome vremeni*, 105.

11   Petelin, *Mikhail Sholokhov v vospominaniiakh*, 2: 231.

12   Sovinformbiuro, "Razmery territorii osvobozhdennoi Krasnoi Armii," *Krasnaia zvezda*, April 3, 1943.

13   This account of the reception is a composite reconstruction created from descriptions by Osipov, *Tainaia zhizn' Mikhaila Sholokhova*, 234–36; Valerii Ganichev, "'Molodaia gvardiia'. 1968–1978. Iz vospominanii," *Moskva*, September 2013, online version http://www.moskvam.ru/publications/publication_963.html (last accessed June 2018); for the same narrative with minor variations see Valerii Ganichev, "Oni srazhalis' za Rodinu: K 100-letiiu so dnia rozhdeniia Mikhaila Sholokhova," *Iuzhnyi Ural* [Orenburg], May 23, 2003; Shakhmagonov, "Bremia 'Tikhogo Dona'," 115–17; and Vladimir Chivilikhin, *Dnevniki, pis'ma, vospominaniia sovremennikov* (Moscow: Algoritm, 2008), 260. For a critical consideration of these testimonies, see Bar-Sella, *Literaturnyi kotlovan*, 230–34.

14   The chronology of the meeting has been the subject of debate. I have dated the reception to late spring or early summer 1943 in connection with a major shipment of medicines and other supplies which was scheduled to be shipped from New York in late April 1943. See TASS, "Deiatel'nost' amerikanskogo 'Komiteta pomoshchi Sovetskomu Soiuzu v voine," *Pravda*, April 21, 1943. This date would also help to explain Sholokhov's frustrated comments about a second front.

15   The reasons for Sholokhov's frictions with Erenburg are complicated. Early in the war Erenburg thought highly enough of Sholokhov and his reputation to propose to the head of the information service a key role for Sholokhov in countering German propaganda. Erenburg proposed that Sholokhov or A. Tolstoi write an article about Jews "debunking

the fable that Hitler's wrath is only directed against the Jews." Ilia Erenburg, *Na tsokole istorii . . . Pis'ma 1931–1967* (Moscow: Agraf, 2004), 291. A few months later, Vasilii Grossman wrote to Erenburg lamenting Sholokhov's "anti-Semitic slander." From the context it is clear that he was referring to some kind of statement disparaging the willingness of Jews to fight. B. Ia. Frezinskii, ed., *Pochta Ilii Erenburga. Ia slyshu vse . . . 1916–1967* (Moscow: Agraf, 2006), 75–6. By the time of their meeting in Moscow, Sholokhov was angry at Erenburg because he believed Erenburg had been involved in spreading some kind of rumors alleging that Sholokhov avoided evacuation in hopes that he and his family could end up in the German occupation zone. Chivilikhin, *Dnevniki*, 260.

16   Osipov, *Tainaia zhizn' Mikhaila Sholokhova*, 235–6.

17   Sholokhov, *Sobranie sochinenii*, vol. 8, *Ranniia proza 1925–7 gg. Ocherki, stati'i, fel'etony, vystupleniia, 1923–1958 gg.* (Moscow: Terra, 2002), 254–8.

18   Sholokhov to Krupin, November 25, 1943, GAKO [Gosudarstvennyi arkhiv Kirovskoi oblasti] f. R-128, op. 1, d. 929, l.162.

19   For the numbers see [n.a.], *O vypolnenii postanovleniia SNK SSR i TsK VKP(b) ot 21 Avgusta 1943 goda "O neotlozhnykh merakh po vosstanovleniiu khoziastva v raionakh, osvobozhdennykh ot nemetskoi okkupatsii"* (Moscow: Izd. Politicheskoi literatury, 1944). See also the coverage of the Supreme Soviet meetings in *Izvestiia* for the first days of February 1944.

20   On the recovery efforts see GARO, f. R-3737, op. 2, d. 476, l. 4–8. On inventories, see GARO, f. R-3613, op. 1, d. 32, l. 2–25. The meeting is mentioned in a letter to Lugovoi, *S kroviu i potom*, 127–28.

21   Lugovoi, *S kroviu i potom*, 127. See also Petr Maiatskii, *Kolokol pamiati: tridtsat' let riadom s Sholokhovym. Vospominaniia* (Rostov: Rostizdat, 2004), 45–46.

22   Lugovoi, *S kroviu i potom*, 127.

23   For the letter of Stalingrad residents, see [n.a.], "Velikomu vozhdiu sovetskogo naroda tovarishchu Stalinu," *Pravda*, February 3, 1944. Several additional articles about the anniversary are published in the same issue.

24   Petelin, *Pis'ma*, 333.

25   Petelin, *Mikhail Sholokhov v vospominaniiakh*, 2: 462; Kotovskov, *Sholokhovskaia stroka*, 45.

26   M. A. Sholokhov, "Oni srazhalis' za rodinu," *Pravda*, June 3, 1944. For his complaint about his muse, see letter to Krupin, August 13, 1944, GAKO, f. R-128, op. 1, d. 929, l. 154–55.

27   I. G. Lezhnev, *Put' Sholokhova: Tvorcheskaia biografiia* (Moscow: Sovetskii pisatel', 1958), 405. Sholokhov to Krupin, April 26, 1945, GAKO, f. R-128, op. 1, d. 929, l. 153.

28   There are various clips of the announcement available on the Internet. For the audio of the announcement, I consulted https://www.youtube.com/watch?v=kYJ9uMtwbRI (last accessed June 2018).

29   For his attendance at the parade, see Osipov, *Tainaia zhizn' Mikhaila Sholokhova*, 253–254. For Stalin's toast, see [n.a.] "Priem v Kremle v chest' uchastnikov parada pobedy," *Pravda*, June 27, 1945.

TWENTY

1   [n.a.] "Novye glavy romana 'Oni srazhalis' za Rodinu," *Moskovskii bol'shevik*, September 25, 1945.

2   Kuznetsov, *Sud'ba i pravda*, 30.

ENDNOTES

3 Stenli Edgar Khaimen [Stanley Edgar Hyman], "Novaia 'Voina i mir' (razmyshlenie)," *Znamia*, no. 9, 1945, 141–149.

4 Documents about the construction are displayed at the writer's home, which is now a museum.

5 A. M. Blokh, *Sovetskii Soiuz v inter'ere nobelevskikh premii: Fakty. Dokumenty. Razmyshleniia. Kommentarii* (Saint Petersburg: Gumanistika, 2001), 478.

6 Murin, *Pisatel' i vozhd'*, 138–40.

7 For the 1947 confidential letter to party committees, see http://www.alexanderyakovlev. org/fond/issues-doc/69339 (last accessed June 2018). See also Blokh, *Sovetskii Soiuz v inter'ere*, 215–21.

8 Dmitrii Buzin, *Alekandr Fadeev: tainy zhizny i smerti* (Moscow: Algoritm, 2008), 71, 86–89, 116–177, 152–153.

9 M. Sholokhov, "Bor'ba prodolzhaetsia," *Literaturnaia Gazeta*, September 4, 1948. On the preparations for the congress, see RGASPI, f. 17, op. 3, d. 1072, and RGASPI, f. 17, op. 132, d. 81. See D. G. Nadzhafov, Z. S. Belousova, ed., *Stalin i kosmopolitizm: Dokumenty agitpropa TsK KPSS 1945–1953* (Moscow: Materik, 2005), 186–189.

10 S. N. Preobrazhenskii, ed., *Aleksandr Fadeev, Pis'ma. 1916–1956* (Moscow: Sovetskii pisatel', 1967), 230–231; Ilia Erenburg, *Liudi, gody, zhizn'* (Moscow: Sovetskii pisatel', 1990), 3: 125.

11 Sholokhov, "Svet i mrak," *Pravda*, May 31, 1949.

12 Stalin to Feliks Kon, July 9, 1929, in I. V. Stalin, *Sochineniia*, vol. 12 *Aprel' 1929-Iun' 1930* (Moscow: 1952), 112–115. I used a second printing. The original volume came out in late 1949.

13 Sholokhov to Stalin, January 3, 1950, in Kozlovskii, Kuznetsov, Ushakov, and Sholokhov, *M. A. Sholokhov, Pis'ma*, 269–270. First published in 1992. Petelin, *Pis'ma*, 354.

14 Shakhmagonov, "Bremia 'Tikhogo Dona'," 49.

15 Bar-Sella, *Literaturyni kotlovan*, 250–51.

16 Artizov and Naumov, *Vlast' i khudozhestvennaia intelligentsia*, 535; Bar-Sella, *Literaturnyi kotlovan*, 250–51.

17 In 1951 Sholokhov became involved in a polemic with Konstantin Simonov over literary pseudonyms. Sholokhov supported an ally who wrote an article with strong anti-Semitic undertones. Much remains puzzling about his role in this incident. Years later Simonov was not fully convinced that Sholokhov authored the polemical response. Intriguingly Sholokhov decided not to include it in his collected works, which were published a few years later. Konstantin Simonov, *Glazami cheloveka moego pokoleniia: razmyshlenniia o I. V. Staline* (Moscow: Kniga, 1990), 190. On the polemic about pseudonyms as a small episode in the history of anti-Semitism in the Stalinist period, see Gennadii Kostyrchenko, *Stalin protiv "kosmopolitov." Vlast' i evreiskaia intelligentsia v SSSR* (Moscow: Rossiiskaia politicheskaia entsiklopediia, 2009), 226–28. Attempts to exonerate Sholokhov of anti-Semitism usually resort to the specious "friend argument" while ignoring the company that he kept. He seems to have been more casually anti-Semitic than virulently or violently so. Several of his stories feature positive protagonists from Jewish backgrounds. He also did not want to be seen as anti-Semitic by the world. In a meeting with Charles Snow and Pamela Hansford Johnson he unexpectedly gave a speech denouncing anti-Semitism. Philip Snow, *Stranger and Brother: a Portrait of C. P. Snow* (New York: Charles Scribner's Sons, 1982), 156.

18   Shakhmagonov, "Bremia 'Tikhogo Dona'," 44–45.

19   Sholokhov, "Pervenets velikh stroek," *Pravda*, July 30, 1952.

20   Petelin, *Pis'ma*, 371.

21   For Sholokhov's regrets that the editor, Konstantin Potapov, went overboard see a letter sent by Sholokhov to the publisher in late 1951, "Pis'ma i telegrammy M. A. Sholokhova," in *Sholokhov na izlome vremeni*, 223–224.

22   M. A. Sholokhov, *Tikhii Don. Izd. ispravlennoe* (Moscow: Goslitizdat, 1953), 2: 112–125.

23   Shakhmagonov, "Bremia 'Tikhogo Dona,'" 49.

24   This section is based on Shakhmagonov, "Bremia 'Tikhogo Dona'," 56–60.

TWENTY-ONE

1   TsK KPSS, "Pravitel'stvennoe soobshchenie o bolezni Predsedatelia Soveta Ministrov Soiuza SSR i Sekretaria Tsentral'nogo Komiteta KPSS tovarishcha Iosifa Vissarionovicha Stalina," *Pravda*, March 4, 1953. The medical bulletins published on subsequent days were signed by doctors and indicated further developments.

2   A. F. Tret'iakov, I. I. Kuperin, P. E. Lukomskii, N. V. Kovalov, A. L. Miasnikov, E. M. Tareev, I. N. Filimonov, I. S. Glazunov, R. A. Tkachev, V. I. Ivanov-Neznamov, "Meditsinskoe zakliuchenie o bolezni i smerti I. V. Stalina," *Pravda*, March 6, 1953.

3   Mikhail Sholokhov, "Proshchai, otets!," *Pravda*, March 8, 1953.

4   Some of the contents of Malenkov's speech were published in [n.a.] "Nesokrushimoe edinenie partii, pravitel'stva, sovetskogo naroda," *Pravda*, July 10, 1953.

5   M. A. Sholokhov, "Imia izmennika prokliato i budet zabyto," *Literaturnaia Gazeta*, July 16, 1953.

6   Sholokhov, "Vechno zdravstvui, rodnaia partiia!," *Pravda*, July 30, 1952.

7   [n.a.] "Piat'desiat let kommunisticheskoi partii Sovetskogo Soiuza," *Pravda*, July 26, 1953.

8   "Piat'desiat let kommunisticheskoi partii sovetskogo soiuza," *Pravda*, July 26, pp. 3–4.

9   Mark Vishniak, "Latest communist rewriting of history," *Communist affairs* 2, issue 6 (1964): 3.

10   Bar-Sella, *Literaturnyi kotlovan*, 167.

11   Shakhmagonov, "Bremia 'Tikhogo Dona'," 80. Bar-Sella, *Literaturnyi kotlovan*, 142–72.

12   Tvardovskii to Sholokhov, February 1954, in A. Tvardovskii, *Pis'ma o literature 1930–1970*, ed. M. Tvardovskaia (Moscow: Sovetskii pisatel', 1985), 90.

13   Ermolaev, *'Tikhii Don' i politicheskaia tsenzura*, 100.

14   Blokh, *Sovetskii Soiuz v inter'ere*, 459, 480. A very important collection of archival documents about Sholokhov's Nobel aspirations was published in 1993. See A. Petrov, "Dokumenty iz arkhiva TsK KPSS po "Nobelevskomu delu" M. A. Sholokhova," *Kontinent* (Moscow), no. 76, April 1993, 233–256.

15   Petrov, "Dokumenty," 235–238.

16   For drinking see RGANI, f. 3, op. 34, d. 196, l. 37, Viacheslav Ogryzko, "Tri butylki kon'iaka v den', ili strasti po Mikhailu Sholokhovu," *Literaturnaia Rossiia* (Moscow), no. 24, July 3, 2015.

17   E. S. Afanas'eva, V. Iu. Afiani, Z. K. Vodop'ianov, ed., *Apparat TSK KPSS i kul'tura, 1953–1957: dokumenty* (Moscow: ROSSPEN, 2001), 324–25, 337–39, 349–52.

18   Blokh, *Sovetskii Soiuz v inter'ere*, 477–8.

19   Shakhmagonov, "Bremia 'Tikhogo Dona'," 81–4.

20   On Kudinov see Priima, *S vekom naravne* (1985), 151–159; Kuznetsov, *Sud'ba i Pravda*, 193–257. I am preparing an article devoted to Kudinov. Some of the information in this paragraph derives from my research in Bulgaria in 2013.

21   Ivan Stadniuk, *Ispoved' stalinista: vospominatel'naia povest'* (Moscow: Patriot, 1993), 257–259.

22   M. A. Sholokhov, "Pis'mo v redaktsiiu," *Inostrannaia literatura*, no. 2, 1955, 224.

23   For dose and diagnosis see RGANI, f. 5, op. 17, d. 535, l. 113; for Suslov see RGANI, f. 5, op. 36, d. 14, l. 149. Both were published by Viacheslav Ogryzko in "Tri butylki kon'iaka."

24   I. V. Strel'chuk, *Alkogolizm i bor'ba s nim* (Moscow: Molodaia gvardiia, 1954); I. V. Strel'chuk, "O novykh sovremennykh metodakh lecheniia bol'nykh alkogolizmom," *Sovetskaia meditsina* 21, no. 5 (1957): 26–33.

25   I. V. Strel'chuk, "Lechenie alkogolikov antabusom," *Nevropatologiia i psikhiatriia* 20/1 (1951): 80–84.

26   Sholokhov's words were recalled by Strel'chuk at a later consultation in 1957. See [n.a.], "Kak TsK prinuzhdal Sholokhova lechit'sia ot alkogolizma," *Sovershenno Sekretno* (Moscow), October 3, 2012.

27   I. V. Strel'chuk, "Opyt differentsirovannogo gipnoterapevticheskogo vozdeistviia v svete ucheniia I. P. Pavlova o dvukh signal'nykh sistemakh," *Zhurnal vysshei nervnoi deiatel'nosti* 3, no. 3 (1953): 353–368. For documentary footage of such experiments, see [n.a.] *Sovetskaia shkola gipnoza*, 1961, at https://www.youtube.com/watch?v=UKBgU9iRIAg (last accessed June 2018).

28   For the committee report on its deliberations, see Utlåtande av Svenska Akademiens Nobelkommitté 1955, archive of the Swedish Academy, Stockholm. The quote is from page 10. For the expert appraisal filed on May 1, 1955, see Nils Åke Nilsson, "Michail Sjolochov (1955)," archive of the Swedish Academy.

29   Shakhmagonov, "Bremia 'Tikhogo Dona'," 89.

TWENTY-TWO

1   For various appraisals of 1956, see Lev Lur'e and Irina Maliarova, ed., *1956 god. Seredina veka* (Saint Petersburg: Neva, 2007).

2   M. A. Sholokhov, *Sobranie Sochinenii*, 8 volumes (Moscow: Izd. khudozhestvennoi literatury, 1956–60).

3   For Sholokhov's meeting with Makar'ev in 1956, see Mikhail Shkerin, "Shtrikhi tragedii vospominaniia A. Fadeeva," *Literaturnaia gazeta*, April 12, 1989. The sections on Makar'ev's life in Norilsk and his efforts to obtain an apartment are from other sources, cited separately in subsequent notes.

4   This description of Makar'ev's appearance and voice are derived from Raisa Orlova and Lev Kopelev, *My zhili v Moskve 1956–1980* (Ann Arbor, Mich.: Ardis, 1988) 55.

5   For Makar'ev's life in Norilsk, see Viacheslav Khantin's reminiscences in Lur'e and Maliarova, 1956 god, 259–261. For the more complete treatment of Makar'ev's biography, see Irina Kargina, *Gorech' polyni: propavshii v 'Podniatoi tseline'* (Moscow: AIRO-XXI, 2010), 86–121.

6   From the documents in Fadeev's archive it is clear that he helped Makar'ev to regain his party membership and made assurances about helping with housing. N. I. Dukushina, ed., *Aleksandr Fadeev. Pis'ma i dokumenty iz fondov Rossiiskogo Gosudarstvennogo Arkhiva literatury i iskusstva* (Moscow: Gor'ky Institute of World Literature, 2001), 201–4. A letter sent to Fadeev by Makar'ev after his return indicates a pent-up desire to tell Fadeev "many interesting things," ibid., 297–99.

7   V. Iu. Afiani et al., ed., *Doklad N. S. Khrushcheva o kul'te lichnosti Stalina na XX s"ezde KPSS: Dokumenty* (Moscow: Rosspen, 2002).

8   M. A. Sholokhov, "Rech'," *Pravda*, February 21, 1956.

9   On Fadeev's relegation to the "penalty box" (i.e., the balcony), see Dmitrii Buzin, *Alekandr Fadeev*, 271–4. According to Buzin, one of Fadeev's allies considered Sholokhov's speech to be a "civilian execution" that could end Fadeev's career in the Writers' Union. Buzin, *Alekandr Fadeev*, 268.

10   A. Gindin, "Pis'mo v redaktsiiu," *Literaturnaia gazeta*, February 28, 1956.

11   [n.a.] "Ot Tsentral'nogo Komiteta: Aleksandr Aleksandrovich Fadeev," *Pravda*, May 15, 1956; Writers' Union, "Pamiati A. A. Fadeeva," *Pravda*, May 15, 1956.

12   Strel'chuk, Gerashchenko, Onsentovich, Markov, "Meditsinskoe zakliuchenie o bolezni i smerti tovarishcha Fadeeva Aleksandra Aleksandrovicha," *Pravda*, May 15, 1956.

13   Shkerin, "Shtrikhi tragedii." See also, Iurii Korotkov "Samoubiistva sovetskikh pisatelei," [1968], republished in *Sovershenno sekretno* (Moscow), October 3, 2012.

TWENTY-THREE

1   [n.a.] "Pochemu kul't lichnosti chuzhd dukhu Marksizma-Leninizma," *Pravda*, March 28, 1956.

2   M. M. Sholokhov, *Ob ottse*, 8.

3   For coverage of the anniversary, see *Literaturnaia Gazeta*, June 16 and 17, 1956.

4   APRF, f. 3, op. 50, d. 510, ll. 42–57, published in V. Naumov, et al, ed., *Grigorii Zhukov: Stenogramma oktiab'rskogo (1957 g.) plenuma TsK KPSS i drugie dokumenty* (Moscow: Fond Demokratiia, 2001), 126–133, 652–3.

5   Sergei Khrushchev, *Nikita Khrushchev: Reformator* (Moscow: Vremia, 2010), 380.

6   Sergei Khrushchev, *Reformator*, 381.

7   [n.a.] "Ia vsem serdtsem veriu v svetlyi razum muzhestvennogo i trudoliubivogo vengerskogo naroda: zaiavlenie Mikhaila Sholokhova korrespondentu gazety 'Nepsabadshag,'" *Pravda*, December 27, 1956.

8   M. Sholokhov, "Sud'ba cheloveka," *Pravda*, December 31, 1956 and January 1, 1957. Mikhail Sholokhov, *One Man's Destiny*, 9–45.

9   [n.a.] "Kak TsK prinuzhdal Sholokhova lechit'sia ot alkogolizma."

10   I deduce this from the delay in implementation of the order. On Sholokhov's alcoholism in those years, see also Khrushchev, *Reformator*, 380–1.

11   M. Sholokhov, "Podniataia tselina," *Pravda*, April 14, 1957.

12   Such a warning would appear to explain why Sholokhov went out of his way to emphasize sobriety in his letter to Krupin cited below.

13   Ivan Tolstoi, *Otmytyi roman Pasternaka. "Doktor Zhivago" mezhdu KGB i TsRU* (Moscow: Vremia, 2009), 128–31.

14   Sholokhov to Krupin, June 4, 1957, GAKO, f. R-128, op. 1, d. 929, l. 138–139ob.

15   This paragraph is based on a close reading of the cryptic official announcements. See [n.a.] "Nepokolebimoe edinstvo," *Pravda*, July 3, 1957; "O plenume TsK KPSS," *Pravda*, July 4, 1957.

16   William Taubman, *Khrushchev: The Man and His Era* (New York: Norton, 2003), 262–67, 371–76. For meat and milk, see William J. Jorden, "Khrushchev Aims to Top US in Food: Sees Soviet Per Capita Lead in Milk and Meat by 61," *New York Times*, May 25, 1957.

17   Mikhail Shkerin, "Order na Arrest," *Pravda Ukrainy* [Kiev], October 1, 1988.

18   Khrushchev's narrative of Stalin's death is derived from Mikhail Shkerin, "Order na Arrest." For a detailed, innovative account of Stalin's death, see Montefiore, *Stalin: The Court of the Red Tsar*, 566–77.

TWENTY-FOUR

1   Petrov, "Dokumenty," 240–41.

2   Peter Finn and Petra Couvee, *The Zhivago Affair: The Kremlin, the CIA and the Battle over a Forbidden Book* (London: Harvill Secker, 2014).

3   Petrov, "Dokumenty," 240–243.

4   Aleksei Ivkin, "Pokazat' klassika chelovekom bylo zapreshcheno," *Izvestiia*, May 25, 1996; Osipov, *Tainaia zhizn' Mikhaila Sholokhova*, 164; Petrov, "Dokumenty," 255–56.

5   Ironically, Sholokhov was not actually a finalist in 1958. See Aleksandr Polivanov, "Pasternak i Sholokhov v nevol'noi bor'be za nobelevskuiu premiiu 1958 goda (po dannym arkhivnykh materialov Shvedskoi Akademii)," (2010) available at http://www.ruthenia.ru/document/549933.html (last accessed June 2018).

6   This paragraph is based on the coverage in *Literaturnaia gazeta*, October 25, 29, and November 1, 1958.

7   See V. Iu. Afiani and N. G. Tomilina, ed., *A za mnoiu shum pogoni: Boris Pasternak i vlast'. Dokumenty 1956–1972* (Moscow: Rosspen, 2001), 158–189.

8   Orlova and Kopelev, *My Zhili*, 60.

9   Kozlovskii, Kuznetsov, Ushakov, and Sholokhov, *M. A. Sholokhov, Pis'ma*, 331.

10   See Afiani and Tomilina, *A za mnoiu shum pogoni*, 257–62.

11   V. Iu. Afiani, et al., *Apparat TSK KPSS i kul'tura 1958–1964: dokumenty* (Moscow: Rosspen, 2005), 119, 205–6; Afiani and Tomilina, *A za mnoiu shum pogoni*, 256–7.

12   Victor Zorza, "Sholokhov: A Writer of the Soviet People," *Manchester Guardian*, April 29, 1959; [n.a.] "Pasternak 'Poet of Old Maids'," *Times* [London], April 29, 1959.

13   Anthony Powell, forward by Ferdinand Mount, *To Keep the Ball Rolling: The Memoirs of Anthony Powell* (Chicago: University of Chicago Press, 2000), 420–424. The quote is from 421.

14   Kozlovskii, Kuznetsov, Ushakov, and Sholokhov, *M. A. Sholokhov, Pis'ma*, 333–334.

15   [n.a.] "V stanitse Veshenskoi," *Literaturnaia gazeta*, September 1, 1959.

16   Harrison E. Salisbury, "Khrushchev Bid to Sholokhov Follows a Dispute over Novel: Sholokhov Rift Believed Ended," *New York Times*, September 1, 1959. See also Harrison Salisbury papers (henceforth Salisbury papers), Series III, Box 181, Folder 16, Columbia University Rare Book and Manuscript Library.

17   M. A. Sholokhov, "O malen'kom mal'chike Garri i bol'shom mistere Solsberi," *Pravda*, March 1, 1960.

18   A. A. Gromyko, *Pamiatnoe* (Moscow: Izd. Politicheskoi Literatury, 1988) 2: 364–367. See also James Billington's report on a meeting with Sholokhov in *Princeton Alumni Weekly*, volume 60, no. 6, October 23, 1959, 25–26.

19   Harry Schwartz, "Sholokhov, in Talk, Derides Pasternak as a 'Hermit Crab'," *New York Times*, September 26, 1959.

20   Georgii Iakovlev, "Kak Sholokhov Khrushcheva obidel," *Vechernaia Moskva*, May 24, 2000. For the volume, see M. Kharlamov and O. Vadeev, eds., *Litsom k litsu s Amerikoi: Rasskaz o poezdke N. S. Khrushcheva v SShA 15–27 sentiabria 1959 goda* (Moscow: Izd. Politicheskoi literatury, 1959).

TWENTY-FIVE

1   See comments in Kalinin, "Veshenskoe leto," 21.

2   After Khrushchev's fall, Sholokhov expressed disdain for the new cult he fostered. See Nikolai Korsunov, *S Sholokhovym . . . : vstrechi, besedy, perepiska* (Orenburg: Orenburg knizhnoe izdatel'stvo, 2000), 109. On Yeremenko, see Zimovnov, *Sholokhov v zhizni*, 45.

3   A. I. Yeremenko, *Stalingrad: zapiski komanduiushchego frontom* (Moscow: Voennoe izdatel'stvo, 1961), 53–56, 64, 135, 139, 144, 250, 289, 325–6, 468, 472, 480, 500.

4   This paragraph derives from my analysis of P. N. Pospelov et al., eds., *Istoriia Velikoi Otechestvennoi voiny Sovetskogo Soiuza, 1941–1945*, 6 vols. (Moscow: Voen. Izd-vo, 1960–65).

5   M. A. Sholokhov, "Voskhishchenie i gordost'," *Pravda*, April 12, 1961 (Ekstrennyi vypusk).

6   Iu. M. Baturin, ed., *Sovetskaia kosmicheskaia initsiativa v gosudarstvennykh dokumentakh 1946–1964 gg.* (Moscow: RTSoft, 2008), 171.

7   [n.a.] *XXII S"ezd Kommunisticheskoi Partii Sovetskogo Soiuza 17–31 Oktiabria 1961 goda: Stenograficheskii otchet* 3 vols. (Moscow: Izd. Politicheskoi literatury, 1962).

8   The quote is from *XXII S"ezd*, 2:582. For Khrushchev on Kirov's murder, see *XXII S"ezd*, 2: 583–84.

9   *XXII S"ezd*, 2:120. The comment was delivered by R. Ia. Malinovskii, the Minister of Defense.

10   For Sholokhov's speech, see *XXII S"ezd*, 2: 161–172.

11   On Hemingway in 1960, see Elena Serebrovskaia, *Mezhdu proshlym i budushchim: zapiski svidetelia* (Saint Petersburg: Lenpoligrafmash, 1995), 2: 88–94. For Furtseva's speech to the congress, see *XXII S"ezd*, 1: 383–398. Her mention of 780 plays is on page 386.

12   For her alleged disparaging remarks and the events that led to her fall from favor, see A. V. Sushkov, "Vysshee rukovodstvo SSSR i 'riazanskoe delo' (1959–1961)," *Vestnik Cheliabinskogo gosudarstvennogo universiteta* 35 (2008): 72–83.

13   N. A. Korneeva, *Ekaterina Furtseva: politicheskaia melodrama* (Moscow: Algoritm, 2007), 209–14; Leonid Mechin, *Furtseva* (Moscow: Molodaia gvardiia, 2011), 272–279.

14   [n.a.] "Postanovlenie XXII s"ezda KPSS o Mavzolee Vladimir Il'ichia Lenina," *Pravda*, October 31, 1961.

15   Petelin, *Pis'ma*, 429–430.

16   TsKhSD [Tsentr khraneniia sovremennoi dokumentatsii], f. 5, op. 33, ed. Khr. 212, ll. 216–7, published in R. Romanova, "Oshibochnye proizvedeniia," *Voprosy literatury*, no. 3, 1996, 291–303.

17   See Nikolai Mitrokhin, *Russkaia partiia: dvizhenie russkikh natsionalistov v SSSR: 1953–1985 gody* (Moscow: Novoe literaturnoe obozrenie, 2003), 156, 159, 241, 251, 259–62, 268–9.

18   C. P. Snow, *Magnanimity: Rectorial Address, Delivered before the University of St. Andrews, April 13, 1962* (St. Andrews, Student's Representative Council, 1962), 23–24.

19   The sole account that discusses Sholokhov's involvement in the Novocherkassk events is Petr Maiatskii, *Kolokol pamiati: tridtsat' let riadom s Sholokhovym. Vospominaniia* (Rostov: Rostizdat, 2004), 170–172.

20   The Maiatskii account avoids particulars about the rebellion. For this account of the actual events I have relied on P. P. Siuda, *Novocherkassk 1–3 iunia 1962 g. zabastovka i rasstrel (na osnove svidetel'stv ochevidtsev i interviu s P. P. Siudoi)*, ed. David Mandel, (Moscow: soiuzmedinform, 1992); Samuel H. Baron, *Bloody Saturday in the Soviet Union: Novocherkassk 1962* (Stanford, Calif.: Stanford University Press, 2001).

21   See especially the coverage in *Pravda* June 1 and 2, 1962.

22   Anastas Mikoian, *Tak bylo: razmyshleniia o minuvshem* (Moscow: Vagrius, 1999), 610, agrees with Maiatskii about the role of Kozlov.

23   [n.a.] "Pered bol'shoi zhatvoi sobranie aktiva rostovskoi oblastnoi partiinoi organizatsii," *Pravda*, June 9, 1962.

TWENTY-SIX

1   For documents on the publication and early responses, see P. E. Spivakovskii and T. V. Esina, eds., *'Ivanu Denisovichu' polveka: iubileinyi sbornik, 1962–2012* (Moscow: Russkii put', 2012).

2   For an interesting account of intrigues in the Kremlin over cultural policies during those years, see V. V. Ogryzko, *Okhraniteli i liberaly: v zatianuvshemsia poiske kompromissa. Istoriko-literatrunoe issledovane* (Moscow: Literaturnaia Rossiia, 2015). Sholokhov involved himself in behind the scenes intrigues as early as April 1962, when he protested the conversion of the daily paper *Literatura i zhizn'* into a weekly. Ogryzko, *Okhraniteli i liberaly*, 16.

3   For important new sources on the events leading up to the Manezh incident, see Ogryzko, *Okhraniteli i liberaly*, 316–32.

4   For a stenographic record, see RGANI, f. 52, op. 1, d. 330, l. 1–149. Published in N. G. Tomilina, ed., *Nikita Sergeevich Khrushchev: dva tsveta vremeni, dokumenty iz lichnogo fonda N. S. Khrushcheva* (Moscow: Mezhdunarodnyi fond, 2009), 2: 533–601.

5   The brief encounter was captured in a newsreel about the assembly. See *Kinozhurnal Novosti dnia/khronika nashikh dnei* no. 51, 1962, available at fil'mfond.rf/kinodokument-11165/ [in Cyrillic] (last accessed June 2018). For Solzhenitsyn's reminiscences, see 60–75.

6   His remarks were subsequently published as "Tvorit' dlia naroda, vo imia kommunizma," *Literaturnaia gazeta*, December 22, 1962.

7   Neizvestnyi gave several interesting and contradictory testimonies about these events over the years. I have generally avoided using them, due to his personal investment in the controversy. Very important details about the assembly were published in the reminiscences of the Armenian director and screenwriter Laert Bagarshyan. These were serialized in the newspaper *Novoe Vremia* (Yerevan), in May, 2012. For official coverage, see *Literaturnaia Gazeta*, December 20, 22, 1962. Other important accounts can be found

in A. I. Solzhenitsyn, *Bodalsia telenok s dubom* (Moscow: Soglasie 1996), 60–70, and M. I. Romm, *Kak v kino: ustnye rasskazy*, ed. Ia. I. Groisman (Nizhnyi Novgorod: Dekom, 2003), 179–196.

8 Ogryzko, *Okhraniteli i liberaly*, 333–336.

9 Serebriakova's accusations strike me as a preplanned move. For Serebriakova as a "Communist believer," see Nanci Adler, *Keeping Faith with the Party: Communist Believers Return from the Gulag* (Bloomington: Indiana University Press, 2012), 94–97. Adler's account has since been superceded by Ogryzko, *Okhraniteli i liberaly*, 561–568. Intriguingly, Sholokhov was in communication with her a few months before the assembly, see Petelin, *Pis'ma*, 438.

10 Tomilina, *Nikita Sergeevich Khrushchev*, 2: 575, 580–585.

11 On the mysteries surrounding Poskrebyshev's exit from the political scene, see Niels Erik Rosenfeldt, *"Special" World: Stalin's Power Apparatus and the Soviet System's Secret Structures of Communication* (Copenhagen: University of Copenhagen, 2009), 441–447.

12 Tomilina, *Nikita Sergeevich Khrushchev*, 2: 580.

13 Solzhenitsyn letter to Sholokhov, December 1962, in S. M. Sholokhova, "Sud'ba Sholokhova," *Literaturnaia Rossiia*, May 23, 1990.

14 Tomilina, *Nikita Sergeevich Khrushchev*, 2: 601–628.

15 Khrushchev's various statements in support of the terror in the 1930s were diligently compiled and republished by a Russian émigré after the Party Congress. See N. Gradoboev, *Destalinizatsiia: razoblocheniia XXII s"ezda KPSS* (Munich: Izd. Tsentral'nogo Ob"edineninia politicheskikh emigrantov iz SSSR, 1962), 93–97.

16 The only record of that meeting can be found among a series of dictations Khrushchev made to his assistants in preparation for a second assembly. RGANI, f. 52, op. 1, d. 331, l. 3–42; published Tomilina, *Nikita Sergeevich Khrushchev*, 2: 601–617.

17 Tomilina, *Nikita Sergeevich Khrushchev*, 2: 611.

18 Ibid., 2: 568.

19 Alexander Werth, *The Khrushchev Phase: The Soviet Union Enters the 'Decisive' Sixties* (London: Robert Hale, 1961), 43–52.

TWENTY-SEVEN

1 Khrushchev was hoping that Sholokhov would speak but did not want to approach him directly. See Tomilina, *Nikita Sergeevich Khrushchev*, 2: 627. He was already planning to use Sholokhov as an example before his assistants brought him their archival revelations. See Tomilina, *Nikita Sergeevich Khrushchev*, 2: 621.

2 A. I. Yeremenko, "V dni geroicheskoi epopee: k 20-letiiu bitvy na Volge," *Pravda*, January 27, 1963.

3 For Solzhenitsyn's reminiscences about the second assembly, see *Bodalsia telenok s dubom*, 70–77.

4 See the KGB report on how information from the first assembly was leaked to the West in Ogryzko, *Okhraniteli i liberaly*, 339–40.

5 The extent to which the official transcripts were retouched is worthy of further study. The quote is from Laert Bagarshyan, "Avtor etoi skul'ptury ne muzhchina, a pederast," *Novoe Vremia* (Yerevan), May 12, 2012.

6   On this point, Bagarshyan's notes strike me as more reliable than Solzhenitsyn's testimony, though they agree on substance.

7   I rely here on the official version [n.a.] "Rech' tovarishcha N. S. Khrushcheva," *Pravda*, March 10, 1963.

8   "Sheboldaev, Boris Petrovich," *Malaia sovetskaia entsiklopediia*, 3rd ed., vol. 10 (Moscow: Bol'shaia Sovetskaia entsiklopediia, 1960), 552. A. Artizov, et al., *Reabilitatsiia: kak eto bylo: dokumenty prezidiuma TSK KPSS i drugie materialy. Mart 1953—fevral' 1956* (Moscow: Mezhdunarodnyi fond "Demokratiia," 2000), 335, 342, 467.

9   Khrushchev may have also known about Sholokhov's letters to Stalin during the Great Terror. They were mentioned in a report issued in February 1963. See Artizov, et al. *Reabilitatsiia: kak eto bylo. Fevral' 1956—nachalo 80-x godov* (Moscow: Mezhdunarodnyi fond demokratiia, 2003), 632.

10   A. Sofronov, "Bessmertnik," *Ogoniok*, July 26, 1964, 10. Both Pogorelov and Lugovoi also spoke to a Moscow scholar. See L. Iakimenko, *Tvorchestvo M. A. Sholokhova: idei i obrazy tvorcheskii metod, zhanry, stil', masterstvo, poetika* (Moscow: Sovetskii Pisatel', 1964), 136–150. For an earlier trial balloon, see Kalinin, "Veshenskoe leto," 19–20.

11   Kozlovskii, Kuznetsov, Ushakov, and Sholokhov, *M. A. Sholokhov, Pis'ma*, 364–66.

TWENTY-EIGHT

1   This paragraph is patterned on the opening scene of Kafka's *Metamorphosis*, but is based on testimonies by the actress Elina Bystritskaia. Ol'ga Kuchkina, "Elina Bystritskaia: Uvidev menia, Sholokhov skazal: 'Vot Aksiniia!'," *Komsomol'skaia Pravda*, October 7, 2007. For a version with minor variations, see Bystritskaia's television interview with Dmitrii Gordon in 2008: https://www.youtube.com/watch?v=OryumPGl8MU&list=PLrfTcf-vdDrCpHiM2rr21naZb3rXgiCAY (last accessed June 2018).

2   See the coverage of the symposium in *Literaturnaia Gazeta*, August 6, 8, 10, 1963.

3   V. A. and O. A. Tvardovskii, "Aleksandr Tvardovskii: Rabochie tetradi 60-kh godov," *Znamia*, no. 9 (2000), online version http://magazines.russ.ru/znamia/2000/9/tvard.html (last accessed June 2018).

4   For a record of Khrushchev's remarks, see Hans Magnus Enzensberger, *Tumult* (Berlin: Suhrkamp, 2014), 20–33.

5   Sholokhov read the text aloud to visitors and solicited their responses. Apparently it was never published and no longer exists. See Petr Maiatskii, *Kolokol pamiati*, 96–97.

6   Petelin, *Pis'ma*, 441. Pamela Hansford Johnson, *Important to Me: Personalia* (London: Macmillan, 1974), 162–4; *Philip Snow, Stranger and Brother: a Portrait of C. P. Snow* (New York: Charles Scribner's Sons, 1982), 156.

7   For Snow's efforts on behalf of Sholokhov see his correspondence, C. P. Snow papers, Series II, Box 105, folders 1 and 2 (letters to Anisimov in folder marked 'Gorky Institute of World Literature'), Box 130, folders 5–9 (O. Krugerskaya), Box 201, folder 21 (D. Urnov), Harry Ransom Humanities Center, The University of Texas at Austin. References in the correspondence hint that Sholokhov could have been apprised of Snow's plans. Intriguingly, Sholokhov sent Snow a letter of greeting from Stockholm, December 15, 1965, Box 184, folder 2, Harry Ransom Humanities Center.

8   Ivan Anisimov, Nicolas Conrad, Michail Kraptchenko, Victor Vinogradov, Gorky
     Institute of World Literature, nomination letter for 1964, Swedish Academy Archive. In
     addition to the nomination letter, Anisimov also provided a biography of Sholokhov and
     enthusiastic appraisals of his novels, Swedish Academy Archive.

9   Pamela Hansford Johnson and C. P. Snow to Swedish Academy, January 15, 1964,
     C. P. Snow papers, Series II, Box 193, folder 11, Harry Ransom Humanities Center, The
     University of Texas at Austin.

10   Elena Serebrovskaia, *Mezhdu proshlym i budushchim*, 2: 99–103. For interview excerpts,
     see V. V. Muratov and Iu. M. Gorodetskaia (Lukina), *Komandarm Lukin* (Moscow:
     Voenizdat, 1990), 330–338; Naum Mar, "Pod Smolenskom, na Donu, v Moskve: Tri
     vstrechi M. A. Sholokhova s komanduiushchim 16-oi armiei general-leitenantom M. F.
     Lukinym," *Literaturnaia gazeta*, September 25, 1985.

11   For the Secretary's report on the deliberations, see Utlåtande av Svenska Akademiens
     Nobelkommitté 1964, Swedish Academy. The comments about Sholokhov are on pages
     2–3. For the expert appraisal see Nils Åke Nilsson (with assistance from Tamara Hed),
     "Michail Sjolochov (1964)," archive of the Swedish Academy. Nilsson paid particular
     attention to passages that were restored by Sholokhov in the first post-Stalin edition of
     Quiet Don. His conclusion that the changes to the 1953 version did not solely originate
     with Sholokhov and could have been introduced by a party functionary appears to have
     helped Sholokhov's candidacy.

12   For the official announcement, see the coverage in *Izvestiia*, October 16, 1964.

13   Zimovnov, *Sholokhov v zhizni*, 23.

14   This section is based on a selection of archival documents related to the plenum which
     Sholokhov would have been entitled to consult as a member of the Central Committee.
     See http://liders.rusarchives.ru/hruschev/category/razdel/pensioner-soyuznogo-
     znacheniya/oktyabrskii-plenum-1964-g-i-otstavka (last accessed June 2018). For a
     personal account by an individual close to Sholokhov, see Mikhail Solomentsov, *Zachistka
     v politbiuro: kak Gorbachev ubiral 'vragov perestroiki'* (Moscow: Algoritm, 2011), 45–51.

15   Zimovnov, *Sholokhov v zhizni*, 153, 253.

16   See Jean-Paul Sartre, "Sartre on the Nobel Prize," trans. Richard Howard, *New York
     Review of Books*, December 17, 1964.

17   Petelin, *Pis'ma*, 458, Petrov, "Dokumenty," 244.

18   Zimovnov, *Sholokhov v zhizni*, 160.

19   Mikhail Solomentsov, *Zachistka v politbiuro*, 52–62.

20   Kozlovskii, Kuznetsov, Ushakov, and Sholokhov, *M. A. Sholokhov, Pis'ma*, 378.

21   For Sholokhov's initial support of Brezhnev, see Korsunov, *S Sholokhovym*, 136. For
     rhetoric of restoration, see [n.a.] "Nezyblemaia leninskaia general'naia liniia KPSS,"
     Pravda, October 17, 1964; [n.a.] "Gosudarstvo vsego naroda," *Pravda*, December 6, 1964;
     "Leninskie idei o nauchnom rukovodstve," *Pravda*, April 29, 1965.

22   V. Molozhavenko, "Ob odnom nezasluzhenno zabytom imeni," *Molot*, August 13, 1965.

23   A. Podol'skii, "Ob odnom nezasluzhenno vozrozhdennom imeni," *Sovetskaia Rossiia*,
     August 14, 1966.

24   Petrov, "Dokumenty," 243.

25   Petelin, *Pis'ma*, 458-9.

26   Petrov, "Dokumenty," 244.

27   Korsunov, *S Sholokhovym*, 49–51.

TWENTY-NINE

1   See E. Rymko, "Mikhail Sholokhov—Nobelevskii laureat iz Rossii: khronika vizita
     pisatelia, interv'iu po povodu vrucheniia Nobelevskoi premii," *Mezhdunarodnaia zhizn'*,
     no. 9, 2002, 160–169. For songs, see E. P. Rymko, "Sholokhov, bezuslovno, zanial mesto
     sredi klassikov, a klassiki ne umiraiut . . ." *Mir Sholokhova*, no. 1, 2014, 84.

2   This section is based on the documents in Blokh, *Sovetskii Soiuz*, 491–493; Petrov,
     "Dokumenty," 245–249.

3   The intellectuals were Helene Zamoyskiej and Gustaw Herling-Grudzinski.
     On this important episode, see Zdislav Kudel'skii, ed., "Nado ustroit' skandal v
     zashchitu Siniavskogo i Danielia," trans. Natal'ia Gorbanevskaia, *Novaia Pol'sha*
     no. 10 (2013), available at https://novpol.org/ru/Skmo4dGDob/NADO-USTROIT
     -SKANDAL-V-ZAShITU-SINYaVSKOGO-I-DANIELYa// (last accessed June
     2018).

4   Peter Grose, "Sholokhov Proud of Role as 'Soviet' Nobel Winner," *New York Times*,
     December 1, 1965.

5   Aleksandr Galich, ed., *Belaia kniga po delu A. Siniavskogo i Iu. Danielia* (Frankfurt am
     Main: Posev, 1967), 45–57; Petrov, "Dokumenty," 250–51.

6   For the Secretary's report on committee deliberations, see Utlåtande av Svenska
     Akademiens Nobelkommitté 1965, Swedish Academy. The comments about Sholokhov
     are on page 11. Because Sholokhov was a finalist the previous year, no expert opinion
     appears to have been solicited in 1965.

7   The British publisher was Mark Bonham Carter. See Philip Shabecoff, "Sholokhov
     Evades Plea for Jailed Soviet Writers," *New York Times*, December 10, 1965.

8   This paragraph is based on photographs and footage of the ceremony.

9   For footage of the ceremony, see the documentary film *Mikhail Sholokh*ov (1975), available
     at https://www.net-film.ru/film-7668/#reel-48414/ (last accessed June 2018).

10   The menu is from https://www.nobelprize.org/ceremonies/menus/menu-1965.html (last
     accessed june 2018).

11   Zimovnov, *Sholokhov v zhizni*, 79.

12   For Österling's speech, see https://www.nobelprize.org/nobel_prizes/literature
     /laureates/1965/press.html (last accessed June 2018). For Sholokhov's speech, see
     https://www.nobelprize.org/nobel_prizes/literature/laureates/1965/sholokhov-speech
     .html (last accessed June 2018).

13   S. Pavlov, "Ideinaia ubezhdennost' molodezhi," *Pravda*, August 29, 1965. For letter
     on Stalin, received before March 1966, see Artizov, *Reabilitatsiia: Kak eto bylo* (2003),
     486–88.

14   Korsunov, *S Sholokhovym*, 106–107.

15   On preparations for the speech, see Zimovnov, *Sholokhov v zhizni*, 211–212.

16   For the text of Sholokhov's speech, see *XXIII S"ezd Kommunisticheskoi Partii Sovetskogo
     Soiuza 29 Marta–8 Aprelia 1966 goda. Stenograficheskii otchet* (Moscow: Izd. politicheskoi
     literatury, 1966), 354–362. The speech was also published in *Pravda*, April 2, 1966.

17 For the KGB appraisal and new archival sources, see Viacheslav Ogryzko, "Na fone protsessa nad Siniavskim," *Literaturnaia Rossiia*, no. 11, 2015 available at http://old .litrossia.ru/2015/11/09469.html (last accessed June 2018).

18 Collective letter of members of philological faculty of Moscow State University, "Net nravstvennogo opravdaniia: pis'mo v redaktsiiu," *Literaturnaia gazeta*, February 15, 1966.

19 See "Pis'mo 62-kh pisatelie v Prezidium XXIII s'ezda KPSS," *Grani. Zhurnal literatury, isskusstva, nauki i obshchestvenno-politicheskoi mysli* 62 (1966), 127–129.

20 The publication Sholokhov referred to is M. Gorky, "S kem vy, 'mastera kul'tury'?: otvet amerikanskim korrespondetam," *Pravda*, March 22, 1932. On "humanists," see M. Gorky "Gumanistam," *Pravda*, December 11, 1930; "Tret'emu kraevomu s"ezdu sovetov," *Pravda*, January 2, 1935.

21 V. A. and O. A. Tvardovskii, "Aleksandr Tvardovskii: Rabochie tetrad' 60-kh godov," *Znamia*, no. 4, 2002, online version http://magazines.russ.ru/znamia/2002/4/tvar-pr .html/ (last accessed June 2018).

22 Galich, *Belaia kniga po delu A. Siniavskogo*, 390–394.

23 For Cossack émigrés, see S. Serapin, "Pamiati F. D. Kriukova," *Rodimyi Krai*, no. 3, 1963, 19–22, and P. K. "Kto takoi Mikhail Sholokhov," *Rodimyi Krai*, no. 2, 1966, 20–23. On young intellectuals, see Harrison E. Salisbury, "Pressures Rise in Soviet for End of Censorship," *New York Times*, October 23, 1967. For Solzhenitsyn, see below.

THIRTY

1 See G. V. Gubanov, *Gagarin na Donu* (Rostov: Al'tair, 2011). For the poem, see Vladimir Firsov, *Stikhi* (Moscow: Molodaia gvardiia, 1972), 59–61.

2 On Sholokhov's statements to the young writers see F. I. Chuev, *Soldaty imperii. Besedy. Vospominaniia. Dokumenty* (Moscow: Kovcheg, 1998), 412–417. See also Chivilikhin, *Dnevniki*, 259–260.

3 Published as "Azure steppe," in Mikhail Sholokhov, *Tales from the Don*, 177–186.

4 Sholokhov's son noticed that sometimes when his father was confronted with praise he would for no apparent reason suddenly be overtaken by a dark mood and would become pensive and taciturn. M. M. Sholokhov, *Ob ottse*, 147.

5 This paragraph presents how Solzhenitsyn's actions would have appeared to Sholokhov's allies in Moscow.

6 V. A. and O. A. Tvardovskii, "Aleksandr Tvardovskii: Rabochie tetrad 60-kh godov," *Znamia*, no. 10, 2003, online version http://magazines.russ.ru/znamia/2003/10/tvard. html (last accessed June 2018). For a survivor's perspective, see Varlam Shalamov, "Novye glavy Sholokhovskogo romana," ed. V. V. Esipov and S. M. Solov'ev, in V. T. Sharlamov, *Sobranie Sochinenii*, vol. 7, *Dopol'nitel'nyi* (Moscow: Knigovek, 2013), 393–399.

7 Solzhenitsyn, *Bodalsia telenok s dubom*, 132.

8 Aleksandr Gladkov, "Dnevnik. 1969 god," ed. Mikhail Mikheev, *Zvezda*, no. 2, 2015, online version http://magazines.russ.ru/zvezda/2015/2/12gl.html (last accessed June 2018).

9 First published in S. M. Sholokhova, "K istorii nenapisannogo romana," *Molodaia gvardiia*, no. 7, 1992, 27; Petelin, *Pi'sma*, 480–1; Kozlovskii, Kuznetsov, Ushakov, and Sholokhov, *M. A. Sholokhov, Pis'ma*, 395.

10 On Sholokhov's persistent attempts to contact Brezhnev, which were dutifully recorded by secretaries of the Central Committee, see A. S. Stepanov and A. V. Korotkov, eds., *Rabochie i dnevnikovye zapisi: Leonid Brezhnev* (Moscow: IstLit, 2016), 2: 305–307, 314, 315, 318, 319, 320, 321.

11 The most important of these provided teasers of developments in the excerpts. See A. Kalinin, "Poezdka v Vioshenskuiu," *Izvestiia*, October 4, 1968.

12 Letter to Brezhnev, December 1968, first published in *Sholokhov na izlome vremeni*, 216–217; Petelin, *Pi'sma*, 483–5; Kozlovskii, Kuznetsov, Ushakov, and Sholokhov, *M. A. Sholokhov, Pis'ma*, 396–7. An article eventually appeared, but it did not compare him to opposition writers, see [n.a.] "Soviet said to ban novel by Sholokhov," *New York Times*, February 8, 1969.

13 The absence of Sholokhov's letter in Salisbury's archive suggests to me that it was intercepted and never reached him. See Correspondence Files, Salisbury Papers, Series II. The Russian scholar who published the letter did not connect it to Sholokhov's attempts to influence Brezhnev. See V. N. Zapevalov, "Vokrug finala 'Podniatoi tseliny': (Neizvestnoe pis'mo M. A. Sholokhova G. E. Solsberi)," *Russkaia literatura*, no. 2, 1994, 220–231.

14 M. A. Sholokhov, "Oni srazhalis' za Rodinu," *Pravda*, March 12–15, 1969.

15 Ogryzko, "Tri butylki."

16 See James F. Clarity, "Sholokhov Continues Soviet Attacks on Solzhenitsyn," *New York Times*, November 28, 1969.

17 Z. B. Tomashevskaia, "Kak i zachem pisalos' 'Stremia'," http://www.philol.msu.ru/~lex /td/?pid=012211 (last accessed June 2018); Solzhenitsyn, *Bodalsia telenok s dubom*, 580–592.

18 Kozlovskii, Kuznetsov, Ushakov, and Sholokhov, *M. A. Sholokhov, Pis'ma*, 408–9.

19 Zimovnov, *Sholokhov v zhizni*, 138–9.

THIRTY-ONE

1 See I. Solov'ev, "Put' predatel'stva," *Pravda*, January 14, 1974.

2 Letter from Salisbury to Solzhenitsyn March 28, 1974, acknowledging a letter sent by Solzhenitsyn, Letter from Solzhenitsyn to Salisbury dated July 12, 1974, Salisbury to Solzhenitsyn July 23, 1974, Salisbury Papers, Series III, box 239, Folder 8.

3 Zimovnov, *Sholokhov v zhizni*, 161–163.

4 For the Mercedes, see Zimovnov, *Sholokhov v zhizni*, 166. For characterization of Salisbury as a connoisseur and detective story remarks, see Letter from Solzhenitsyn to Salisbury dated July 12, 1974, Salisbury Papers, Series III, box 239, Folder 8. In the same letter Solzhenitsyn provided some comments about Lidiia Chukovskaia but declined to write a preface for a publication about her being prepared by Salisbury. For the prepublication copy, see Solzhenitsyn to Salisbury, July 31, 1974, Salisbury to Solzhenitsyn August 13, 1974, and Salisbury's telegram in response August 28, 1974, ibid.

5 There is no direct testimony that the KGB tried to warn Sholokhov. However, a curious cluster of circumstantial evidence makes such a conclusion plausible. First an important and otherwise comprehensive publication of KGB and Politburo documents related to Solzhenitsyn features a strange lacuna for the very months when Solzhenitsyn was

preparing to launch the plagiarism charges. The visit of Central Committee Secretary and head of the Cultural Department Vasilii Shauro to Vioshki roughly coincided with the actualization of Solzhenitsyn's publication plans and his correspondence with Salisbury. Uncharacteristically, Sholokhov's assistant was shut out of that meeting. Three weeks after Shauro's visit, a letter to Sholokhov from one of his allies made cryptic references to "mudslingers" and a need to defend *Quiet Don*. Finally, the Cultural Department appears to have been involved in a search for Kriukov's remaining papers. For the strange publication lacuna, consult A. V. Korotkov, S. A. Mel'chin, and A. S. Stepanov, eds., *Kremlevskii samosud (sbornik dokumentov)* (Moscow: Rodina, 1994). The text skips from July 1974 to June 1975, 500–502, 503–508. On Shauro's visit, see Zimovnov, *Sholokhov v zhizni*, 176. For the letter, see Petelin, *Pis'ma*, 516–517. On the search for Kriukov's papers, see Kuznetsov, *Sud'ba i pravda*, 586–87.

6   Aleksandr Gladkov, "Dnevnik. 1974 god (iul'-dekabr'), ed. Mihail Mikheev, *Neva*, no. 11, 2016, 167.

7   Using his publishing connections, Salisbury was able to procure prepublication selections from the Reshetovskaia book. These were being shopped around to Western publishers by Soviet intermediaries. He shared them with Solzhenitsyn. See Salisbury letter to Solzhenitsyn August 13, 1974, Salisbury Papers, Series III, box 239, Folder 8.

8   Harrison Salisbury, "Solzhenitsyn Questions Authorship of Classic Novel by Sholokhov, a Fellow Winner of the Nobel Prize," *New York Times*, September 1, 1974. For the cable from Moscow, Clurman cable dated September 9, 1974, Salisbury Papers, Series III, box 239.

9   D*, with a preface by Aleksandr Solzhenitsyn, *Stremia 'Tikhogo Dona' (Zagadki romana)* (Paris: YMCA Press, 1974).

10   No official Soviet appraisal from 1974 has ever been published. The appraisal presented here is mine, but it is informed by conversations with Russians who read the book during the Soviet period. For a significant, early critical response in the West, see Herman Ermolaev, "Riddle of the Quiet Don: A Review Article," *The Slavic and East European Journal*, 18/3 (1974): 299–310.

11   Proponents of Kriukov's authorship have made major discoveries and advanced the discussion far beyond the preliminary conclusions proposed by Medvedeva-Tomashevskaia. They have demonstrated a number of key parallels between parts of *Quiet Don* and Kriukov's prose. At the very least the notion that Sholokhov never read Kriukov must be dismissed. At the same time, studies devoted to Kriukov often undervalue the importance of argumentative prioritization: many parallels that they discuss do not appear significant to an objective eye. I am convinced that a Kriukov substratum can be identified in *Quiet Don* but have not yet encountered any decisive line of argumentation that would completely overturn Sholokhov's overall authorship claims. An early study emphasized quantity over quality, see M. T. Mezentsev, *Sud'ba romanov* (Samara: P.S. Press, 1994). Subsequent studies demonstrated intriguing convergences between *Quiet Don* and Kriukov's stories, phrasing, imagery, use of Cossack folklore and knowledge of historical events. The most important of these is A. G. Makarov, S. E. Makarova, *Tsvetok-Tatarnik: v poiskakh avtora 'Tikhogo Dona' ot Mikhaila Sholokhova k Fedoru Kriukovu* (Moscow: AIRO-XX, 2001). New discoveries appear regularly on Andrei Chernov's interesting

website devoted to Kriukov: https://nestoriana.wordpress.com/category /федор-крюков/ (last accessed June 2018). Several important articles by Mikhail Mikheev have provided a balanced analysis and acknowledged Sholokhov's agency. See for example, M. Iu. Mikheev, "*Kuler lokal'*, ili ornamental'nost' v khudozhestvennoi proze: dialektnye vkrapleniia u Kriukova i Sholokhova," *in Variativnost' v iazyke i kummunikatsii: sbornik statei*, ed. L. L. Fedorova (Moscow: Rossiiskii gumanitarnyi universitet, 2012), 361–394.

12 Konstantin Priima argued in 1963 that several passages in *Quiet Don* were taken from Lagutin's 1925 memoir about the civil war. Lagutin's fascinating story is the subject of my short book, *Knocking on History's Door: The Incredible Life of Iakov Lagutin* (forthcoming).

13 *Stremia 'Tikhogo Dona,'* 89–90.

14 See envelope from Information Department of the Soviet Embassy postmarked October 9, 1974, and enclosure. Vladimir Molovazhenko, "A few words for Solzhenitsyn," Salisbury Papers, Series III, box 239, Folder 8. For the London version see the *Times Literary Supplement*, October 11, 1974, 1126.

15 For Sholokhov's reaction, see Ivan Zhukov, *Ruka sud'by: Pravda i lozh' o Mikhaile Sholokhove i Aleksandre Fadeeve* (Moscow: Voskresen'e, 1994), 23. For Solzhenitsyn's expectations of Soviet outrage, see Solzhenitsyn to Salisbury August 15, 1974, Solzhenitsyn to Salisbury, September 3, 1974; on the press conference plans, see Solzhenitsyn to Salisbury, October 11, 1974, Salisbury Papers, Series III, box 239, Folder 8.

16 Kozlov, *M.,A. Sholokhov*, 15–18.

17 Petelin, *Pis'ma*, 92.

18 Al'bert Beliaev, *Literatura i labirinty vlasti: ot "ottepeli" do perestroiki* (Moscow: [s.n] 2009), 144–171. See also Norbert Kuchinke, "Ein solches Buch wird nicht geklaut: Spiegel-Interview mit Sowjet-Autor Konstantin Simonow," *Der Spiegel*, no. 49, 1974, 173.

19 After late October 1974 there was a long lull in Solzhenitsyn's correspondence with Salisbury. There was a brief revival in 1977 when Roy Medvedev published a book about the controversy. See Solzhenitsyn to Salisbury April 11, 1974 and Salisbury to Solzhenitsyn, October 14, 1977, Salisbury Papers, Series III, box 239, Folder 8.

20 Zimovnov, *Sholokhov v zhizhi*, 176, 183–84, 191–2, 199–200, 208–209.

21 M. M. Sholokhov, *Ob ottse*, 42–43.

22 Ibid., 43.

23 Zimovnov, *Sholokhov v zhizhi*, 210–1.

24 M. M. Sholokhov, *Ob ottse*, 44.

THIRTY-TWO

1 For the seventieth birthday festivities, see (TASS), "Gordost' sovetskoi literatury: iubileinyi vecher, posviashchennyi 70-letiiu so dnia rozhdeniia M. A. Sholokhova," *Pravda*, May 24, 1975.

2 On Brezhnev's health, see E. I. Chazov, *Zdorov'e i vlast': vospominaniia kremlevskogo vracha* (Moscow: Tsentropoligraf, 2015). On Brezhnev's dental surgery, see his letter to Suslov on May 19, 1975, first published in Aleksandr Dobrovol'skii, "Nebrezhnye dnevniki Brezhneva," *Moskovskii komsomolets*, December 18, 2015.

3 Korsunov, *S Sholokhovym*, 107; S. M. Sholokhova, "K istorii nenapisannogo romana," in *Sholokhov na izlome vremeni*, 108.

4   G. Kh'etso, "Moia vstrecha s Sholokhovym," *Voprosy literatury*, no. 5 (1990), 30–39;
     K. I. Priima, "Vstrechy v Vioshenskoi. Zarubezhnye uchenye u Sholokhova," *Don*,
     no. 5 (1981): 135–141. See also N. I. Stopchenko, "G. Kh'etso i K. I. Priima–poborniki
     tvorchestva M. A. Sholokhova: vzgliad iz XXI veka," *Kul'tura i tsivilizatsiia*, no. 1 (2016),
     255–272.

5   Geir Kjetsaa, "Storms on the Quiet Don. A Pilot Study," *Scando-Slavica* 22 (1976): 5–22.

6   Ibid., 23.

7   Petelin, *Pis'ma*, 523–5.

8   In a discussion of the letter the Russian nationalist scholar Sergei Semanov claimed credit
     for taking "those materials" to Sholokhov in August 1977. Subtle hints in his account,
     such as particular attention to a change in the letter's tone and repetition of "under some
     kind of influence," indicate that scholars would be wise to explore links between the letter
     and Semanov's activities of that period. See S. N. Semanov, *Brezhnev: pravitel' 'zolotogo
     veka'* (Moscow: Veche, 2002), 187, 189.

9   Petelin, *Pis'ma*, 525–533.

10   L. P. Logashova, ed., *Tikhii Don: Uroki romana. O mirovom znachenii romana M. A.
     Sholokhova* (Rostov: Rostovskoe Izdatel'stvo, 1979).

11   Zimovnov, *Sholokhov v zhizhi*, 237.

12   On *Malaia Zemlia*, see Andrei Sidorchik, "Triumf literatora Brezhneva. Kto sdelal
     genseka velikim pisatelem," *Argumenty i Fakty* (Moscow), March 31, 2015. Sholokhov was
     appalled by flattery of Brezhnev. See Zimovnov, *Sholokhov v zhizhi*, 187.

13   M. M. Sholokhov, *Ob ottse*, 16.

14   These events were covered by the Western press of the period and are well remembered by
     Russians who lived through that era.

15   V. G. Levchenko, ed., "Posledniaia volia pisatelia," in *Sholokhov i sovremennost'. Sbornik
     statei i dokumental'nykh materialov*, ed. V. V. Vasil'ev (Moscow: Nasledia, 1995), 199–200.

16   Anatolii Kalinin, "Zhivaia voda 'Tikhogo Dona'," *Sovetskaia Rossiia*, November 12, 1987.

17   For press coverage of Sholokhov's funeral, see TASS, "Pokhorony M. A. Sholokhova,"
     Pravda, February 24, 1984. The secretary of the Central Committee was M. V. Zimianin.
     On his role in 1969 edits, see S. M. Sholokhova, "K istorii nenapisannogo romana," in
     Sholokhov na izlome vremeni, 106.

18   For documentary film footage of the funeral, consult https://ok.ru/video/251693304413
     (last accessed June 2018). For reminiscences, see Nadezhda Volkova, "1984: proshchanie s
     Sholokhovym," *GorodN* (Rostov), February 28, 2013.

19   Kuznetsov, *Sud'ba i pravda*, 20; Evgenii Belzhelarskii, "Rukopisi ne vrut," [Interview with
     S. M. Sholokhova], *Itogi* (Moscow), April 13, 2011 online version http://www.itogi.ru
     /iskus/2011/15/163984.html (last accessed June 2018).

AFTERWORD

1   On the demise of the Putin puppet, see Dmitrii Gordon's interview with Viktor
     Shenderovich, available at http://bulvar.com.ua/gazeta/archive/s39_32539/3838.html/
     (last accessed June 2018).

2   One of the most significant early articles to advance plagiarism charges was published
     by an Israeli researcher. This fact may have spawned such odd rumors. See Z. Bar-Sella,

ENDNOTES

"'Tikhii Don' protiv Sholokhova," *Daugava* [Riga] no. 12 (1990): 94–107; No. 1 (1991) 53–62; no. 2 (1991) 40–57. The article first appeared two years earlier in the periodical *22* [Tel Aviv].

3 Lev Kolodnyi, *Kak ia nashel 'Tikhii Don': khronika poiska* (Moscow: Golos, 2000).

4 Iu. Buidy, "'Tikhii Don' techet na Zapad?" *Izvestiia*, February 25, 1998.

5 Kuznetsov, *Sud'ba i Pravda*, 39–44, 809.

6 Nataliia Gevorkian and Andrei Kolesnikov, "Zheleznyi Putin," *Kommersant*, March 10, 2000; Nataliia Gevorkian and Andrei Kolesnikov, Natal'ia Timakova, *Ot Pervogo litsa. Razgovory s Vladimirom Putinym* (Moscow: Vagrius, 2000). For commentary at the time about the differences between the two versions of the interview, see Sergei Ivanov, "Pupovina Kondrata Maidannikova," *Itogi*, no. 12, March 21, 2000.

7 On Putin's official visit to Sholokhov's home and grave, see http://kremlin.ru/events /president/news/33426/ (last accessed June 2018).

8 A. Flegon, *Vokrug Solzhenitsyna* (London: Flegon Press, 1981), 2: 752.

9 An even more remarkable turnabout took place in 2011. Roy Medvedev, the author of one of the most important and interesting skeptical Russian studies devoted to the authorship question suddenly changed his mind about Sholokhov. Compare Roy Medvedev, *Problems in the Literary Biography of Mikhail Sholokhov* (Cambridge, U.K.: Cambridge University Press, 1977) to Roy Medvedev, *'Tikhii Don': zagadki i otkrytiia velikogo romana* (Moscow: AIRO-XXI, 2011). Someday a future historian will explain this shift as part of a larger intellectual trend of the Putin era.

10 Golfo Alexopoulos, "Portrait of a Con Artist as a Soviet Man," *Slavic Review* 57/4 (1998): 774–790; Sheila Fitzpatrick, *Tear Off the Masks: Identity and Imposture in Twentieth-Century Russia* (Princeton, N.J.: Princeton University Press, 2005).

11 Sholokhov's family continues to exert protective control over his remaining unpublished letters and papers. I have generally avoided discussing his family life or delving into his alleged extramarital affairs since the available evidence is neither abundant nor cross-verifiable. If the unpublished secret police files on Sholokhov are as detailed as those on Andrei Platonov, which have been partially published, then many fascinating revelations may eventually come to light.

382

INDEX

INDEX